A TOWERING CONTROL

A TOWERING CONTROL

The Story of Britain's Airfields

KENNETH P. BANNERMAN

ISE

First published in 1990.

IS Enterprises,
PO Box 379, Clarkston, Glasgow G76 8AD
(for communications)

British Library Cataloguing in Publication Data

Bannerman, Kenneth P. (Kenneth Peacock) *1963-*
A towering control : the story of Britain's airfields.
1. Great Britain. Aerodromes.
I. Title.
387.7360941

ISBN 0-9516298-0-8

Printed in Great Britain by McCorquodale (Scotland) Limited, Glasgow.
Phototypeset by Newtext Composition Limited, Glasgow.

Contents

Acknowledgements

The author would like to thank the following for their assistance with information and/or photographs:

R.J. Flavel, Librarian/Archivist, The Automobile Association, Basingstoke, Hampshire; L.J.E. Goldfinch, Wiltshire; Mrs Bernice S. Harby, Fareham, Hampshire; R.M. Maywood, Peterborough; W.H.C. Reynolds, Chingford, London; R. Sims, Cirencester, Gloucestershire; C. Walker, Wiltshire; the staffs of the Public Record Office, Imperial War Museum and RAF Museum.

As a result of the many requests made via dozens of regional publications, many people kindly sent information and/or photographs which could not be immediately used in the preparation of this book but will be invaluable in the forthcoming *Airfields of Britain* series, notably D. Alder, Miss H. Alpin, J.W.G. Cocke, T.H. Hislop, D.F.J. Kent, Mrs W. Layzell, Mrs C. Peach, A. Pearcy, Mrs A.L. Twigg, D. Vincent, P. Ward and J. Whittington.

Many thanks as well to the hundreds – if not thousands – of anonymous people all over Britain who provided priceless snippets of information about 'their' local airfield. Any opponent of our disused airfields in particular would be well advised to talk to all of them encountered during the author's operational intrusions: our airfields are infinitely more popular than ever before.

And as for those of you who failed or refused to help with this scheme? You ought to be utterly ashamed of yourselves for denying a tremendous number of people the chance of a potential job.

Do you or anyone you know have historical/technical/architectural/social photographs of any British airfield – military or civil, active or disused – dating from 1905 to the present? The author would be most grateful to receive examples for the *Airfields of Britain* series. Originals will be returned if requested. Write to: *IS Enterprises, PO Box 379, Clarkston, Glasgow G76 8AD.*

Introduction

Not so long ago, they were still Britain's forgotten superstars. Nobody seemed interested in them. If mentioned, it was usually in a dismissive way. Like other classic unsung heroes, it was only past the eleventh hour when people really began to appreciate the astonishingly brilliant work they had achieved.

We are talking about the airfields of Britain, now fast becoming recognised as this country's premier historical sites. Fact: we have the world's most historical airfields. Fact: we have more airfields per square mile than any other country in the world. Forget those worthless, useless, deadly dull and pretentious castles or stately homes: this is real history. Since their advent in 1909, at least 1,700 British airfields have existed at one time or another. What a story it is – wars, frequent crises, non-stop action . . .

This book, the first of its kind, covers every aspect of British airfield life. Past books supposedly dealing with this fascinating subject have consistently failed to do this. Although bearing good intentions, they adopt an air of pretentiousness, bombarding the reader with facts and figures past the point of overkill. Other books desperately lack both purpose and synchronisation, while many are so unbelievably vague. Their facts and figures are deluged with errors to make matters worse.

Now you have the chance to read a co-ordinated history. Facts, figures, specification numbers and all the rest have been virtually pared to the bone. A section on airfield terminology is designed to cut out all the waffle which far too often prevails elsewhere. Even the term 'airfield' itself is used as much as possible to retain consistency.

In another new move, *A Towering Control* has been split into three sections. The first details the lives and times of Britain's airfields, showing how they gradually managed to carve out their own unique place in history. Aircraft have always needed airfields, but you will see how many things far outwith aviation dictated to our airfields for long enough. Instead of the three Rs, there were the five Ps: politicians, planners, pacifists, the Press and what the Romans called pecunia – money, or rather the lack of it.

However, the airfields of Britain carried so much power, thanks to their tremendous success at local, regional, national and worldwide level, that their increasingly awesome strength was evident even before World War Two. A phenomenal amount of luck, good and bad, has also played a huge part in their lives. So too to a certain extent has the mystery element, which proves how terribly history has neglected our airfields. Amazingly, no-one even knows for sure which was Britain's first ever airfield.

The second section of this book deals with every aspect of airfields, from runways and hangars to unit movements and even airfield names. This is designed to give you easy reference whenever you visit an airfield. Heavy emphasis is placed on the military side, as civil airfields do not display great regularity, but the former often show exceptions here and there as well. This need to qualify everything applies to all areas of British airfield history and development in general, just one of many reasons why they are so fascinating.

There follows the third and last section, never previously attempted, which tells of the shocking fall and subsequent rebirth of the legions of disused British airfields. At the end of this personal but considered assessment of what has happened over the years since November 1918 I have also given numerous suggestions – already proven – as to how you could help in their continued fightback. Here again, the tactics of past books have been avoided. They tend to say, 'Britain's disused airfields – what a tragedy.' This book says, 'Britain's disused airfields – what a tragedy, what can we do to conserve them?' That's the difference. Radical, extremely hard-hitting, necessary – and not before time.

This book will precede a series, *The Airfields of Britain,* which will be the most thorough study of these sites ever seen. Again you, the reader, will be saved from the boredom, trivia and sheer uncertainty which litter previous books on the subject. It may be wise to invest in the latest editions of Ordnance Survey 1:50,000 series maps as airfields are shown in reasonable detail.

If our airfields were human, it would be interesting to ask them this question: how many wars have you fought? Most military ones would probably say at least five; some sites involved more with civil aviation could say as many as nine. Quite apart from both World Wars, they could include the periods after 1918, 1945 and 1957, when politicians – whether they were Communist or Conservative, Labour or Liberal, nationalist or anarchist – tried unsuccessfully to eliminate them. Civil airfields could also add their difficult pioneering days at different times down the years and the start of World War Two, when hostilities stopped civil operations for a while.

Of course, our disused airfields have fought the longest war of all – against the ungrateful. Past comments referring to them have been utterly scurrilous. This anti-disused airfield campaign is thankfully on the wane but a lot of provocation, ignorance and sheer lack of gratitude still exists. A typical example of the former trait once occurred in a book about Orkney, where its author disgracefully described our supersites as slums needing to be obliterated from the landscape. Would he have been able to say that – indeed, say anything – if Britain had been captured with no airfield cover in 1940? Perhaps there is too much free speech today.

As for more subliminal opponents, take the case of a famous golf commentator who once said on television, 'There's Turnberry's memorial, to all those brave men who died in World War Two.' What exactly is wrong here, you might ask? Had he not become so immersed in his golf, he would have noticed the men died during World War One . . . Perhaps unintentional, but more serious was the occasion this same gentleman was talking to the late, great Sir Douglas Bader. After asking him if he served at Turnberry, a rather inane question to which Bader brilliantly replied, 'I was only as far north as Coltishall, old boy,' the commentator said, 'Yes, they've turned an old runway into a car park.' Is that all he could say about an airfield which faithfully served its country in both World Wars? Now you see why more and more people are springing to the defence of our airfields. Such remarks, whether deliberate or not, must be eradicated for good.

Why do Britain's airfields, especially disused ones, attract so much opposition? It is conclusively proven that there is enormous interest in them both at home and abroad. Maybe the reason lies with the frightening levels of pacifism today. Proof of this is shown by the Establishment's total ignorance of our airfields. Is it fashionable to do so to keep in with the pacifists? Or is it a convenient excuse to brainwash particularly the young with computers and similarly pernicious devices? Pacifists might reply that this revives the 'damn good war' argument. This laughable statement shows yet again their extreme lack of gratitude. Sure, we all want peace, but which brilliantly successful and later betrayed sites made and continue to make that possible?

One task which for long enough did not seem possible was the 'simple' matter of publishing this book. Another book could easily be written about how your intrepid author fought for well in excess of a decade a truly one-man battle against quite frightening odds. Derison, blatant obstruction, crippling red tape, severe technical difficulties, threats of various kinds and even the narrow avoidance of an aircraft accident resulted in some of the most clandestine operations ever seen having to be effected, activities which might be told one day. It is nothing short of scandalous that the extremely meticulous preparation needed for this overall strategic campaign only succeeded at the fifth attempt, for this book could have appeared as early as 1983. Being so young with such a dire lack of general back-up has maybe been the biggest problem of all. But, as with many things in life, if you are technically, artistically, fundamentally, financially and – above all – morally correct, you will ultimately always win. Any of our airfields bear testimony to that basic fact.

The biggest tragedy in the British airfield story is how they have never been acclaimed. In World War Two, USAAF Groups won Distinguished Unit Citations as rewards to give just one example, but our airfields have received absolutely nothing. Perhaps you may have noticed one expression which has already cropped up several times in this book and will appear again and again: 'our airfields'. And quite right too, for they are yours, mine and everyone else's. Why, they might even be the Government's as well!

So read this book, take up this most thrilling pastime already enjoyed by millions but, more than anything else, do your bit to get your local airfield or airfields in general the proper recognition they deserve. Britain has the world's greatest airfields: any foreigner will tell you that, yet many people at home either cannot or will not accept this fact. Our airfields have done and continue to do so much for us in so many ways that Britain would quite literally collapse if they disappeared. Imagine an economy in ruins, millions upon millions of jobs down the drain, no cultural or social values and the military collapse of not just Britain but certainly Europe and perhaps even the entire free world. For Britain to be without airfields is just unthinkable. That is why I have come to tremendously appreciate them. Hopefully you will too. If not, you ought to.

Kenneth P. Bannerman

February 1990

Britain's Other Language

As aviation developed, it almost become inevitable how a separate aeronautical vocabulary would emerge. Some people have gone as far as saying that this has turned into a new language. You may have noticed the odd other aviation book attempt to give a list of abbreviations and thought 'what a bore.' In short, you are right! When an author decides to attempt such a section, he usually manages to confuse not only the reader but himself as well by using some incredibly vague terms. Many of these are to do with administrative matters, of little interest value to most people. Other terms bear hardly any relevance to Britain's airfields, while some more are rapidly skated over without giving their full meanings. One-off experimental units are classic examples, remaining as highly obscure abbreviations to easily baffle the reader. The latter, with one or two necessary exceptions, have been excluded from the list below as a result.

British airfieldspeak can prove utterly baffling to the uninitiated, and so the following list has been heavily pruned down. If you still think this is bad, another list twelve times as long could be prepared with ease. These terms relate both to this book and the forthcoming *Airfields of Britain* series. As simplicity is always the best policy, they are laid out in alphabetical order for easy cross reference purposes. One or two fairly obvious terms such as RAF are omitted, as have certain choice examples which can only be described as being best confined to the barracks. All relate to the RAF unless stated otherwise.

Term	*Meaning(s)*
AA	Anti-Aircraft; or Automobile Association (civil)
AAC	Army Air Corps
AACU	Anti-Aircraft Co-operation Unit

A & AEE	Aeroplane and Armament Experimental Establishment
AAP	Aircraft Acceptance Park; World War One airfield where new aircraft were tested before transferral to squadrons
AASF	Advanced Air Striking Force; RAF element in France during 1939/40
ACHU	Aircrew Holding Unit
ADDL	Aerodrome Dummy Deck Landing (FAA); name given to special type of training, whereby airfields simulated aircraft carrier decks
ADGB	Air Defence of Great Britain; alternative name for RAF Fighter Command, used 1925-36 and also during 1943-44
AFS	Advanced Flying School
AFTS	Advanced Flying Training School
AGS	Air Gunnery School
AI	Airborne Interception (type of radar)
ALG	Advanced Landing Ground; temporary airfield with minimal facilities for fighter use. Common in southern England during 1943-44
ANS	Air Navigation School
Anti-*Diver* patrol	One intended to destroy V-1 flying bombs
AONS	Air Observer Navigation School
AOP	Air Observation Post; term always associated with the Auster artillery spotter aircraft
AOS	Air Observer School
APC	Armament Practice Camp
ASR	Air-Sea Rescue
ASU	Aircraft Storage Unit
ATA	Air Transport Auxiliary; World War Two aircraft ferrying organisation
ATC	Air Traffic Control; or Air Training Corps
AuxAF	Auxiliary Air Force (renamed RAuxAF 1947)

Baedeker attacks	Luftwaffe bombing raids carried out in 1942 upon towns and cities of historic importance
BAT Flight	Blind (sometimes Beam) Approach Training Flight; common training unit at airfields from 1941, instructing pilots how to use beam approach systems for safe landings in poor weather. Oxfords normally used as equipment.
BDTF	Bomber Defence Training Flight; World War Two unit, equipped with ageing fighter types, for affiliation duties with bombers
BEA	British European Airways
BG	Bomb Group (USAAF)
B&GS	Bombing and Gunnery School
BOAC	British Overseas Airways Corporation
CAG	Civil Air Guard; training organisation formed out of flying clubs. Active 1938-39
CCRC	Combat Crew Replacement Center (USAAF, roughly the equivalent of an RAF OTU).
CFS	Central Flying School.
Circus	Daylight bomber mission, with heavy fighter escort, intended to lure enemy aircraft.
C&M	Care and Maintenance; broadly speaking, used to describe an airfield's state when it is in the process of closing down, or without aircraft, or undergoing reconstruction work. Yet C&M can have various meanings, as there may be still some aeronautical link such as gliding or missiles. Best to remember with this term that regular flying could return at the site concerned.
CND	Campaign for Nuclear Disarmament; pacifist organisation.
Con Flight	Conversion Flight; element active during middle of World War Two supporting RAF squadrons switching from twin-engined to four-engined bombers.

CPF	Coastal Patrol Flight; name given to several Tiger Moth anti-submarine units during 1939/40.
CU	Conversion Unit.
D/F	Direction Finding; term applied to numerous ground stations, providing safe radio navigation for aircraft.
DZ	Dropping Zone; area set aside to allow men or supplies to land by parachute.
E/A	Enemy Aircraft.
ECM	Electronic Countermeasures; various forms of devices or methods to confuse enemy radar systems.
EFTS	Elementary Flying Training School.
ELG	Emergency Landing Ground; either denoting a crude site or a specialised World War Two airfield with a huge runway.
E&RFTS	Elementary and Reserve Flying Training School; preceded the EFTS.
Exercise *Spartan*	Large joint RAF/Army exercise of February/March 1943, to test airfield mobility of squadrons.
FAA	Fleet Air Arm.
FG	Fighter Group (USAAF).
FIDO	Fog Investigation Dispersal Operation; costly but effective petrol-burning device installed during World War Two at 15 airfields to clear fog around site.
FIS	Flying Instructors' School.
FPP	Ferry Pilots Pool.
FRU	Fleet Requirements Unit (FAA); dogsbody element (usually a squadron) used for mundane duties, notably target towing.
FTS	Flying Training School.
FTU	Ferry Training Unit.
FU	Ferry Unit.
Gardening	Aircraft sea minelaying operations.
GC	Gliding Club (civil).
GCA	Ground Controlled Approach; talk-down

	radar to aid pilots while landing. Developed during World War Two, in use post-war.
GCI	Ground Controlled Interception; ground radar, used in World War Two to vector night fighters to E/A target.
Gee	Medium-range radio aid of World War Two, transmitted from the ground, aiding navigation and target identification for RAF bombers.
Gp	Group.
Group Pool	Training unit of 1939/40, consisting of RAF squadrons, which evolved into the OTU.
GS	Gliding School (ATC).
GTS	Glider Training School.
HCU	Heavy Conversion Unit (succeeded the Con Flight).
HD	Home Defence; collective term for World War One British-based fighter units and their airfields.
HE	High Explosive (bomb).
HGCU	Heavy Glider Conversion Unit.
Highball	Bouncing bomb developed for the Mosquito. Never used in action by No 618 Squadron because, incredibly, it was too good.
HTCU	Heavy Transport Conversion Unit.
H2S	World War Two airborne radar navigational and target identification aid used by RAF bombers.
IRBM	Intermediate Range Ballistic Missile (as in Thor).
JG	Jagdgeschwader; Luftwaffe day fighter wing.
KBB	Kite Balloon Base; 'airfield' sited at various ports during World War One, from where ships towed away balloons to search for U-boats.

K site	Decoy airfield, used in World War Two to divert enemy raiders away from real airfields. KQ sites also had flashing lights to attract night attacks.
LFS	Lancaster Finishing School.
LNSF	Light Night Striking Force; bombing element consisting of RAF Mosquitoes of No 8 Group.
MAEE	Marine Aircraft Experimental Establishment.
Mandrel	Airborne radar jamming system, employed by the RAF's No 100 Group.
MAP	Ministry of Aircraft Production.
MCA	Ministry of Civil Aviation.
Met	Meteorological.
MoA	Ministry of Aviation.
MoD	Ministry of Defence.
MT	Mechanical Transport; general term applied to vehicles. Also referred to as Motor Transport but the latter strictly incorrect.
MU	Maintenance Unit.
NAAFI	Navy, Army and Air Force Institutes (canteen for servicemen).
Nickel	Propaganda leaflet dropped from aircraft; term can also be used as a verb.
NJG	Nachtjagdgeschwader; Luftwaffe night fighter wing, as in the dreaded I Gruppe (squadron)/NJG 2.
Noball	Name for either a V-1 or V-2 site.
(O) AFU	(Observers) Advanced Flying Unit.
Oboe	Blind bombing radar system of World War Two, whereby one ground radar station showed the true compass course of an aircraft route, and a second the point of bomb release.
OCU	Operational Conversion Unit (succeeded the OTU).
Operations:	
Crossbow	Offensive against V-weapon sites 1943/44.

Dodge — Ferrying home of troops from Italy during 1945.

Exodus — Ferrying home of former prisoners of war during 1945.

Gisela — German codename for the infamous intruder attack of March 3/4 1945.

Haddock — Force of Wellingtons sent to southern France in June 1940, with intention of bombing Italy. French fears of retaliation prevented many sorties, and thc Italians suffered negligible bomb damage.

Manna — Food dropped to starving Dutch in April/May 1945.

Market — Arnhem airborne operation of September 1944.

Starkey — Spoof invasion of the Pas de Calais area in August/September 1943, intended to test the Luftwaffe air defences. Largely unsuccessful.

Varsity — Large airborne operation of March 1945, involving towing gliders over the River Rhine.

OPMAC — Operation Military Aid to the Community; post-World War Two scheme which resulted in the construction of several Scottish airstrips.

ORB — Operations Record Book; military records, which can be obtained via membership of the PRO.

ORP — Operational Readiness Platform; widened section at ends of main runway for quick reaction by fighters and other aircraft. Devised after World War Two.

OS — Ordnance Survey; for this and subsequent books, maps are 1:50,000 scale.

OTU — Operational Training Unit.

(P) AFU — (Pilots) Advanced Flying Unit

PFF — Pathfinder Force; World War Two RAF element which marked enemy targets to assist main attacking force.

PRO	Public Record Office; where aviation documents are held. Based in London, these can only be obtained if you hold a Reader's Ticket.
PSP	Pierced Steel Planking; most successful of World War Two's metal runway types.
Pundit	Letters in signals square or lights flashing in Morse Code giving an airfield's identity.
Q site	Decoy airfield, consisting of flashing lights, to attract Luftwaffe night bombing attacks.
RAAF	Royal Australian Air Force.
RAE	Royal Aircraft Establishment.
RAFGSA	Royal Air Force Gliding and Soaring Association.
RAFVR	Royal Air Force Volunteer Reserve.
Ramrod	Escorted daylight bombing raid, intended to destroy a certain target.
Ranger	Long-range offensive mission to attack any targets of note in a set area.
RAS	Reserve Aeroplane Squadron (RFC).
RAT Flight	Radio Aids Training Flight.
RAuxAF	Royal Auxiliary Air Force (AuxAF until 1947).
RCAF	Royal Canadian Air Force.
RFC	Royal Flying Corps (preceded the RAF).
RFS	Reserve Flying School (succeeded the EFTS).
Rhubarb	Low-level fighter operation in cloudy weather against short-range targets. Unpopular with many pilots, as considered wasteful.
RLG	Relief Landing Ground.
RNAS	Royal Naval Air Service (1914-18); or Royal Naval Air Station.
RNZAF	Royal New Zealand Air Force.
Rodeo	Fighter sweep.
Rover	Patrol, usually by Coastal Command aircraft, to look for enemy shipping.
RS	Radio School (World War Two); or Reserve Squadron (World War One, RFC).

r/t	Radio telephony (for communication between aircraft and ground).
SAM	Surface-to-Air Missile.
SAR	Search and Rescue; effectively the modern way of describing ASR.
Scarecrow	Coastal patrol flown by DH6s in 1918 to primarily frighten off U-boats.
Scatter Scheme	RAF plan of late 1939, in which bomber squadrons withdrew to rearward airfields as a temporary safety measure to avoid anticipated attacks.
SFTS	Service Flying Training School.
SLG	Satellite Landing Ground; extra aircraft storage area. Not to be confused with satellite airfields.
SMT	Square Mesh Track; like PSP, another common type of World War Two metal runway.
SOC	Struck Off Charge; the dreaded term for an aircraft, meaning retirement and, for most, the melting pot.
TAF	Tactical Air Force.
TCG	Troop Carrier Group (USAAF).
TDS	Training Depot Station; type of World War One training airfield.
TS	Training Squadron (RFC/RAF).
TT	Target Towing.
Turbinlite	Term applied to Havocs and Bostons fitted with airborne searchlights. They would use radar to intercept enemy aircraft, then illuminate them for accompanying Hurricanes. Several Flights became Nos 530-539 Squadrons on September 2 1942, but better radar and negligible operational success forced all *Turbinlite* units to disband on January 25 1943.
USAAF	United States Army Air Force (renamed US Air Force 1946).
Window	Strips of tin foil, dropped by bombers to jam enemy radar. First used in July 1943 with devastating success against Hamburg.

PART ONE:
The Triumph

A Swift Upbringing

Born 1909, ailing by 1912 but off to war two years later: such was the dramatic early life of that unique phenomenon called the British airfield. How different it all was to the extremely protracted time flying took to establish itself in this country.

Man had not even begun to think about airfields when first attempting to fly. He was too busy trying to lift off the ground. The dim and distant past produced many 'birdmen' who jumped off towers and other high buildings or cliffs with disastrous results. Bladud, father of King Lear, killed himself this way in 843 BC. Perhaps better remembered is the flying monk of Malmesbury in Wiltshire, said to have flown more than a furlong about 1020 AD. Alas, heavenly assistance was not on his side as he crippled himself on landing.

Flying became a much more practical proposition when manned balloons first appeared in France during 1783. If the word 'airfield' is taken in its loosest context, a place where aircraft take off and land, title for earliest site in Britain must go to the Comely Gardens in Edinburgh. Here James Tytler tied himself like a log beneath a barrel-shaped hot air balloon on August 27 1784 to fly in a wildly unchecked fashion. Hardly anyone bothered to notice him, unlike another event later the same year on September 15 when a staggering 150,000 people turned up at Moorfields in central London to watch Italian balloonist Vincenzo Lunardi make a two and a quarter hour flight to the Hertfordshire village of Standon Green End, north of Ware. Considerable farce overshadowed this fine achievement, for drunk workmen became so incapacitated they could not pump hydrogen into the balloon at first. The crowd then rioted in a separate incident and caused a grandstand to collapse. A large punch-up completed quite an eventful day!

Foreigners continued to advance the cause of British flying on January 7 1785 when Frenchman Jean Pierre Blanchard and American doctor John Jeffries, despite having to throw away many of their clothes overboard to conserve weight and keep airborne, first crossed the English Channel. Napoleon soon considered using balloons to invade England. Unlike that other proposed invasion of 1940, there was not a British airfield in sight. Balloons only needed a field and some (hopefully sober) helpers as winchmen.

Fixed-wing pioneers such as Sir George Cayley and Percy Pilcher, one of German Otto Lilienthal's hang-gliding disciples, also had no use for airfields in the 19th Century. Sloping ground or suitable hilltops were good enough for them. Speculation continues to rage about whether a later Cayley glider was in fact equipped with a small engine. We know for certain his machine flew about 500 yards across a valley at Brompton Hall near Scarborough in June 1853 and led to the famous incident where his coachman/pilot resigned after crashing. The inventor's granddaughter, who witnessed the flight, still intriguingly told in later years of how the aircraft was 'started up'. Although Cayley and some aides followed tradition by pulling it down a slight hill, the elderly pioneer was a recognised world authority on air engine theory. So did the first powered flight anywhere in the world occur in this remote part of Yorkshire instead of Kitty Hawk in North Carolina, where the Wright brothers took off from 50 years later?

Even the intrepid American duo had taken no chances by choosing a hill for their experiments. Airships, though, were a different proposition. Their immense size meant they required large areas devoid of obstructions. Gales became another problem and wrecked several early airships. For once, Britain did not wait until the last minute to solve these and other difficulties. The Balloon Section of the Royal Engineers formed in May 1890 at Chatham, later moving to Aldershot, but this combined factory and school found its second site wanting as well. Therefore, in the early months of 1905, another move was made to a piece of Army land in Hampshire now revered throughout the world: Farnborough. An airship shed was erected in May and in September 1907 *Nulli Secundus,* the Army's first dirigible, took to the air. Further craft necessitated more airship sheds to be built.

Not everyone was interested in airships. Other pioneers stuck with trying valiantly to overcome the massive problems associated with fixed-wing flight. Airfields continued to have no relevance in their thinking. One of these was Horatio Phillips, the first great aerodynamicist, who was greatly concerned with lift in aircraft. Having built a model in 1891, his thoughts turned to full-size construction like Cayley.

Claims that his Phillips II subsequently became the first British aircraft to fly in 1907 at Streatham in southern London cannot be verified. His machine was extraordinary as it possessed four 'Venetian blind' wing structures in tandem. Supposed to have flown about 500 feet, the Phillips II had good lift at the expense of control. Its strange multi-wing design also meant that visibility was extremely poor. Here was one man who had enough problems without having to worry about airfields.

Two other pioneers were busy at work during the same year. One was Samuel Franklin Cody, a colourful American who would soon gain British nationality. His base was Farnborough, where he later made the first true flight in Britain on October 16 1908. A few months earlier, on June 8, future founder of the great Avro aircraft company Alliott Verdon Roe had hopped at Brooklands motor racing circuit in Surrey. As the authorities there made life difficult for him, Roe soon moved to Lea Marshes in east London where he became the first Briton to fly a totally British aircraft on July 13 1909. No sooner had he managed this than legal proceedings were threatened. But by then the original British airfields had already come into use.

Where was our first site? The airfields of Britain abound with mysteries but this is the eternal conundrum which will almost certainly never be solved. Other inexplicable matters such as Stonehenge (the prehistoric monument, not the Great War airfield), the life of King Arthur and who exactly was Jack the Ripper are nothing in comparison! We can at least discount Farnborough, although that great place still remains our oldest active airfield, as it was not originally earmarked for this role. Most organisations, including the Guinness Book of Records, state our initial airfield opened in February 1909 at Shellbeach (better known as Leysdown) on the Isle of Sheppey. There is no doubt it was the first organised airfield in Britain, but many consider Leysdown was just edged out for the title by Fambridge, north of Southend. Could it have opened in 1908 instead and only become publicised in February 1909?

Deeply probing research into the ultimate airfield mystery ostensibly seems to provide an answer. Fambridge became known to the British general public on February 23, while Leysdown was originally mentioned four days later on the 27th after the Aero Club announced that it had just finalised arrangements for its use. It would thus appear that Fambridge wins hands down. But, as will be seen, the airfields of Britain have provided so many surprises in their time that nobody can be absolutely certain of this fact. Corroboration of any kind in 1909 only came from the mass media, and even then reports of airfield activities had to be taken with a pinch of salt because of newspaper flippancy or barely latent political bias.

What a tragedy it is that most other countries know where their earliest airfield existed – and Britain does not. France can always say that its – and the world's – initial site opened at Issy-les-Moulineaux in 1907. Britain has by common consent the greatest airfields of any country in the world, yet we can only grasp at straws in trying to find which one served as cradle for a massive army of others.

Official indifference to airfields was already becoming quite apparent. A suggestion made in the House of Lords during March 1909 loudly hinted as much, while still trying to sound benevolent:

> 'Helpful work could be accomplished by observant people in many parts of the country by compiling lists of places which might be suitable for aeroplane practice grounds and natural aerial harbours. For the first purpose extensive treeless plains would be required, sheltered as much as possible from the wind. Careful note should be made of the prevailing winds and their average power. At the foot of a hilly region well-sheltered valleys can frequently be found . . . If observant and scientific people all over the country took up the quest . . . a number of new and admirably suitable grounds could be found.'

The authorities were in other words saying that have airfields if you wish, but someone else has to do the donkey work and do not rely upon us for support. Determined individualists would just have to plough yet another lonely furrow.

Although another aviation or aeroplane trials ground – as airfields were initially described before the now archaic word aerodrome became accepted – had also arisen near London at Dagenham, where the Ford motor company now has its famous factory, Fambridge and Leysdown proved the more important sites. Various pioneers used the former, created by Noel Pemberton Billing, an eccentric but clever visionary who went on to found the Supermarine company. Leysdown had two purposes by serving as opening base for the Short company and holding the Aero Club. Among many famous personalities who belonged to this second organisation was J.T.C. Moore-Brabazon, holder of the earliest British private pilots' licence. He also became the first Briton to make powered flights in his homeland at Leysdown during April/ May 1909 as operations both here and at Fambridge finally managed to get under way.

Despite the undoubted enthusiasm of people like himself, Brabazon and other early users soon discovered how unsuitable were their airfields. Fambridge, Leysdown and Dagenham all suffered from extremely poor landing grounds which were very rough and often riddled with drainage ditches. This was a great pity, especially as the first two places both had good hangars and support facilities in workshops and accommodation. All three airfields had closed by the spring of 1910 but this was not the end of the British airfield story: it had only just begun.

The first aviation meeting in England was held at Doncaster racecourse in Yorkshire during October 15-23 1909. Inspiration again came from France and its spectacular aerial displays at Reims in August of the same year. Vast British crowds now came to see their first aircraft as flown by Sam Cody and other pioneers. This meeting proved a great success, as did a second event held almost simultaneously at Blackpool, although bad weather hampered that particular occasion. Louis Bleriot's arrival at Northfall Meadow near Dover Castle after crossing the English Channel on July 25 1909 had sensationally brought aviation to the notice of the British general public; these two meetings emphasised this fact. The aircraft had arrived. Where was the airfield?

Up until now, air shows and related events had taken place on specially hired grounds. A meadow or playing field suited pilots adequately, even if officialdom did not always take kindly to impromptu exhibition flying given without notice. Doncaster became significant as many racecourses would be converted into airfields in the future. One existed to the east of Hull at Hedon, and Lanark racecourse became Scotland's original airfield. Such was nationwide interest in aviation generally that a week of flying displays at the latter in August 1910 brought along 200,000 visitors, enough to make even the greatest football stadium in the world at Hampden Park cringe with envy. Lanark nevertheless began experiencing similar difficulties as its southern counterparts and quickly folded in 1911.

All was not lost, for in August of that year a rising aerial star named Claude Grahame-White purchased a large stretch of farmland in north-west London. Hendon duly became one of the all-time British airfield greats; most people now recognise it as home of the RAF Museum. Grahame-White turned his dream into a highly profitable ongoing concern before long, a place where aerial displays formed only part of a most lucrative market.

Hendon can rightly claim to be forerunner of the modern airfield, not just in Britain but anywhere in the world. A good landing area plus well laid out hangarage and support facilities made it different from preceding sites. No more would any airman have to sign a chit for some fuel at the first place he landed – usually unintentionally. This legendary place became the first airfield to serve London, and also achieved fame in a variety of other ways. Specially printed cards and letters flown to Windsor during September 9-26 1912 as part of the latest coronation celebrations gave Britain its original air mail service. As Claude Grahame-White had already pioneered night flying on April 27/28 1910 in the course of his epic duel with Frenchman Louis Paulhan in the London-Manchester 24 hour air race, this was another 'novel' activity which Hendon showed could be feasible.

Only now could the airfields of Britain say they were prominent to any degree, though not quite established as such. If Fambridge and Leysdown had jointly paved the way for future airfields, it was left to the Greater London superstar to iron out many of their previous shortcomings. Hendon introduced to Britain such daring feats as aerobatics and parachuting before World War One. Demonstrations of aerial bombing or 'bomb throwing', to use the then somewhat frightening term, hinted at more aggressive airfield uses in years to come. Although Hendon was not directly involved, it had a hand in yet another achievement. A familiar face there was Horatio Barber, who is reputed to have carried the world's first air cargo during July 1911 in Sussex from Shoreham to Hove – a humble box of Osram lamps.

British civil aviation had at last struggled to its feet. Private flying was by now relatively commonplace, thanks to the efforts of various still-unknown places like Castle Bromwich on the edge of Birmingham. Flying schools and aircraft factories also tentatively appeared on the scene. Claude Grahame-White, surely one of the greatest entrepreneurs ever seen, did not waste time by setting up similar organisations at Hendon.

A marked increase in flying naturally meant accidents were more likely to occur. Aircraft were exceptionally frail machines then, with engines often underpowered, unreliable or both. Aeronautical theory, regardless of whether it was in construction, navigation or flying techniques, frequently proved to be extremely limited. Last, but far from least, there was the problem almost as old as man himself: lack of money.

Financial short cuts in a multitude of ways sometimes spelt disaster, though not every air crash was attributable to sheer carelessness. Bad luck prevailed in a fatal crash involving the Honourable C.S. Rolls during a flying display in the Bournemouth suburb of Southbourne on July 12 1910. The Rolls-Royce company had lost one of its two mainstays in probably the most noteworthy accident of the pre-war period. Rolls had the dubious honour of being the first of countless British airmen and women to lose his life at home in a crash. Sam Cody became just another fatality when he crashed at his beloved Farnborough on August 7 1913.

Early British airfields did not escape the odd disaster either. These tended to come under both the self-inflicted and accidental categories. On the negative side, some sites continued to be so terrible that their users were simply asking for trouble. Acton and Park Royal in Greater London were two typical examples. Fate proved particularly cruel to Port Meadow, in the vicinity of Oxford, by dealing it two hammer blows in less than two years. A bad fire at Barrhead near Glasgow in April 1912 resulted in another disaster to ensure a tragic end for the second Scottish airfield after Lanark.

All these combined destructive forces were palpably the reason why considerable uncertainty loomed large over airfield activities by 1912. Their numbers had steadily increased since 1909, reaching double figures by the spring of 1910. Now the total of active airfields stuttered around the 23/24 mark after falling back slightly. They badly needed to branch out into other areas of aviation to progress further and fully establish themselves.

Different kinds of new airfields happily began to emerge as developments started to take place on the military side of British aviation. These could be traced back to manoeuvres at Larkhill in Wiltshire during September 1910 when a trio of biplanes participated. The Air Battalion of the Royal Engineers formed at Farnborough on April 1 1911, but 1912 became far more important as the Royal Flying Corps evolved from it on May 13. This newer force was in truth a twin element, for the RFC split into Military and Naval Wings, with the latter under Admiralty instead of War Office control. A naval flying school had already been established at Eastchurch, Leysdown's nearby enigmatic successor, although training had occurred for some months previously. Naval authorities were somewhat wary of their new 'experiment' but soon grew to accept its supreme usefulness.

Three events during the middle months of 1912 became important milestones in the life of the Military Wing. Its first three squadrons formed on May 13, then the Central Flying School came into being at Upavon in Wiltshire on June 19. The initial batch of pupils included Robert Smith-Barry and Hugh Trenchard, two men destined for far greater things and later to have major says in military airfield development. Now forgotten pioneer neighbour of Upavon Larkhill held the inaugural Military Aircraft Trials shortly afterwards, where a biplane built by Sam Cody was voted surprise winner following extensive tests for design and performance.

One machine disqualified from this competition actually easily outclassed its opponents. The Royal Aircraft Factory BE2 biplane from Farnborough was a Government entry, and so could not participate at Larkhill, but enjoyed revenge by serving as the main RFC aircraft type in the early years of World War One.

As the whole of Britain had to be defended against any possible aggressor, the RFC quickly realised how it had to be mobile. Many more airfields were needed to supplement the solid base which Farnborough, Larkhill and Upavon provided. No 2 Squadron immediately silenced doubts about mobility by flying from Farnborough to Montrose on Scotland's east coast in February 1913. Its new home was not the Montrose of two World Wars' service, as is so often stated, but a more southerly temporary site at Upper Dysart which lasted for about a year. The complete transferral of squadron aircraft was achieved in thirteen days without too much hassle. Perhaps this achievement might not sound the most remarkable in aviation history. However, in the British airfield story, it showed how they could be nationwide and not just confined to Salisbury Plain.

Almost a year had passed when the RFC airship element was suddenly transferred to Admiralty control. The Naval Wing was but one small step from gaining independence as the Royal Naval Air Service on July 1 1914. Meanwhile, the old Military Wing had been busy at another Salisbury Plain military airfield during June and July. Netheravon acted as a concentration camp or exercise area: a mass of tents, supported by a vast array of aircraft, helped to refine service operating techniques and create realistic war conditions. Little did the participants realise how close war would be in coming.

First hint of the horrors to come appeared with the assassination of a relatively obscure Austrian member of royalty and his wife by a fanatic. It was only over a month later on August 3 that the resultant sinister turn of events directly affected the airfields of Britain. A ban was placed on civil aviation and, next day, Britain entered World War One.

The mood of young men in this country verged on glee as they hoped to see some chance of action. To them the Hun was easily beatable.

In comparison with the other two armed services, it is highly questionable if the RFC and RNAS were in quite the same celebratory mood. Five main air powers existed at the outbreak of World War One – Great Britain, France, Germany, Russia and Austria-Hungary – and Britain was scrambling with Austria-Hungary to avoid bottom place of this quintet in terms of aircraft/airship strength. This country could only count on 113 front line aircraft (63 RFC, 50 RNAS) and six airships of all shapes and sizes, so the scene on our positively minute number of military airfields was fairly chaotic by August 1914.

A desperate lack of aircraft standardisation had dogged our airfields right from the beginning. No aircraft type could say it reigned supreme from 1909 into the early years of World War One. Designs were as diverse as night and day both at military and civil level. The fact 25 different types entered for the Military Aircraft Trials at Larkhill surely proved this alone. Along with Brooklands, Britain's first military airfield could still be said to have started laying the long road to aircraft standardisation. The Bristol aircraft company at Filton set up a flying school at each airfield, where trainees flew the Bristol Boxkite, broadly based on Henry Farman's biplanes. Four-fifths of British pilots available for military service would be Bristol-trained by the advent of World War One.

Britain would still not be the same without its eccentrics, and true to form many designers tried to turn theory on its head by building weird aircraft which had little or no hope of flying. Scot George Davidson placed great faith in a vertical take-off monoplane driven by fans that would power the machine to good altitude until it was able to glide forwards. This machine would then go through the same process again at a lower height. Davidson unbelievably intended his 'Air-Car' to serve as an airliner – had airline meals existed, they would not have been thrown in, more thrown up – and even discarded the notion of airports by proposing his aircraft land on tall platforms.

One equally odd aircraft which did fly was an annular or circular winged monoplane created by Cedric Lee and George Tilghman Richards. After testing annular biplane gliders, their first powered machine crashed because of engine failure on its maiden flight at Shoreham on November 23 1913. A second machine also came to grief but the third performed very well until Lee crashed it into the River Adur alongside Shoreham soon after World War One began. Fate seemed to be telling airfields and aviators alike that aircraft had to become more regular.

Although one or two types such as Bleriot monoplanes became more noticeable as a result at British airfields, any numerical superiority was totally lost after August 1914. Both home air elements nevertheless rallied to give what support they could. The RNAS was quick off the mark on friendly ground, mainly due to the flamboyant nature of Charles Samson. Eastchurch's commander had served as one of the four original trainee airmen at the Kent airfield over three years earlier. Leading the famous Eastchurch Squadron, Samson and his men proceeded to Skegness' first airfield by the Burgh Road, staying there for three weeks before returning south and crossing to France. The RFC was slower in responding domestically but faster in international terms when aircraft of Nos 2, 3 and 4 Squadrons managed to gather at Dover (St Margaret's) on August 12. They soon flew across the English Channel, quickly followed by No 5 Squadron, thus trail-blazing the way for many more units.

This aerial exodus to France did not help British airfields in the short term. They had virtually run out of aircraft! As 37 machines had passed through Dover (St Margaret's) on August 13, 63 altogether flying to France that month, military bases then in existence were left with very few types on charge. Aircraft still at home formed the most astonishing hotchpotch of equipment.

Related problems only made the situation worse. As early British squadrons had a wide mixture of types for nearly a year, so flying instruction was difficult. This factor, plus probably a lack of appeal in the job, led to an initial shortage of groundcrews. Available mechanics endured many a nightmare trying to keep this ragbag of aircraft serviceable; their small numbers made aircraft movements on airfields at best irregular in due course.

The airfields of Britain were hence forced to adopt a training role. Flying instruction would become their primary function throughout World War One. Reserve Aeroplane Squadrons were created to give would-be pilots *ab initio* training before they moved to an operational squadron. Existing airfields such as Brooklands, Castle Bromwich and Shoreham converted to instructional duties, while totally new stations like Catterick in Yorkshire and Gosport in Hampshire came into use. A few civil organisations also helped churn out new aircrews but the lack of a set training system only resulted in considerable chaos.

Trainees soon realised how such a diversity of aircraft types would not be conducive to good instruction. The Maurice Farman S.7 and S.11 biplanes, known as the Longhorn and Shorthorn respectively as the latter had no skids or front elevator, had become more numerous at training airfields. Yet these were poor aircraft, showing why accidents on or near airfields had now become commonplace. Our always unpredictable weather has just been one of ten causes which have made countless aircraft crash. One can also include engine or structural failures, human error, take-off or landing accidents, mid-air or ground collisions plus fires/explosions – not to mention enemy action. Airfields have rarely been to blame for any of these mishaps, though hardly a day has gone by since without some accident or general commotion. Great War training airfields had only seen the beginning of it.

We can now only marvel at how our airfields entered a war just five and a half years after their conception. A similar comparison would be to imagine a boy reaching that age and going into the armed services instead of school. Their progression from birth to any semblance of military activity came at lightning speed.

Semblance was undoubtedly the right word to use early on in World War One, for the still tiny British airfield band could only ostensibly offer an air of efficiency. Much of their problems still centred around the many aircraft types which used them. Brooklands was the place to be where aircraft standardisation at last became a permanent fixture when No 8 Squadron formed on January 1 1915 with BE2cs, the first unit to do so with just one aircraft type. BE2 variants soon found themselves jacks of all trades despite being intended for reconnaissance duties. Although many have since tended to rubbish the Farnborough-designed type, it proved far better than its predecessors excluding the marvellous Avro 504 biplane.

Squadrons operating these and other types soon became common on British airfields as they worked up to operational readiness before flying to the Western Front. As French-based RFC and RNAS units enjoyed top priority in the supply of aircraft, therefore those forces at home continued to struggle with a mixture of types.

The dire plight of trainees was made far worse by an almost in-built lack of flying theory on the parts of their frequently disgruntled instructors, who taught them in a cumbersome parrot fashion. Dual controls hardly existed in aircraft either and so the sorry list of fatal crashes kept increasing. Airfield personnel almost became numbed to near-daily accidents.

Many aircrews feared crashing at base and, as they described it, being 'roasted' in the process of becoming trapped amid fabric and struts.

Utter confusion was not restricted to flying schools. The Admiralty, tasked with the aerial defence of Britain from September 3 1914, soon proved incapable of carrying out its new role. A large airship station at Kingsnorth in Kent had just been commissioned as well but a lack of equipment prevented much activity in those first few months of wartime.

The marine airfield position was even worse. Although some stations had arisen since the end of 1912, a year or so after the first successful seaplane flight in Britain at Lake Windermere in the Lake District, things were still terribly disorganised by August 1914. It seems odd how water-borne flying started fairly slowly in this country, for little preparation was needed at a marine base in comparison with a landplane one. Planners had long learned the cardinal rule that you never launched aircraft from a houseboat equipped with a catapult, as American Samuel F. Langley twice tried to do with disastrous results in 1903. His machine – ironically called the Aerodrome – was not even a seaplane: Langley thought water offered a safer landing. Now nearly all available British machines had to operate from Felixstowe, Grain and Great Yarmouth on the south-eastern coastline of England because of their operational, range and servicing limitations. A war was the last thing they needed.

Unfortunately for British marine and landplane bases, the German Navy did not show much consideration for their wishes of a peaceful time. Huge gaps existed along the whole eastern side of Britain which enemy capital shipping could exploit. German North Sea operational planners had no worry about opposing aerial defences at that time. A large enemy cruiser force thus sailed along England's north-eastern coast on December 16 1914 and shelled the towns of Hartlepool, Scarborough and Whitby. Over 150 inhabitants were killed. The airfields of Britain did not respond. How could they?

Further events showed how toothless the Admiralty was. Eight days after the shelling incident, a German seaplane dropped an HE bomb in a garden at Dover. A second air raid next day on the same general area again resulted in no casualties but Britain had experienced its first taste of strategic bombing. Worse was to come on the night of January 19/20 1915 with the first German Navy Zeppelin raid which left four dead in East Anglia. More largely unopposed raids on London and the east coast during 1915 killed and injured many other people. The general public voiced their frustration at this 'gross impertinence' which rained death from the skies. It was fairly obvious that the Admiralty was hopelessly unable of aerially defending Britain. Too much emphasis had been placed at airfields on training, especially for reconnaissance.

After Hendon had led the way yet again by mounting the first night patrols over London in September 1914, some airfields were set aside as a result for defensive duties in early 1915. Operating conditions then bordered on the diabolical. Aircraft equipment was poor, co-ordination and weaponry availability negligible. Among offensive implements available about this time for anti-Zeppelin operations could be counted rifles, grenades – and grappling hooks. These were meant to rip away at the structure of an enemy airship but, to do this, a pilot first had to reach a similar altitude, and most fighters were unable even to achieve that stage of an operational flight.

Problems for defenders multiplied further as Zeppelins usually operated at night. Their airfields would be lit by a few oil canisters to 'assist' them take off and land. This was dangerous enough as a number of pilots became disorientated in darkness and often crashed with fatal results. Once airborne, pilots were on their own: no radar, no r/t, nothing. Such a highly unsatisfactory state of affairs lasted until March 1916.

By then the authorities had had enough of the cack-handed Admiralty defensive supervision of Britain. Changes had already taken place, notably the phasing out of vastly inferior aircraft types at all airfields. Flying schools now possessed better equipment, although airfields continued to witness some dubious training techniques. Control passed to the RFC, a move which did wonders for that increasingly distinctive institution called the British airfield.

Co-ordination

Home Defence was the all-important new term in the spring of 1916. Something had to be done about persistent Zeppelin attacks. These cigar-shaped monsters roamed over most parts of Britain with ease, even daring to penetrate north-east England and southern Scotland. Fatalities and injuries among the British population were not huge by later standards. Morale still kept slipping. How could the country be properly defended?

The number of British airfields greatly increased during 1916, with a big chunk of these new arrivals being intended for Home Defence. Racecourses were quickly adapted for flying needs as they had useful naturally flat landing areas. The idea of an aerial racecourse – for that was the literal Greek translation of the word aerodrome – was now reality instead of a dream. Yorkshire sites became particularly prominent: those at Beverley, Doncaster, Knavesmire, Pontefract, Ripon and Thirsk were all impressed for RFC service and saw at least limited use.

Dozens of other fresh airfields opened along the eastern coastline from Kent to central Scotland and also well inland as several new HD squadrons formed. The previous practice of placing two aircraft each at ten airfields around London had too little an impact and made a mockery of co-ordination, a highly important part of the formula for outstanding success which all of our airfields needed a war to discover. A typical HD squadron now had available a headquarters, three Flight Stations and as many as twenty landing grounds. All three types of airfield were notable in their own ways, not least because HQ sites did not always have to be an airfield, as was the case with No 39 Squadron's HQ at Woodford in Essex between June 1916 and December 1917. Flight Stations had limited support facilities in a few huts for air and groundcrews plus some small hangars.

Of the numerous HD airfields, though, landing grounds

were easily the most amazing. It is still difficult to comprehend just how many existed during World War One. They were virtually everywhere and sometimes popped up in the most unlikely of places. Some had very short lives, others were hardly used but each one was necessary.

Landing grounds had first appeared before World War One, only they were not officially recognised as such at that time. Mechanics had sped ahead of Claude Grahame-White by motor car to previously arranged staging posts during the 1910 London-Manchester air race. His successful opponent Louis Paulhan touched down at a presageful place in Staffordshire called Lichfield in the course of their friendly battle. Military aircraft before World War One badly needed landing grounds as well. The line of naval aircraft stations which the Admiralty announced on October 10 1912 it was able to create were effectively landing grounds, although some of these like Cleethorpes and North Berwick were never actually used in the event.

Use of these airfields depended on the vagaries of the machines employing them. Aircraft were unpredictable pieces of equipment easily capable of suffering mechanical difficulties. Their short operating range was another problem. Pilots therefore had to find a safe place where to land in an emergency. Landing grounds were split into three classes, depending on the amount of obstructions surrounding them and the quality of their runway surfaces. Two further classes defined whether they were lit or unlit for night or day availability respectively. Conditions alone were very primitive: at best, a landing ground would possess a couple of wooden huts, a few personnel and some necessary stores should any aircraft land. This was sheer luxury for some HD squadrons as many landing grounds consisted of a single airman sitting by a telephone in a farmhouse! When one of these remarkable airfields was used, its landing area would be cleared of animals which normally kept the grass down.

The whole concept of landing grounds must seem antiquated in this sophisticated age we live in today. Maybe so, but there is no doubt these mostly unsung heroes saved innumerable lives. One must always remember that parachutes were prohibited in all British aircraft except static observation balloons during World War One to deter cowardice or even possible defectors. (The RAF only fully introduced them in 1921). Almost as a reward, a number of landing grounds would be revived in the future for their gallant service. For example, four sites in south-east Scotland and north-east England belonging to No 77 (HD) Squadron were West Fenton, Woodbridge, Eccles Tofts and Horndean. They in turn eventually became far better known in World War Two as famous fighter airfield Drem, fighter-bomber Operational Training Unit station Milfield, night fighter OTU base Charterhall and its satellite Winfield.

In the south, a Flight Station destined to become an airfield superstar helped turn the tide in Britain's war against the Zeppelin. A BE2c pilot had engaged the Schutte-Lanz SL.11 during the night of September 2/3 1916 and destroyed it with machine-gun fire. William Leefe Robinson of No 39 (HD) Squadron was awarded the Victoria Cross for his actions. He was based at Sutton's Farm, just east of London, which later evolved into the immortal fighter airfield of Hornchurch. Ironically, the SL.11 was a German Army airship – Zeppelins belonged to the Navy – but the invincibility of airships as bombing craft had disappeared for ever. No 39 Squadron destroyed another Zeppelin and helped finish off a third in one night later on in September to enforce this point.

Although great courage had undoubtedly been displayed, one factor still obvious was the lack of standardised training at airfields. William Leefe Robinson and his contemporaries were dare-devil fliers who happened to be in the right place at the right time. In their early flying days, instructors were often pilots resting after action on the Western Front, men who had no great taste for teaching 'rookie' pilots. Those who were lucky enough to train at Upavon's CFS at least had 50 flying hours under their belt but most other pilots were rushed through their particular courses. If the theoretical shortcomings of new aircrews bore signs of concealed apparence at home, they became yawningly obvious once on the Western Front as German fighters made new intakes look like easy meat. Both aircraft and men were now not just confined to general reconnaissance duties.

In stepped Robert Smith-Barry, one of the original batch of trainees at Upavon back in 1912. He determined to revolutionise flying training when given charge of No 1 Reserve Squadron at Gosport in December 1916. Smith-Barry wanted flying instructors to be properly trained as such and all available aircraft to have dual controls. Another of his innovations was the Gosport Tube, a famous device intended to allow better communication between crewmembers. Astounding results led to creation of the School of Special Flying and much better flying standards at airfields overall. Pilots could now expect a fair chance of survival unlike before, when at one point life expectancy was unbelievably measured not in weeks, days or even hours but minutes . . . It was a case of unfortunate timing how Smith-Barry's legendary training notes of May 1917 came a month after 'Bloody April', when the RFC suffered dreadful losses in action. Better crews and aircraft would be on their way from British airfields.

Part of the renewed optimism lay in advances in aircraft design and manufacture. British firms had knuckled down to producing aircraft in quantity from 1916; some numbers of French machines like Caudron trainers and Nieuport fighters had been needed beforehand to bolster units until production fully geared itself up. Not surprisingly, production centred on Greater London, where the first totally intended (albeit unsuccessful) works had opened at Barking Creek in 1909. Cricklewood now accommodated Handley Page instead, while Brooklands held Martinsyde, Sopwith and Vickers (also based at Joyce Green) and Hendon Grahame-White plus Airco. Various other factories were spread throughout Britain, notably Blackburn at Brough near Hull and also Bristol, based north of the city at Filton. Places like these mainly produced aircraft under licence for other companies.

Experimentation became most important too as a direct result. Busy land and marine research airfield Grain was arguably the main British base in this field. It soon had opposition, for a small test unit moved from Upavon to a new airfield close to Ipswich called Martlesham Heath in January 1917. This eventually brought about formation of the Aeroplane and Armament Experimental Establishment, a famous evaluation unit still in existence today.

Airfields showed themselves to be excellent places both for production and testing. They offered huge working areas plus complete secrecy. Aircraft Acceptance Parks had to be established in a second spin-off, places where these thousands of new machines emerging from factory airfields could be tested before transfer to the military authorities.

Another co-ordinated system seemed to be in force. But was this really the case? If Grain was supposedly the top test airfield in this country, what was Farnborough doing? The inspiration of British flying, although busy in other spheres, was suffering from severe procedural problems. Its Royal Aircraft Factory remained at loggerheads with the authorities for most of World War One and, not for the first time, there were grave doubts about government control. In theory, the Factory was forbidden to build aircraft as this would clash with private aircraft company interests. It weaved round the problem by seeming to repair damaged aircraft, when in fact placing new types under construction. Cover for this clandestine activity was to give types unusual prefixes: BE or

Bleriot Experimental, FE or Farman Experimental, SE or Santos Experimental and so on. As these examples demonstrate, the general ploy was to completely confuse the authorities by naming an aircraft after an aviation pioneer. Who would have then guessed that BE stood for general purpose duties or SE for fighter purposes?

The aeronautical dunces of Parliament raged in frustration at how Farnborough had completely outwitted them. It was a brilliant ruse, not least because the Royal Aircraft Factory created some of Britain's best World War One types. The BE2 was joined by the FE2 series of fighters, RE8 reconnaissance type and SE5A scout. When permission was grudgingly eventually given for aircraft production, so much time had been wasted that it was too late, as Farnborough had too small a manufacturing capacity. Such prolonged nit-picking had almost totally obscured the little fact a global conflict was still going on.

Some might say that the Farnborough saga of World War One is why MPs have been so anti-airfield in policy ever since. Military airfields became the source of much adverse comment in Parliament at this time. Frequent questions and verbal sniping occurred about land requisition, airfield construction and sundry issues. Even niggly problems such as allegations about a great wastage of petrol at bases were publicly paraded out of all proportion. Great official concern arose about airfield expenditure as a result of the Loch Doon scandal, when a proposed training airfield in south-west Scotland turned out to be so costly and pathetically misplaced that MPs were all but baying for blood when this ridiculous scheme was eventually abandoned. The huge majority of British airfields fortunately proved immensely better but that did not stop petty-minded politicians having a right go at them.

One of their few political friends was already well known to them, for Noel Pemberton Billing was elected to Parliament in 1916. He has since been accused of wasting Parliamentary time but in reality the gallant Noel made brilliant intrusive actions by keeping thoughts fully on aeronautical affairs. Here was a man who knew what he was talking about, having only created a firm which later produced a little aircraft called the Spitfire and then organised the world's first strategic bombing raid on airship sheds at Friedrichshafen in November 1914. Or did other MPs not like him just because he founded one of the first two British airfields?

The Government – and everyone else – had a far greater matter than Farnborough to worry about by 1917. No sooner had the average Briton thought he had seen the end of strategic bombing by airships than a new threat arose. Gotha entered the national language, a general term applied to German fixed-wing bombers. Nearly all previous activity had been confined to Zeppelins, still spasmodically active, but aircraft raids on south-east England became increasingly frequent from March 1917. A total of 24 earlier small scale German aircraft attacks between December 1914 and early 1917 had only served as a bearable nuisance. Home Defence squadrons on their airfields in and around London were now in for one almighty shock.

The first Gotha raid on London during May 1917 had to be aborted due to bad weather, but Folkestone and a then little known Kent airfield called Lympne were bombed instead to leave 80 people dead. Luck sided with an airfield for once as Lympne was spared from casualties and even endured only negligible damage. A second attempted raid on June 5 saw AA defences account for one bomber but 66 fighters achieve nothing. The crunch came on June 13 when a 14 strong force of Gothas reached London in broad daylight to kill 160 civilians and injure another 432 around Liverpool Street railway station, near where Vincenzo Lunardi's balloon had taken off from in 1784. Many were furious that home defences were unable to destroy an enemy machine.

Desperate measures had to be taken. SE5s of No 56 Squadron were summoned from the Western Front eight days later to Bekesbourne in Kent; they left on July 5 after seeing no action. London was not to know this was a disastrous move, for Gothas visited again two days later to cause more death and destruction. Despite a bigger than ever defensive presence of 95 fighters, only one bomber was destroyed by a resident of another Kent airfield at Throwley. Again a fighter squadron was recalled, this time No 46 to Sutton's Farm; again no action occurred during its brief stay. Feelings had become so high there were isolated instances of irate civilians physically and verbally attacking off-duty airfield personnel.

The old problem of co-ordination had reappeared to dog our airfields. This was solved by vastly improved links between them, AA defences and searchlights. Remedies brought rewards as RNAS fighters at Manston and Walmer in Kent each shot down a Gotha during August 1917; the RNAS, as ever competing fiercely with the RFC, did not want to miss out on the action either. The German biplanes duly switched to night operations but discovered organised British fighters still coming after them. Airfields were no more like ancient battles or fair-weather friends for, if they had kept active in other times of the year and not just summer, certainly they had much preferred daylight beforehand to darkness. This explains why the first night flight by a British military aircraft took another three years to transpire after Claude Grahame-White's heroic journey. Even this later trip of April 16/17 1913 only involved the 13 mile flip from Larkhill to Upavon and back by a pilot of No 3 Squadron. Now HD fighters frequently ventured out into dark British skies.

While London and the south-east continued to see some bad bombing raids, 147 people losing their lives on September 3 1917 alone, Gothas began displaying considerable vulnerability. They left Britain well alone after a disastrous raid on London during May 19 1918 when participants among 84 defending fighters destroyed three aircraft. Remarkably accurate AA fire shot down three more of the attackers. The airfields of Britain had helped to save their country from further punishment. One of these was an unknown site on the southern outskirts of London, credited with a victory in the May 19 rout. It was called Biggin Hill.

If HD airfields had needed some time to shatter the mythical Gotha, in many ways Germany's World War One equivalent of the Stuka, they had sorted out its Zeppelin fleet quite a while before. Although nearly a year had elapsed between the first interception of a Zeppelin and William Leefe Robinson's historic kill, more gallant efforts soon saw several airships tumble earthwards in huge balls of flame as RFC and RNAS aircraft pumped tracer bullets into them. Victory was complete when a Great Yarmouth-based Airco DH4 shot down the LZ.70 over the North Sea on August 5 1918 in what turned out to be the last attempted Great War bombing raid on Britain. This event proved doubly fitting as on board was mastermind of the Zeppelin bombing campaign Peter Strasser.

Home Defence personnel must have felt as if they had gone to the edge of hell and back. Until 1918, their airfields had mainly relied upon the Royal Aircraft Factory threesome of the BE2, BE12 and FE2 series types. All lacked adequate ceilings to tackle Zeppelins; while Avro 504Ks were introduced in January 1918, it was only with the Sopwith Camel's coming shortly afterwards that HD airfields now held an efficient defensive fighter.

Operations, which involved aircraft patrolling over their designated airfield, proved equally fearful or frustrating. Some squadrons – especially in the north – spent their whole wartime existence without shooting down any enemy aircraft. Night operations became the most dreaded as HD personnel had to learn by trial and error. Initial sorties early on in 1916 tended to see infinitely more crashes than good luck but, by the summer, HD airfields could hope to see each one of their residents departing and returning more safely. Accident levels were certainly well down in the last twelve months of World War One.

Provided no enemy aircraft had been spotted during a night patrol, a pilot would fly back to his airfield. He would fire a green flare to indicate his arrival, await a similar response from the ground and then land between crude runway 'lights'. This all seems so primitive, yet HD airfields were informed of enemy aircraft movements in a process involving observation posts, who told localised operations rooms and then via the defence controller to the airfields themselves. It was this useful technique which over two decades later helped fighter airfields win the Battle of Britain.

German bomber depredations meant airfields too were more than likely to be subjected to this new phenomenon of aerial bombardment because of their distinctive outlines. Eastchurch became our first airfield to be attacked, on August 9 1915, but only a handful of sites encountered enemy raids afterwards. Those few attacks which did occur caused hardly any fatalities and little damage. Various reasons were responsible, such as the limited operating radii of enemy landplanes, while Zeppelins indulged in some woeful navigation and highly exaggerated bombing reports. One stated how not only a hangar was hit at Kensington (?) but also ships blown out of the water, factories destroyed and hundreds killed: bombs had really fallen either on fields or in the sea. On a sadder note, the solely effective Great War enemy attack on an airfield happened on July 4 1917 when Gothas killed seven mechanics at the famous marine base of Felixstowe. The Suffolk station and its brethren would still achieve more than ample revenge.

Whereas Germany had taken the aerial war to Britain, necessitating RFC fighter airfields, the RNAS (known with the RFC as the Royal Air Force from April 1 1918) was just as concerned with maritime patrol duties. U-boats had enjoyed such tremendous success since the German Admiralty declared unrestricted submarine warfare in waters around Britain on February 4 1915 that they managed to enforce food shortages here. As aircraft could help to quell this menace, many new coastally positioned airfields arose from the mid-war period.

Heavy reliance was initially placed upon airships as they were able to be on station for long periods. Most lighter-than-air craft saw little action but proved excellent deterrents. Stations for their use were developed in such differing places as Mullion (Cornwall), Capel (Kent), Llangefni (Anglesey), Howden (Yorkshire), Luce Bay near Stranraer and Longside to the north of Aberdeen. Airships were split into rigids and non-rigids: most famous of the former was the R.34, which post-war flew from East Fortune in eastern Scotland to America and back to Britain during July 2-13 1919 almost unrecognised to make the first double Atlantic crossing. This was an infinitely better improvement in comparison with nearly eight years earlier when the R.1 left its shed at Barrow-in-Furness and promptly collapsed! Non-rigids, on the other hand, came into use during 1915 and at first consisted of the Submarine Scout or SS type. The larger plus improved Coastal or C class type followed, then the big North Sea or NS class in February 1917. Best known of all individual non-rigids was the C.9: its home was Mullion, top British airship patrol station and the only one to see really major action against U-boats.

Only at patrol airfields were aircraft relatively standardised from the start of World War One. The story was much the same with flying boat and seaplane bases, the 'Spider Web' patrols (so named after the shape of routes aircraft flew) from Felixstowe, Great Yarmouth and other marine sites passing into legend after their introduction in April 1917. Britain was most fortunate towards the end of World War One to have two successful seaborne types in the reliable Short 184 and John Porte's Felixstowe series of flying boats. The Short floatplane entered service in 1915, while Felixstowe F.2as and F.3s meant marine bases had truly effective machines from late 1917. So aggressive were Felixstowes that some of their crews took on Zeppelins with great success. Two more seaplanes fairly common at marine airfields were the Sopwith Baby and long-running Fairey III series. All were needed as U-boat activity reached new heights after February 1917.

Unfortunately, the aircraft which the RNAS possessed were not matched by an equally good organisational structure. Even allowing for a small number of squadrons and Flights, most RNAS aircraft came under control of an airfield such as Great Yarmouth. This was despite the fact that airfields sorted themselves out in mid-1915 to form Commands controlled by the Senior Naval Officer in their area. RNAS stations thus operated more or less oblivious of what each other was doing to make constant anti-submarine monitoring patchy. They tried their best to disprove the old saying that no man (or airfield) is an island.

Co-ordination was needed yet again. It finally started to appear when the convoy system was introduced in May 1917. Aircraft attacks on submarines rose markedly as a result: 169 sightings and 106 attacks in 1917, plus 192 and 130 respectively during the first nine months of 1918. Inside instead of outside forces later made their mark as well once properly numbered Flights were introduced in April 1918 (300 class for flying boats, 400 class seaplanes and 500 class landplanes) before RAF squadrons arose in the summer.

Putting aside these shortcomings, the RNAS more than earned pass marks for its airfields. Most were favourably equipped with hangars and support facilities. Cranwell or HMS *Daedalus* in Lincolnshire became Britain's biggest airfield in World War One, while various airship and marine bases had adjoining landing grounds for resident or visiting landplanes.

Many British coastal airfields in addition saw two of the most unlikely aircraft types imaginable latterly enter the U-boat war. Airships had been originally envisaged to use harbours: they never did but manned kite balloons towed behind destroyers out of vital ports to look out for submarines became unexpectedly successful in action.

Kite Balloon Bases would soon be joined by an even odder force. After being declared obsolescent for training duties, a large number of Airco DH6 biplanes were given the task of flying Scarecrows or coastal patrols from early 1918. This tactic developed from a ploy used for part of 1917 when a few Sopwith 1½ Strutter bombers temporarily filled a gap in home anti-submarine defences by flying from south-westerly English and Welsh bases at Mullion, Pembroke and Prawle Point. DH6 pilots found their new role crashingly boring as they mounted endless patrols from most parts of Britain. Carrying a tiny bomb load, units saw just as little action as their airship counterparts but U-boat attacks on Allied shipping dropped considerably in 1918. Submarines simply would not dare attack ships while aircraft were present overhead.

The little ex-trainers, airships, flying boats, seaplanes and kite balloons had all performed extremely well in the face of adversity. Poor weather was always a problem and claimed many lives. Combats with enemy seaplanes proved rare at first but the spring and summer of 1918 saw Felixstowe and Great Yarmouth flying boats frequently battling it out with German machines based not far away at Zeebrugge in Belgium. Combats occurred too in the English Channel and RNAS/RAF seaplanes had to receive fighter protection.

A most modern aircraft type also to see maritime patrol service would be operated from one more northerly part of Britain. No 246 Squadron at Seaton Carew in Yorkshire held most of the few Blackburn Kangaroos in RAF use. Although in action for only the last few months of World War One, the world's first wholly effective anti-submarine patrol landplane had managed to help sink a U-boat by November 1918.

One regrettable fact all Allied patrol airfields had to accept was how they could not be credited with many U-boat sinkings. Only six out of 178 U-boats sunk overall in World War One were destroyed solely by home aircraft, with six more shared victories (including two by kite balloons) and another 41 enemy submarines damaged to varying degrees. The first to be destroyed by an aircraft was UC-36 in the North Sea on May 20 1917 when a Curtiss H-12 flying boat from Felixstowe attacked it. As this occurred in the same month as introduction of the convoy system, one cannot help but wonder what might have happened if this tactic had been introduced earlier. Bombs carried aboard aircraft proved very inferior too and crews really required nothing less than a direct hit on the surprisingly strong hull of a U-boat in order to sink it.

Confirmation of a U-boat kill proved the real problem: aircrews were able to report back at base how their attacks resulted in oil slicks, wreckage or even dead bodies floating in the water. But rarely could they be certain of a kill unless seeing the U-boat break up. Range limitations often meant aircraft could not hang around long enough to witness what happened next. Mullion epitomised the sheer frustration involved by putting in thousands of hours of hard work and only being able to credit itself with a single 'probable' kill. Official figures undoubtedly conceal the fact that our airfields sank or all but finished off many enemy submarines in reality.

Perhaps more than any other role, even Home Defence or training, it was maritime patrol work which produced a mushrooming of airfields in Britain during World War One. The days when planners limited themselves to Salisbury Plain because of its isolation and proximity to the Army had long gone. No more did the cavalry complain about wasted galloping land either – they would not have dared. Most parts of Britain, with the exception of most of western Scotland, had some sort of airfield presence by the latter stages.

Although most airfields in Britain lay on its eastern side, others arose in virgin territory. Aircraft production centres began appearing around Glasgow, Manchester and Southampton to feed the voracious demands of this rapidly emerging industry. Factory airfields would turn out a grand total of 55,000 machines during the conflict. New machines such as the Armstrong Whitworth FK8 reconnaissance type, Airco DH4, 9 and 9A day bombers plus the Sopwith Dolphin fighter among others now left for the Western Front or became assigned to training airfields much further inland. Foreigners conversant in the mother tongue began making their presence felt at these new stations. Australian airmen arrived at Leighterton and Minchinhampton in Gloucestershire, while Canadians came to Upper Heyford in Oxfordshire before going south to old stager Shoreham.

Airfields also made their inimitable mark on the smaller islands of Britain. The Isle of Wight was a particularly good example, where several sites were used for a whole variety of purposes. To the extreme west, the Isles of Scilly had a most important flying boat base in Tresco, whereas at the other end of Britain Orkney became equipped with a mixture of airfields, most having some connection with the critically important Fleet Anchorage at Scapa Flow. Even Shetland entered the scene by allowing a fledgling flying boat station to open at Catfirth in mid-1918, a KBB already on the islands at Gremista thus now having a little company in this formerly airfieldless area.

Welsh and Irish readers will no doubt have noticed how hardly any mention has been made of their airfield involvement so far. The simple reason is that no site existed in either country before World War One; those which did during the conflict only came into action fairly late on. Wales only had a handful of airfields from mid-war but the important airship stations of Llangefni and Pembroke gave good service and would also see World War Two use as Mona and Carew Cheriton respectively. Ireland, as it was in pre-Free State days, owes its aeronautical existence to one man. A young RFC officer named William Sholto Douglas was ordered to travel around Ireland in a BE2c during mid-1917 while recovering from severe injuries received in a flying accident. His mission was to select a number of training airfields. Douglas, who became Marshal of the RAF in 1946, chose some excellent sites. Four of his choices have gained much significance since flying started at the end of 1917. Aldergrove and Collinstown have become the airports for Belfast and Dublin, while the Irish Army Air Corps has its airfields at Baldonnel and Gormanston. Both Northern Ireland and the Republic fail to realise the massive aviation debt they owe to Sholto Douglas.

In the last year of fighting, the Americans despatched a fair number of US Navy flying boats and seaplanes to four Irish bases. The country's entry into World War One had brought great hopes among the other Allies. America had manpower, industry and generally a fresh approach to its armed services. However, unlike in the next world conflict, its aerial contribution proved very small. Various difficulties were responsible, mainly involving production problems and logistics. A certain climatically pleasant Scottish airfield was not around to help America this time.

American forces still gamely tried to assist the war effort in Europe in whatever way they could. Scotland's east coast saw limited activity by US fighter units as they worked up before moving to France; the marine base of Killingholme in Lincolnshire accommodated a number of USN flying boats; but most American airmen were based on the south coast of England. Eastleigh, nowadays far better known as Southampton Airport, served as an AAP for the USN and performed some good work before World War One ended. Other nearby bases at Ford, Goring-by-Sea, Rustington, Southbourne (no relation to the site where Charles Rolls died pre-war) and Tangmere were intended as Training Depot Stations. They had unluckily arrived too late on the scene, either not reaching full operational status or completion of construction. Two neighbouring colossal airfield superstars of days ahead had at least taken their first faltering steps on the road to supreme glory.

Cautious activities of foreigners were really only a minor diversion for British Great War airfields. As we have already seen, it was training which filled the majority of their time. The decreasing enemy aerial threat allowed HD squadrons in more operationally distant parts of Britain to largely transfer to training duties by 1918. Now the aforementioned TDSs established themselves to at last end the agonies of disorganised instruction. Stamford in Cambridgeshire saw No 1 TDS form in August 1917, the same month as the School of Special Flying was created at Gosport. Trainees could breathe a huge sigh of relief. Gone were the days of Reserve Aeroplane Squadrons, renamed Reserve Squadrons on January 13 1916 and Training Squadrons on June 1 1917. The latter now usually linked up in pairs to become TDSs. These airfields could be easily identified with their superb flying equipment of the Avro 504 trainer, supplemented by more advanced aircraft types. Each also possessed a large number of aeroplane sheds or hangars, a mixture of the two best known World War One types in the permanent Belfast and temporary Bessoneau.

TDSs were not just the only training innovations, for new kinds of schools formed at airfields to keep pace with aircraft development. Fighter, bomber and navigation training elements gradually came into being. Kent typified the trend by having aerial gunnery establishments at Dymchurch and New Romney/Littlestone, while a wireless school existed at Penshurst. An unexpectedly resuscitated Leysdown held the Pilots and Observers Aerial Gunnery and Aerial Fighting School: some Great War training units bore ponderous names. All this varied activity would prove crucial for both future military and – albeit more indirectly – civil airfield/aviation needs.

The end of World War One witnessed another equally notable development at Bircham Newton in Norfolk: RAF heavy bombers were sensationally going to bomb Berlin. No 166 Squadron had received a few examples of the Handley Page V/1500, a development of the highly successful 0/100 and 0/400 bombers. The V/1500 was Britain's answer to the German Giant, collective name for various enemy bomber types which even dwarfed Gothas. Giants had enjoyed remarkable success over Britain by not losing a single machine in action and dropping the heaviest bombs seen in World War One. Fate played against No 166 Squadron when bad weather delayed its proposed raid on November 9 1918. Another attempt planned for the 11th was cancelled because of the Armistice.

This was the final wartime act of note the airfields of Britain became involved in. Although over four years of hard fighting had brought much misery, a lot of good also came out of World War One. Our airfields of this era contributed an immense amount in this respect. Each helped both its country and aviation in six major ways which must be explained.

First and most obvious, the advent of standardised training meant flying would be infinitely safer in the future. Airfields showed how they could now successfully protect Britain as well, for south-eastern bases in particular were primarily responsible for halting enemy bombing raids. It is incredible to think that attacks might not have even reached conception if Count von Zeppelin had been forbidden to organise lotteries to raise money for replacement airships. Our airfields finished with a kill tally of nine airships, seven Gothas, a number of seaplanes and were instrumental in the destruction of two more Zeppelins. Such a score may not seem much today but their sheer being was vital as enemy raids tied down large numbers of aircraft and personnel. Bombing killed 1,414 Britons and injured over 3,000 more: while German bombers thus had mainly a psychological effect, there is no doubt about how many more innocents would have met a swift end had adequate defences not existed.

Airfields could be thirdly credited with managing to end the U-boat threat by constantly guarding surrounding British waters. Maybe British maritime patrol bases had not produced tremendous results against enemy submarines, but foreign sites proved utterly hopeless in comparison. Their help in introducing new technologies, such as in personal safety and weaponry, was another good development for the years to come. The aircraft industry also brought a whole new type of employment to tens of thousands of grateful people, and could have performed even better had it not been greatly troubled by the problem of developing good engines. The DH9 day bomber became a major direct casualty by suffering terribly from its BHP piston engine; if any aircraft needed a landing ground, it was a DH9.

Lastly, but perhaps most important of all, the airfields had managed to iron out most of their own problems. Was it only nine and a half years since Fambridge, Leysdown and their ilk had first appeared? In those early days, airfields suffered from some quite dreadful problems: limited acreage, far too uneven landing areas, waterlogging, insufficient support facilities, obstructions and adverse wind conditions. Sometimes a site simply lay in the wrong place. Now most of these shortcomings had been cleared up.

This was not to say that all wartime airfields were flawless. Flooding was not unknown at bases and, while the masses of gallant landing grounds did not disgrace themselves, some were clearly chosen without much thought. Prolonged use in and after wet weather resulted in muddy conditions: the hard runway was still another 20 years in coming.

Joyce Green, on the eastern boundary of London, was one such sub-standard airfield. It alone proved one of the worst airfields Britain has ever had the misfortune to see. Too narrow, bordered on two sides by rivers, often swathed in mist as a result, obstructed and possessing a landing surface where duckboards bridged drainage ditches, Joyce Green had a terrible accident rate. An unusual array of activities here consisted of training, Home Defence, wireless experimentation and flight testing by Vickers. Joyce Green astonishingly still lasted for eight years.

Thankfully, Britain was generally spared of such appalling airfields. All bar a few rogue sites played a massive part in their country's victory. From less than 40 in existence by August 1914, wartime saw over 500 airfields be present at one time or another. 1915 had seen the number of airfields in Britain more than double, then treble this figure in 1916, but the autumn period of that latter year had proved the crucial turning point as airfield totals rocketed upwards. Home Defence had undoubtedly been the cause, as it was for the consolidation apparent during 1917. Now over 300 airfields were available, yet stagnation had set in: numbers actually fell back slightly in late summer as many westerly and northerly HD landing grounds closed early as their aircraft made a tactical exodus eastwards. But dramatic increases in numerical strength again became evident from the spring of 1918 to see British airfield totals average out at about 410 between June and the Armistice. The general introduction of aviation to Ireland had naturally helped in the spring; so too had the appearance shortly afterwards of new anti-submarine landplane and marine sites, quickly followed by equally fresh supportive bases for airships; and the same to a lesser extent with additional TDS airfields in the summer. Active strength now held steady for the last few months of fighting.

The overwhelming rise in numbers of airfields would become mightily impressive in another and more subtle way. Already they had shown how most areas of aviation could be taken on with at least reasonable efficiency. Only the role of transportation eluded airfields – that was a job for peacetime.

Historians frequently tend to ignore completely how the air war greatly affected World War One. They prefer instead to look at land and sea battles but, if one looks clinically at these areas of warfare, what did the Somme, Jutland and many other clashes achieve apart from total stalemate?

The British airfield success story thundered along from strength to strength in comparison: the side show had become the star. Military importance was undeniable. If we are charitable and say that it might be going too far to say they won it single-handed, for let us not forget that other Great War sensation the tank, airfields certainly defended Britain when help was desperately needed to counter enemy bombing raids. Their aircraft might not have got anywhere near the raider which bombed Dover on December 25 1914, but at least airfields had tried their best to further the war effort, rather than playing football with the enemy.

More importantly in terms of the offensive capabilities of airfields, few acknowledge just how crucial their war was with the U-boat during World War One. German submarines were a big enough problem in World War Two but, in the previous conflict, they were deceptively deadly threats. Had no British airfields responded, not even by sending out those old DH6s, it is no exaggeration to state that marauding U-boats could have eventually starved Britain into surrender. The high and mighty in authority, no doubt enjoying their virtually unrestricted diets, rarely bothered to see how Mrs Bloggs was having to queue for hours on end to gather together a few meagre morsels. A combined lack of food and fuel became the real reason for Germany's capitulation once the tables were turned and our airfields returned fire on behalf of the people who really mattered – even if the ordinary man, woman and child in the street did not fully comprehend what was happening. Despite for once being unopposed, U-boats scurried home across the North Sea to their bases in October 1918 and never re-emerged.

War has always had its happier moments. The World War One airfields of Britain were no different: the good-natured banter among personnel, friendly links with the neighbouring civilian population and occasional light-hearted bizarre incidents. But nobody remained contented with their lot by the end of 1918, not least the airfields. Pacifism filled the air. No sooner had the average British airfield won one battle when a second arose. The battle for survival . . .

Down – And Almost Out

First to go were the landing grounds. Bearing hardly any installations, they fell like flies following World War One. Many had closed at the Armistice or just after in line with Government policy. One can more often than not now pass a disused landing ground today without noticing it. Once the Ministry of Munitions' Disposal Board acquired these sites they quickly disappeared, which explains why the vast majority are now only flat fields. The situation has reached a stage where some landing ground sites cannot be determined with any degree of certainty. These unfortunate examples have been lost for good.

1919 was undoubtedly a sickening year, and not just for landing grounds. Countless numbers of more permanent airfields throughout Britain shut down and hurriedly faded into oblivion. Most of their buildings were wooden, so it was not too difficult for a farmer or landowner to get rid of them. Machrihanish on the Kintyre peninsula area of western Scotland symbolised this lurid trend by closing in March 1919, having only opened the previous July. Seemingly secure airfields sited all over Britain formed a huge fatality list during the main killing period. After the immediate slump caused by the Armistice, their numerical strength diminished to a third of the total available in 1918 by the end of 1919. Vast areas of Britain suffered terrible maulings. Huge parts of the English countryside became aeronautical deserts; Scottish and Irish sites were reduced to a trickle, even such illustrious places as Montrose of No 2 Squadron fame succumbing; and our surrounding smaller islands became deprived of airfields almost overnight. Probably the worst sector was Wales, stripped of its airfields except for Shotwick in Flint, later renamed Sealand, marginally inside the Welsh border. General activity would not return there until the late 1930s.

This woeful situation was still infinitely better than the horrifying prospect Germany faced in May 1920: all of its airfields were to be destroyed. Fortunately for them – and, with the benefit of hindsight, Britain's sites as well – eradication never quite reached totality.

Certain types of home airfields meanwhile endured certain trends, although by 1920 the net result was the same: widespread slaughter. Home Defence airfields generally lasted until mid-1919 before following the same sorry paths as their faithful landing grounds. TDSs managed to last a little longer, thanks to their excellent hangarage, and the same could be applied to AAPs. Many examples of these two airfield types could still be seen for some time after they closed.

Coastal airfields were not so lucky, a factor largely caused by their positioning in remote areas. For example, Padstow and Westward Ho in the extreme south-west of England could hardly hope to survive in the long-term. Even so, easily the most surprising of all airfield types to be felled were airship stations. These places had controlled sub-stations (sometimes called mooring-out stations) during 1918. Built at more obscure locations to create better dispersal, cut down on travelling distance to operating sectors and avoid possible poor weather conditions, woodland usually enveloped these simple supportive airship bases to offer camouflage. Sub-stations soon closed down into peacetime, but few foresaw how parent stations would also be quickly axed. Whether it was Capel in the south or Longside in the north, most airship bases ceased to function during 1919 and the early part of 1920, frighteningly heavy losses arising in the former year. Their vast hangars seemed to present no problems to scrap merchants as many an auction would demonstrate.

The Armistice of November 1918 also cruelly ended the hopes of various airfields still under construction. Two have already been mentioned in the previous chapter: Catfirth and Southbourne. At least the Shetland flying boat base saw some flying in the final wartime months, though a great deal of construction work was still required. Its Sussex counterpart was not even able to accommodate aircraft in its TDS role. The majority of what constituted Southbourne had been built but lay unused until disposal.

It would have been interesting to see how our incomplete airfields might have fared if fighting had continued for a while longer. Places which come to mind included Southbourne's near-neighbours Goring-by-Sea and Rustington, non-starter American AAP Oldham or the aborted airship station of Moreton in Dorset. One far more fortunate site – albeit in the long run – turned out to be Flookburgh in Lancashire. Intended to succeed the established airship station of Barrow-in-Furness, it never did but served successfully in World War Two under the different name of Cark.

This band of incomplete British airfields could have reached full maturity had events turned out differently. But it was not to be. To use that extremely well-worn term, people had suffered 'the war to end wars'. Everyone was more concerned with peace, not forgetting the disastrous influenza outbreak which claimed the life of airship conqueror William Leefe Robinson among millions of others. Our airfields had become the champions but outside forces then delivered them such a fearsome punch from which they very nearly failed to recover. Rarely has such a travesty of justice occurred to compare with these times – and it would not be the first time either.

Despite all the assorted difficulties, the real problem was a dire lack of money. Such an overwhelming win as that just enjoyed by Britain had left an exceptionally bitter taste for the solely financially minded in peacetime. World War One as a whole had ferociously eaten up money on a daily basis. Up to March 1916, as its military airfields began to gain major importance, Britain was spending £5 million per day; this gross figure had risen to nearly £7 million expended every 24 hours in May 1917. Undoubtedly our airfields had played a big part in this increase but were well worth the expense as their brilliant victory showed. Now Germany stood bankrupt, while Britain and its other allies lay heavily in debt. The announcement on February 1 1922 that this country's dead weight debt for 1921/22 stood at a mind-boggling £7,585,409,690 was not exactly something to be proud of.

Cash shortages did nothing to assist aircraft companies as many folded under the severe financial strain. Famous companies such as Sopwith and Martinsyde stopped trading at their factory airfields as military contracts for thousands of new RAF types disappeared with the advent of peace. Lack of work inevitably meant a lack of jobs and vast numbers of workers sadly had to become redundant.

There was still hope for the future, provided a company took at least one of the following three actions. First, if it had shown enough foresight, the company would have bought its premises long ago. It could then ride out any financial storm once the depression was in full flow until better times appeared by sitting on its own assets. Second possibility would be to diversify and manufacture non-aeronautical products. Claude Grahame-White at Hendon managed to keep going in this way by producing cars and even prefabricated furniture.

No doubt a true airman like him thought little of such dull work, but what else could be done at the turn of this new decade?

Of course, there was always option three – the desperate option. A company could always pray for a miraculous saviour to buy its assets. Former Sopwith test pilot Harry Hawker dramatically rescued his old Brooklands firm in November 1920 after it had closed only two months earlier. All Sopwith had to do was to change its name to that of Hawker, whose tragic reward would be to die in an air crash at Hendon on July 12 1921.

No new aircraft construction resulted in hindering experimental airfields as well to make life quiet at Farnborough, Grain and Martlesham Heath. They had already tried out some frustrating proposals in their time but now these bases literally had a testing period.

Activities on British airfields were not completely subdued. RAF stations in Ireland continued to be fairly busy by accommodating army co-operation squadrons. Each unit proved its worth in helping to stem trouble as outbreaks of violence reached new peaks. Squadrons tended to remain as one force or occasionally detach a Flight to another airfield. The Anglo-Irish Treaty of 1921 created Northern Ireland and the Republic, vastly reducing the RAF presence in the new southern country, though a few sections remained until February 1922. Britain employed military facilities in Eire for another 16 years but left its airfields well alone once the constitution was drawn up in 1922.

Back on the mainland, the RAF was finding life almost unbearable. Its airfields kept on closing in the early 1920s due to starvation of money, men and materials. Casualty percentages made those incurred in trench warfare during World War One seem positively moderate in comparison. A major shock occurred at the beginning of 1920 when Great Yarmouth suddenly shut down. So much did personnel who had served at Great Yarmouth like the place that several reunions were held in post-war years; unlike then, this is a common activity today. At least one person is recorded as saying how staggered he was to see that his favourite old haunt had mostly disappeared. Did he say this in 1963, 1973 or fairly recently? In fact it was 1923 . . .

A different kind of threat to British naval aviation and related airfields came from another marine airfield in every sense of the term. The aircraft carrier had quietly slipped into view, a real life floating airfield which could potentially restrain land-based operations yet further. Its ability to allow aircraft to take off into any head wind, no matter what direction, was one particularly unappreciated advantage. After America had pioneered the use of this vessel during 1911/12, Britain decided to adopt the idea too and commissioned HMS *Argus* as its first Royal Navy aircraft carrier in September 1918. No 185 Squadron formed in October at East Fortune with Sopwith Cuckoo torpedo bombers in compliance but the Armistice prevented this unit from seeing action. How both it and HMS *Argus* might have fared if they had is only irrelevant supposition, although aircraft carriers would not give airfields great problems. The former would nevertheless make one big change by becoming the new front line and turn coastal airfields into shore-cum-training stations.

If inland RAF stations had no say in this matter, they still had more than enough problems to contend with. Was there going to be any end to the British airfield annihilation? The reviled 'Geddes Axe' of February 1922, named after the former Director-General of Military Railways and Minister of Transport Sir Eric Geddes, became about the last straw. Again the ghost of Loch Doon indirectly reared its ugly head; perhaps the proposed £5½ million saving might never have been needed had Britain's worst ever airfield stayed only as an untried plan. Certainly £1 million of this total was directly aimed at airfields to stop them in their tracks. Every other part of the RAF, from aircraft to wages and even motor vehicles, similarly fell by the wayside as officialdom cut down heavily on spending relating to all aspects of British life.

As a result of this economy-obsessed report, incredible in itself as Geddes had gained notoriety for being a big business spender during World War One, RAF manpower dropped to a tenth of its former size. This was strangely almost exactly the same fraction the total of military and civil airfields slumped to in active strength. Numbers had fallen back into double instead of treble figures in the spring of 1920. Further closures in a steady decline during 1921 now brought an average of only 50-55 airfields available at any one time during 1922-24 as dormancy replaced the period of killing. Persistent pressure on the ever-changing Prime Ministers and Governments of the day by Army and Navy interests to either abolish the RAF altogether or have the other two armed services absorb it, the first attempt at extinction coming in February 1922 as the Geddes Report was published, still fuelled scary rumours of impending shut-downs at many an airfield.

Nearly every RAF station struggled to survive in the early

1920s. Squadrons returned from their wind-blasted, questionably permanent and generally horribly inadequate French airfields without aircraft as cadres pending disbandment, or just managed to survive in reduced Flight form. Flying had cut back everywhere to severe levels, and a fair amount of evidence shows that large numbers of aircraft were simply left to rot unattended on airfields. Some machines were even unceremoniously burned or dumped. Wasteful authoritative forces could not have cared less if they salvaged any valuable spare parts from aircraft, as many resourceful groundcrews tried to do.

Worries did not just end with the mismanagement of aircraft. Now the greatest ever passive enemy of our airfields, the British Press, effected terrible damage by almost wholly turning a blind eye to the utter carnage and chaos going on. Reporters had already got in a great deal of practice during World War One by all but completely ignoring the tremendous events and advances happening at home bases, so in that sense nothing had really changed. But pacifism had since become the 'in thing' and, as Britain's airfields kept hanging on to the ropes for dear life, newspapers were not interested in losers.

Even so, being typical of the perverse Press, losers still remained good copy if they could be seen to languish in the gutter through no fault of their own. Reporters did not have to look far. The armies of RAF personnel demobbed from airfields added to the already grievous unemployment situation. Men fortunate to remain at stations were accused of extravagance. A series of fires which looked far more like arson attacks caused by disaffected personnel and even isolated mutinies only made matters worse. And then there were continued fears about attacks on airfields from Suffragettes, though the actions of these militant women proved empty threats as in every other area of life in Britain at this time.

Short of actual closure or a savaging from the Press, the next worst situation for an airfield would be for the drastic stage where the site was too good to be dropped but unable to serve any useful present or foreseeable purpose. An ominous new term called Care and Maintenance – better known to all as C&M – thus had to come into force in order to save a little more precious money and please that man Geddes. Grain then closed in 1924 after its excellent experimental work to make 1921-24 surely the worst years ever seen in RAF history, but the service could be consoled as its future now seemed secure.

Two bright spots on the horizon ensured this fact, for the efforts of Minister of Air Winston Churchill and Chief of the Air Staff Hugh Trenchard resulted in Cranwell training cadets and Halton in Buckinghamshire apprentices from the early 1920s. Both airfields became crucial places where to train new generations of RAF personnel, and remain so. There would be a steady stream of highly qualified pilots, while equally large numbers of mechanics meant that a shortage of them as seen in the early days of World War One would not happen again. Much of the credit must go to ex-Upavon trainee Trenchard, who fought tooth and nail to retain the independence of RAF airfields, aircraft and personnel who used them. It only shows how out of touch officialdom has always been when dealing with aeronautical affairs in general that the training of boys at Halton might have been abandoned had the Geddes Report got its way. Only problem with Trenchard's policies was that as he placed most squadrons overseas, this meant continued thin times at home RAF bases. There was still a long, long way to go.

As British military airfields had found it virtually impossible to keep going, what chance would their civil counterparts have? After the Civil Aerial Transport Committee had made tremendous evaluation of every area of airfield operations in its report of January 1919, civil aviation in this country restarted on May 1 after its wartime absence with an ambitious idea. A number of ex-military airfields were listed for use as Continental 'link' sites. Some of these earmarked places, like the former HD landing ground at Cullingworth near Bradford, were most unexpected choices to put it mildly. This plan came to nothing, as mainly did a domestic idea to bring civil aircraft to recently derequisitioned RAF airfields. An official *ad hoc* approach to this scheme resulted in no proper control being exercised.

Support for civil activities came from an unusual source. The incumbent Under Secretary for Air, Major-General J.E.B. Seely, stated in the House of Commons on June 5 1919 how urgent it was to have more landing grounds and good telephone communications between airfields. Seely took this issue further by writing to everyone involved in local authority to hunt out sites for emergency landing purposes. But they apparently never bothered . . .

A more determined attempt to rectify matters saw the Air Ministry place airfields into six separate categories. Although the rapidly changing aeronautical situation resulted in terms being given different meanings as time passed, the initial list was as follows:

List	*Meaning*
A	Service aerodromes only available for civilian machines in emergency
B	Service stations available also for civil use
C	Stations temporarily retained for service purposes, but available also for civil use
D1	Aerodromes licensed for all but larger types of aircraft
E	Stations no longer in use by RAF. Passed to the Government Surplus Property Disposal Board, and will be relinquished as soon as the Government property thereon has been disposed of

The five above types each proved important in their own right as events showed. No airfield wanted to fall to List C as the shadow of death, otherwise known as List E, hovered ominously near. But it was a miniature army of brand new sites also introduced at this time in 1919 under a sixth category which have become some of the vaguest in British airfield history. Brean Down, a stretch of sand close to Weston-super-Mare named after a peninsula, was but one place mentioned; another existed to the south of Middlesbrough at Linthorpe. Both were described as List D2 types or 'aerodromes licensed as suitable only for Avro 504K and similar types of aircraft', a commonly used airfield category of that period as so many of these biplanes were to be seen in relation to other types. Whether some List D2 places were even actually used is greatly open to doubt: Brean Down did see limited flying but most others were lucky to briefly hold one or two aircraft.

No matter the level of their sophistication, Britain's civil airfields could not hope to succeed for the first few years after World War One. Flying of this nature had not reached the position where it could be truly described as nationally popular. Although 92 airfields were licensed for civil use by the end of October 1919, the large majority lay in the vicinity of towns and only temporarily required by firms carrying passengers on short flights, usually for joy-riding purposes. In other words, List D2 sites held what little advantage there was to be gained in numerical supremacy.

This subject of numbers became one of the few benefits made evident by Air Ministry List D2 and other civil airfield variants as they tried furiously to stop the overall total of active British sites from falling like a stone. The amount balanced out at 190-200 in mid-1919 but fell away again in the autumn as the summer holiday season ended; another rally in strength orchestrated by civil airfields occurred a year later until quickly subsiding once more. Absolutely nothing seemed to be going right for our airfields in general.

Pioneering flights became another facet of civil aviation which restarted in peacetime and similarly tried their best to assist our ailing airfields. The Smith brothers left a foggy Hounslow in Greater London on November 12 1919 for Australia in their Vickers Vimy biplane *G-EAOU;* the joke its registration stood for 'God 'elp all of us' could have applied to airfields too, for similar exploits achieved little in reversing their tale of woe. Alcock and Brown's historic Atlantic crossing on June 14/15 of that year certainly bore no significance when their Vimy crashed into an airfieldless Irish bog!

Air races never quite caught on again to such a feverish extent after World War One either. Maybe the general public had simply become more accustomed to seeing aircraft. Matters were not helped when the first Schneider Trophy contest held in Britain at Bournemouth during September 1919 turned into an absolute organisational fiasco. Lack of interest later saw the Oxford-Cambridge air race, centred around Hendon and won by Cambridge, never be revived after its inaugural competition on July 16 1921. The only flying competition to gain prominence was Britain's most famous, the King's Cup, first won by Captain F.L. Barnard in an Airco DH4A during September 8/9 1922. Many airfields helped to generate themselves considerable publicity by acting as control points where pilots checked in along the 810 mile course.

Another move which many thought might advance the cause of civil aviation and airfields was the availability of thousands of war-surplus aircraft on the open market. Such hopes would not be realised. Incredibly low prices – an aircraft could be bought for £1 or less in some cases – failed to stop most going straight to scrap dealers. Cars and motorcycles were conversely being exchanged for high prices: it just did not make sense. Surviving aircraft which kept intact fared little better for, although joy-riding was officially encouraged, their entrepreneurial pilots found all the associated costs of flying crippling. Charging passengers a guinea a head was obviously not enough. Barnstormers loved using holiday beaches or any old field in the 1920s but early pleasure flight operators after World War One did not survive for long, especially with the slump of 1921. A brave try by ubiquitous Avro 504s of the Avro Civil Aviation Service to link Manchester and Blackpool via Southport from May 24 1919, in what became Britain's first scheduled domestic air service, stopped after less than five months on September 30.

This task of transporting people from one place to another had proved a real problem for British airfields following World War One. When it had been officially announced in April 1919 that civil flying was to be allowed again, the Air Ministry received many applications for licensing of proposed airfields all over Britain. No doubt many of their supporters were looking further ahead to making money out of transport services. Most sites had never even seen use as airfields but officials still inspected every one. However, many suggested places were hopelessly unsuitable for flying purposes.

Despite this setback, airfields were not to blame for a lack of aerial transportation – aircraft were. Claude Grahame-White's Charabanc biplane had carried nine passengers for nearly 20 minutes at Hendon on October 2 1913, but aircraft structures were generally so frail that not many people could be lifted at one go. The world's first scheduled passenger service in America during 1914 could only take one person alone at a time.

It was left to the military to show what could be achieved when RAF Handley Page 0/400s made over 200 flights between Lympne and France from April to November 1918 while carrying hundreds of passengers and some goods. More 0/400s and DH4As of No 1 (Communications) Squadron then ferried officials and documentation between Hendon and later Kenley in Greater London and Paris in conjunction with the Versailles peace conference from December 1918 to September 1919; DH9As of No 120 Squadron would fly mail sorties from Lympne and nearby Hawkinge to France and Germany during March-August 1919 as well. From these small beginnings arose the role of communications; hardly a military airfield since has not seen a machine appear on this unsung but quite vital duty.

Realisation soon dawned how RAF aircraft could not be relied upon for all transport duties. Neither could small independent firms – only large civil companies. Most significant of the immediate post-war period easily became Aircraft Transport and Travel Limited; it had already formed as far back as October 5 1916 in anticipation of making money out of transporting people. This company was based at Hounslow, just along from what is now Heathrow, a primitive place which became the original terminal airport in Britain. Early on August 25 1919, a route-proving charter flight took to France the unusual cargo of a journalist, newspapers, grouse, leather and some Devonshire cream. AT&T Ltd mounted the world's first daily international service over the same route later that day when pilot Cyril Patteson flew four passengers on the trip. Each person paid £21 as a one-way fare. This was a costly business not everyone could afford and AT&T Ltd did not survive to see the revolution in passenger air travel by ceasing services in December 1920. A London-Paris air mail service from November 10 1919 was however another of its innovations; the sight of mail-carrying civil transports appearing at airports during night hours have since become familiar to all.

Hounslow was a poor site for an airport but did introduce one most important innovation in Customs facilities. Checks upon imports became a natural progression as Britain linked itself more and more with the Continent. Customs was retained on March 29 1920 when the title of London Airport switched to a new place called Croydon, built out of two World War One airfields joined together. Apart from the arguable exception of Birmingham's Castle Bromwich, the young upstart soon showed how an airport could operate profitably. The King's Cup and other activities helped in addition to build up interest in airports, especially as the former involved flying from Croydon to Glasgow's airport at Renfrew and back.

Pioneer airline operators from Croydon and the rest still had to struggle to establish themselves. Foreign companies began price cutting and by February 1921 all scheduled British air services had ceased; Croydon found itself only being used by overseas airlines for a short period. Meteorological services were so unheard of in the early 1920s that pilots were left to their own devices while airborne. Navigation also failed to operate on a set basis as airliners resorted to following distinctive landmarks such as railway lines. More efficient communication began to appear in 1920 when Handley Page airliners started carrying Marconi radio sets. Contact could now be easily made with other airfields along airliner routes.

As an extra precaution, a few emergency landing grounds were developed for airliners of this period. Nobody could still be too sure about the reliability of aircraft engines. One unforgettable AT&T Ltd London-Paris flight resulted in 22 forced landings! Although Lympne served as one emergency site, the Kent airfield became far more notable for events achieved in another sphere of British civil aviation. Its famous light aeroplane competitions of 1923-26 paved the way for extensive private flying in this country. Each contest was held over a number of days some time in late summer or early autumn, the first being slightly different in trying to find a suitable motor-glider. Many entrants were cleverly designed but not really practical for civil needs as they were underpowered, too light and not strong enough for poor weather flying.

Among entries barred from the competition – in several ways the civil equivalent of Larkhill 1912 – was a sturdy two-seat biplane which originally flew on February 22 1925 at Stag Lane alongside Hendon. The de Havilland Moth had arrived, undoubtedly the world's first practical light aircraft. Its firm had to thank a private individual and another aircraft company saviour named Alan Butler for single-handedly pumping a considerable amount of money into the old Airco concern. He subsequently hit the jackpot by becoming chairman, whereas Lympne's winners such as the English Electric Wren and Gnosspelius Gull in time turned out the losers. The Moth was superior to these and other aircraft types in so many respects, not least because it did not cost much to buy and maintain.

What might now be regarded as the most important aircraft ever seen on our airfields soon reached production status. Revitalised or totally new British sites opened as a result for flying club use. The Lancashire Aero Club at Woodford near Manchester – itself a new airfield and a real one this time as opposed to the former World War One Essex Home Defence HQ – became the first organisation to accept a Moth in July 1925. An extremely influential future airfield pioneer by the name of Alan Cobham sat at the controls of the aircraft.

We can therefore safely say that 1925 became the turning point for Britain's airfields; in boxing terms, they had only risen at the count of nine. Numbers now steadily increased as the physically and psychologically shattered survivors gathered strength after their collective near-fatal knock-out blow. Yet one of their few champions was to be seen no more, for Claude Grahame-White had clashed with authority once too often and left Hendon for abroad, a bitter man. RAF stations continued to keep an extremely low profile, so it was left to civil airfields to take the reins for the next decade. Their ride would possess more than a few bumps too but be a cakewalk compared with the military nightmare of before.

Britain's first airfield: Fambridge *(above)* or Leysdown *(below)*? The mystery continues.

(above) Racecourses did much to help our airfields, few more so than Lanark, Scotland's first airfield.
(below) Here Britain's airfields lost their parochiality. The memorial at Dover (St Margaret's) to Nos 2, 3, 4 and 5 Squadrons.

(above) Improvisation often had to rule in the early days of World War One. Victorian defence installation Fort Grange helped out training pioneer Gosport with accommodation. *(Mrs B.S. Harby)*
(below) Cullingworth, just one of Britain's innumerable now forgotten Great War landing grounds.

(above) An RNAS Sopwith Pup at Chingford in 1917. The irregular markings, society ladies, lack of security and encroaching houses: a classic World War One scene of British airfield eccentricity. Co-ordination still had to arrive. *(W.H.C. Reynolds)*
(above right) In the gloom of one of East Fortune's airship sheds lurk the R.29 rigid plus NS.7 and NS.8 non-rigids. Such lighter-than-air craft proved excellent passive deterrents against U-boats *(RAF Museum)*.
(below right) A more aggressive opponent of German submarines was the Felixstowe F.2a, like this No 228 Squadron machine at Great Yarmouth on February 27 1919. *(RAF Museum)*

Bristol Fighters of No 141 Squadron return to Biggin Hill after an enemy bombing raid *(above)*. Our airfields had made it. *(IWM)*
But had they? Support buildings today at fellow Home Defence station Stow Maries *(below)*, extremely rare survivors of another age when extinction seemed a possibility for the entire British airfield population.

(above) Sandy airfields have usually not enjoyed great success – but in the 1920s almost any type of airfield was welcome. The List D2 joy-riding site of Brean Down today.
(below) The pupil pilots of No 5 FTS put on a brave face in 1927 at Sealand, Wales' only major airfield of that shocking decade. *(RAF Museum)*

(above) The early 1930s saw our airfields' power really begin to show, both at civil and military level. An unusual control tower at Barton, Britain's first municipal airport, and still going strong. *(below)* Hawker Harts beside yet another new airfield of that era, Peterborough/Westwood. An A hangar is under construction. *(R.M. Maywood)*

(above) Heston, the airfield that saved Britain. Not that anyone today would guess . . .
(below) And how: the Hurricane and Spitfire prototypes at Hendon's New Types Park during the RAF Display of June 1936. Would over 34,000 more of these machines have followed but for Heston and Neville Chamberlain? *(RAF Museum)*

(above) Once the Phoney War had ended, our airfields wasted no time in hitting back at Germany. A Handley Page Hampden I of No 49 Squadron bombing up at Scampton in June 1940. *(IWM)*
(above right) Soon the Luftwaffe recognised its real collective threat. A C hangar at Driffield after receiving special attention on August 15 1940. *(RAF Museum)*
(below right) Quiet today but far from forgotten: Battle of Britain airfield superstar Hawkinge.

(above) Armstrong Whitworth Whitleys under construction at Baginton near Coventry in 1940. *(IWM)*
(below) The hordes of aircraft resident in Britain during World War Two had to be stored somewhere. Satellite Landing Grounds such as No 22, alias Barnsley Park in Gloucestershire, played an unusual but effective role.

A Peaceful Resurgence

Another country would have encountered hardly any aerial opposition had it attacked Britain in the early 1920s. How frightening now it is to think that only one RAF fighter squadron existed to defend the population from April 1920 until the spring of 1923. No 25 Squadron was based at Hawkinge and operated Sopwith Snipes. Not at full power because of inevitable spares problems, even it stayed away from Britain for a while to leave the country defenceless. The Snipes resided in Turkey between September 1922 and October 1923 to deal with disturbances there: only on November 1 1922 did No 56 Squadron reform at Hawkinge with more Snipes.

And what would Britain have relied upon to hit back at the strategic targets of this invader? Four, *four* Vickers Vimy heavy bombers of No 100 Squadron at Spittlegate in Lincolnshire. The governing authorities could thank their lucky stars these and other diabolical facts were not then revealed. Imagine the huge public outcry had a similar situation occurred today.

Those on high also had a lot to answer for as regards the general states of British military airfields. No money still existed to allow spending on new equipment or facilities, so most RAF stations had to make do and mend. Airfields such as Aldergrove, Digby in Lincolnshire and Cattewater (known from 1929 as Mount Batten) alongside Plymouth – three big stars of days ahead – could count themselves as most fortunate to survive these thin times.

1925 at least offered better things with formation of the Auxiliary Air Force and Special Reserve. Both formations operated on the basis of relying upon territorials but the Auxiliaries employed far more part-time volunteers, whereas Special Reserve squadrons like No 502 at Aldergrove held a more even balance of regular/reserve personnel in order to gain operational status more quickly. (All five Special Reserve units were absorbed into the AuxAF from May 1936). Ironically, the RAF now had to depend upon civilians to man its precious few airfields and aircraft. These spare time or 'weekend' fliers would still have a considerable say in reviving Britain's poorly military airfields.

Far greater numbers of civilians were not unnaturally involved with the civil aviation scene, though this area of flying also remained fairly restricted as a whole during the 1920s. State subsidisation brought about formation of Imperial Airways on April 1 1924; the efforts of Aircraft Transport and Travel Limited had not been in vain. As this much needed new intercontinental airline company expanded after a strike had nearly caused irreparable damage, so too did its centre of operations. Croydon witnessed vast rebuilding work to allow London to have the world's first purpose-built international airport. In came such revolutionary items as its famous control tower. A superstar prepared to state its position as the world's most celebrated airfield of the inter-wars period. Upper sections of society began to compare Croydon with the Derby and similar events, a place where they could see and be seen. Many aerial pioneers like Amy Johnson preferred to use the airport as their starting or finishing points, thereby adding to the magical atmosphere of this place. Perhaps the airports of today are more efficient but they could never hope to match the sheer excitement Croydon generated in its heyday. No wonder this place became one of the most popular British airfields of all time. One wonders at times what aeronautical publications of the period would have done without it!

Early airports were simple affairs as they consisted of little more than hangars and a few office buildings. Croydon began in this fashion before introducing the features normally associated with an airport today. Terminals arose to allow much improved organisation for arriving or departing passengers. Security became necessary as a result, and was also required to watch over the increasing amounts of light air freight passing through. Easily the main difference was seen in airfield acreage. Croydon and other airports had to rapidly expand their landing areas to cope with more intensive airline operations and bigger aircraft. Imperial Airways became typical by keeping to a policy of using large airliner types such as the three-engined Armstrong Whitworth Argosy biplane.

At the opposite end of the civil scale, tiny flying club airfields began to attract great support in Britain. Light aircraft along the lines of the de Havilland Moth only required small grass landing areas. Hangars were not absolutely vital at this stage, for folding-wing Moths could be feasibly kept in large household garages. Any suitable field could be used by the recreational airman but many of these were not airfields in a true sense. Not officially designated as such, they saw little use in the process and even then often only by a single aircraft. It is often said how the Wright brothers' test site at Huffman's Prairie became the world's first ever airfield, not Issy-les-Moulineaux, yet the American place was better described as the prototype private airfield. British pilots, especially those at the top end of the social scale, now followed on from this example and liked to have their own private airstrips. One of the best known became the eccentric Duchess of Bedford, who possessed her own little airfields at Woburn Park in Bedfordshire, Wispers Midhurst in West Sussex and Cairnsmore House in south-west Scotland.

A sizeable group of obscure and hardly used sites which did become recognised civil airfields were assisted by an unexpected source – the Automobile Association. Realising how aircraft were still prone to mechanical and structural failure, the organisation marked down a large number of temporary landing areas; landing grounds had suddenly come back into vogue. Having ironic origins in a suggestion made during March 1913 that marked landing places might be provided by the AA's great rival the Royal Automobile Club, the basis of this idea was first voiced in August 1926 before the AA announced its plans during May 1928; a general service began a year later, and a Register of Aircraft Landing Grounds appeared from the autumn of 1932. Support facilities were all but nil as in World War One, for sites consisted of fields whose owners agreed to their use in return for a small fee. Ploughing often dictated affairs!

Despite being rather an unusual system, pilots having to be warned about such unlikely obstructions as haystacks, the idea of patrolmen going out in their vans to remote spots to aid stranded airmen worked just as well as the normal AA procedure of attending to broken down cars. When they reached their height in the early 1930s, AA civil landing grounds were scattered over most of Britain, though the great majority existed in southern England. Wispers Midhurst became one when the Duchess of Bedford decided to open up her most southerly port of call for everyone and not only herself. Never greatly publicised in their time, the masses have forgotten these humble places. Banbury, Daventry and Rhos Ucha do not ring any bells now with the general public in the same way as Biggin Hill does. Extremely few AA civil landing grounds lasted to achieve great fame: one rare exception became Ronaldsway, today the Isle of Man's airport.

More permanent British civil airfields had to thank two distinguished men for their steady expansion. One was Sir William Sefton Brancker, the Director of Civil Aviation, whose energetic leadership helped create new airfields and organisations. Known to have a thorough dislike of red tape, Brancker's simple policy was to get things moving without all the crippling administrative fuss. He visited many civil airfields in person and persuaded local authorities as best he could to construct more. Here was one general who did not sit in his gaudy stately home. For once our airfields had authority on their side.

While Sefton Brancker effectively served as the motivator, operator was the highly popular Sir Alan Cobham. Knighted after a pioneering flight to Cape Town and back during 1925/26, Cobham determined to make the ordinary British citizen air-minded. His National Aviation Days or 'air circuses' travelled the length and breadth of Britain from 1932 to 1935 for several months each year and used fields or convenient spaces converted into short-term airfields; while the sites of many shows are known, it is sad that Cobham never bothered in his autobiography to say exactly where these displays took place. Aerobatics, aircraft oddities and spectacular stunts formed part of each show but the main objective was to take vast numbers of ordinary people into the air.

The National Aviation Days became tremendously successful in due course and made a lot of money all over Britain as flying occurred virtually every day in a punishing schedule. Cobham's air shows were also instrumental in laying the foundations for many new airfields. He had a particularly good eye for suitable landing areas which offered a lot of space. A large number of military and civil airfields owe their existence to Cobham – hardly surprising when in 1932 alone he and his merry men visited 170 British towns. One temporary site, for example, was a place in Cornwall called Trebelzue: it is now known as St Mawgan, a famous airfield and one of the RAF's most vital stations.

It was thanks to people like Brancker and Cobham that numbers of British airfields began to increase again. A total of 237 airports, airfields and landing grounds were stated as active by July 1927, a figure since regarded as highly dubious and probably bolstered markedly by private airstrips. Further figures quoted how 77 licensed civil airfields were available in January 1929, 90 a year later, 127 civil and 48 RAF airfields in April 1930, 129 and 50 respectively in December and 122 civil in January 1931. The procedure of short licensing for civil sites meant that 206 licences had been issued in 1928 and 320 in 1929, apart from renewals in each case. So how our airfields were faring could not be assessed for certain. But nobody could deny their quiet resurgence.

This country still had a long way to go to match other major aviation countries. America possessed an equal 1927 total of 3,806 sites, though it must be added that the US-inspired term 'airfield' had even more flexible connotations than in Britain; a more realistic figure was 800 equipped civil airfields by May 1929. Another report of six months earlier had revealed how America held 391 municipal airports, while Germany miraculously possessed 254. And how many Government-owned sites did Britain have? Just five. Home airfields, both at civil and military level, urgently required help from officialdom in its entirety and not only Brancker – and were not getting any. Of the 127 British active civil airfields in April 1930, 117 had been privately owned.

Any official encouragement there was seemed to concentrate instead during the late 1920s and early 1930s to the increasing numbers of flying clubs. A variety of airfields throughout Britain accommodated establishments bearing the names of either towns, cities, counties or regions. Organisations such as the Herts and Essex Aero Club at its tiny airfield of Broxbourne flourished. Flying costs were not too expensive but Sefton Brancker introduced a good incentive scheme where clubs could earn substantial yearly amounts depending on the number of people trained to licence standards. The number of hours flown would also be taken into account. This scheme managed to help the causes of pilot availability, flying clubs and their airfields in the long-term.

1930 brought more hope to civil airfields until ending on an extremely sour note. One era was about to begin, another would be drastically finished. Gliding became established in Britain during this year after a false start. The *Daily Mail* newspaper, long a relatively honourable exception in the already prolonged Press anti-airfield witch-hunt, had sponsored a competition back in October 1922 for the longest flight by a glider. Held at Itford Hill, lying between Lewes and Newhaven in Sussex, fierce competition arose between the numerous entrants. A Frenchman won but, despite the presence of thousands of excited spectators, gliding inexplicably saw no further major interest here for another eight years.

Yet another foreigner was badly needed to pave the way ahead. The great Austrian glider pilot Robert Kronfeld can be credited with resuscitating British curiosity in this form of activity, a man who would become another naturalised Briton like Sam Cody and later also die while furthering the cause at Lasham in Hampshire during February 1948. Gliding clubs quickly formed thanks to his trail-blazing displays. The London Gliding Club at Dunstable Downs in Bedfordshire started a new breed of airfields and soon became the centre of pre-war gliding in Britain. This club continues today, as do several other veteran organisations – the Derby and Lancashire GC at Camphill, Midland GC at Long Mynd and Yorkshire GC at Sutton Bank. Although glider airfields have usually tended to be small in acreage, right from the start many came equipped with reasonable support facilities. There would be a clubhouse for the members, a hangar or two plus stores for equipment. Sites have never needed to only be hills, though Cedric Lee and George Tilghman Richards found the higher parts of Westmorland good enough where to test their annular biplane gliders before World War One.

While gliders now began to establish themselves, the autumn of 1930 abruptly ended British airship participation. Problems with lighter-than-air craft might be said to have started in World War One. Quietly efficient Great War service was possibly overshadowed by the lack of offensive power among RNAS/RAF airships during their maritime patrol duties. No non-rigid had definitely sunk a U-boat, and only one rigid (the R.29) saw action, though it had helped on September 29 1918 to sink the UB-115. One of the East Fortune-based airship's two earlier attacks had frightened another enemy submarine so much that the vessel accidentally ran into a mine and sank. But the ignorant in power still tended to view airships overall as pea-shooters trying to knock down a brick wall without acknowledging their excellent deterrent value.

Airship stations in Britain hence rapidly dwindled in number during immediate peacetime. Only three military sites – East Fortune, Howden and the experimental base of Pulham in East Anglia – had sheds still open for craft by December 1919, this dire situation becoming even worse when East Fortune closed in February 1920. More ammunition for the anti-airship lobby's cause now came when they belatedly discovered the relative inability of a rigid to land in bad weather, conveniently ignoring how a non-rigid could by quickly deflating itself. Landing a rigid also required a lot more men for ground handling duties but the development of mooring masts early on in the 1920s to save housing an airship after every flight shot down more criticism.

Unfortunately, the weight of authority told in the end. The flak having to be endured by not only airships but their stations as well began to render critically heavy damage when the R.38 suffered structural failure on approach to Howden on August 24 1921 and crashed into the River Humber, killing 44 men on board. Americans were among the fatalities, but this tragedy did not give their descendants any qualms about using non-rigid airships in World War Two to fly over the eastern Pacific and hunt for Japanese submarines. US blimps beat aircraft with ease when it came to immediate operational availability in addition to emphasise how Britain threw away yet another good idea.

Visionaries here continued regardless to have their feasible dreams. There were hopes in World War One that airships could employ cliffs and other geological formations as bases for peacetime uses; quarries were also suggested as sites. It was thought that all would only need to be excavated, have roofing constructed or recesses in rocks bored. But so great had been the post-war rundown just three airship stations remained in Britain by the late 1920s – Howden, Pulham and Bedfordshire production centre Cardington. Even this trio of sites had suffered bouts of closure or inactivity at one time or another in recent years.

Lingering Government interest in airships as passenger carrying craft subsequently resulted in Cardington and Howden each building a large all-new rigid dirigible. Howden constructed the R.100, while Cardington gave birth to its even larger sister the R.101. In turn popularly dubbed the 'capitalist' and 'socialist' airships, both were declared ready by 1930. The successful R.100 made a perfect tour to Canada and back but its government-controlled sister had to endure a nightmarish development period. Speed remained all important in authoritative minds at the expense of safety; in short, the R.101 should never have flown. It nevertheless staggered away from Cardington on October 4 1930 in spite of much concern for, of all places, India. Early next morning, the craft crashed in France. Among the 48 fatalities was loyal ally of Britain's civil airfields Sefton Brancker: people noticed how uncharacteristically nervous he seemed shortly before take-off, and it was later revealed Brancker knew all was not well with the airship.

The resultant shock which swept Britain somehow seemed to criticise nobody when the Government should have been blasted for its blithering incompetence. There were no prizes for guessing who received the fatal bullet instead. Our blameless airship stations duly shut down with incredible speed as everyone in high office wanted to forget about them. Cardington was fortunately able to adapt to different aeronautical roles. Gigantic hangars and an adjacent landing area for visiting aircraft helped no end to make this highly distinctive place become recognised by the general public as the greatest of all former airship bases, an odd and sad state of affairs considering the sheer heroics displayed by Mullion in World War One and Cardington's comparative lack of history.

Further high-level lack of basic aeronautical theory arose about this time as British civil airfield expansion steadily progressed. Suggestions had often appeared for 'town' or 'city' airfields during the 1920s, with their adherents not being too sure what they exactly meant, but local authorities at last correctly saw the advantages of having an airport. Enthusiasm among the general public seemed to be immense, so councils tried to cater for their needs. But a lack of money ensured developments arose with dreadful slowness: some kind of a minor miracle was needed.

Prayers were duly answered in 1929. Sir Alan Cobham planted seeds in many local authority minds when he provided personnel with numerous flights all over Britain as part of his pro-airfield survey tour campaign. No sooner had he finished in early October than Cobham spent the next month spreading his expert knowledge. Good intentions immediately abounded once Cobham left his official guests to get on with it but were not matched by either planning expertise or sites chosen by councillors. So arose that curious 1930s phenomenon called the municipal airport, most of which were not airports in the strict sense of the term as they lacked international aircraft traffic and Customs facilities. An extreme lack of long-term planning in general led to poor sites and organisation. Municipal airports often did not have a firm financial and economic base either, strange when recalling how they were described as 'business assets' as far back as July 1920.

Many councils had quite simply bitten off far more than they could chew. As a result, British municipal airports enjoyed only mediocre careers at best. Hedon from the early days of flying proved a case in point; another good example became Worcester as, though destined to serve as a World War Two training airfield, it closed shortly into peacetime and has never reopened. Leicester's original airport of Braunstone met a similar end. The first municipal airport in Britain at Barton alongside Manchester shows typical airfield logic by still being active today, yet it is not an airport either.

The 1930s became notable for the number of decidedly odd proposals for airfields which were aired. Already the 1920s had occasionally seen curious suggestions such as railway station and even golf course airfields, while the alleged advantages of Hyde Park in London remained a favourite topic for long enough, but now plans in this new decade came thick and fast. Certain wildly extravagant ideas never reached their envisaged targets: the 1,000 civil airfields in operation as hoped for by National Flying Services Limited never happened, and this primarily training-orientated organisation which branched out too far eventually went into receivership during 1933. Among the many officially approved but unbuilt sites was Oswestry, and the plans hopeful for fruition in May 1934 remained evident two years later. With all due respect to that fine part of Shropshire, quite what the local authorities hoped they could achieve will always remain a mystery. Another typically ill-conceived plan occurred in October 1935 when the Rossall School at Fleetwood in Lancashire stated how it was going to acquire an aircraft for instructional purposes. The school would alter and extend its racket courts into an airfield!

Mercifully, not everyone proved inept at choosing airfield sites. The Channel Islands received the first of their three permanent airports in 1935 when Alderney opened; all three continue in use today. As Sir Alan Cobham had already demonstrated, airfield site selection was best left to the experienced individualist. Nowhere was this better illustrated than in northern Scotland. The terrain created tremendous difficulties, as did highly variable weather in this area. People wanted a service, but how could any exist if no airfields were available?

Their saviour was former barnstormer Captain Edmund E. Fresson, who formed his Highland Airways in 1933. He managed to establish regular passenger services between Inverness and both Orkney and Shetland. Fresson's potentially profitable routes did not go unnoticed by big business as his airline became Scottish Airways in August 1937. He also created considerable history in mounting the first regular internal air mail service in Britain on May 29 1934 by flying from Inverness (Longman) Airport to Kirkwall/ Wideford and back. Thanks to Fresson, his marvellous efforts gave rise to several new airfields, notably the present day Inverness and Shetland Airports at Dalcross and Sumburgh. This unrecognised genius helped aviation in other ways by effectively inventing the standard military airfield runway layout and also taking the then unusual step of dropping supplies to islanders by parachute.

The aviation scene in northern Scotland was not entirely a one-man show. Midland and Scottish Air Ferries under John Sword did not become so successful but can still be credited with opening up the Western Isles. Northern and Scottish Airways further developed the various routes, its chief pilot David Barclay helping to found these Hebridean sites. He even spent his holidays looking for possible landing places – now there was dedication. Mention must lastly be made of Eric L. Gandar Dower of Aberdeen (later Allied) Airways. Like Fresson, with whom a bitter rivalry arose to such levels that they built separate airfields alongside one another at Thurso, one of Britain's worst municipal airports, he too flew routes to Orkney and Shetland. But Gandar Dower's major achievement became the creation of Dyce: Aberdeen's airport has since become the busiest heliport in the world.

Two more civil biplane types were similar to the Moth in being everyday sights at these and many other British civil airfields; both were also de Havilland products. The twin-engined Dragon and its more powerful development in the famous Dragon Rapide were used by numerous internal airline operators. Both aircraft were familiar to Fresson and company but started passenger services with Hillman Airways out of Essex during 1933/34, first at Maylands before switching to Stapleford Tawney. Fickle fate would again intervene as Edward Hillman died of a heart attack at the all too early age of 44 to sour this otherwise successful story.

Money started rolling in during the early 1930s as civil airfields showed the way in British aerial activity. Airliners such as the Dragon and Dragon Rapide confirmed how no more worries remained about carrying only one or two people at a time. Aircraft structures had become much stronger and engines more dependable. Imperial Airways thrived, joined on the home airline front on October 1 1935 when Highland Airways, Northern and Scottish Airways, Hillman Airways, Spartan Airlines and United Airways amalgamated to become known as British Airways. A proliferation of money inevitably brought greed and then crime, as shown earlier that year in March when Croydon witnessed a gold robbery. The criminals were quickly arrested, though, and unlawful activities continued to be virtually absent at airfields as before because of exceptionally tight security measures.

It had surely become apparent by now how British airfield expansion seemed largely confined to the civil side of aviation. Certainly Cobham, Fresson and other individualistic pioneers were successfully putting airfields on the map. The same could be said for larger concerns such as Railway Air Services Limited, who displayed the great power of railway companies without having to resort to the farcical railway station airfields of the 1920s. But what had happened to the military?

Following the horrors of those frightening first few years after World War One, the RAF was content enough to stabilise its position. More scandalous Parliamentary attempts at abolishing the RAF had occurred, first in March 1927 under the leadership of well known pro-Suffragette and therefore presumably anti-airfield Labour MP George Lansbury, then another failed Labour assault in March 1930. The Air Ministry sensibly retained certain disused airfields during this unsettling time; greater availability of money meant these sleeping warriors could be reopened. Not every Great War period airfield had been subjected to such appalling butchery in peacetime: future superstars like Boscombe Down, Tangmere, Waddington and Wittering (the former Stamford of TDS fame) slowly reopened one by one as the 1920s gradually slipped away. In relation to this period, there was not so much expansion but refurbishing. Military airfields looked much the same as they did in World War One; even their aircraft had not changed all that much.

Four main types of RAF airfield then existed, namely those for fighters, bombers, army co-operation and coastal reconnaissance aircraft. Trainers would not be particularly evident until the mid-1930s. Military bases had witnessed relatively little advance in aircraft design from the end of World War One up to that time. The Avro 504 had personified the classic biplane with its fabric construction, fixed undercarriage and tail-skid. This forced RAF airfields to house at first large numbers of two general purpose machines which had greatly distinguished themselves in the conflict, the Bristol F2b and Airco DH9A. Despite becoming gradually faster, RAF fighters still remained two-gun biplanes. The Sopwith Snipe, successor to the legendary Camel, was followed by a long line of basically similar designs, especially the Armstrong Whitworth Siskin, Bristol Bulldog and Gloster Gauntlet. This last type led to the popular Gloster Gladiator, which with the beautifully streamlined Hawker Fury signalled the peak of fighter biplane development.

All three other categories of military airfield slowly developed likewise. Each type was hindered like fighter stations by seeing no new aircraft type enter RAF service after World War One until 1923/24. Two-seat single-engined biplanes continued to give the Army aerial support from airfields mainly in the Salisbury Plain area, while smaller numbers of rather cumbersome biplanes served at several central or eastern England heavy bomber stations. Among aircraft at these places could be included the Vickers Vimy of Alcock and Brown fame plus a later company product in the Virginia. Last RAF biplane heavy bomber proved to be the exceptionally ungainly Handley Page Heyford. Flying boats of this period such as the stately Supermarine Southampton were also awkward in build but became slightly more numerous when arranged into squadrons instead of Flights after 1929. So few flying boats of any one type were still built in the 1930s to make maintenance at marine bases difficult. French flying boat and floatplane stations did not learn the same lesson experienced by Britain later on and ultimately paid dearly for this policy.

Not surprisingly, fighter bases received virtually all the attention of these four airfield types. Already famous and eventually immortal Tangmere found itself becoming probably the most glamorous military airfield in Britain during the first half of the 1930s. Yet this place typified its brethren by still possessing Belfast hangars and other World War One era support facilities.

Only at light bomber airfields in Britain in the period between both World Wars from 1918 to the mid-1930s did technological advances in aircraft astonish with their revolutionary aspects. Introduction of the Hawker Hart to RAF service with No 33 Squadron at Eastchurch in February 1930 gave this country almost overnight a bomber which could outpace contemporary fighters. So successful was the Hart that military airfields started accommodating general purpose machines again, all derived from the Hawker machine. The Audax and Hector soon appeared at army co-operation bases, and the Hind was an improved Hart. One could also count the Demon, helping to revive the two-seat fighter strategy started by the Bristol F2b. Many RAF airfields held members of the Hart family by the 1930s. But even these aircraft still had tail-skids, while their airfields still continued to be grassy and still remained fitted out with old buildings. Had technology really advanced?

Life was different, almost unreal for most of the 1930s at military airfields in Britain. Operations revolved around a curious and highly cumbersome zonal system over the country. Service life carried on at a very leisurely pace as RAF airfields largely kept open only during daylight hours. All personnel, except those on guard duties, worked from around eight o'clock in the morning until late afternoon. Wednesday afternoons were religiously set aside for sport. Many RAF stations even closed for a fortnight or month during the summer while their units were absent on leave or at firing camps: presumably no dastardly enemy would attack during a chap's hols. Every aircraft looked either gleaming or colourful, a stark contrast to their worn old airfields. Numerous coats of paint at least helped the latter keep up a good appearance.

For all these outward signs of slumber, the RAF was still looking into the future. Temporary airfields devised as summer camps enabled squadrons to train in near-operational conditions. Armament Training Camp sites such as Catfoss in Yorkshire, North Coates and Sutton Bridge in Lincolnshire and Weston Zoyland in Somerset would later become permanent airfields.

Apart from the Annual Air Exercises, the RAF's other highlight each year was its Pageant (later called Display) at Hendon which always drew huge crowds. Here the general public could see breathtaking flying displays and, more importantly, new aircraft types coming into service. Their evaluation was undertaken by the A&AEE at Martlesham Heath, always a busy and interesting place. Martlesham was assisted by nearby Orfordness, undoubtedly one of the most mysterious airfields Britain has ever had on account of its isolated geographical position. Foresight was evident – if one hunted around a bit – but their usual enemies of money, politics and dogged pacifism otherwise forced Britain's military airfields to snooze on.

This easy-going arrangement lasted until the summer of 1934. It would prove a supremely crucial year, being probably the most important in British airfield history, even if only military ones were affected. What became known as the Expansion Period had started. Future RAF airfields coming into service would now be larger than those of the World War One era, become totally self-supporting and possess brick buildings on all airfield sites. Elegance became the keyword in construction as this new breed blended in well with the landscape, not least because of their stylish hangars which centred on the distinctive C type.

Rapid expansion resulted in many more military airfields appearing during the next few years. Overall totals of both RAF and civil airfields, which had risen since 1925 in a step fashion by increasing for the first six months of a year and then remaining dormant or even marginally slipping, now kept going steadily upwards from 1936. The Expansion

Period had opened the flood gates to allow 20-25 new airfields to open each year, instead of 10-15 as happened before the mid-1930s.

Various 'new' military bases coming on stream were really former World War One sites revived after years of disuse, almost certainly thanks to the long memories of planners. Among their ranks could be spotted Britain's unofficial roving airfield ambassador Montrose. One or two sites almost magically arose from the ashes to become known by another name, the old Australian Great War haunt of Minchinhampton turning into Aston Down. It was notable too how the late generation of World War One TDS airfields enjoyed a gradual revival from the mid-1930s onwards; one of these was Eastburn in Yorkshire, similarly undergoing a change of name like Aston Down and becoming far better known as Driffield. Other airfields appeared on completely new locations, Mildenhall in Suffolk marking its opening by acting as departure point on October 20 1934 for the famous MacRobertson England-Australia Air Race. Many similar new sites would become big stars in later years.

Regardless of whether military airfields were original or redeveloped, protests by the local civilian population suddenly increased. Opponents of Sunday flying, the Council for the Preservation of Rural England and the Anti-Noise League only created nuisance value, yet still enough to gain notice by others. Civil airfields could already tell their aggressive brethren about some bizarre experiences, such as the time in 1927 when the curious mixture of a man armed with a shotgun, the 'Sunday brigade' and Poole Rural District Council combined to stop recreational flying at Ensbury Park on the outskirts of Bournemouth. Now the 1930s saw militarism replace pacifism – and this fact worried many people. Civil sites continued to be rated as fair game by protestors: 34 Communists were arrested at Renfrew on May 21 1933 following anti-war demonstrations, laughable as they were objecting to a pageant held by the Scottish Flying Club. But this barely co-ordinated harassment was increasingly lunging towards the military's way.

Perhaps because of complaints from their constituents, MPs again started asking every conceivable kind of question about RAF station activities as their predecessors had done during World War One. In no way did they let up, and airfields had to be constantly wary of inevitable 'questions in Parliament'. Of greater concern became further Labour murmurs about abolishing the RAF. At the other end of the political scale came complaints from poultry farmers about how their hens were irregularly laying eggs. And nowhere did opposition become more considerable than that shown spectacularly by Welsh Nationalists in September 1936 when they effected an arson attack on an incomplete training airfield at Penrhos in north-west Wales.

All of these convicted or unchecked criminals and more law-abiding objectors were all wrong, for airfield construction work had to go on. From Germany came alarming news of airfields arising in demilitarised zones, an allegation denied in April 1934. Less than a year had passed when a new air force called the Luftwaffe came out from under the covers. A certain gentleman named Adolf Hitler threatened: Britain's greatest threat beforehand was thought to be France. So our new RAF bases justifiably thumbed their noses at all of their detractors. In any case, the moaning anti-airfield army at home did not fancy openly clashing with military bases; they had not the guts to do so, unlike with civil ones. This was shown by the occasion building of one proposed site resulted in rejection because – shock, horror – the locals would move away!

To prepare for the real unthinkable, far greater emphasis was placed on training later on in the 1930s. Flying Training Schools became Service FTSs as if to recognise the military buildup, and formation of the RAF Volunteer Reserve on July 30 1936 greatly helped in building up the ranks of prospective pilots. Training airfields sometimes mixed pre-war with the emerging Aircraft Storage Units but this proved an unsuitable combination as both jobs were so unlike one another. The RAF naturally did its best in the training role but civil airfields also played a major part in flying instruction. A new organisation known as the Civil Air Guard formed on July 23 1938 to contract flying clubs to churn out new pilots. Provided each student paid a certain amount in fees, the Government would fork out the remaining cost. The vast majority of clubs participated in this scheme which turned out a militia force in all but name. 'Cags', as they became known, proved excellent long-term assets.

Civil aviation otherwise kept going as if everything was normal. Our more peaceful airfields thrived with internal and external airline services, taxi or charter aircraft to carry passengers across irregular air routes, flying clubs, private pilots and increasing numbers of gliders. Odd new aircraft appeared as Spaniard Juan de la Cierva gave to the world the autogiro, a cross between an aircraft and a helicopter which needed only short take-off and landing runs on airfields. Frenchman Henri Mignet invented the first homebuilt aircraft, the Pou-du-Ciel or 'Flying Flea', but crude amateur construction techniques made these tiny monoplanes so dangerous that they were banned in Britain after a series of fatal crashes on or near a number of airfields.

Majestic Short 'C' Class Empire flying boats of Imperial Airways meanwhile epitomised the generally healthy state of British civil aviation as they operated in full flow by 1937. Working out of their new terminal at Hythe in Hampshire, these graceful machines offered previously unheard of luxury to passengers on long distance flights. First class mail could now be flown to all parts of the British Empire without surcharge as well.

Such tranquility did not suffice. Nobody realised that the 1937 RAF Display at Hendon would be the last, not just because the authorities had announced in January 1938 how the famous site had become too small for flying exhibitions. Menacing activities abroad brought about the Munich Crisis in September, and Britain looked set for war. RAF squadrons travelled from their idyllic inland airfields to designated war stations, sometimes placed hundreds of miles away on the various coastlines of Britain. Especially for the Auxiliary Air Force units, not used to such unstable situations, it proved an extremely anxious period.

The airfields of Britain were able to relax somewhat as a general exodus home occurred in early October once the enemy threat had receded. Prime Minister Neville Chamberlain arrived back at Heston in western London to triumphantly wave his piece of paper with Hitler's signature on it. Much scorn has since been hurled at Chamberlain and this document but, as regards Britain's airfields, his conciliatory actions became a positive godsend. Military stations – and therefore aircraft – would have twelve more months of construction and preparation time.

If aircraft are considered first, the RAF could phase out its obsolescent multi-purpose biplanes in favour of newer types. Re-equipment had already started, as No 48 Squadron at Manston had received the first Avro Anson coastal patrol aircraft in March 1936. Here was not only a monoplane but one with the luxury of a retractable undercarriage. Even the old tail-skid had disappeared, replaced by a wheel, thus heralding the end of lifting an aircraft's tail and placing its skid in a wheeled trolley before pushing out the machine to the apron or grass of an airfield.

Slowly but surely, more monoplanes forced biplanes out of British military bases. Army co-operation squadrons acquired Westland Lysanders at their inland sites, first of which became

Old Sarum in Wiltshire. Another great advance seemed to have occurred with arrival of the Fairey Battle in Bomber Command. This single-engined type was followed by the twin-engined Bristol Blenheim, of which even more was expected. After employing heavier interim types such as the Handley Page Harrow and Vickers Wellesley monoplanes, Bomber Command stations in central and eastern England also saw three promising medium bomber types in the Armstrong Whitworth Whitley, Handley Page Hampden and Vickers Wellington move in from the late 1930s. And then came two attractive monoplane fighters on the scene during 1937/38, known as the Hawker Hurricane and Supermarine Spitfire.

Would it be fair to say that Neville Chamberlain has become the most misjudged Briton of all time? It would appear so from this formidable list of modern aircraft stationed on our airfields. A wit of the time described his Munich agreement with Hitler as 'the peace that passeth all understanding'. Yet there was plenty of sense in Chamberlain's apparent folly. He must be the only pacifist in history to have won a war.

It must rank as one of the greatest injustices of all time how history has subsequently treated this supposedly harmless man. Nobody today recalls how Chamberlain lowered tax four times in a row as Chancellor of the Exchequer, then raised it because of rearmament – and nobody complained. This act and the way he carried it off typified his sheer subtle genius. Furthermore, contrary to his ostensible pacifism, Chamberlain was about the only major Government politician to support the policy of total rearmament. Still Hitler cursed the by now deceased ex-Prime Minister during his final days in the bunker, knowing all too well how the Third Reich could have rapidly overrun Europe but for the Munich Crisis. Germany could have too, for it basically possessed the same military equipment as in September 1939, while surrounding air forces were ten times worse than their poor states by the time of invasion. Having demolished Poland and then swept through the Low Countries, France would have fallen in six days, not six weeks as the Armée de l'Air was a complete shambles by late 1938. Yet Britain could not afford to boast in aeronautical terms either.

Although subsequent events did not treat Czechoslovakia kindly, to prove how Chamberlain was correct, ponder these points. Had Germany attacked Britain in the autumn of 1938, RAF biplane fighters would have mostly defended this country. Furies, Gauntlets and Gladiators then ruled friendly airspace, whereas Hurricanes remained relatively few in number and the Spitfire had only entered service in August with No 19 Squadron at Duxford in Cambridgeshire. Any offensive capability was essentially weak; one would have to question just how ready were British bomber units, for their airfields still had to register a single raid on enemy territory. With the exception of RNAS Dover (Guston Road) on two occasions in February 1915, no site in this country had at all because of the limited operating range and offensive qualities of aircraft. This is why the RAF's Independent Force of light and heavy bomber squadrons had to operate from airfields in eastern France during 1918.

What now seems even more frightening is how many critically important British airfields would never have reached completion but for Neville Chamberlain and Munich. The list is most impressive: Drem, Kirton-in-Lindsey II and Middle Wallop, vital Battle of Britain fighter stations; Lincolnshire and Yorkshire heavy bomber stars Binbrook and Leeming; Benson, king of the photo reconnaissance or PR airfields; St Eval, arguably Coastal Command's greatest base; famous north of Scotland duo Kinloss and Lossiemouth II; and the three major East Anglian multi-purpose airfields of Wattisham, Watton and West Raynham. What a stream of big guns – and these places only formed the tip of an almighty iceberg.

Another late starter became the great Welsh storage airfield of St Athan. Aircraft companies worked flat out at their factory airfields as a direct result of the Munich Crisis to produce huge quantities of more modern military aircraft. They had long learned how to employ much more metal in aircraft as dictated by the Air Ministry in 1924, following potentially serious shortages of high-grade timber experienced in World War One. Of considerable help later on was an expansion of the shadow factory scheme from April 1938, whereby new manufacturing centres would be built at national expense and controlled by acknowledged aircraft companies. If ASUs like St Athan had therefore not reached completion, where would these brand new machines have resided in readiness?

Technological advances at British airfields and in the aircraft which so desperately needed them had made dramatic advances between 1934 and 1939. Public interest in airfield activities greatly increased, as shown by massive attendances at 78 RAF and civil sites during the latest Empire Air Day on May 20 1939, five years after this event was introduced. About 850,000 people visited military bases, an enormous rise from the 421,000 in 1938. One million visitors in total had also seen concrete runways and perimeter tracks slowly begin to overwhelm grassy landing areas, those last vestiges of the biplane era. The aircraft stationed on airfields at last began to show how they could attack *and* defend. Ceilings doubled, speed and weight trebled, range quadrupled plus engine power and bomb loads quintupled: aircraft had improved considerably since 1918 to help both themselves and their airfields.

Far less obvious were the organisational changes which dictated to our airfields and now had to be refined. The RFC had been divided into Brigades and Wings during World War One. Groups and Areas then arose when the RAF formed in 1918, and this had led to the creation of Air Defence of Great Britain on January 1 1925, which later split into the Fighting and Wessex Bombing Areas. Now these organisations became Commands on July 14 1936 in a move which gave RAF airfields better identification of purpose. As the French inexplicably placed their airfields relating to a geographical basis, the Fighting and Wessex Bombing Areas evolved into Fighter and Bomber Commands respectively, Coastal Area changing into Coastal Command and Inland Area likewise to be known as Training Command. Maintenance Command would later form on April 1 1938 in recognition of the increasing importance of aircraft preparation or storage.

There is no doubt that the airfields of Britain had become extremely influential in making such ostensible and more hidden changes. The days of only 15 or so years before when they collectively wondered if next day would be their last seemed a totally different world – but then it was. Britain was now gearing up for war, not running down for peace. Despite the severe confusion civil totals created, 1930 and a new decade had seen active airfield numbers once more rise above the 100 mark for sure. The Government probably realised the difficulties involved and started counting only 'permanent' sites, 50 licensed civil airfields, landing grounds and marine bases being present at the end of 1930, 57 a year later, 68 in December 1932 and 79 twelve months after that. Further steady increases since early 1935 resulted in the overall military/civil figure threaten to reach 300 by mid-1939. The airfields were fast becoming masters of their own destiny. Not even events such as the disastrous world financial slump as the 1930s started could produce any dire long-term effects. Yet this towering control had been admitted officially away back in January 1920 as airfields in Britain bore severe signs of a terminal decline. They ruled supreme in aviation: they dictated to aircraft.

Every type of aircraft now had to take into account its own

little airfield-related quirks as proof of how times had irrevocably changed. Design factors usually related to take-off, landing or approach procedures, greatly revolutionised by the introduction on aircraft wings of trailing edge flaps and leading edge slots to cut down on the possibility of stalling near airfields. Earlier worries about biplane struts affecting visibility on the ground disappeared with the numerical ascendancy of monoplanes; it would not be long before 'bubble' canopies arrived for even better all-round vision. Aircraft undercarriages increased both in width and strength; fuselages – particularly in the rear half – toughened up as well; metal propellers replaced wooden ones to reduce wastage in crashes; and even the development of such unlikely aircraft components as bomb racks developed with airfields in mind. Most aircraft were now equipped with radio telephony sets too, creating that almost unbreakable umbilical cord between them and watch or control towers at airfields which aircraft had always badly needed but largely been deprived of until now. One of the most unexpected airfield-related involvements became how flying boats had to change their hulls and floats from wood to aluminium. Soaking water at marine bases could surprisingly add considerable weight to an aircraft and thus restrict its performance.

Such a passive, if not downright open presence made its mark in another way as Press commentating on civil and military airfield activities once more reached a high daily frequency. All too clearly the losers had become winners again. Part of this change in attitude could be put down to social values for, while flying was viewed as primarily a leisure time activity for the rich before World War One, developments since 1919 had shown how civil airfields could create enormous benefits for everyone. Day to day life became increasingly easier by such simple measures as speeding up the transportation of people and goods, whether for business or recreational purposes, or air ambulance services mounted between airfields for people living in remote areas.

Military airfields joined in the fun from the early 1930s as reporters watched them like hawks. Newspapers feverishly announced RAF squadron and school unit movements, changes of command at stations, telephone numbers, night flying practice, levelling operations and obstruction notices for many years. This incredible openness continued almost to the day war was declared. Spies never had life so easy: all they had to do was read the daily papers!

Along with civil airfields, military ones had also successfully attacked the scourge of unemployment but, best of all, they had fought back virtually from the dead without firing a single shot in anger. Our airfields blew away their innumerable critics without resorting to the violence of the kind they had suffered after World War One. Intensive media interest was thus a reward of sorts.

One only had to read 1930s newspapers and magazines or look at cinema newsreels to see the many photographs and films of airfields and their activities which spoke in volumes far better than words ever could. The British nation watched with hope as Neville Chamberlain shuttled to and from Heston, the place where Sidney Cotton was soon unofficially pioneering the latest airfield art of sending aircraft out on PR operations across the North Sea towards German objectives. But the increasingly apparent enemy was hard at work too by building up a vast photographic catalogue of important British targets. And at the top in terms of priority stood the places Germany knew as flugplatzen.

This false start to World War Two in the Munich Crisis heralded a new era for British military airfields. Although the Press continued to glamourise them, in reality austerity had replaced expansion. The sheer flashiness Expansion Period stations exuded had gone, shocked by a false alarm. Leisurely operating hours disappeared overnight, hangars and support buildings became camouflaged plus ground defences vastly improved in comparison with before. Aircraft changed as well: formerly painted with bright colours or left in a natural metallic finish, drab green and brown colours now covered every home-based resident. Both airfields and aircraft alike now generally resorted to a simpler approach without all the trimmings.

Farmers and landowners somehow still failed to realise that the final countdown was on. Even by February 1939, when war was a question of not if but when, still they complained about the acquisition of farming land. Still the old moans and innate selfishness predominated as both parties completely ignored local authorities, who quite rightly thought that new airfields would be excellent for jobs.

A general uneasiness also held sway at civil airfields. Municipal airports continued to open, the last to officially do so being Burnaston for Derby in June 1939 and the big Central Scotland Airport at Grangemouth (alongside today's famous oil refinery) next month. Perhaps fittingly, the latter's honoured guest was none other than Hugh Trenchard, to whom many RAF airfields owed almost everything. The peaceful resurgence carried on but war clouds were about to unleash their greatest storm. Violence would soon have to reign instead.

For many civil airfields in particular, World War Two would abruptly end their participation in the British airfield story for ever. Germany's invasion of Poland on September 1 1939 created immense changes throughout this country. Civil aviation ceased to exist and immediately closed numerous airfields of this nature. Airliners were spirited away to safer areas, while flying club aircraft were either locked up in their hangars, dismantled for storage or requisitioned by the military. On the military side of aviation itself, all reservists were called up following general mobilisation on August 31, and the large number of RAFVR Elementary and Reserve Flying Training Schools abolished to become Elementary FTSs or disbanded to assist those schools already in service. A highly important future new organisation called the Air Transport Auxiliary formed and all remaining married quarters at RAF airfields were evacuated.

Next day, the war stations came alive again as RAF squadrons ready for action moved in. Croydon became downgraded to serve as an aide of Kenley; for the world's most famous airfield – or any other for that matter – life would never be the same again. Surprisingly, the number of British airfields had dropped considerably to make a mockery of the expansionist years. Fourteen years hard work had effectively been wiped out in two days, bringing active levels back to what they were in the mid-1930s. Totals were not going to hold up as had happened at the start of World War One. If one lunatic had got his way in 1939, every airfield would have been abandoned and aircraft turned into floatplanes for launching by catapult. But this all too real fall in strength only proved a temporary setback. World War Two would provide the airfields of Britain with eternal glory.

Immobility, Then Immortality

World War Two began for ten Midlands-based Fairey Battle light bomber squadrons of No 1 Group a day early on September 2 1939. Travelling to bases in France, the large Advanced Air Striking Force would find a colossal difference between their new foreign airfields and former comfortable British stations.

Nevertheless, this country was also beginning to possess greater numbers of more spartan airfields. They were known as satellites and had actually been devised three years earlier. Did Home Defence Flight Stations, Great Yarmouth or airship sub-stations of World War One have any influence? Certainly the practice forced landing grounds of the 1930s had played a part. Candidate for title of original satellite airfield seems to have been Alconbury in Cambridgeshire, dating from May 1938, though one could always argue how Eastchurch acquired the prize back in the autumn of 1909 when it supported Leysdown. Any serviceman hoping to find another base bathed in unashamed luxury like his previous one was undoubtedly in for a rude awakening.

In the initial stages of World War Two, satellites consisted of little more than dispersal areas for aircraft. Machines now dispersed around the perimeter instead of lining up in neat rows. Chances of a successful enemy air attack involving strafing or fragmentation bombs would therefore be greatly lessened. Parent stations continued to deal with aircraft necessities such as arming, refuelling and overhauls, although as war progressed each satellite achieved increasing independence. Soon only the latter task remained prevalent, and by mid-war most satellites had broken away to become self-accounting, able to maintain their own administration.

A good proportion of early British satellite airfields comprised of former civil sites. Realising the need for more airfields in general, the Air Ministry requisitioned many hurriedly silenced places in just as short a time. The lucky ones were places with fair acreage which offered reasonable expansion for future requirements. Gliding sites stood no chance of revival, as did tiny flying club airfields dotted about here and there. Their more fortunate civil brethren would largely remain silent for a while, though only to allow extensive reconstruction work. If aircraft did land, they simply did so to make use of the landing area for dispersal purposes.

Civil airfields witnessed another stroke of good luck when civil aviation was allowed on a limited scale in late October 1939. No flying of this variety existed in World War One as aircraft could do nothing worthwhile: now someone had to transport important passengers, freight and mail, hence formation of the National Air Communications organisation. As Croydon no longer continued to be available for civil duties, various other airfields shared the chores of internal and external services. The outlying Scottish islands had to be served, so Scottish Airways faithfully met the special needs of Orkney, Shetland and the Western Isles. Operations mainly emanated from Longman and Renfrew, and became particularly appreciated for their air ambulance flights. The Western Isles would be later honoured with a regular mail service too.

Further south, Shoreham became the unlikely British base for overseas flights, also maintaining links with the three Channel Islands airports. Croydon's airliners had meanwhile been sent to western England. Their new base was to be Whitchurch, at that time Bristol's airport, while Exeter would help out with civil operations as well. Although many remaining home air services used the excellent Dragon and Dragon Rapide airliners, both West Country airports became lumbered with an odd array of civil aircraft types. Among these were a few examples of that tremendously popular ex-Croydon anachronism, the Handley Page HP42 biplane airliner. Despite performing sterling service on transport flights to and from France, this type highlighted Britain's dire lack of indigenous modern transports, a flaw which was never corrected in World War Two. At least more modern machines remained on hand at Poole in Dorset, acting as replacement flying boat terminal for the vulnerable Hythe.

Radical changes, cutbacks and evacuations were not just confined to civil airfields in Britain. The military authorities also had to revise their network of airfield operations. New bases began to emerge, being a mixture of totally new ones, civil conversions, more former Great War sites or compromises between the Expansion and austerity eras. Wartime tended to make airfields infinitely more functional.

Even so, a handful of airfields conversely had to be evacuated because they were far too open to attack. A&AEE and its marine equivalent MAEE at Martlesham Heath and Felixstowe respectively fled to safer airfields at Boscombe Down and Helensburgh on the Clyde as experimental units reached new heights of importance. Martlesham would soon see glory in other ways but Felixstowe became virtually mothballed for the duration of World War Two. No more flying occurred ever again after September 1939 at Martlesham's ever-odd assistant of Orfordness.

Another precautionary measure was the *Scatter Scheme* of late 1939, whereby RAF bombers would withdraw to rearward bases if attacked in eastern England. Western and central England, Wales and even the Isle of Man accommodated small detachments of Hampdens, Wellingtons and Whitleys on exercises during the next few months. The first fortnight of World War Two proved particularly noteworthy as fears of Luftwaffe attacks sent bombers on their opening unusual travels. Carew Cheriton, Jurby, Kidlington and Squires Gate – to take but four examples – had never even seen bombers before. It all served as good practice for many airfields, though, as they were given the opportunity to adapt to RAF units of greatly varying size and aircraft.

Various exercises were about all our airfields could do, for Britain lay firmly in the grip of the so-called 'Phoney War'. Any action to be seen occurred in France, to where Hurricane, Blenheim, Lysander and Gladiator squadrons of the Air Component supporting the British Expeditionary Force travelled during September-December 1939. The winter of 1939/40 proved excrutiatingly bad in addition, being one of the worst ever seen in Europe. Personnel found life quite immobile on British airfields as a result but made good use of their time by preparing for the inevitable artificial storm. Construction and consolidation went hand in hand into the spring of 1940 and defied the atrocious weather conditions. More airfields on the scene, especially satellites and Relief Landing Grounds for training units, meant active levels got back to what they were immediately before World War Two by the early summer of 1940.

Constant patrols over our surrounding waters became most important early on in World War Two to make up for the general monotony. These duties in turn produced the occasional slice of action. Fighter airfields were tasked with this job to an extent, Spitfires from Drem and Turnhouse in eastern Scotland destroying the first enemy aircraft over Britain in World War Two on October 16 1939, though naturally landplane and marine bases of Coastal Command bore the brunt of maritime operations. A Lockheed Hudson patrol bomber of No 224 Squadron at Leuchars in Fife had beaten its neighbours further down the Scottish east coast by becoming the first home-based aircraft to claim an aerial victory earlier on in the month.

For all Britain's massive pre-war expansion programme, many operational biplanes still remained in service at home, none more so than in Coastal Command. Among these were some ancient Vickers Vildebeest torpedo bombers, but biplanes dominated especially at flying boat bases. The popular Supermarine Southampton had led to other types, notably the Saro London, Short Singapore and Supermarine Stranraer, all three of which still kept active by September 1939. Salvation was already at hand as the great Short Sunderland monoplane had now entered the RAF. This military development of the serene Empire boats so familiar at Hythe pre-war had ousted biplanes by mid-1940, soon joined by the American Consolidated Catalina. A new land-based monoplane torpedo bomber in the Bristol Beaufort also began to make its mark at airfields, despite recurring problems with its two piston engines.

Several airfields around the British coast additionally served as home to Coastal Patrol Flights between December 1939 and May 1940. Each saw de Havilland Tiger Moth biplane trainers enter service as unarmed anti-submarine types! It bore more than a slight resemblance to the DH6 *Scarecrow* coastal patrols of World War One. While the Tiger Moths achieved even less than their earlier company stablemate, they proved to be better than nothing.

Many had noticed how far more operationally practical American-built aircraft such as the Catalina now inhabited British airfields in greater numbers. Protests in official circles arose over introduction of the North American Harvard trainer to RAF service at Grantham (formerly Spittlegate) in January 1939. This reliable Lincolnshire base had also served as the Tiger Moth's first port of call in its more accustomed role of basic trainer over seven years earlier. For all this operational stagnation, it was just as well the 'Phoney War' existed as it allowed scores of British airfields to re-equip with newer aircraft types in relative peace.

Of these newcomers, two types easily stood out from the rest. Hurricanes and Spitfires filled countless airfields from the start of World War Two. Few sites had not accommodated one or both types by the end of fighting. Airfields holding Spitfires grabbed most of the attention but, despite its undoubted greatness, the Spitfire was not quite the wonderplane as most people still see it. As it possessed a narrow track undercarriage, unlike the Hurricane, this meant the Spitfire could not fly from *any* airfield. Once on terra firma, a non-existent forward view forced it to 'fish-tail' or weave from side to side while taxying. Both the Hurricane and Spitfire tended to be nose heavy on the ground as well on account of their powerful piston engines but the Hurricane enjoyed much better forward visibility. Production of the special elliptical wings for Spitfires proved difficult at first too, and the story has been often told of how fuselages stood idly by at Castle Bromwich's factory during 1940 as they waited in vain for a pair of wings.

Yet another major airfield-related shortcoming in later years was how the Spitfire had limitations as a fighter-bomber. Its glycol coolant tank under the nose proved exceptionally vulnerable to ground fire: one bullet piercing this component would see the engine seize up in minutes. Therefore, if a pilot suffered this kind of damage, his only real hope was to race across the English Channel and land at the nearest friendly airfield available.

Allowing for these deficiencies, the legions of airfields equipped with Spitfires gave superb service throughout World War Two, active from the conflict's first day to its last. Any Army criticism about lack of protection from fighter airfields over Dunkirk during the Allied evacuation of May 25-June 3 1940 was both wrong and ill-advised, as Spitfires were too precious to send to rudimentary French airfields, while Hurricanes remained too busy coming or going across the English Channel between these and British bases. South-eastern fighter stations could also point to taking a heavy toll of Luftwaffe bombers attacking shipping.

Two types of British airfield, at least on the surface, did not seem to be so active as fighter ones – but both had perfectly good excuses. One was that under Fleet Air Arm control. What a long uphill struggle the Royal Navy had required to endure since its RNAS had disappeared into the RAF in April 1918. The service was determined to regain its own air arm and achieved this feat in April 1924, though the FAA continued to be heavily dependent on RAF help. Airfields did not become involved at this time as FAA units technically only existed on aircraft carriers. Having gained autonomy when transferred from RAF to Admiralty control on July 30 1937, another couple of years passed before the FAA could claim self-sufficiency and complete mastery of both its own stations and shore-based aircraft. Only now could the Navy move in its own inimitable direction.

In the early months of World War Two, the FAA was content enough to quietly build up its airfields and training establishments. A few very solid bases already existed for special naval needs, notably Ford and Lee-on-Solent on the south coast of England, but the FAA badly required newer aircraft. Previous types had been little more than hand-me-downs; by September 1939 many biplanes were still on charge. Best naval fighter available was only the Gloster Sea Gladiator, while the new Blackburn Roc turret fighter monoplane proved a total disaster in service. Little more proof was needed to show how FAA airfields needed a while longer to gather their strength.

RAF bomber airfields seemed initially idle too along with naval ones, certainly in their intended role. Bomber Command in reality primarily concerned itself with training and dropping propaganda leaflets over enemy territory. Ten Whitleys of Nos 51 and 58 Squadrons from Linton-on-Ouse in Yorkshire had delivered *Nickels* on the first night of World War Two. By September 27 1939 a total of 18 million leaflets had already been dropped on Germany; this figure had risen to 65 million when *Nickelling* was temporarily suspended on April 6 1940. No Bomber Command aircraft succumbed to action during this period but crews undoubtedly hated this job which, in their eyes, served to achieve nothing except provide the enemy civilian population with what became politely known as 'bumf'. Midlands airfields meanwhile saw a number of bomber squadrons amalgamate into Group Pools, the forerunners of Operational Training Units. Bombs were largely left alone until the spring of 1940 because unsuccessful anti-shipping strikes had culminated in a disastrous attempted daylight raid on Wilhelmshaven on December 18 1939 and forced a switch to night operations. Not until the night of March 19/20 1940 did RAF bombers attack German soil, and even then only in retaliation for the death of a civilian on Orkney.

Only with the German invasion of Norway in April did Bomber Command airfields come fully into action. Hampdens from Scampton and other Lincolnshire bases soon made the first *Gardening* sorties on April 13/14, groups of six aircraft soon becoming common on such sorties. Tactics had changed from the days when airfields sent out aircraft in World War One only to detect enemy minelaying ships or spot mines for subsequent destruction. Even the FAA, which was not to be noted for its operational forays from British airfields in World War Two, spectacularly aided the Allied cause when

Blackburn Skua dive bombers based at Hatston in Orkney sank the German cruiser *Konigsberg.* This little base could proudly claim to have notched up the first major enemy ship sunk in the conflict.

Generally, though, Britain's airfields concerned themselves far more with the main territory of Europe than Scandinavia. Their days of studious boredom suddenly ended on May 10 1940 with the massive German assault west. East Anglian bomber airfields sent out large Blenheim formations to assist the Low Countries, seeing ragged survivors return from the carnage. The first RAF strategic bombing raid followed on the night of May 15/16. Life hotted up as airfields in south-east England became more involved in the Battle of France. At first offering aerial support, their role changed to that of safe havens for RAF aircraft fleeing from France. Blenheims and Lysanders gratefully flew back across the English Channel around May 19/20, with Lympne being a particularly prominent temporary reception point.

The increasingly chaotic situation worsened in June. Flying training on airfields in southern England was considered too dangerous, so schools moved north out of harm's way. As ever with our airfields, anomalies appeared: why Fairoaks on the western fringes of London was never cleared of its Tiger Moths remains unexplained. Possibly the reason in this case was that Fairoaks had too limited an acreage to accept bigger aircraft but possessed support facilities far too good to waste. The dangers of training still became all too evident during the following year when a bombing raid in April created considerable damage and destroyed three Tiger Moths.

A handful of south coast airfields enjoyed nowhere near the same general good luck. The sites concerned looked so potentially defenceless that a major military presence seemed just too dangerous. Two marine bases would be affected: while Portland in Dorset had to totally close, flying activity at Calshot was dramatically reduced. This was a tragedy for the famous and geographically distinctive Hampshire RAF station, greatly involved in assisting Britain to win the Schneider Trophy air race outright in 1931. However, as the Isle of Wight had been deprived of most of its civil airfields in September 1939, the fates of Calshot and Portland were not totally unexpected.

More evacuation followed on June 15 1940 as the remaining AASF Battles made for the first British airfield available. Their war had turned into an utter nightmare: terrible French airfields, horrifically heavy losses in action and then a headlong retreat via places barely describable as airfields. As for the dwindling RAF French-based fighter force, its Hurricanes would form only a small part of one of the weirdest of all British airfield stories.

Since the outbreak of World War Two, the Channel Islands had preyed on many official minds. Each one had certain advantages and disadvantages. Being optimistic, the military authorities decided to use their airports. Alderney was extremely unsuitable for anything other than civil aircraft but Guernsey and Jersey did see limited RAF/FAA use. These two larger airports became more valuable during June as Germany continued its lightning advance into France. Both received most surprising visitors on the 11th because of events in southern France. Two Wellington detachments of Nos 99 and 149 Squadrons, normally based at Mildenhall and Newmarket Heath in East Anglia, had been frustrated by French forces in trying to carry out Operation *Haddock*. (A few bombing sorties on Italian targets were eventually effected). A substitute force of 36 Whitleys from parts of five squadrons stationed in Yorkshire hence arrived and, having refuelled at Guernsey and Jersey, a number of these angular bombers proceeded to reach Italy. Only now did the Hurricanes of Nos 17 and 501 Squadrons finally appear on June 17, but they quickly left to allow airliners to withdraw a large number of civilians to England between the 19th and 21st.

The amazing Channel Islands airfields saga had by no means ended. Another twist next day saw Alderney become the only British airfield in history to have its landing area completely and intentionally spiked. Guernsey and Jersey would also gain dubious honour as our only sites to be captured by the enemy when German transports landed without encountering opposition on July 1. The Luftwaffe subsequently transformed both airports in order to hit back at their own side in a novel form of countermeasures. The RAF then used counter-countermeasures to bomb Guernsey several times! Used to some extent by Luftwaffe fighter units in the Battle of Britain, only communications aircraft called afterwards.

The Battle of Britain itself immortalised many of our airfields. Obscure places the general public had never heard of before became household names – and all this despite oppressive censorship. Most people today tend to associate the Battle with four things – Hurricanes, Spitfires, south-east England and the beginning of the *Blitz*. Of course they were important, but the most crucial features of all became our airfields, with radar a good second. Historians wrongly dismiss this fact far too often. The airfields of Britain simply had to be attacked and knocked out if a German invasion was to take place. Army and Navy elements were powerless at this time, as only airfields could save Britain. All acted as this country's foundation stone: the whole structure would collapse if they failed. There were endless possibilities should this happen, far too many to list here. It is sufficient to say how not only Britain but the whole world relied upon them.

One must also remember how every British airfield played a part in the summer of 1940, not forgetting all RAF Commands and not just mentioning Fighter Command. This book now recalls the Battle of Britain as viewed by the real heroes, our airfields, instead of reviving the usual less significant or completely false myths.

Having made evaluative bombing attacks on airfields since shortly after the Dunkirk evacuation ended in early June 1940, Luftwaffe aircraft movements over Britain started to greatly increase. The Battle of Britain began as such in July with home sites now enduring more than the odd enemy raid. To dispel myth number one that only airfields in south-east England were involved, Montrose became one of Britain's worst hit bases that month. Going even further north, Gladiators of the Sumburgh Fighter Flight made an epic journey almost comparable with No 2 Squadron's trip from Farnborough to Upper Dysart in 1913 during late July by travelling from their Shetland base to Plymouth's airport at Roborough. The Battle of Britain now possessed its only Gladiator fighter squadron when the Flight was renamed No 247 Squadron on August 1.

Roborough and many other south of England airfields also helped out as anti-invasion patrol bases. Lysanders scoured various coastlines daily to see if any German landings had occurred, no doubt helping to bring about the formation of Army Co-operation Command on December 1 1940. Even training airfields became willingly involved by allowing fair numbers of ageing types to be converted into emergency bombers with the aid of temporary bomb racks. Certain sites would act as rendezvous points for these suddenly aggressive aircraft should the need arise. Invasion fever gripped Britain as a whole – nothing could be left to chance.

One of the biggest worries at this period remained how enemy paratroops could try and capture an airfield intact. The Germans had already successfully achieved this tactic in Norway by seizing the vital Oslo/Fornebu airfield, an event which is worth briefly recounting in itself. Plans had stated that German paratroops should capture the site as Messerschmitt Bf 110 heavy fighters strafed it; once Junkers

Ju 52/3m transports had brought in conventional troops, the Bf 110s would land at Fornebu as short on fuel. The actual operation turned into a farce as poor weather first resulted in the paratroops never arriving. Norwegian Gladiator fighters then put up a stiff fight before an understandable error on the part of a troop-carrying transport pilot, who thought the paratroops had captured Fornebu, resulted in his machine coming under a hail of bullets as it tried to land. The Bf 110s by now had to land or else crash; their crews took the first option and, by dismantling machine guns from their fixed positions once on the ground, captured Fornebu on their own before other troop transports could arrive.

Although this event occurred in another country, it illustrates three points. Nobody could deny the Germans' bravery or their supreme improvisation at getting out of a muddle. But what is most evident is that if German forces could capture intact an airfield in Norway, a country renowned for its difficult landscape, there was no reason why such an event could fail to happen in much flatter Britain.

The answer to combat this problem proved simple. All significant British airfields duly received a scatter site – no relation to the *Scatter Scheme* – or ELG of sorts in mid-1940 in case a major airfield was captured or destroyed. The idea was that friendly aircraft would withdraw and hopefully operate from their nearby crude emergency field. All were thankfully never needed; aircraft usually never even actually landed and so scatter sites are vague in terms of records. This is why historians normally do not include them in any official listings.

Our planners should not have worried so much about such drastic measures, for the Luftwaffe mainly concerned itself during July and the initial days of August with attacks on shipping in the English Channel. Raids of this nature reached a crescendo with an assault on Convoy *Peewit* on August 8. Airfields throughout Britain helped protect convoys as best they could. One of these was the forward base at Hawkinge, which accommodated Boulton Paul Defiant turret fighters of No 141 Squadron at West Malling in Kent. They were massacred in action on July 19 but the RAF paid little heed to obvious warning signs as more Defiants of No 264 Squadron would fall around Rochford, later known as Southend, towards the end of August. All this was at a time when each airfield would need every bit of help it could find.

Heavy Luftwaffe attacks on British airfields started on August 12. Enemy bombers prepared for their latest primary targets, just as they had done with airfields in Poland, Norway, Denmark, the Netherlands, Belgium and France. *Eagle Day* served as Germany's codename for the 13th, and some southerly British sites suffered enormous punishment during that afternoon. But Andover, Detling and Eastchurch did not hold fighters. The Luftwaffe had made its first big mistake, one it did not immediately recognise either. Smaller but considerable attacks on the 14th, even reaching Northern Ireland, were followed next day by the fiercest fighting yet as seven separate assaults were made on Hampshire, Kent, Suffolk and also Yorkshire. Although fighter stations such as Martlesham Heath were badly damaged, Driffield of Bomber Command became another major casualty.

Further huge attacks on August 16 and 18, the first seeing small raids extend into the Midlands, savaged more airfields: these included Ford, Gosport, Lee-on-Solent and Thorney Island on the south coast. Yet none of these places held RAF fighters, except perhaps Thorney, and even there the link was tenuous as its 'fighters' were Blenheims of Coastal Command. It was tragic how these and other unrelated airfields should have suffered but their agonies undoubtedly released a fair amount of pressure off fighter airfields. Ford and Thorney Island could furthermore be consoled by being partly instrumental in the Luftwaffe's general withdrawal of its fearsome Junkers Ju 87 dive bombers; few were seen over Britain after August 18. Stukas found airfields perfect targets – provided no RAF fighters appeared to harass them.

Only limited attacks materialised on British airfields from August 19 until the 23rd because of poor weather. The bane of every site for many years previously had suddenly turned into an ally to give each one a few days breathing space. As August lengthened, the Luftwaffe altered its tactics on the 24th by now determining to hit the RAF fighter airfields of No 11 Group in south-east England. Of prime importance were its seven sector stations – Biggin Hill, Debden, Hornchurch, Kenley, Northolt, North Weald and Tangmere – which formed a protective ring around Greater London. Each member of this magnificent seven, the real Magnificent Seven, also controlled satellites and forward airfields nearer the coast like all fighter sector bases. If the Luftwaffe could wear down the sector stations, overall control would diminish.

The Battle of Britain began to reach its cataclysmic climax as enemy aircraft launched murderously furious aerial attacks on August 24, 26, 30 and 31, then on every day in September until the 6th. As regards the seven key bases, six were heavily damaged. Only Northolt escaped major punishment thanks to its excellent camouflage, an art still in the process of refinement. Biggin Hill and company could nevertheless continue to operate with makeshift repairs. The RAF also continued to make good use of its rearward airfields further north, so that tired squadrons could withdraw to places like Catterick, Coltishall, Digby, Drem and Kirton-in-Lindsey II and be replaced by fresh units. Duxford in No 12 Group was the closest base of this type to the main action. It too was bombed to some effect but was about as far as the Luftwaffe hordes could reach. Should anyone have been in doubt, there was always Wittering just up the road.

This stage of the Battle also became notable for Luftwaffe bombing raids on factory airfields. By attempting this tactic, Germany hoped it might be able to dry up the supply of RAF fighters. Brooklands, Castle Bromwich, Eastleigh and Filton had unpleasant visits but damage was then mainly confined to human lives lost. Production remained barely affected to allow fresh machines to keep rolling off assembly lines.

In spite of this happy situation, constant pounding of fighter and other airfields was beginning to take its terrible toll. Eastchurch and Manston had to be virtually abandoned. Ground personnel worked frantically through night hours to patch up heavily cratered landing areas. A rate of one vitally important site a day was being pummelled into near total destruction by Luftwaffe aircraft during the first week of September. While bombs and bullets remorselessly zeroed in on their targets, Messerschmitt Bf 109s employed 'free chase' tactics to keep everyone on their toes. RAF fighters refuelling and rearming back at base between sorties now did so at great risk. Many airfields were being gradually worn down under this almost incessant onslaught. Stray bombs caused concern, but the Luftwaffe inadvertently created extreme psychological havoc with its bombs which *failed* to explode. German bombs were renowned for not detonating: one-third of those dropped on Warsaw in September 1939 alone proved duds. This partly explains why the amount of airfield damage, apart from isolated instances, was nowhere near as bad during September 1-6 1940 in comparison with before. Not that bomb defusing experts were to know . . .

Problems were not all caused by the Luftwaffe. A major difficulty lay in the fact that Spitfires, numerically vastly inferior to Hurricanes, could not be easily repaired. Only five airfields were suitably equipped to patch them up. Duxford was naturally one of these few exceptions but groundcrews were far more used to the old style of fabric aircraft construction which Hurricanes possessed.

Airfields needed every kind of assistance to defend themselves, and various bases not even remotely related to

Fighter Command thinking entered the fray. Factory, training and MU airfields created usually unofficial Flights on lines very similar to those used by the Escadrilles Légères de Defense in France before its collapse in June 1940. One shortcoming was that these elements, along with other 'foreign' home sites accommodating Fighter Command detachments, were not linked to the main operations system, yet several officially unrecognised fighter units achieved quite remarkable success in action.

Another type of help had a French connection – only a far stranger one. Right from the Battle of Britain's beginning, Luftwaffe aircraft had constantly struggled to operate from their mediocre captured airfields in France, just like the RAF Battles of only a few months previously. Poor support facilities hindered operations, and grassy landing areas gave problems as well. Was this the reason why French 1930s era fighter types had notoriously weak undercarriages? Like its aircraft, France's airfields were quantitatively strong but qualitatively highly suspect, yet one cannot forget the unorthodox (if unintended) passive assistance they gave their distant cousins across the English Channel.

Although the vastly superior airfields of Britain were only just hanging on, they would soon be relieved. German bombs had accidentally landed on London during the night of August 24/25; RAF bomber stations immediately replied by hitting back at Berlin. So great was German anger that the Luftwaffe switched its aerial assault from our airfields to London on September 7. It became an excellent example of how emotion can cloud clinical priorities, and in any case the Luftwaffe was a tactical air force instead of a strategic one. If Britain lacked indigenous transport aircraft, Germany could have done with some heavy bombers.

Daylight aerial battles ensued over the capital during the next eight days. September 15 saw Fighter Command throw every available aircraft into battle to perilously leave no reserves. RAF losses were heavy – but their airfields had become much safer places to reside at. What perhaps helped more than any other factor was the blundering interference of Luftwaffe chief Hermann Goering. He had completely turned the tide by brushing aside experienced advice; defeat was being snatched out of the jaws of possible victory. In the attacks on Poland, Norway and elsewhere, each battle had not been for the country but for its airfields, and the same applied with Britain. Germany had initially realised this absolutely critical fact but then somehow lost its way. In terms of planning, the Luftwaffe was both strategically and tactically all over the place during those first few days of September.

Hitler became desperate as the proposed invasion of Britain on September 15 passed its deadline. Two days later he postponed Operation *Sealion* until further notice. Bomber and Coastal Command airfields gave him more cause for concern by despatching their aircraft on night raids against French ports and destroying many German invasion barges. Once *Sealion* had been effectively abandoned on October 12, the Battle of Britain finished by November as attacks on airfields were reduced to hit and run raids in the future. During October and November, the frequency of raids had actually become greater than at the Battle's height, but now were restricted to either one or a few enemy aircraft at a time.

All of our airfields had saved the current superpowers in the United States of America and Russia from facing Germany on their own. South-easterly bases had borne the brunt of fighting but every area had become involved. Fighter stations in the rest of England, plus those in Scotland, Wales and Northern Ireland kept far from idle by managing to destroy a not inconsiderable number of enemy aircraft too. Fighter airfields on the eastern England-Scotland border such as Acklington, Drem and Usworth proved particularly vital when they fended off aircraft of Luftflotte V on August 15; Danish and Norwegian-based Luftwaffe types never again attacked in daylight. Apart from the involvement of army co-operation plus Bomber and Coastal Command landplanes, flying boats from Mount Batten to Sullom Voe in Shetland plodded to and fro barely noticed above surrounding British waters. Their maritime patrol work was no less necessary than fighter operations in order to protect Britain.

Of the main human participants, most met unusual fates. For a start, both Hitler and Goering finished up as the big losers but still survived to fight another day. But it was in Britain where the sparks really flew. Victors of the Battle of Britain had been Air Chief Marshal Hugh Dowding and Air Vice-Marshal Keith Park, heads of Fighter Command and No 11 Group respectively. Both had led the line brilliantly despite the lack of help from Air Vice-Marshal Trafford Leigh-Mallory of No 12 Group in central England. He favoured the 'Big Wing' approach of using squadrons in one big assembly as had happened during the 1920s and 1930s; so too did legless air ace Squadron Leader Douglas Bader. The fact Dowding had the misfortune to fall out with the Air Ministry did not help his cause either, and by November Leigh-Mallory decided to seize his chance to shoot down both Dowding and Park: incredibly, he thought their tactics were totally wrong.

So out went the two masters, hurried on their way by Bader and, unfortunately, Air Vice-Marshal Sholto Douglas.

The sole person to emerge with total credit out of this severe official bloodshed became Air Vice-Marshal Christopher Brand. He had not found life easy as his No 10 Group only arose as the Battle of Britain was already in progress. Fighter airfields under Brand's command in the south-west of England also proved thin on the ground but included the fearsome parent-satellite partnership of Middle Wallop and Warmwell, which took a heavy toll of attackers. Their leader had shown how to spectacularly destroy enemy aircraft long before, for by sheer chance Brand had shot down one of the Gothas on May 19 1918 while based at Throwley.

As with the leading RAF servicemen, home politicians more indirectly involved in the British airfield saga met similarly odd destinies. Prime Minister Winston Churchill thrived and turned out to be the biggest winner of them all. Nobody could question his benevolence and helpfulness towards aviation in Britain down the years. Yet Churchill had blotted his copy book by helping to sink Dowding and Park: he liked to think on a grandiose scale, and Leigh-Mallory's ideas unquestionably appealed to him. Our airfields meanwhile did not regret the passing in 1940 of George Lansbury, turning his abolitionist theories into the utter sham they always had been, but the biggest tragedy of all occurred in November when their unlikely ally Neville Chamberlain finally succumbed to his long terminal illness. At least he had been spared long enough to see the Battle of Britain reach its conclusion. Churchill claimed the glory, yet the real glory belonged to this broken and almost forgotten figure.

And what of our heroes themselves? How much fame and publicity had they gained? That was a difficult question to answer. Extensive censorship meant no airfield could be named, of course, even though the Press had no qualms about naming enemy airfields as had frequently happened in World War One or the Germans British ones on occasion. The Air Ministry would only make vague references to such things as 'aerodromes in Kent' or 'an aerodrome in East Anglia'. But tales of their deeds soon passed along the grapevine outwards from the local inhabitants so, if the civilian population did not have firsthand knowledge of airfields and their activities, everyone quickly came to respect them.

More intricate details could be found in the often delayed communiques issued by both sides. The Air Ministry and German High Command frequently tended to exaggerate – the 'raiders suffered heavy losses on September 7' statement issued by the former was optimistic to say the least – but each organisation, contrary to later mode of thought, did often spout considerable truth. A German communique issued on September 3 said how on the previous day '. . . our bomber and fighter squadrons attacked enemy aerodromes in the South of England. Hangars and barracks were destroyed and fires were caused at Hornchurch, Gravesend, Eastchurch, and Detling . . .', events which really did happen. Similar levels of reasonable truth were shown by the Air Ministry on the 7th, that fateful day for the Luftwaffe, when it described how '. . . an aerodrome in Kent was unsuccessfully attacked, but a bomb which fell in the neighbourhood caused some casualties, details of which are not yet available.' History now shows that place was none other than Hawkinge: yes, several villagers in an air raid shelter were tragically killed by a stray device but no, damage to the airfield was in truth worse than admitted.

Part of the beauty in looking back at history is wondering what might have happened if leading policy decisions had been different. The Battle of Britain is no exception. Six questions immediately come to mind:

1. Could the airfields of Britain have totally wilted if the Luftwaffe had kept on attacking them? There is a slight chance that attrition tactics might have won in the end, for major airfields like Biggin Hill were starting to struggle to hold even a limited complement of fighters by the beginning of September. Lympne among others had only become an ELG in all but name, and certain bases simply remained open by sheer will-power when they perhaps could have taken a leaf out of Driffield's book in August and closed for the rest of 1940. But any Luftwaffe hopes of major success continued to be slim so long as the British radar network lasted to warn fighter airfields. The enemy had given up attacking radar stations as they were difficult to destroy. Only one (Ventnor on the Isle of Wight) was put out of action during the Battle of Britain.
2. Might Luftwaffe reconnaissance of British airfields have been better? The answer to this question is undoubtedly yes. There was something seriously wrong when Upavon could be counted as a fighter station despite the last RAF fighters leaving this famous training base over six years earlier. Of major attacks incurred upon ten airfields on August 16 1940, only three could be rated as fighter bases. Coastal

Command Thorney Island and FAA Lee-on-Solent should not have received bombs; nor should have the experimental centres of Gosport and, as if this was incredible enough, Farnborough. Three Oxfordshire airfields were also raided but none of these held fighters either; Stanton Harcourt had not even opened. What was the use of spectacularly destroying 46 aircraft at training/MU station Brize Norton? Many Luftwaffe bombing sorties were therefore wasted against non-operational or tactically irrelevant airfields when more profitable havoc could have been created at front line ones.

3. Was the Stuka prematurely withdrawn? Certainly it had suffered dreadful losses and it seems that crews were being held back for future use in easier aerial climes. Poor range hindered Ju 87s too but they had caused fearful damage to airfields such as Detling and Tangmere during their short sojourn over Britain to prove the sheer cost effectiveness of dive bombers.
4. What if the Luftwaffe had employed its 'free chase' tactics more? Bf 109s had performed poorly in a bomber escort role because of their poor range. A change in tactics saw them achieve considerable success against RAF fighters in the period around September 15 when Hurricanes and Spitfires were caught unawares low on fuel and ammunition. Greater use of the pretty-pretty but tremendously awkward Fighter Command 'Big Wing' procedure favoured by Leigh-Mallory would have left airfields dangerously exposed and let in marauding Bf 109s. They in turn could have allowed back in the dreaded Stukas.
5. Had the Luftwaffe blunted the British fighter airfield threat, could Germany have successfully mounted a seaborne invasion of Britain? The answer to this question is surprisingly no. Enemy assault barges were terribly inferior compared to the Allied landing craft of four years later. Even if Fighter Command bases had eventually failed to cope, Bomber, Coastal and emergency Flying Training Command attacking aircraft might well have slaughtered the invasion fleet. Aircraft belonging to the first two Commands were already destroying many barges at their anchorages.
6. Why did the Germans not risk their hand by dropping small groups of crack paratroops into coastal British airfields to try and capture them? This idea had worked in Norway as we have seen. Nobody was a

greater fan of experimentation than Hitler either, yet it is probable he feared that the combination of British air supremacy and the English Channel were difficulties just too great to be tackled. Imagine, though, what might have happened if German assault troops had dropped in on Hawkinge, Lympne and Manston. The latter airfield in particular was virtually helpless at the turn of August and September. No British site possessed co-ordinated ground defence elements to counter invasion forces as well. Nobody has ever seriously considered this point before, and it remains surprising to this day why Germany never attempted a paratroop assault. Given the right conditions, this measure just might have come off.

Perhaps the easiest path to glory for Germany lay in following the tactics of the Oslo/Fornebu operation – but with one or two differences. Suppose enemy reconnaissance aircraft had sited crude airstrips in the Romney Marsh area of Kent: Germany had pioneered the technique of operating at short notice from temporary landing grounds. Paratroops would have secured these landing areas, let fighters land, and then allowed in Wehrmacht troops to establish this beach-head. Although attacks on British airfields would have needed to reach new heights, this plan could have worked had each shattered site stayed out of action for only a few hours. One brilliantly co-ordinated gigantic raid of split second timing might have temporarily crippled dozens of home airfields. Another certainly did almost five years later.

Was this plan impossible? Only less than three years later did revolutionary and yet equally rudimentary airfields known as Advanced Landing Grounds begin appearing in Romney Marsh and other southern areas of England. And more than a few troops stayed there for another invasion . . .

Much speculation has also revolved around whether Hitler really wanted to defeat Britain. The success of Dunkirk may have been down more to good luck in his decision not to send the Panzers on to the beaches. It does now seem likely that he hoped both Britain and Germany would attack Russia. The Russians certainly failed to learn British airfield dispersal tactics when they lost 1,811 aircraft or 70 per cent of their strength on numerous forward airfields during the opening day of Operation *Barbarossa* on June 22 1941. The figures for that black day in the annals of Russian history almost make the Battle of Britain look like a skirmish: 66 airfields attacked; 1,200 aircraft destroyed in the morning, 800 of them on the ground; 1,489 of the overall total (mostly fighters) destroyed where they stood by dusk. Red Air Force machines simply stood in neat rows just waiting to be annihilated. It was as if both these aircraft and their airfields were saying 'eat your heart out' to Brize Norton and some other devastated British airfields in a perverse kind of way.

One issue amid all this extreme hypothesis was not in doubt. The airfields of Britain had been enormously successful in their most testing period in history. Their development in only 31 years was nothing other than incredible. Now they were showered in everlasting glory. Many sites had become famous; the 'Magnificent Seven' and a number of other airfields had taken a step further and gained immortality. New aircraft types kept appearing, one of these being a versatile American type called the Douglas Boston or Havoc – a tricycle undercarriage aircraft at that – but our airfields could beat any obstacle thrown at them. They had taken on arguably the world's greatest air force and utterly massacred it. The awesome phenomena had the world at their feet. Who could possibly guess what the future held for them?

Going Forward By Standing Still

Harsh: only one word was needed to describe the winter of 1940/41. Perhaps not quite as bad as the first winter of World War Two – but still bad enough. Adverse weather still did not stop massive airfield construction all over Britain. Countless thousands of construction workers, many of them imported Irish labourers, slogged against the elements to create many more airfields. This latest generation had even fewer frills than the early austerity breed, except in one sense. As winter had played havoc with grass landing areas, concrete runways now came into widespread use. It would be a slow process, especially when converting grass airfields, but concrete made both operations and ground conditions much easier.

Hardly a part of Britain now did not have airfields. Although World War One had shown how they could be spread out, its later counterpart proved this point more fully. Whether the unlikely area was a Scottish island, Cumbria, the moors of Derbyshire or remoter parts of the West Country, airfields would almost certainly be there. Any reasonably large and flat piece of land could suffice. Even Northern Ireland, for long enough the planners' bogey area because of its climate and terrain, had a number of new airfields under construction by late 1940. Before World War Two, airfields there had consisted of the evergreen Aldergrove and little else, but not now. Coastal Command had particular interest in Northern Ireland as it badly needed a suitable base from where the Atlantic Ocean's vital Western Approaches could be patrolled in the RAF organisation's fight against German U-boats.

Among new sites in Northern Ireland arrived five examples of an unorthodox new type. Aircraft storage in Britain was the job for big ASU or MU airfields, placed further north or inland to avoid enemy air attacks. Easily distinguished by their vast arrays of hangars, storage bases frequently held hundreds of aircraft over a wide acreage. As the Battle of Britain warmed up, however, it reached a point where MUs also became choked with aircraft. These places could only expand so far.

So was born the Satellite Landing Ground, bearing little or no resemblance to the HD landing grounds of World War One. Although SLGs also possessed few buildings or facilities, they were not intended for emergency use. Each site was a heavily camouflaged supplementary dispersal area where the Kembles and Kirkbrides could off-load some of their charges.

An old friend of Britain's airfields was directly responsible for creating this different kind of site. Sir Alan Cobham had led a group of resting RAF pilots to select SLGs in the autumn of 1940. Several hundred possible sites were initially chosen, over 50 of these primitive grass airfields (certain facilities like fire-fighting were not available) being earmarked for use; some of those rejected later turned into full airfields. Slade Farm in Oxfordshire became the first SLG to open in December 1940; the rest mainly followed during 1941 and appeared in some really peculiar places. Woburn Park, former home of the by now mysteriously disappeared Duchess of Bedford, dropped its AA civil landing ground past and turned into the biggest SLG of all.

Policy changes resulted in a small number of SLGs adopting different roles, such as Langford Lodge, Maydown and St Angelo in Northern Ireland which later saw use by the USAAF, FAA and RAF respectively, while training units occasionally used other sites of this kind. Not every SLG was successful, Low Eldrig to the south of Stranraer being just one example, but most did their job well. All were so shrouded in secrecy at first that sheep or cattle placed in fenced-off areas to aid camouflage easily deceived pilots. It still remained odd how these unrecognised airfields – SLGs became true unsung heroes as they were deliberately not featured on Air Ministry airfield maps – tended to suffer from problems with intruders until dog handlers were brought in. A lack of enemy air activity enabled greater numbers of aircraft to arrive at SLGs later on in World War Two for a total of 100 or more at any one time in storage to be common. Types could range from single-engined fighters to four-engined heavy bombers. One cannot help wondering how RAF personnel managed to cram so many aircraft into such tiny sites on seeing a former SLG today.

Training and second-line airfields also proliferated in Britain from 1941 by opening up in less familiar parts, if not quite as extreme as SLGs: the West Midlands was but one typical area. This further twist had partly resulted from the withdrawal of trainers out of southern England in mid-1940. Training Command had wisely managed to quickly settle the administrative hassle involved by already splitting into Flying Training and Technical Training Commands on May 27. OTUs now existed for most aircraft roles, with fighter and bomber establishments not surprisingly taking up a lot of room. Bomber OTUs had an exceptionally wide range of activities, flying day and night training missions, *Nickels* and the odd bombing raid to give pupils experience. Wellingtons formed the bulk of equipment until World War Two ended, and rapidly ageing Whitleys were able to keep going into 1944.

So much importance was placed upon instructing fresh bomber crews that considerable fine tuning became necessary for consistent airfield operations. Bomber satellite stations soon took on more basic training duties, leaving advanced training and operational experience raids to their parents. Satellites were consoled by holding different aircraft in target towers and fighter affiliation types as well as bombers. Unusual terms like ¾OTU appeared, meaning that the unit had three-quarters of the strength of aircraft available, normally about 54.

Many other non-operational British airfields saw still less daring aircraft, instead providing their unsung yet invaluable services for various forms of aerial warfare. Apart from pilot instruction at all stages, training airfields existed for navigators, observers, engineers, radio operators, gunners and a wide range of specialist requirements such as flying instructor training. As most schools had a large number of aircraft available, often over 100, they had Relief Landing Grounds on hand for the dispersal of Flights. RLGs were comparatively simple sites furnished with few buildings in their earlier days. Yet another bad winter of 1941/42 and the resultant waterlogging saw these airfields being more extensively used. Larger airfields also became RLGs as war progressed, depending on the local situation, so the term was latterly a loose one. By then they were better described as satellites, though it became notable how many 'big' airfields fell back to being satellites.

At the outbreak of World War Two, Britain's training airfields had largely settled on the aircraft types which would serve them until hostilities ceased. Tiger Moths, Ansons and Harvards had been joined by the Airspeed Oxford and Miles Master monoplanes. The Hart, related members of its family plus other increasingly old biplane types like the Avro Tutor were also present but gradually phased out during wartime.

A pattern can be seen at training airfields if one tries to distinguish between aircraft types and instructional units which operated from them: one or two types could be seen in the main at each. EFTSs (the pre-war E&RFTSs) flew Tiger Moths and lesser numbers of the Miles Magister, though this monoplane had dwindled in quantity by late on in World War Two. Schools for more advanced training operated Ansons, Masters and Oxfords. Harvards were still around too, popular like the others, except among local inhabitants near airfields who dreaded its noisy engine. It was surely the loudest aircraft our airfields have ever experienced! Otherwise, Masters and Oxfords equipped SFTSs and their (Pilots) Advanced Flying Unit successors, while Ansons formed the flying equipment of Air Navigation Schools, (Observers) Advanced Flying Units and Air Gunnery Schools. These latter units also flew Miles Martinets in order to pull target drogues over various bays near their home bases for Ansons to shoot at. Radio training at Yatesbury in Wiltshire and similar airfields differed from others by holding Percival Proctor monoplanes and de Havilland Dominies or militarised Dragon Rapides, and Oxfords dominated the numerous Blind Approach Training Flights scattered over most of Britain from 1941. Only Flying Instructors' Schools did not standardise on any particular aircraft type, but naturally these units required a variety of aircraft for such an advanced task.

A big change occurred in 1941 when the Commonwealth Air Training Scheme was introduced. This took the majority of pilot training away from Britain. Trainees still needed basic and advanced instruction, so after ground training a hopeful pilot would proceed to an EFTS at home before travelling to an SFTS abroad. Once back in Britain, he would have to serve at a (P) AFU and then an OTU prior to passing the grade. Bomber pilots required further advanced instruction at a Heavy Conversion Unit and a Lancaster Finishing School in turn because of the heavier aircraft they would be using. Wartime training at airfields had become a complex affair, but this was surely better than the supreme disorganisation which lasted for most of World War One.

Various support airfields assisting their training brethren did not settle on certain aircraft types either. Nowhere did this apply more than with those involved in anti-aircraft co-operation. This duty had existed since Army, Navy and AA gun positions had required target towing aircraft to provide their personnel with something to shoot at. Future developments brought other tasks, including bringing aircraft into contact with ground troops while flying simulated attack sorties. AA co-operation was essentially a dull job but just as vital as the next one.

A few Anti-Aircraft Co-operation Units were initially detailed with trailing drogues over Britain in the early stages of World War Two. Unfortunately, by 1941 these elements had become split into so many Flights and diverse airfields that planners had more than a few sleepless nights in trying to keep track of them. AACUs thus gradually split into independent Flights and eventually squadrons, placed in regions of Britain for better administrative control. While detachments continued to be numerous, each now lay within fairly easy reach of the HQ airfield.

AA co-operation airfields could always be readily picked out, leaving aside their drogues, for most of their resident aircraft had seen much better days. A failed light bomber in the Hawker Henley soldiered on for long enough, joined by Defiants among others. American Vultee Vengeances also kept quite common at these bases as the RAF rather short-sightedly disapproved of dive bombers in Europe. This was despite the fact that Vengeances saw successful front line service in the Far East. Easily the best type available was the aforementioned Martinet, not least because it had been specifically designed for this mundane duty.

As virtually every non-operational British airfield in World War Two held some veteran aircraft, crashes became inevitable. The war effort sacrificed all other considerations, so accidents in and around airfields ranged from the farcical to tragic. Trainers making circuits and bumps or touch-and-go landings often suffered undercarriage collapses if landing heavily. Wearisome engines and uncertain trainees brought more chaos to second-line stations, which had to battle through all kinds of weather. Many bomber OTU and HCU aircraft took off from airfields on 'safe' cross-country flights to then disappear without trace. Others met their end within sight of home, airfield personnel becoming accustomed to blazing wrecks momentarily lighting up their otherwise darkened bases. The scene looked just like World War One again, except that night flying was now accepted by all.

Unlike the Great War, though, training airfields in particular had to adjust to some frightening new facts of life. Dangerously close balloon barrages were bad enough, but now sites had to contend with roaming enemy aircraft. The summer of 1941 saw Luftwaffe intrusions reach their peak. Although a number of trainers were shot down in airfield circuits, far more damage resulted from interrupted training schedules.

The prime culprits of this real and psychological terror were Junkers Ju 88s belonging to I Gruppe of Nachtjagdgeschwader 2. Absolute pandemonium ensued as these aircraft played around with recognition lights at airfields, fired flares and tuned into RAF r/t chatter. Airfield air and ground personnel began experiencing a kind of frightened exhileration, never quite knowing what might happen next. The success of I/NJG 2 became obvious for all to see but, on October 13, Hitler abruptly ordered General of Night Fighters Josef Kammhuber to cease intruder operations over British airfields. It would appear the Fuhrer viewed the attacks only as 'experimental' without appreciating their real worth. But that was typical of old Adolf: just as the Panzers had Moscow at their mercy and then were suddenly diverted south to Kiev, so the removal of I/NJG 2 added to his catalogue of tactically small yet deceptively large strategic mistakes. Training airfields could now operate a bit more easily.

To have any chance of catching Luftwaffe intruders, radar first had to spot them, and one task which involved both training and support airfields was the testing of radar. Calibration units were necessary to make sure that the unseen eye stayed continually up to scratch. Airfields used again became numerous as detachments likewise spread out in certain regions. Signals Wings had to slowly evolve into squadrons like AACUs. Aircraft used for radar calibration proved equally varied, ranging from elderly Hurricanes and Blenheims to de Havilland biplanes and even autogiros.

On the operational front, radar strangely proved one of the few weak points for Britain's airfields in the first two years of World War Two. Robert Watson-Watt's invention had performed brilliantly in ground stations during the Battle of Britain but AI radar sets in night fighters were initially few and highly troublesome. Tangmere was credited with the world's first radar-assisted kill when, after much struggle, a Blenheim of the Fighter Interception Unit destroyed a Dornier Do 17 bomber one night in July 1940. However, as Luftwaffe bombers flew at night during the *Blitz,* fighter stations could not do very much until AI radar developed both in quality and quantity. Blenheims, Defiants, Hurricanes and the promising new Bristol Beaufighters often took off without radar aids – regardless of whether by design or default – and still managed to destroy raiders, yet were all limited in what they could do. Spitfires, on the other hand, showed themselves to be most unsuited to night flying. A detachment of No 92 Squadron at the training RLG and unlikely Battle of Britain hero of Bibury in Gloucestershire had shown this to be the case as early as August/September 1940, after which ground accidents on airfields at night became frequent.

The result of all these shortcomings was that most of the Luftwaffe *Blitz* raids on Britain therefore passed largely unopposed. Kill tallies as in those achieved during the attacks on Coventry in November 1940 and Clydebank in March 1941 proved almost embarrassingly small. Gallant efforts by heavy AA defences could in effect do little more than frighten enemy bombers above: there was going to be no repetition of the gunners' Gotha massacre of May 1918.

Night fighter airfields had their own worries about air raids as defensive operations were largely mounted from satellites until the summer of 1941 to save parent bases any major distress. This was a good tactical move, for it seems that the Luftwaffe had plans by November 1940 to attack RAF night fighter airfields more often, though enemy intentions were not met by considerable action. Wittering suffered several nights of terror and heavy damage in May 1941 but that was about all.

Bomber Command airfields also had to endure hardship because of radar as operations became much more difficult due to the lack of such aids. Only excellent navigation allowed a safe passage to the target and back home, let alone being able to hit it. German industry thrived as medium bombers wandered about like blind men in a field. Problems continued at home as bomber bases came under attack by I/NJG 2 and more standard Luftwaffe bombing elements. The fear experienced at training airfields spread eastwards as bombs set hangars on fire and guns strafed support facilities at the Feltwells and Honingtons, Marhams and Stradishalls and many other airfields. One favourite enemy ploy became attacking RAF bombers as they landed or flew in their particular airfield circuit, a tactic which enjoyed some success as tired aircrews prepared to mentally wind down after a tiring night's work.

Still the German High Command continued to issue communiques describing bombing attacks, in which Britain's airfields prominently featured. A typical example was this report, relating to Luftwaffe activities during the night of May 11/12 1941:

> 'On Sunday night our air force attacked many aerodromes in southern England and the Midlands. Fierce fires were kept going in hangars and barracks, as well as among technical facilities and fuel depots. At several aerodromes bombs were dropped among heavy bombers on the ground.'

This series of claims were described by the Air Ministry '. . . as usual, grossly exaggerated.' Government statements furthermore stated that damage was not considerable except at one or two points and few casualties endured, though these included some killed. Such comments were not entirely true, as enemy munitions did score several spectacular localised successes. Bomber Command airfields such as Marham bore out this fact. Surprisingly, all this mayhem could have been prevented as decoding had already revealed by January 1941 how the Luftwaffe had deliberate plans to attack bomber airfields – if not all British ones. The former thus had to soldier on regardless. Ironically, the only factor in Bomber Command's favour was that Luftwaffe bombers seemed so intent on attacking airfields in eastern England Germany meanwhile did not bother to build up its defensive night fighter force for long enough.

By day, the airfields of Britain were enjoying more luck. RAF operations had switched after a short breather from a defensive to offensive nature in December 1940. Southern fighter airfields, now mostly finished with major repair work, could hit back at the enemy by carrying out *Circuses, Rhubarbs* and other curiously named set piece operations. If our airfields might not have been able to win World War Two yet, they could at least give their Luftwaffe equivalents a taste of what British sites had suffered since the early summer of 1940.

Night activities by RAF fighters slowly began to bring dividends too as No 23 Squadron at Ford introduced intruder missions as a new form of aggressive activity in December to give German-operated bases further problems. This idea of harassing enemy aircraft on or near their airfields was not of German origin as one might have thought with I/NJG 2 around but a British one instead, having its beginnings in the escapades of No 151 Squadron's Sopwith Camels during 1918 when they played merry hell with Belgian Gotha bases. But radar again conspired to limit success over 22 years later as AI sets were forbidden to be installed in intruders lest they fall into German hands should an aircraft crash or be shot down over enemy territory.

East Anglian-based light bomber squadrons of No 2 Group also dared to venture out into the open from 1941 by participating in *Circuses*. Aircraft from British airfields had not attacked ships during World War One because of range and offensive weaponry limitations; now World War Two brought anti-shipping raids over the English Channel. These achieved occasional successes but heavy Blenheim losses. The faster Boston showed itself to be a more elusive target and produced better bombing results in due course. Two more American types would appear at No 2 Group airfields mid-war in the North American Mitchell (another tricycle undercarriage aircraft for airfields to deal with) and the fairly unsuccessful Lockheed Ventura, although both became nowhere near as common as the Douglas machine.

Rearward British airfields kept far from idle either by maintaining their primary roles as convoy patrol, rest and working up bases. It was at these 'quieter' places where displaced servicemen from Australia, Canada, New Zealand, South Africa, Poland, France, Czechoslovakia, the Netherlands, Belgium and Norway were able to form. Only in March 1941 was it announced that hordes of airmen from occupied countries in Europe now served with the RAF. Stations in central and northern Britain provided solid bases for them, the first of which became Eastchurch, where refugee Polish airmen arrived at in December 1939. Many foreign servicemen struck up close friendships with the local population which have lasted to this day, thanks to the airfields.

The great majority of Commonwealth or Allied squadrons became equipped with fighters and bombers. Certain airfields or areas were thus held aside for their initial use in some cases. Evacuated Dutch squadrons had already entered RAF Coastal Command service in June 1940 at Pembroke Dock and Carew Cheriton in south-west Wales, even flying examples of their own Fokker seaplanes for a short period from the former base. Bramcote in Warwickshire acted as cradle for four Polish bomber squadrons at about the same time, and Polish-manned fighters would later become familiar both at Northolt and its satellite Heston, the airfield Neville Chamberlain had known so well. French Halifax heavy bomber units would eventually settle at Elvington in Yorkshire, while their fighter pilot countrymen tended to form in southern Scotland. Catterick became another starting point for fighters, this time flown by Norwegians, who by 1942 had established strong roots at North Weald.

Nevertheless, it was the Royal Canadian Air Force which

made the greatest impact on British airfields during the early years of World War Two, after having first arrived in squadron form at Old Sarum in February 1940. Canadian fighter squadrons latterly had Digby as their own little slice of home where many new units came into being. Biggin Hill and Kenley also became favourite haunts as RCAF Spitfires headed south to see some action before going north again. From the spring of 1941, RCAF bomber units began making their presence felt too as they firmly encamped in Yorkshire. These colourfully named squadrons such as No 420 (Snowy Owl) and No 426 (Thunderbird) were in for a long war.

Despite ever-increasing activity with help from abroad, British airfields did have one purely home-based task which could not be described as a growth industry by 1941. Civil aviation was almost inevitably struggling on its feet. Services had become extremely limited, apart from Scottish island routes and those mounted from Whitchurch which both kept in reasonable shape. Germany's sojourn on the Channel Islands had killed off civil aviation at Shoreham, and British Overseas Airways Corporation flying boats at Poole were left with little more than occasional trips to America. This new organisation had formed on April 1 1940 by amalgamating Imperial Airways with British Airways. The Associated Airways Joint Committee subsequently replaced the National Air Communications element on May 5 to encompass all airline companies except Scottish Airways. Such reorganisation was welcome as civil flying reached a low ebb; it was better to have one or two chiefs control only a handful of Indians.

Just because civil airliners wore no military markings did not ensure them immunity from enemy air attack. A de Havilland Dragon is thought to have met this fate in June 1941 on the Cornwall-Isles of Scilly service between St Just and St Mary's. This particular route was thought to be so filled with risk that it ceased during November and led to St Just's controversial closure, leaving a large section of land without airfields of any sort. Critics have said how British civil aviation in World War Two was extremely primitive; this was true to an extent but it had to be because of prior military demands at airfields.

The civil scene was not diminishing everywhere. A spectacular new route opened in 1941 between Sweden and, of all places, Leuchars. Lockheed Hudsons and Lodestars gradually became too slow on this most dangerous service, so de Havilland Mosquitoes superseded them two years later. Mostly unmarked, these tremendously swift British machines carried mail and one passenger per mission, but the Mosquitoes' most famous payloads were vital ball-bearings for British industry. A mixture of incredible bravery and luck kept the Sweden-Scotland service going, usually managing to outwit German fighters along the way.

All British airfields did not have to suffer the same constant enemy pressure after May 1941, for the Luftwaffe had withdrawn most of its bombers east to attack Russia. One final big strike on London during the night of May 10/11 left nearly 1,500 people dead, then a free-for-all on airfields resulted next night in what almost seemed a farewell 'present' from the Luftwaffe. The evening of the London raid had seen fighter stations fail to destroy yet another unwelcome visitor as it flew south of Glasgow. But then its pilot abruptly baled out: Deputy Fuhrer Rudolf Hess landed by parachute near the village of Eaglesham with proposed peace plans. Only less than a week earlier he had appeared to act strangely at a Reichstag speech given by Hitler. The authorities here dismissed Hess as a lunatic, though soon Russia accused Britain of not revealing all it knew as the Luftwaffe slaughtered Red Air Force airfields. And it could have been all so different, if only a British airfield had done its duty and destroyed a single Messerschmitt Bf 110.

One group of airfields were without doubt pleased to see the back of the Luftwaffe. Aircraft companies such as Supermarine had learned the painful lessons of keeping their production centres together like eggs in one basket and now dispersed their factory sites. Manufacturing had long left the Greater London area since World War One but Luftwaffe bombing during the Battle of Britain and after had created a delayed action effect and affected production for some time. The last thing needed was a string of unrealistically large orders as Hitler landed on German factory airfields, but for once our authorities recognised the peculiar ins and outs of aeronautical affairs and allowed companies time to regroup. Military airfields often helped out by setting aside an enclave where civilians could assemble or modify aircraft. Civilian maintenance repair depots, operating on roughly the same principles as World War One Aircraft Repair Depots, also brought little airfields into play. The Bartons and Broxbournes became just as important as their more spectacular brethren.

The absence of major bombing attacks on larger sites meant construction and operations could continue relatively unmolested. New airfields were opening at the astonishing rate of one every three days. Wartime necessities meant speed became of utmost importance, in spite of obvious regards for safety. It was unheard of for an airfield to open absolutely complete as building work would normally have to be finished on certain areas. Construction sometimes went on for months more and deprived personnel of even the most indispensable items of life like water. New stations therefore had to be occasionally pressed into service as temporary ELGs or RLGs while they found their feet.

Many active airfields also had to close mid-war, but for them it was to allow builders to lay hard runways. New aircraft types such as the superb multi-purpose Mosquito virtually demanded that concrete appear. Yet RAF units, especially training ones, could still use former sites out of action as RLGs even though they were officially closed. Ground establishments were present as well, notably Battle Schools to give aircrews anti-PoW training, so even supposedly dormant airfields defied their inactive tag by providing at least an ancillary service.

One needs hardly say that the rush to produce more airfields provided Britain with the odd clanger. Although there now existed hardly any 'disaster' airfields in this country on the scale of Loch Doon, Yorkshire was most unlucky to possess two real terrors. The older site was Cottam, so diabolical that its main claim to fame was as a bomb dump; nearly as bad was Acaster Malbis, which heavy bombers would have found impossible to use operationally because of its adverse geographical position. Some grass airfields still had to cope with flooding, others with concrete suffered from excessive wear and tear, but it must be said that planners had mostly learned from past experience. If most airfields endured niggly faults from time to time, they were still immensely improved in comparison with earlier British sites.

Hard though it might seem to appear, one common factor became evident throughout the period from November 1940 to the beginning of 1942: airfields looked as if they were not achieving much. Whether that was the case or not depended on a personal point of view. There was certainly enough evidence to show how they had stayed quiet in an operational sense. Military bases had not grabbed the headlines by mounting any huge bombing raids, defending home ground with spectacular success or sinking any enemy capital ships. But no blame could be attached to them as Britain was essentially weak after the summer of 1940. Its airfields needed some time too to build up their strength once more. Regardless of what the politicians or public thought, the best course of action was thus to perform a containment job on

German forces and hope for better times.

Yet our airfields had kept busy behind the scenes in working out training procedures and developing new kinds of sites for both new roles and new friends. Great theoretical advances occurred while the practical offensive situation became bogged down in stalemate. Co-ordination had helped to finely tune most types of airfield or their roles as had happened during World War One.

One of the last forms of activity to receive this treatment before the start of 1942 was air-sea rescue or ASR for short. Many airfields had to be set aside for rescue duties as, though each one served as a dependable home for aircraft, it could only do so much for each resident. Aircraft still remained prone to accidents, poor weather and now enemy fire. Army co-operation Lysanders had flown spotter patrols from numerous bases after mid-1940 when they had little else to do. Proving successful in finding ditched aircrews, Supermarine Walrus amphibians were later added to actually lift stranded personnel out of the water instead of letting them wait for a rescue boat to come along. The authorities fortunately saw the value of ASR and created squadrons to replace Flights, Coltishall's satellite Matlaske becoming home for the first ASR squadron (No 278) in October 1941. Airfield operations still remained much the same as numerous ASR detachments often ranged far from the squadron HQ to cover every part of Britain. Aircraft types became not just restricted to Lysanders and Walruses as Defiants, Spitfires and airborne lifeboat carrying Vickers Warwicks soon appeared. More substantial airfields had to be brought in as a result to accommodate these higher performance machines.

The ASR story epitomises to perfection what happened in those first fourteen months after the Battle of Britain at our airfields: little or no action but plenty of planning, no glory yet non-stop development. Historians would have most people believe that this period of World War Two was totally irrelevant instead of describing the hard background work involved. By January 1942 the airfields of Britain had all but finished their planning, finalised their techniques and revved up as they prepared to go back to the war in Europe. All they had to do was win it.

Their Biggest Splash Of All

1942 became busier than ever before for the airfields of Britain. Not everyone viewed their exploits as successful, for there still seemed to be no end to the aerial deadlock as fighter sweeps and daylight bomber raids from southerly bases continued to harass enemy positions. The grotesquely ambitious Dieppe Raid of August 19 saw RAF fighters cram into every available south-easterly station to support Canadian troops attempting to land ashore and be mauled by Luftwaffe fighters. But it is with an earlier action that we must first concern ourselves, for it offered our airfields the chance to once more grab the limelight after a sixteen month gap. They never again sank back into relative obscurity.

The so-called 'Channel Dash' of February 11/12 1942 became one of the great exploits in naval history when a German armada of ships audaciously stormed the English Channel to reach friendly waters. This event would have been notable enough but for the fact that among them could be numbered the famous battleships *Scharnhorst* and *Gneisenau* plus the heavy cruiser *Prinz Eugen.* British airfields were alas again none too successful in trying to stop these vessels, though the action finally showed beyond doubt how totally different airfields could co-operate in one set piece move.

RAF fighters were once more called upon to raise large numbers of aircraft as the German dreadnoughts became apparent. They enabled the FAA to fly a heroic but murderously unsuccessful torpedo attack with Fairey Swordfish biplanes out of Manston. Flight leader Lieutenant-Commander Eugene Esmonde later received a posthumous Victoria Cross. So ended another of the FAA's rare operational ventures, for the Navy preferred to view its airfields in Britain as training, working up and shore bases while aircraft stayed away from their carriers, far too vulnerable around British waters. Any suitable action, so the organisation basically rightly thought, was to be seen on the seven seas.

Provided naval airfields were built as such from the outset, all differed too as regards their runways, control towers and hangars. Even the airfield itself was also referred to by its 'ship' name (almost without exception a bird) and a satellite being known as a 'tender'. Therefore, to give an example of each, Ballyhalbert in Northern Ireland served as HMS *Corncrake* and its tender Kirkistown as HMS *Corncrake II*.

Aircraft at FAA airfields now began to show great individuality. Several types more associated with RAF bases inhabited naval ones but others kept strictly to the latter. The Fairey company provided several types in particular: the Swordfish and its replacement the Albacore which ironically went out of service earlier, then later on in World War Two the Barracuda monoplane torpedo bomber and Firefly fighter to succeed the earlier Fulmar.

Three more fighter types became even more prominent at shore bases. The Spitfire turned into the Seafire when given an arrestor hook and one or two other modifications at Hamble in southern England. From America came two products from the Grumman company, first the Martlet and then the Hellcat. One of the former – better known to all as the Wildcat – became the first US fighter to destroy an enemy aircraft while in the hands of No 804 Squadron at Skeabrae in Orkney during December 1940.

Whether all of these aircraft types were used for operations or training, many airfields throughout Britain became used to seeing small groups of FAA aircraft passing through on short stays. Life at FAA airfields was certainly different: busy in training but quiet operationally. Aircraft based at their static aircraft carriers did not often attack battleships; perhaps the Navy should have after Hatston's victory over the *Konigsberg* in 1940. One could always argue how Eugene Esmonde's attack had failed disastrously, but how could he have possibly won with no effective RAF fighter escort, dozens of enemy fighters, heavy AA fire and two of the most fearsome battleships then afloat?

Bomber Command had also tried to sink the *Scharnhorst, Gneisenau* and *Prinz Eugen* without success. In its more accepted sphere of operations, this branch of the RAF was busy trying to become accustomed to its new four-engined heavy bombers. Airfields had to acquaint themselves with Short Stirlings, Handley Page Halifaxes and Avro Lancasters too as hard runways were now vital for the 'heavies'. Huge numbers began invading eastern England, although twin-engined bombers still greatly outnumbered the titanic trio for the first Thousand Bomber Raid on Cologne on the night of May 30/31 1942. This event was notable for how airfields in different RAF Commands tried to work together in one huge task, albeit with little success like the 'Channel Dash'. Coastal Command stations were willing to send out 250 aircraft until the Admiralty belatedly forced them to withdraw their offer. Army Co-operation and Bomber Command Blenheims, plus some Fighter Command types, helped to intrude over enemy airfields, while Flying Training Command managed to add four Wellingtons to the 1,043 strong total of attacking Bomber Command aircraft drawn from front line and operational training airfields.

This assorted help would soon not be needed anyhow as four-engined heavy bombers were rapidly coming to the fore. The last of Britain's twin-engined bomber types had been the Avro Manchester, from which the Lancaster was directly developed, a sort of latter-day DH9 so dogged with engine trouble a sick joke arose that Manchesters had to be stationed in Lincolnshire as it was the best available forced landing area. Crews found life quite difficult on bomber airfields during 1942 as conversion from twin-engined to four-engined types had to be carried out at their own station. Squadron Conversion Flights were too unwieldy for their own good: HCUs replaced them at non-operational airfields from the autumn of 1942. By then the Pathfinder Force had moved into Wyton and other Cambridgeshire sites to allow better bombing results. Radio or, as they became much better known post-war, ECM or electronic countermeasures units would not long be installed on various bases in East Anglia and Lincolnshire when the special duty and support squadrons of No 100 Group formed in December 1943. Bomber support always had a spooky edge to it, not least as No 100 Group's existence was not publicly revealed until November 1944.

Bomber Command airfields had suddenly adopted an air of supreme sophistication in trying to outfox Luftwaffe fighters. Strangely named devices – especially *Gee, Oboe, H2S, Window* and *Mandrel* among others – allowed RAF bombers an improved chance of getting to the target, accurately bombing it and safely returning to base. The familiar term 'Maximum Effort' would be called on many an occasion at bomber stations.

Many more bombers, then fighters arrived in Britain from mid-1942, wearing very different colour schemes. The Americans had at last officially moved in to succeed the volunteer *Eagle* fighter units. While Britain recovered from the culture shock, its airfields quickly adapted to the needs of their new visitors. The first USAAF bases were under their ownership but far from ready, as represented by Grafton Underwood, Molesworth and Polebrook in the east Midlands. So badly prepared were the Americans initially that their opening bombing raid had to be mounted in an RAF Boston from Swanton Morley in Norfolk on June 29 1942. Grafton Underwood and Polebrook were thus not able to carry out the first daylight attack proper until August 17, a day after it was openly announced how the USAAF had taken over various British airfields; American fighters had already operated with RAF ones over the French coast since August 11. Other airfields subsequently transferred their services as the months progressed, while completely new ones appeared out of nowhere. American engineers and more local labourers worked side by side to turn Britain into one huge landing area. No wonder one US pilot visiting early on described airfields in this country as being '. . . thicker than fleas on a dog's back.'

Today, many people often think that East Anglia became America's home from home during World War Two; in reality, airfields under US control existed in most parts of Britain. American heavy bomber forces stretched well into the east Midlands, able to do so thanks to the excellent ranges of Boeing B-17s and Consolidated B-24s. Douglas C-47 transports were accommodated in various central counties of England and also Lincolnshire, which held in addition a fighter training establishment at Goxhill; another existed at Atcham in Shropshire. Going further away, Northern Ireland heavily supported the 8th and 9th Air Forces by providing useful areas for training duties. Among its ranks was ex-SLG Langford Lodge, designated a Base Air Depot for storing or modifying operational aircraft. Burtonwood and Warton across the Irish Sea in north-west England served in the same role, and advanced depots were established further south on the fringes of East Anglia. One cannot forget either the small but significant part played by the US Navy units based in such diverse areas as Devon and south-west Wales, or by US Army light communications types such as Piper L-4 Grasshoppers which could use just about any open field. The USAAF could have employed many more airfields in southern Scotland and Northern Ireland as well if it had wanted to.

It would still be the glamorous USAAF heavy bomber stations which managed to grab most attention in wartime. Surrounding local inhabitants became used to seeing B-17s and B-24s leave their bases to form into tight flying formations. Crews favoured this tactic as they thought it could provide concentrated machine-gun fire and hence dispense with escorting fighters. Increasingly heavy losses proved them badly wrong as became sadly all too obvious back at base. So great was the density of airfields in Britain that even finding the right one to return to proved too much at first for some American bomber crews! Flying Fortresses still always had terrific help from their grounded fortresses: so safe were they that only one B-17 was lost on the ground at a British airfield (Great Ashfield in Suffolk) to enemy action in World War Two.

Fighters still had to serve as an answer to the problems suffered by USAAF heavy bombers in the air over enemy territory. Lockheed P-38 Lightnings and Republic P-47 Thunderbolts soon came to Britain but both found life hard in action over Europe and so became less common. The Bell P-39 Airacobra – a disaster in RAF service at the unlikely combination of Duxford and Acaster Malbis – was another earlier visiting US fighter type, though it quickly left with other British and American aircraft via Cornish airfields for North Africa to take part in the Allied landings there in November 1942. RAF fighters thus had to help escort American heavy bombers to take some pressure off the struggling P-38s and P-47s, the first of which later inhabited Midlands airfields in a reconnaissance role, until the effective North American P-51 Mustang could arrive on the scene. Douglas A-20 Bostons and Martin B-26 Marauders provided America's lighter bombing element in Britain before moving to the Continent in late 1944.

Even with the necessary wartime security, it became fairly obvious to the civilian population how the Americans transformed many of Britain's airfields. Perhaps the Expansion Period had ended but these friendly foreigners represented a form of rich austerity which the RAF could not hope to match. USAAF personnel always seemed to have large aircraft, large quantities of food – and large wallets. Some found it difficult at first to settle in remoter parts of the British countryside but all eventually established excellent relations with the surrounding communities. As for American-owned airfields, each could be picked out by their greater number of hardstandings for the large numbers of aircraft available. The USAAF comprised of Groups divided into squadrons, normally four for Bomb Groups and three for Fighter Groups.

To reach Britain, the Americans and their thousands of aircraft first had to make the long and hazardous haul across the Atlantic Ocean. Canadian-built aircraft types such as Lancasters needed to do so as well. This was where ferry pilots came in. After the first transatlantic ferry flight reached Aldergrove in November 1940, ATA Ferry Pools formed at 15 airfields throughout Britain from where male and female pilots could effectively operate. Once an aircraft had been collected, the pilot could either fly the machine straight to its operational station or to a suitable repair-cum-modification centre. Anson, Dominie and Fairchild Argus taxi aircraft for ferry crews became common sights while whisking personnel off towards their latest assignments.

The ATA performed magnificent service during World War Two by flying 308,567 sorties in over 100 different aircraft types. British and American aircrews greatly helped by either bringing aircraft from America and Canada or ferrying them out to the Middle East and India. Portreath in Cornwall was heavily used as a transit point for this latter task. Airfields now had to accommodate Ferry Training Units as well to instruct, kit out and despatch fresh aircraft and their crews. Although White Waltham in Berkshire served as headquarters for the ATA, top ferry airfield in Britain was the mighty Prestwick. Blessed with a phenomenally good weather record, it became our main transatlantic terminal from 1941. A total of 37,000 ferrying flights passed through the Scottish airfield, including the first B-17 for the 8th Air Force on July 1 1942. Prestwick's role had started in usual eccentric British airfield fashion when a Hudson overshot Aldergrove on November 29 1940 and landed here instead!

Hordes of incoming aircraft, added to those produced by numerous factories both at home and abroad, continued to saturate Britain with airfields. Their numerical supremacy had become almost frighteningly impressive. Having passed the 300 mark during July 1940 as training aircraft fleeing northwards created a noticeable increase in active strength, spring 1941 saw the total of airfields go beyond 400 and scratch 500 at the year's end. Only another twelve months had passed when the 600 barrier had been broken after the rise had temporarily flattened out in the autumn of 1942. Many airfields were expected to perform dual roles but some became overloaded virtually to breaking point with tasks. Prestwick came into this category, and another typical example was Lichfield in Staffordshire. At one point, Lichfield had eight different jobs to do (bomber OTU, MU aircraft preparation/storage and packing, ATA ferrying, mail transportation and experimental flying, centralising Flying Control and catering for diverting aircraft) as its worn runways and perimeter track could testify to.

Fortunately, not every British airfield remained overburdened. Already preparations were in hand for the invasion of Europe, thanks to the USAAF giving home airfields still greater hitting power, so many sites stuck rigidly to their respective tasks. 1943 would be best remembered for the big one-off operations and exercises. Bomber airfields undoubtedly stole the show, starting on March 5/6 when RAF Bomber Command commenced what became known as the 'Battle of the Ruhr'. Another massive assault started just thirteen nights later as the 'heavies' called the opening shots in the 'Battle of Berlin' by attacking the 'Big City' itself. While the Ruhr bombardment ended on July 14 after a punishing schedule of 43 raids, attacks further east relentlessly continued until the night of March 24/25 1944.

It appeared to be one raid after another for RAF and USAAF stations along eastern England from the spring of 1943 over the next twelve months. No 617 Squadron's dambusting raid in May immortalised Scampton, followed by the first 'shuttle' mission by Bomber Command on June 20/21 when Lancasters bombed Friedrichshafen and flew on to North Africa. Three nights later these aircraft attacked the Italian naval base at Spezia while returning to Britain. USAAF bombers would also fly to Africa that month to bomb the Ploesti oilfields in Rumania. In turn came the hugely successful Hamburg firestorm raids of July, another effective attack on the experimental weapon centre at Peenemunde on August 17/18 plus two disastrous USAAF daylight 'shuttle' raids on Schweinfurt on August 17 and October 14. Until North American P-51s complete with drop tanks under their wings could reach East Anglian airfields in December, American heavy bombers remained too vulnerable over Germany. More success was enjoyed with the first mass raid on Berlin a month later.

The sanctimonious moralists whined as usual about the effects of area bombing and how thousands of innocent people continued to die amid the carnage. Strategic bombing raids launched from British airfields could not win the war in their opinion. How wrong they were. Former German Armaments Minister Albert Speer, no less, went on record later in life as saying that six or seven raids on big German targets on a scale similar to Hamburg could have finished his country. British airfields could have easily provided a rapid aircraft turnaround to fulfil Speer's prophecy, but the authorities wasted yet another opportunity . . .

Enormous activity at heavy bomber airfields did not mean

that fighter ones were left out in the cold during 1943. When not dealing with nasty Focke-Wulf 190 fighter-bomber raids on coastal towns in southern England, many RAF fighter and fighter-reconnaissance stations took part in Exercise *Spartan*. Although primarily an Army Co-operation rehearsal, it also gave units the chance to constantly switch airfields, something they would have to do once in Europe. Apart from being involved in Operation *Starkey* in September, fighters found themselves visiting Armament Practice Camps more often. These airfields offered pilots realistic weapons training during very short courses. Weston Zoyland became one of the most prominent APC bases, and old Eastchurch would later give Hawker Typhoon fighter-bomber units vital practice in using rocket projectiles.

Fighter and bomber airfields had become not the only ones to have such a single-minded approach to World War Two. Reconnaissance was of incalculable importance to the Allied cause, frequently unarmed Spitfires and Mosquitoes flying at high altitudes to photograph enemy installations. The shabbily treated Sidney Cotton had pioneered work in this field at Heston before war had even started, but it was Benson which would become recognised as the unquestioned king of the few true PR airfields in Britain. Its satellite Mount Farm proved a loyal lieutenant, as did Leuchars and St Eval. Meteorological units became equally important and dispersed, with the Hebridean airfield of Tiree being a surprising backbone in this role. Other airfields in East Anglia, Northern Ireland and Wales gave assistance, though met Halifaxes later became not so single-minded by having a secondary anti-submarine role.

In the more atmospherically stable Midlands shires of England, different activities were evident as transport fleets built up on their centrally positioned airfields. Inevitably present was the world's greatest ever aircraft. Call it what you like – DC-3, C-47 or Dakota – Douglas' 'Gooney Bird' had invaded both RAF and USAAF transport bases. Britain had previously suffered from a dreadful lack of military machines to carry people and supplies, so the appearance of this twin-engined monoplane was most welcome. No 271 Squadron at Doncaster IV showed in June 1940 how this country had relied upon the most unbelievable heterogenuous mixture of aircraft types. This unit then had available Bristol Bombays and Handley Page Harrows, two monoplane bomber-transports and the best aircraft currently available, a few Handley Page 42s and a Ford Trimotor – not forgetting a handful of Italian-built, ex-Belgian Savoia-Marchetti S.73s! To offset this crazy situation, the RAF brought Halifaxes and

Stirlings to transport airfields mid-war. Both types performed well but C-47s/Dakotas still held the ascendancy, regardless of whether the British or Americans owned them. Lyneham in Wiltshire rapidly established itself as Britain's top transport airfield, not least because of its involvement with carrying VIPs, and remains in this position today.

More standardised transport airfields in turn allowed glider training in the Midlands, notably Oxfordshire, to finally get properly moving. This type of wartime activity had started dreadfully in Britain, partly because planners seemed unsure how best to operate gliders and partly due to truly inept initial equipment. Civil gliding had somehow continued here and there until mid-1940 to further confuse the situation. These actions were totally senseless, and prosecutions still occurred as late as February 1941 when owners were rightly hammered. The choice of airfields for the Glider Training Squadron also hindered matters, for Manchester's airport at Ringway was too crowded, Side Hill near Newmarket hopelessly misplaced and Thame too small. But the GTS persevered with this third site in Buckinghamshire (which, oddly enough, gliders still use for pleasure) and tried to make the best of it. Miraculously revived Avro 504s were not exactly everyone's idea of a glider tug.

A better move was selection of the General Aircraft Limited Hotspur glider for use at Glider Training Schools later on. Its tug was initially the Hawker Hector biplane until more modern Master monoplanes appeared. By 1943 training had become far more organised. Gliders finally proved their military worth when towed from Britain over the Bay of Biscay en route to Gibraltar and North Africa for the Allied landings in Sicily during June 1943. The only problem was that so many of these engineless craft remained at home and required a lot of space; Airspeed Horsas and other types had to be stored somewhere for future needs. Help came in usual unexpected airfield style when 20 or so sites undergoing extensive reconstruction work in eastern England stood in as temporary storage areas during 1943/44. Each held 32 gliders at a time under the control of No 2 Heavy Glider MU at Snailwell in Cambridgeshire.

Gliders and their tugs only formed a small part of the varied activities on British airfields as mayhem resulted in friendly airspace. Thousands of movements occurred every day, carefully organised to allow sufficient time for both operational and training aircraft. Perhaps the airfield construction business had peaked but 1944 saw well over 700 sites in use. Bentwaters would be last to open at the year's end:

so good were World War Two airfield construction techniques that the Suffolk airfield still remains in front line service as a USAF base.

Despite this massive presence, diversions by straying aircraft were becoming a serious problem. It was far from unknown for heavy bombers based in eastern England to divert to areas such as west Wales or northern England and hamper normal airfield activities in these parts. Big aircraft did not help the situation either by trying to land at too small airfields. Lost training aircraft presented even more problems because of their war-weariness. Emergency Landing Grounds turned out to be the answer, massive airfields consisting of extra-long, extra-wide runways and little else. A site just along from Bentwaters at Woodbridge became the first ELG to open in November 1943, followed by two more in the spring of 1944. Carnaby in Yorkshire was another totally new airfield, unlike the venerable Manston. All three soon proved their worth by helping to save thousands of aircraft and crews until the end of fighting. 'Cuckoos', as airmen called strays in wartime days, now did not have to hunt around for a temporary nest. Crude ELGs of much smaller size on various outlying Scottish islands such as Fair Isle provided further help during World War Two.

A second new type of airfield to appear about the same time could hardly have been more different. Southern England possessed over 20 Advanced Landing Grounds from the summer of 1943, very primitive temporary sites for fighter operations. The term ALG had already been used since early on in World War Two to denote airfields placed nearer the scene of operations for fighters but now had quite different connotations. Whereas no-one can say two British airfields have ever been alike, ALGs tried their best to disprove this theory. While certain minor alterations existed among some of them, each basically consisted of two metal runways, a few Blister hangars and hardly any other buildings as tents were thought adequate for air and groundcrews. Only about half of these ephemeral sites saw service during the latter half of 1943 for, although fighters used them on some operations, the main purpose was to see how ALGs would cope under wartime conditions. As the vast majority proved successful, working parties spent the winter of 1943/44 strengthening their runways and generally making improvements. ALGs were not designed for winter use in any case.

As RAF and USAAF fighters moved into these supertemporary special airfields from April 1 1944, British airfield activity reached fever pitch as D-Day loomed ever nearer. USAAF fighters and bombers had just flown over

Berlin for the first time a month previously, while Operation *Crossbow* was in the process of finishing after having started on December 20 1943. These constant attacks on missile sites had proved a much needed change for Bomber Command after its slaughter during a raid on Nuremberg on the night of March 30/31 1944. RAF and USAAF 'heavies' anyhow now kept fully occupied during May and June in effectively paralysing the German communications network in France.

Night fighter airfields similarly let rip as they at last overcame most of AI radar's problems and eradicated failed schemes like *Turbinlite*. Hope had arisen for them as far back as May 1941 when combined British defences managed to destroy 23 Luftwaffe bombers during the final big London raid. Beginning to enjoy consistent success during the *Baedeker* attacks of 1942, night fighter stations then proceeded to take a heavy toll of enemy raiders during the so-called 'Baby Blitz' of early 1944. The opening raid on London on January 21/22 saw 16 out of 95 bombers destroyed. Bases meant to take on attacking Luftwaffe aircraft had to exist over large tracts of Britain but could be handsomely rewarded, provided their Beaufighter and Mosquito residents were prepared to travel far afield to receive a plot on their radar screens.

The equally scattered British intruder airfields also turned the corner in 1944 as the planners finally allowed radar in RAF aircraft for use over enemy territory. The recently developed bomber support role now saw night fighter airfields become still more offensive as their aircraft duelled with defensive Luftwaffe night fighters over German airspace with great success. This task was specially assigned to a few Norfolk bases under No 100 Group. Attacking operations now mainly started from the parent station in a total opposite of earlier days.

As for airfields more accustomed to daylight operations, sites holding fighter-bombers came more into play. Each accommodated several units which softened up German tactical defences. Ground attack duties brought tremendous success to our airfields – and the Army was nowhere to be seen: no more the cheap Dunkirk jibes.

Units had similarly become more noticeable for airborne forces duties, yet another role airfields had to adopt. The feasibility of this task was first shown when paratroops captured vital enemy radar equipment in the famous Bruneval Raid of February 27 1942, mounted from Thruxton in Wiltshire. RAF squadrons and USAAF Troop Carrier Groups later spread out over a wide area of central and southern Britain, airfields existing for them in Lincolnshire and much of the Midlands. Thorough training in and around these places in readiness for D-Day saw vast numbers of transports exercise on most days by either dropping paratroops or towing gliders. RAF stations employed Dakotas, Halifaxes, Stirlings and Armstrong Whitworth Albemarles as troop carriers or glider tugs and the USAAF C-47s. Gliders available consisted of Horsas, tank-carrying General Aircraft Limited Hamilcars and American Waco CG-4As, known as Hadrians in RAF service. As so many servicemen resided at airborne forces airfields, where to put them often posed big problems.

The months of waiting for all concerned slowly turned into weeks, the weeks into days. More than ever our airfields turned into villages or small towns. But each one was not just any ordinary place. Every airfield became totally cut off from the outside world: no personnel allowed to leave, extreme restrictions placed upon personal mail and absolute secrecy. This last factor tended to shoot itself in the foot as home-based aircraft were smothered in black and white stripes, so destroying that most useful passive airfield aid camouflage. Nobody seemed to care much all the same, only wishing the invasion to be over and done with. The tension became unbearable.

Germany did not fully know what was about to hit its French-based forces by the start of June. The British airfield armada had reached its all-time peak of over 730 sites, with another 30 or so used on an occasional basis; Driffield then resurfaced after another period of reconstruction work to add to this total. Less than five years of some amazing escapades had seen airfield strength treble – and this did not include nearly another 50 (mainly primitive) airfields which had closed during 1940-44, 14 on C&M or closed to flying, five closed for reconstruction, six new ones being built, a couple of ALGs in reserve, or the three captured Channel Islands airports. That unique airfield quality of unpredictability remained as strong as ever for, while front line bases were packed with aircraft, a few places stood deliberately open for emergencies. Four of the 'Magnificent Seven' – Biggin Hill, Hornchurch, Kenley and North Weald – lay either quiet or closed to flying. Only five airfields may have been undergoing rebuilding work, but what a roll of stars: Ronaldsway, Coltishall's two satellites Matlaske and Ludham (surely a bad tactical move there) and famous Expansion Period Oxfordshire bomber OTU station Abingdon. True to form with our airfields, of course, it was a complete opposite to the Battle of Britain when Abingdon's satellite Stanton Harcourt had been the one not open at a crucial period of history. But most surprising of this temporarily silenced quintet was none other than the premier bomber airfield itself: desperately unlucky Scampton would not be able to reopen for over another month.

A front line force of 271 RAF squadrons and five Flights, 104 USAAF Groups and six independent squadrons, twelve FAA squadrons plus one US Navy Wing and a squadron strained at the leash on their airfields for the signal to attack. Britain became top heavy with all these units positioned towards the south, Scottish airfields being fairly quiet except for a few RAF squadrons concentrating on Norway. The Americans preferred to keep their airfields almost exclusively occupied with just one task, but British and Allied bases juggled with two or more roles at once, so it was not uncommon to see RAF fighters mingle with ASR types, or Lancaster heavy bombers staying with Mosquito light bombers, hence six of the 50 RAF heavy bomber stations operating in a shared capacity. This overwhelming aerial force split into 136 RAF, 105 USAAF, 1 FAA, 1 US Navy and 7 other mixed airfields as follows:

Role of Airfield	*RAF*	*USAAF*	*FAA*	*USN*	*Totals*
Fighter	15+5	13+2	--	--	28+7
Fighter-bomber	10+7	16+1	--	--	26+8
Fighter-reconnaissance	3+1	--	-+1	-+1	3+3
Heavy bomber	44+6	41-	--	---	85+6
Medium bomber	1+1	8-	--	--	9+1
Light bomber	1+6	3-	--	--	4+6
Night fighter	2+4	--	--	--	2+4
Intruder	4+6	--	--	--	4+6
Bomber support	4+1	--	--	--	4+1
ECM	2+2	-+1	--	--	2+3
Airborne forces	8-	16-	--	--	24
Strike/anti-shipping	2+4	--	1+2	--	3+6
Maritime patrol	9+3	--	-+1	1-	10+4
PR/reconnaissance	2+1	4-	--	--	6+1
Meteorological	4+3	1-	--	--	5+3
ASR	5+7	-+1	--	--	5+8
Special duties	1-	2-	--	--	3
	117+57	104+5	1+4	1+1	223+67

At long last D-Day arose, and most of Britain's airfields became tremendously busy from the night of June 5/6 1944. Bomber Command stations were detailed to attack coastal targets or drop a mixture of dummy parachutists and fiery devices east of Le Havre to create a false airborne landing, the numerous central transport bases followed by despatching their gliders and paratroops, then Allied fighters and light bombers from countless southerly airfields set to work on Normandy; another 256 RAF gliders came as reinforcements in the evening. Many south coast airfields such as Hurn, just one of Sir Alan Cobham's pre-war discoveries and now otherwise known as Bournemouth Airport, became exceptionally busy as single-engined fighters and fighter-bombers choked them. ALGs saw more fighters swamp these deceptively small sites. Lee-on-Solent became one of the most noteworthy of all invasion airfields as an Air Spotting Pool formed at this FAA station to assist naval gunners. The RAF, FAA and USN all grouped together here to emphasise how D-Day was a combined effort. More importantly, our airfields could not be faulted: with the exception of an accident at Bodney in Norfolk which combined the usual mixture of tragedy and farce when a USAAF P-51 deigned to flatten the control tower, they had performed brilliantly.

Even at airfields far away from where the main action lay, personnel stood at readiness in case their services were required. The *Saracen Scheme* was revived once again as fighter OTUs turned into temporary squadrons to cover any unexpected emergencies. This system worked by changing the unit's number, so No 61 OTU at Rednal in Shropshire could quickly become No 561 Squadron to give but one example. These OTUs were not called upon as events transpired but perversity would still dog some airfields in the West Country and eastern England by leaving them largely vacant for no real reason over the D-Day period when all could have seen useful employment.

Only a day had passed when the first Allied airstrip in Normandy reached completion near Bayeux. Fighters could quickly transfer to their crude new abodes to support the military landings. The Second Tactical Air Force had been created for this particular reason on June 14 1943, comprising of the old Army Co-operation Command and light bombers of No 2 Group as well as numerous fighter units. Fighter Command had resorted to using its inter-wars Air Defence of Great Britain name on November 15 as a result, though it would return to its original title on October 15 1944. This minor confusion was nothing compared to Second TAF units as they rather confusingly split into groups known as Airfields, being wisely retitled as Wings not long before D-

Day. The US 9th Air Force also served in this army support role.

Life on British airfields slowly but surely became quieter once Allied forces had secured a foothold in France. Transport bases still remained busy by resupplying ground units and ferrying out casualties in their thousands to designated airfields near hospitals, RAF Transport Command bringing back 20,000 wounded by mid-August alone, yet the departure of especially tactical front line aircraft transformed more southerly sites into rest and re-equipment areas. Training aircraft, safe for so long on their northern and western airfields, could now dare to venture south. Even BOAC felt able to transfer its terminal from Whitchurch to Hurn on November 1 1944.

Taylorcraft Auster Air Observation Post or AOP light aircraft could at last leave Britain too for the Continent after a considerable period of endless exercises up and down the country. Old Sarum acted as birthplace for many of these artillery spotter squadrons, the first of which had formed back in August 1941. AOP units had landed at scores of places but many Auster ALGs could not be described as true airfields as these places only consisted of insignificant grass fields which stayed in use for a few days at a time.

Most ALGs of the fighter variety were suddenly left without aircraft either, leading to their general closure soon afterwards, but a few like Newchurch in Kent remained active until the autumn of 1944 to help counter a new threat. Despite the success of the Peenemunde raid and Operation *Crossbow's* ransacking of the Pas de Calais area, V-1 missiles started penetrating the south of England one week after D-Day. Fighter airfields in this area had to mount non-stop anti-*Diver* patrols, while bomber stations further north were forced to resume attacks against *Noball* targets in Europe. Fast fighter types such as Hawker Tempests and Mosquitoes were needed to catch these weapons; it was one of the latter type, belonging to No 605 Squadron at Manston, which became the first fighter to claim a V-1 on June 15.

Although home-based fighters could claim to have destroyed 1,900 of these missiles by September, with AA defences using special proximity fuses and barrage balloons between them knocking out almost as many, more than enough V-1s still managed to reach London and its surrounding regions. Airfields could do nothing about the terrifyingly fast V-2 rockets except send out aircraft to bomb their launch sites. Night fighter stations suddenly had to cope with V-1s being launched from Heinkel He 111 bombers instead of from the ground and heading as far north as Manchester. Furthermore, the sheer unpredictability of these winged devils adversely affected airfield operations so much that a few in south-east England had to temporarily close to flying. Biggin Hill and Hornchurch became the most notable casualties; this period marked the start of a lingering death for the old Sutton's Farm of World War One glory.

Into the autumn of 1944 and beyond, airfield life in some other parts of Britain slackened to a more long-term degree. These changing times were first felt almost inevitably at training and support level as certain roles had increasingly little value. Calibration was one such example because radar stations now had to monitor far fewer Luftwaffe aircraft in British airspace and therefore did not need to be checked so often. Not so much work simply existed for training and support units to do. Various airfields up and down Britain such as Forres in northern Scotland, Newtownards in Northern Ireland and Rhoose in south Wales devoted to second-line duties were already being relegated to ground duties, going on C&M or even closing altogether.

Allied advances in Europe also gave RAF Special Duty squadrons less work. Tempsford in Bedfordshire became associated with this clandestine and highly dangerous activity, an austerity period airfield but still superbly equipped in relation to the obscure enemy-occupied foreign landing grounds its aircraft frequently used that made even Great War HD landing grounds seem luxurious. A wide variety of types had flown from Tempsford to support Resistance forces in Europe by equipping them with weaponry and sundry equipment plus ferrying in and out agents. The best known aircraft available for these duties were modified Lysanders, though they had to be stationed further south at Tangmere because of their short ranges.

Range served as the main reason why a number of airfields in the southern half of East Anglia and parts of southern England suddenly became vacant in late 1944. USAAF 9th Air Force fighters plus light and medium bombers had found nearer European bases from where they could operate more effectively. TCGs made the same discovery not long afterwards.

Transport airfields suffered further frustration in September when fog enveloped them during Montgomery's second monumental mistake after Dieppe alternatively known as Arnhem. All helplessly stood and watched disaster follow disaster – if only the FIDO fog-clearing device could have been available at a few more British airfields. Poor weather was a major factor why this amateurishly planned airborne assault on the Netherlands failed so badly. Gliding instruction had to be instantly reinstated at several training airfields to compensate for heavy losses.

Events looked to be generally doing no favours for Britain's airfields, not because aircraft kept leaving them or that Arnhem had turned into such a fiasco, but that they were the victims of their own supreme success. It showed as the total of active British sites dropped below 700 during September 1944, this magic figure having been reached earlier that year in March after another steady upward surge since early 1943. But an almost instantaneous decline had become noticeable as June ended: despite new ALGs and some revived sites such as Scampton helping to keep losses to a minimum over the summer, airfield strength started to seriously wane. Now the ALGs had closed and less prominent or headline-making airfields showed slight signs of frailty. Even before D-Day on June 1, a dispirited Airfield Controller at Sawbridgeworth in Hertfordshire had suggested tying a bottle of whisky to the windsock in hoping to attract visitors. Frustration such as this was all too obvious. Britain's airfields had done everything for their country: now their country was doing nothing for them in return. But so much still had to be achieved . . .

Whereas people today talk about the north-south divide, the last year of World War Two saw an east-west split develop among the airfields of Britain – with the usual exceptions. Those sites in the eastern sector still enjoyed the good life by keeping heavily involved in the fighting. Heavy bombers weighed down with bombs, fuel and ammunition continued to drone down the runways at Scampton, Waddington and many other airfields in East Anglia, Lincolnshire and Yorkshire on their way to pound Germany. More Lancaster and Mosquito squadrons formed late on in 1944 to intensify their already massive strength. Bomber Command even contemptuously flaunted weakening Luftwaffe fighter opposition by making daylight raids in addition to night ones from the autumn. Its aircraft could afford to take this measure as enemy fighters had lost the use of their outer ring of radar stations. A raid by over 2,000 British and American heavy bombers into Germany on October 14, with only 29 losses, emphasised both how day bombing had become viable once more and also the increasing dissipation of Luftwaffe opposition.

USAAF B-17s had meanwhile totally chanced their arm on June 21 by making a 'shuttle' raid en route to Poltava in Russia. This event proved one gamble which did not ultimately pay off as Russian non-co-operation was followed by an enormously effective Luftwaffe bombing raid. Not many Fortresses returned to their far more pleasant bases in East Anglia.

This was also, along with Kent, the only one of the three areas mentioned above to now see major offensive fighter activity. Fierce and constant attacks soon had to be made upon Dutch flying bomb sites in early 1945 in addition. APC airfields elsewhere still remained fairly busy as well, though transitory fighters had to come from abroad for firing courses before returning to Europe.

One fighter type easily noticeable on front line British airfields both in RAF and USAAF hands had long made a great impact. It was the North American P-51 Mustang, not the Allison-engined variant as operated by RAF Army Co-operation Command and Second TAF squadrons since mid-war but a more streamlined version powered by the Rolls-Royce Merlin. Greenham Common in Berkshire became the first British airfield to see this superb new machine in November 1943; soon P-51s were busily escorting heavy bombers deep into Germany with great success.

If ever there was an individual aircraft type which operated from Britain's airfields during World War Two and single-handedly changed the course of the conflict, it would have to be the famous American fighter. Mustangs showed how they could easily fend off Luftwaffe fighters over their own territory. However, their greatest worth had much to do with airfields, though not British sites but German ones instead, for carefully planned staggered bomber escort patrols saw Mustangs attack anything in sight on their return legs. Pilots rarely wasted remaining ammunition as non-operational Luftwaffe aircraft came under fire. So ferocious were these incessant snap raids that Germany had to scrap considerable amounts of its training programme: trainees could not flee to safer airfields like their British counterparts over four years earlier.

Another major problem for the Luftwaffe at this time was how its airfields tended to be far more inferior to those in Britain. Only one-tenth of bases under its control possessed hard runways for a start by the end of 1944. Facilities became ever more primitive, non-stop bombing raids kept depriving their aircraft of fuel, and marauding Allied fighters led by Mustangs strafed them almost daily. Allied air elements on the Continent did not have technically great airfields either but remained content in the knowledge how they could always fall back to their tremendously reliable former bases in Britain if need be.

Much of the remaining wartime action could be found far away from the mainland of Europe on coastal and northern airfields in this country. Right from the beginning of World War Two, Coastal Command's war with the U-boat had been a long and difficult affair. The 'Spider Web' tactics of World War One were totally inappropriate for this second conflict, along with the bombs still carried on aircraft at first. Developments in anti-submarine warfare came thick and fast: our airfields had their work cut out to keep up with them.

Britain had initially relied upon Mount Batten, Pembroke Dock, Sullom Voe and other marine bases to endlessly patrol its coastal and outer waters. To a Sunderland of No 228 Squadron from Pembroke Dock fell the honour of sharing in the first U-boat kill on January 30 1940. Their land-based equivalents like Bircham Newton or St Eval were then ineffective in comparison because of the poor bomb loads carried by Ansons. The American-built Lockheed Hudson proved quite an improvement, and maritime patrol airfields on dry land gradually began to claim ascendancy over their marine friendly rivals. But typically the British airfield form book was thrown out the window when Bomber instead of Coastal Command claimed the first U-boat to be sunk unaided in World War Two when a Blenheim of No 82 Squadron at Watton attacked one on March 11 1940. Even this victory had a sour taste as the submarine concerned was later raised, only to be sunk again for good by a Royal Navy ship.

Allowing for this minor setback, U-boats continued to be in their element as colossal tonnages of Allied shipping succumbed to enemy torpedoes and gunfire. Germany undoubtedly held the upper hand in this area of fighting for the first three years of World War Two. A variety of problems meant that Coastal Command only claimed its first outright kill on November 30 1941 when a Whitley of No 502 Squadron from St Eval caught the *U-206* in the Bay of Biscay. As Britain required every patrol aircraft available to combat submarines, Bomber Command airfields found themselves unexpectedly releasing medium and heavy bombers until well into 1942. Aircrews used to bases in eastern England suddenly found being temporarily posted to 'strange' places like Kinloss or the emerging Devon airfield star of Chivenor. Bomber personnel tried their best but this stopgap situation could not go on for ever.

Aircraft with even longer ranges than Sunderlands,

Catalinas, Hudsons, Wellingtons or Whitleys were needed on a permanent basis, particularly for the area known as the 'Atlantic Gap' where U-boats operated with near-impunity. Liberators and Halifaxes therefore began appearing at coastal airfields from Cornwall to northern Scotland; joined by smaller numbers of Fortresses, airfields holding these three types turned the tide. What U-boat crews previously called the 'happy time' soon turned into a bloodbath.

British maritime patrol airfields were arguably the most underestimated of all in World War Two, considering the highly important job each one had to do. Action proved intermittent – crews could go a whole tour of operations without witnessing any – but, when they did, it was fierce. The weather could be an extra enemy, as was the case in Northern Ireland which became so important in Coastal Command plans. An occasional Luftwaffe aircraft on the prowl brought more problems and airfields had to adopt new tactics by accommodating long-range fighters. Clashes with Junkers 88s and 290s, Focke-Wulf 200 Condors and Arado 196s might not have happened every day; these aerial encounters were still far more common than the limited number of RNAS/RAF battles with German seaplanes in World War One. U-boats fighting back above as well as below the waves saw greater RAF use of defensive armament, Leigh Light illumination equipment, Air-to-Surface Vessel or ASV radar and sonobuoys dropped to pick up underwater noise in order to beat the submarines. Airfield groundcrews now constantly fitted depth charges instead of bombs, even though these more suitable weapons had been invented as far back as 1917.

By mid-1943 victory at last became apparent to ensure that U-boats faced a losing battle. Kill tallies at British airfields rapidly increased, Bomber and Coastal Command *Gardening* of the Baltic late on in World War Two taking its toll of U-boats as well. Britain was not renowned for its mines, or torpedoes for that matter, but enough of the former made their mark as the loss of 759 German surface vessels in north-west Europe with a total tonnage of 721,977 tons showed. It had been a close run thing, though, as the schnorkel air-breathing device fitted on submarines could have destroyed air supremacy had Germany introduced this revolutionary item earlier.

Not all maritime patrol airfields in Britain existed to the west and north. Eastern bases were vital for North Sea operations. North Coates had its famous Strike Wing from 1942 for torpedo or rocket projectile-equipped Beaufighters to wreak havoc with enemy shipping. Similar Beaufighter or

Mosquito Wings arose at Langham in Norfolk plus Banff and Dallachy in northern Scotland during the second half of 1944. These last two airfields concentrated on Norway and enjoyed great success, yet still fought out many battles with Luftwaffe fighters. Anyone who thought that only south-eastern parts of Britain experienced any heavy action in those closing wartime months was sadly mistaken. Yes, the airfields around our various shores could say with pride how they never gave up during World War Two. It was fitting how Castle Archdale, an Irish marine base on Lough Erne, sent a Sunderland of No 201 Squadron on the war's last anti-submarine patrol on June 3/4 1945. Just as our airfields had started World War Two early, so they did not finish until after the cessation of fighting.

While all of Britain's airfields prepared for peacetime, each still had to overcome some big obstacles in the last three months of fighting. One hindrance disappeared in February 1945 when Balloon Command disbanded on the 5th after 6¼ years of existence because enemy aircraft had become extremely rare over Britain. Barrage balloons had proved their worth but at the same time always tended to hinder local airfield activities.

February was nevertheless easily dominated by another huge heavy bomber raid mounted from the eastern counties on the night of the 13th. This attack on Dresden has since become controversial both for the heavy fatalities among German civilians and whether Dresden itself was of any major military importance. The blunt answer is that it was for two reasons: first, the German city had never been bombed before, but of greater note was Dresden's position as an extremely important communications centre.

More controversy arose during the even more eventful month of March – and this time our airfields became the centre of attention. It had all stemmed from the Luftwaffe's policy towards attacking British sites since May 1941. Raids had considerably dwindled that year until the dreaded I/NJG 2 left for abroad in October; further catatonic, unco-ordinated and mostly ineffective assaults then followed between 1942 and the early summer of 1944. All subsequently fell silent as home airfields were spared from the effects of strafing and HE, incendiary, oil and the particularly nasty 'butterfly' bombs. Heavy bomber stations above all felt the benefits of a peaceful time and operated almost at will. Only nine out of 805 aircraft failed to return from Dresden on February 13/14 1945. Everything seemed good: somehow just too good.

The day – or rather night – of reckoning lay not far off.

Events on the night of March 3/4 had started well enough as RAF heavy bombers returned home from yet another massive raid, this time on an oil plant at Kamen near Dortmund. But, unknown to them, a big Luftwaffe intruder force of Ju 88s and Messerschmitt Me 410s had tagged along behind as part of their Operation *Gisela.* Dozens of airfields were thrown into confusion as enemy aircraft bombed anything in sight throughout East Anglia, then machine-gunned targets at will as they swept over Lincolnshire and Yorkshire – where the real damage occurred – before flying back to base. Daylight revealed how 27 airfields had endured raids, the greatest ever number in Britain from just one attack, and 22 RAF aircraft destroyed while either airborne or on the ground.

Further research into those few hours of utter havoc brings forth a few more surprises. Not the least of these turns out to be how the authorities here not only heavily played down the incident but totally ignored it altogether. No losses were mentioned, and only damage to civilian property stated. One therefore has to say that not every detail of this story has probably still arisen. Sceptics go further by continuing to suggest how RAF losses might have in fact reached a total of 70. Who can blame these albeit unproven allegations of yet another potential official cover-up? Certainly the ill-fated Luftwaffe fighter attack on Continental airfields during January 1 1945 (Operation *Bodenplatte*) had given an early warning of what could happen in Britain. But then it already had: pinprick but successful intrusions had occurred near USAAF heavy bomber airfields in East Anglia during the first half of 1944.

Bomber Command gained some kind of revenge on March 14 1945 when a Lancaster of No 617 Squadron at Woodhall Spa in Lincolnshire first dropped in action an example of the colossal 22,000 pound *Grand Slam* bomb on the Bielefeld viaduct in Germany. Yet small Luftwaffe intrusions continued on home airfields, though with little end result, until the night of March 20/21 when enemy aircraft bombed Britain and its top military sites for the last time; another isolated attack still had to come on the 30th. Who knows what might have happened if the Luftwaffe had attacked far earlier and in far greater strength as seen in the Poltava raid.

Perhaps mindful of what was going on in supposedly peaceful Britain, the Allied tactical air forces in Europe mounted a massive assault on Luftwaffe airfields and their aircraft from the 21st to 24th. Overseas RAF and USAAF elements managed to virtually wipe out any aerial opposition and allowed Operation *Varsity* to proceed on the latter date.

RAF and USAAF airborne forces units – the former having become so unemployed their aircraft indulged in tactical bombing missions during early 1945 – left for the River Rhine from their newly-acquired forward bases, the East Anglian airfields made largely redundant in late 1944. Here lies another wartime myth for, while the British end of this operation worked to perfection, glider casualties proved so heavy over their landing zones that they were never used in anger again. European airfields had concentrated so much on knocking out the Luftwaffe that they had forgotten about AA defences, and German ground fire let rip with everything it could muster to destroy ten gliders and damage 300 others.

For all the success of Operations *Gisela* and *Varsity* enjoyed by Germany, the boot remained very much on the other foot. Home-based fighter units ran up tremendous scores of Luftwaffe aircraft both in the air and especially on the ground. The Americans in particular encouraged Fighter Groups to shoot up fuel-starved machines: it reached the point where just one unit was claiming an awesome 100 kills or more in a single day. Then the No 100 Group Mosquitoes from East Anglia followed up by torching these luckless airfields with incendiaries and the new napalm bombs.

British heavy bomber airfields again made their mark in April as Germany contracted further. German military ships and submarines, like their aircraft compatriots, were raided mercilessly as they lay stranded in dock areas. Little Staughton in Bedfordshire could be credited with sending the last aircraft to bomb Berlin on April 21, then stations struck their final blow four days later as the USAAF bombed Czechoslovakian targets, while Bomber Command visited the island of Wangerooge and Hitler's mountain retreat at Berchtesgaden, where Neville Chamberlain had gone for preliminary discussions back in 1938. RAF Lancasters also raided an oil refinery at Tonsberg in Norway that night. The 'heavies' now had to temporarily switch to Operation *Manna* on April 29 and drop over 6,600 tons of food and clothing for Dutch civilians until May 8, though Mosquitoes of Nos 8 and 100 Groups continued bombing attacks until the night of May 2/3.

Coastal Command airfields stayed in action even longer by keeping a look-out for German midget submarines which had been giving nuisance value. Mosquitoes from strike airfields had run riot in April by sinking 26 U-boats in the Kattegat area of water between Denmark and Sweden. No 210 Squadron at Sullom Voe remained active to the end by sinking the *U-320* on May 7 to close Coastal Command's excellent wartime account. Unlike in World War One, our airfields had not missed their chance at the close of fighting by effecting a veritable turkey shoot on U-boats.

Most British airfields were by this time not concerned with extravagant missions, preferring to quietly tie up the loose ends. Factory and experimental sites, some of the most crucial of any type, always kept looking into the future. In their eyes, 1945 was just the same as any other year.

The same could hardly be said for hundreds of other British airfields. Each of them, from the superstar glamour base to the humblest training site, had participated in at least part of nearly six of the most spectacular years ever seen. Barring a tiny number of sites quite unsuitable for flying, every airfield served Britain brilliantly. Easily the most significant factor in their country's victory, all had single-handedly saved Britain and then shattered Germany. To list the achievements of each one in turn would require a book in itself!

Now many of you may say that these are sweeping statements. But the proof is there for all to see. Nobody can possibly doubt the unparalleled heroics of fighter airfields during the Battle of Britain, or how they subsequently fired back at Germany while everyone else stood still. The dogged persistence of aircraft stationed in Britain to wrest supremacy from U-boats in the Atlantic Ocean cannot be denied either.

Yet, when assessing the strategic value of all British airfield types in World War Two, fierce arguments rage on and on about one group more than any other. What did the heavy bomber bases in eastern England actually achieve? The answer is far more than they have ever been given credit for. RAF and USAAF airfields could have obliterated Germany but were severely hindered by problems outwith their control: one shudders to think what might have resulted if the airfields of Britain in general had not created so much clout for themselves. Aircraft never came in enough numbers to heavy bomber airfields, were transferred to other tasks such as U-boat patrols or ferrying fuel to France or supplies to the beleaguered troops at Arnhem in late 1944, and generally lacked a certainty in planning. Bomber airfields had to constantly shift priorities from strategic to tactical targets, back to strategic ones and so on. 1944 proved a bad time, with a mixture of attacks on air, oil, population, transport and V-weapon targets. If only these places had been allowed to take out one German city at a time as had happened during 1942 and 1943, then an overall win was most certainly on. Bomber bases could also point to devastating attacks on oil targets, as shown by the helpless ranks of Luftwaffe aircraft forced to stand on their airfields towards the end of World War Two.

Looking further afield, the airfields of Britain only gain even greater significance when considering what occurred elsewhere in the world at this time. Hitler greatly overstretched his forces, so North Africa had to give way sooner or later, and it was the thousands of aircraft sent from Britain which finally snapped this weak link. The later invasion of Italy bore little meaning as that country possessed little strategic significance and had not wanted to enter World War Two in the first place. Russia's great winning role only became possible because of tactical mistakes by Hitler and a huge numerical superiority on the Russians' part, considerably helped by the activities of RAF and USAAF heavy bomber airfields which kept millions of Germans at home, a ploy learned from the Gotha raids of World War One.

Fighting in the Far East and Pacific similarly tends to be given far greater notice than it deserves. Some terrific airfield battles developed: who will ever forget Hickam Field in Hawaii and Wake Island at the time of Pearl Harbour or Midway in 1942. But when the USAAF base at North Field on the island of Tinian sent out two Boeing B-29s to drop the atomic bombs on Hiroshima and Nagasaki in August 1945, it made all the previous years of close quarter combat and horrendous losses on both sides seem a tragic waste. The throwaway comment once made that Japan might have surrendered back in 1942 had Jimmy Doolittle dropped the bomb on Tokyo during his famous attack may sound distasteful today, yet there is a lot of truth in this statement. Even if Japan had not then capitulated, it would have lost very quickly because of spreading all three armed services too thinly, as Germany had done by moving on to North Africa.

So, for all of these reasons, our airfields could hold their heads high and say how they really mattered. Brilliant air operations won Britain World War Two, not the Army because of its extremely heavy reliance upon aerial support from 'back home'. The Royal Navy had fought valiantly but its worldwide presence meant the service could not create colossal impact: air power helped, thanks largely to the passive support from FAA stations in Britain. And the victory could have been greater still if politicians had not stuck their unwelcome oars in at many an airfield, farmers not severely disrupted airfield planning, the vagaries of radar and the weather never happened, or the Allied armies in Europe stopped squabbling after D-Day and not let the Russians advance as far west as they did. Airfields were therefore deprived of using *Highball* and other exotic weapons. If a different kind of government had taken Rudolf Hess seriously, they could have set off to attack Russia on the ultimate missions: anthrax bombing and chemical spraying.

Air Chief Marshal Arthur Harris of Bomber Command must take some blame as well among home planners for his dislike of the Halifax, a much better aircraft than he gave it credit for. Although a great supporter of airfields, the attitude of Harris meant constant chopping and changing in Halifax production and thus reduced airfield effectiveness. He should have looked at the hardly unchanged Hawker Typhoon, a type which recognised airfields with its wide track undercarriage, strong fuselage and 'bubble' cockpit canopy, and the phenomenal success it achieved in action. One also has to criticise Harris for his insistence on 'spoof' or diversionary raids mounted in profusion which, despite saving many RAF lives, often diluted the effects of bombing attacks.

But for these setbacks and others on a more localised scale, the 1,000 airfields in Britain as envisaged pre-war by National Flying Services Ltd might have become reality. It is quite impossible to say briefly how astonishingly well the superlative 800-plus did perform. Nobody will ever know for sure how many thousands of enemy aircraft our airfields definitely or probably destroyed, the millions of tons of bombs dropped, the exact tonnage of enemy shipping and submarines sunk, or the countless ground targets such as tanks and trains blown up. The numbers of *Nickels* placed over enemy territory proved infinitessimal: the Americans, statistically-minded as ever, recorded how their East Midlands-based Night Leaflet Dropping Squadron (alternatively known as the 406th Bomb Squadron) alone dropped almost one and a half billion!

On the passive as opposed to active side of airfield operations in World War Two, their contribution is even harder to assess. How many lives PR, training, transport, ASR and meteorological bases saved in their own distinctive ways could never possibly be estimated. About the only calculable area became our airfields' adoption of unit gardens – the service equivalent to civilian allotments – on spare ground to help out the food situation. World War One had latterly seen airfields growing food around their perimeters, but now production had increased in value from £62,500 in 1941 to £166,156 in 1942 and £285,147 in 1943; acreage increased from 4,200 acres in 1942 to 7,200 in 1943 alone. Such a fine auxiliary job was done both voluntarily and in the spare time of personnel, yet RAF messes always remained well stocked up with food and helped add an extra air of self-sufficiency to airfields. The Duchess of Gloucester said on October 12 1943 when opening the RAF Horticultural Exhibition and viewing the fruits and vegetables assembled: 'It seems incredible that barren-looking airfields could possibly grow all these things.' But then our airfields could do just about anything at this time and win handsomely – a towering control indeed.

It should not be said that their victory was still achieved at a stroll. Tens of thousnds of personnel paid the ultimate sacrifice either on or while operating from their home bases. Our airfields had similarly suffered, with well over 1,000 effected or attempted bombing, strafing and circuit attacks by Luftwaffe aircraft. Many aircraft fell on or in the vicinity of their havens, and those enemy bombs or bullets which failed to hit their targets often scored against the surrounding civilian population. Nevertheless, Britain's airfields made sure that their German equivalents were mercilessly pounded from 1944. Nor did they have to suffer the ignominy of Russia's airfields, blown apart in the greatest one-day anti-airfield operation the world has ever seen, or the everlasting shame of the sites in the country which invented airfields. Amazingly, five different air forces had bombed the airfields of France – those of Britain and the Commonwealth, Germany, America, Italy and the French themselves.

All these activities had been quite breathtaking. However, if one had to sum up the performances of Britain's airfields, two words must be used. As this chapter and previous ones have demonstrated, our airfields had no peers when it came to adaptability and versatility. World War Two forced them to adapt from guardians to defenders, then to instructors and finally attackers. Unlike pre-war, airfields had to be on guard 24 hours a day, regardless of whether a forthcoming event was humdrum or special.

British airfields also had to adapt to the profusion of aircraft types which appeared at them throughout World War Two. Many sites had to be greatly extended in order to squeeze in larger machines. They had done everything possible to safely accommodate aircraft by greatly advancing technology, developing Flying Control and introducing such futuristic items as mass-produced hangars and concrete or metal runways, but still their visitors remained prone to various mishaps. Still aircraft 'pancaked' or ground looped on landing; still they became involved in the most unaccountable of accidents right to the end of fighting. Just one of innumerable examples occurred at East Kirkby in Lincolnshire on April 17 1945 as victory lay within grasp. While RAF ground personnel loaded one of No 57

Squadron's Lancasters, several bombs prematurely detonated, triggering off others. Three personnel died as a result, plus five Lancs destroyed and many others damaged. Yet this same airfield became involved from April 26 in Operation *Exodus* by bringing ex-PoWs back to various bases in central England. Such was daily life at wartime British airfields: one minute sad, the next happy – but never dull.

As for versatility, whatever task anyone asked of an airfield, as in the case of airborne forces duties, it tackled the job with tremendous success. Even the arrival of foreign forces, complete with their own special needs, presented little or no problem. No type of installation has shown itself to be so multi-purposeful before or since. Witness how vastly different aircraft could reside on an airfield at the same time – fighters and AA co-operation types, or RAF Coastal Command and FAA aircraft to give but two examples. Detachments or great numbers of small independent units were almost unheard of pre-war: now 'lodgers', as they became known, could always be found some enclave on an airfield. Certain sites became odd job places because of this on occasion but all served a useful purpose.

Should anyone still be doubting these conclusions about adaptability and versatility, let us consider just one airfield out of hundreds of contenders. Lossiemouth II in northern Scotland was originally designed as a base for FTS aircraft, but in World War Two easily coped with widely differing roles. On the non-operational front, 'Lossie' held a bomber OTU and an MU, the second of which also required an ATA ferry unit in tow. Room still existed for various squadrons or detachments, mainly of medium and heavy bombers present for anti-shipping duties. As if this was not enough, Lossiemouth still found time to wage a long personal war with the mighty German battleship *Tirpitz,* and finally helped to sink it on November 12 1944. Assistance came from nearby Kinloss and Milltown, all three of which would never have seen the light of day had it not been for the brilliant stalling actions of Neville Chamberlain.

World War Two British airfield life naturally was not entirely all about action and activity, success and stardom. Many are the stories to be told about the eccentric, quirky or downright odd happenings which occurred at them. Each airfield had its own peculiar ground or circuit conditions. Its personnel often waged psychological battles with the frequently grumpy local farming and civilian fraternities, outwitting them time and time again in a morally unquestionable manner the selfish farmer/landowner contingent especially utterly deserved. Ju 88s had a most unfortunate tendency to land at our airfields: sites as far apart as Chivenor, Dyce, the current Bristol Airport at Lulsgate Bottom, Oakington and Steeple Morden in Cambridgeshire and Woodbridge received most unexpected visits. Even these places could not beat the time four Fw 190s arrived in error at West Malling one night in April 1943. Pembrey in south Wales had invited in another example earlier on in June 1942, and maybe this training airfield did more than any fighter one to combat the powerful Luftwaffe fighter.

As ever, the mysteries abounded too: the aircraft which never returned, clandestine operations which officially never happened, or the famous personalities who were never seen again. What happened to Britain's top reconnaissance pilot Adrian Warburton when he took off from Mount Farm in April 1944? Or famous American bandleader Glenn Miller after he left Twinwood Farm in Bedfordshire in December of that year? We shall never know but issues like these show how our airfields are so compulsively interesting.

Amid all the extensive victory celebrations, one small but highly significant event passed unnoticed. No 529 Squadron was a calibration unit, based in May 1945 at Henley-on-Thames, a little airfield north-east of Reading. When the squadron received a Sikorsky Hoverfly I, it became the first in RAF service to operationally use a helicopter. This weird new type of flying machine posed one of the greatest threats yet to British airfields, not least for its ability to take off and land from almost any undesignated landing area.

Peace seemed an even more ominous coming. Like a shipyard completing its latest ship, an air of uncertainty hung over Britain's supersites. What on earth would happen next? Our airfields had felt a massive axe fall on them after World War One. But now? The future looked mistier than ever before.

Another Uneasy Peace

War in Europe was over. Germany was finished – and so would be the lives of many British airfields. Contrary to popular belief, the number of closing airfields became not as bad proportionately in comparison with after World War One. Only about one in ten sites had survived the terrible post-war cutbacks following November 1918; now the survival rate was approximately one in every three. Casualty figures still proved bad enough.

The airfields were allowed to gloat at their victory – Bomber Command aircraft flew 'Cook's Tours' for home-based groundcrews to see damage over Germany – but only briefly. Various jobs still had to be done. Heavy bomber stations had to immediately participate in Operations *Exodus* and *Dodge* plus an evaluation of German radar systems, while Britain had the little matter of recapturing the Channel Islands and its three airports on May 9 1945. Refurbishment was so fast that Guernsey and Jersey were able to link up with Croydon again before the end of June and reconnect each other by July. Alderney took longer to see aircraft again after the island's unorthodox use as a concentration camp but returned to the fore in early 1946.

Far too many other airfields would sadly never enjoy any further activity. As extensive training was not required for at least the immediate future, many second-line sites hurriedly closed down in the summer of 1945. Numerous RLGs all over Britain from Denham to Stracathro and in between closed on the same day (July 9) in what appears to have been a policy move. Few RLGs of the basic wartime variety lasted long into peacetime.

The Americans began to depart from Britain about this time as well to leave their purpose-built bases silent and empty. Huge aircraft formations passed through transit point airfields at Prestwick, St Mawgan and particularly Valley in Anglesey during the next few months. US heavy bombers reached the Welsh base just nine days after VE Day, becoming the first USAAF aircraft due home after this time for proposed operational use in the Pacific. Most Canadian squadrons followed them, especially those equipped with RCAF Lancasters, and for them it was also not just a case of going home. The Canadians were to form a major part of *Tiger Force,* intended to bomb the Japanese mainland. Those two revolutionary superbombs taken away from Tinian and dropped on a couple of cities in the first half of August 1945 would stop *Tiger Force's* participation.

The Japanese surrender did not prevent a large number of British airfields from adopting a new activity. Trooping flights were considered necessary on numerous routes to the Middle and Far East. Southern England witnessed by May 27 a marked increase in movements by Dakotas, Halifaxes, Stirlings and sundry aircraft types. All came under the control of RAF Transport Command, formed on March 25 1943 out of Ferry Command, which had itself formed on July 20 1941. Much of the current busy activity was ironically due to policy changes in northern England. As soon as Germany had surrendered, Bomber Command Halifax squadrons on Yorkshire airfields switched to Transport Command on May 7 before going south. HCUs made the same first step by being renamed Heavy Transport CUs on August 1. It seemed as if Britain was trying to atone for its lack of transports during World War Two.

Our airfield scene elsewhere looked far from bright. Once more the cause lay outwith their control. A Coalition Government had existed in Britain from May 1915 to October 1922 and again from August 1931. It is noticeable how airfields in this country enjoyed hugely better times during this combined total of over 21 years with the exception of those first four dire years after World War One. No inter-party squabbling meant no vested interest; even Prime Minister J. Ramsey MacDonald, despite coming under heavy fire for not supporting Britain's attempt to win the Schneider Trophy outright in 1931, did his bit by creating the first Lossiemouth airfield at Kinneddar. But now time had progressed to May 23 1945, barely a fortnight after VE Day, and Winston Churchill had scrapped the Coalition in favour of a Conservative government.

Little more than two months had passed than the seemingly impossible happened. Make no mistake, people were amazed, if not positively frightened, by the ease with which Labour won the July 1945 election: Churchill had looked such an absolute certainty to retain office. The party of George

Lansbury, the party which more than any other bore terrific malevolence towards aviation in general, had gained power. Bad times surely lay ahead for the airfields under its control – and so it proved.

Proof of the effects of ceasing a political Coalition and then the emergence of Labour could be seen in active airfield figures. Although there had only been a slight numerical decline in the last months of World War Two, with 650 airfields still active by March 1945, the trickle turned into a flood as totals fell to under 600 in June, less than 500 in August and below 400 in December. While transport bases flourished, their bomber brethren suffered as aircraft and personnel changed Commands. Bombers were naturally big aircraft and, as their homes had to be equally large, the authorities thought it wasteful to completely shut them down at once. All remained a good short-term investment in military hands after closing to flying by acting as ancillary establishments. Britain's bigger airfields were excellent areas for storing all kinds of surplus military equipment.

Peacetime gave these places some more unexpected jobs to do. Aircrew Holding Units or ACHUs arose to deal with the vast numbers of servicemen who would have to be dispersed for release, further training or posting. Constant changes in personnel at active airfields, never mind inactive ones, gave considerable problems for the first couple of years after World War Two. Resettlement Units were established for Polish servicemen, while a major housing shortage for persons either returning home from abroad or displaced such as Lithuanians gave airfields the opportunity of offering fine temporary accommodation. Sites involved were officially designated as 'emergency' housing but perfect enough for most people. One particularly arrogant Government Minister inadvertently summed up the feelings of his fellow officials, no doubt used to their disgraceful stately homes, as he tried in vain to paint a wildly contrasting picture by saying: 'Of course, people can be housed at airfields, but who wants to stay at them?' Yet another excellent use for redundant airfields was to act as administrative centres for RAF ground units. Even in their death throes, many sites could offer almost anything – except flying.

Such was the perverse situation which confronted so many airfields immediately after World War Two. This was not altogether surprising, as most areas of aircraft activity had gone into decline. Squadrons generally suffered heavy reductions in numbers of men and aircraft; the late 1940s often saw a number of units on one airfield. There was now little need for AOP or radar calibration units. The same could be applied to ferry units in the long run, especially as the ATA had disbanded on November 30 1945. Airfields home to Czech, French and other Allied air forces watched personnel depart to their own countries, leaving the tragic Poles in East Anglia and Lincolnshire. Unable to return home because they would suffer imprisonment by the Russians, Polish airmen soldiered on into 1947 until their last squadron disbanded at Coltishall during January before permanently settling in Britain. Most military flying boat bases meanwhile endured an even quicker demise, and ASR forces on various coastal airfields were decimated as the new Lancaster-equipped maritime reconnaissance squadrons ostensibly looked as if they could deal with rescue duties on their own – incorrect thinking as soon became apparent, for Britain's favourite heavy bomber struggled in its new role. The official reason for all these and other cutbacks was rationalisation, a fancy way of saying that the authorities were being extremely mean with their money.

As usual with politicians, though, this official stance failed miserably in terms of consistency. Severe financial restrictions forced Britain's airfields to close in droves. But then came news from Germany in November 1945 of the first permanently British-manned sites being employed there. What an incredible change in fortunes from the days after World War One when officialdom recommended obliteration of every enemy airfield. The losers had not only been rewarded but still survive in some cases today, whereas the colossal winners were castigated. It is often said these days how Germany won World War Two instead of Britain at least in economic terms, a statement which is all too depressingly true, and the same could be argued for the airfields in both countries.

However, one group of home military airfield types did remain more fortunate. As Expansion Period stations consisted of brick construction and possessed greater yet more comfortable support facilities, our authorities preferred to keep them instead of more spartan austerity period sites. This shows why big airfield stars like Church Fenton, Cottesmore, Finningley and Honington have managed (with the odd hiccup) to survive in the RAF. Nevertheless, even Expansion era airfields had undergone a long war and sometimes took time out in immediate peacetime to have what was described as 'a good clean up'. Another petty problem proved the shocking winter of 1946/47, when a number of airfields in eastern England had to rely upon parachute dropped supplies to keep going because their landing areas were buried under deep snow.

While Expansion Period airfields largely continued as they were, peacetime brought a massive new change to general airfield life: jet aircraft were here for good. These machines had already made an impression in RAF service after the Gloster E.28/39 experimental type first flew at Cranwell on May 15 1941, Culmhead in Somerset being the unlikely site for the first Gloster Meteor fighter squadron (No 616) during July 1944. Colerne in Wiltshire and later Molesworth also became important as No 1335 CU helped piston-engined fighter pilots convert to jets. Fighters and, to a lesser extent, bombers powered by this still strange type of engine would form the backbone of the RAF in future years.

Jets had made so terrific an impact that even mundane daily activities at airfields took on a whole new meaning. Engines of this nature did not need to be maintained and checked so frequently by groundcrews in relation to piston powerplants. Low grade aviation fuel proved another advantage. More specialised measures had to be taken as well, one typical example being the introduction of Mirror Aerodrome Dummy Deck Landing training at FAA airfields to cope with the new-fangled art of jet aircraft on carriers. This technique replaced the familiar Deck Landing Control Officers or 'batsmen' present during World War Two.

Undoubtedly the most direct result of all this revolutionary thinking was that grass airfields in particular stood the least chance of continued activity among military bases. Jets could take off from grass, as the prototype Supermarine Attacker fighter showed at the company's test facility of High Post in Wiltshire, but the durability of this natural runway surface under such conditions had to be rated as doubtful. Whereas World War Two had made the grass military airfield obsolescent, now it was quite obsolete. Hawkinge became a classic example. So too did Heston: the site which had pioneered or greatly forwarded such futuristic ideas as blind landing systems, runway lights, PR and Customs facilities at civil airfields as opposed to airports among other things succumbed to its one anachronism. This was a sad end to the place which had saved its fellow airfields' bacon in 1938.

Aircraft factories were also forced to adapt to these changing times, often having to acquire new flight testing sites or greatly expand their old ones. Precursor of this dramatic aeronautical alteration Gloster found it had to test company products more and more from Moreton Valence in Gloucestershire instead of Brockworth. Supermarine moved from High Post to Chilbolton in Hampshire, a real World War Two odd job airfield if ever there was one as it had taken on nine different tasks, while Vickers had to give Brooklands a hard runway and increase nearby Wisley's status.

Airfields in this country had to be bigger than ever when the Americans reappeared in Britain from July 1948 after a gap of nearly two and a half years, initially operating at three bases in eastern England. Boeing B-29s looked large enough, but certain heavy bomber stations then had to accommodate the almost impossibly huge Convair B-36. British airfields now needed countless thousands of more square yards of concrete to allow in these monsters as the Cold War silently raged on in earnest. Thankfully, this problem had been anticipated as early as 1944 when a handful of bomber stations in East Anglia closed prematurely in World War Two for tremendous expansion. These included Lakenheath and Marham, which followed Scampton's example by inviting United States Air Force Bomb Groups back to Britain over four years later.

Many had feared that airfield runways at these places and elsewhere would have to be several miles long for safe jet operations. One wartime plan actually suggested an amazingly long stretch at the experimental base of Thurleigh, nowadays called Bedford, which would have swallowed up the nearby airfields of Little Staughton and Twinwood Farm! Jets fortunately did not require such immense take-off runs.

If the airfields of Britain were busy enough trying to cope with these odd new aircraft without propellers, they still found time for other tasks. Squadrons of the Auxiliary Air Force (known as the Royal Auxiliary Air Force from December 16 1947) had reformed on May 10 1946 after excellent wartime service, airfields near large centres of population once more holding part-time fliers. Virtually every unit tended to operate piston-engined fighters before eventually exchanging them for Meteors and de Havilland Vampires. A small number of RAuxAF Auster AOP squadrons helped keep Army aviation in Britain alive as well.

MU airfields also remained busy – if for the wrong reasons. In their infinite wisdom, the authorities had seen fit to dispose of many thousands of military aircraft. What did it matter if a heavy bomber had gallantly flown over 100 operational sorties? It was no problem to declare the machine as Struck Off Charge of SOC, then cart it off to a painful death at the hands of a blow torch at an MU site. Although SLGs had disappeared by the first half of 1946, to be replaced by Sub Storage Sites which largely served the same purpose but were full airfields, storage bases became packed with aircraft ready for scrapping. Just one site could have several hundred types put into every available space; it was not even unknown for an MU to hold over 1,000 aircraft at a time. Whether they comprised of fighters or bombers, gliders or even most interesting captured enemy aircraft, the melting pot gratefully yawned open for them.

The resultant mindless destruction as ordered by the authorities made two factors become all too distressingly clear. Control alone proved inconsistent: while every chance was taken to seize aluminium, wooden gliders were wastefully burnt where they stood. No foresight was given to aircraft preservation either and a number of types have tragically left us for good: the Short Stirling and Handley Page Hampden bombers are two examples which come to mind. Hordes of other machines slowly rotted away at MUs to keep these airfields fully occupied until the late 1950s.

One kind of aircraft remained conspicuously absent from these converted and totally blameless killing grounds. As has already been said, transports were enjoying peacetime life. Still they increased in number into the late 1940s as new types such as Avro Yorks and Handley Page Hastings appeared, necessitating some austerity period airfields to remain longer than expected in use. A year-long service from September 1945 between Blackbushe in Hampshire and Prestwick also helped pioneer all-weather flying.

All this activity could not have come at a better time with the Berlin Airlift of July 1948-October 1949. Apart from showing the advantages of air freighting, this mercy mission hammered home the need for a large number of transports and their airfields. Now transport bases did not have to be potentially sited only in central England: almost anywhere would do, a place where squadrons could be firmly settled before flying off to some far-flung area.

Transports also became instrumental in the rebirth of British civil aviation. How BOAC was able to mount flights to Australia from Hurn after May 31 1945 still rates as something of a minor miracle. However, civil activity as a whole only slowly reappeared. Once the general ban on this type of flying had been lifted on January 1 1946, private and charter operations immediately restarting, official policy was to try and derequisition military airfields or reopen civil ones for more peaceful uses. This was easier said than done, and many sites took their time to open for civil aircraft. Former training RLG Denham stood among those which happily returned to activity but then this grass site had enjoyed considerable light aircraft experience pre-war. Technology meant other airfields unfortunately looked unsuited for post-war civil operations, primarily because of their limited landing areas. So great became the suspended animation at some civil airfields that World War Two tended to make the memories of people increasingly hazy. Luftwaffe bombing and dubious fires claimed a few more, and no disused civil airfield met a more farcical end than Thurso when the Army demolished it by error in 1940.

Wiping away the scars of war therefore turned into a long process. The grandiose plans given to civil aviation in Britain from about 1942 as victory seemed increasingly likely never really stood a chance. Langstone Harbour alongside Portsmouth ranked as a major favourite amid the various planning proposals for airfields which failed to reach fruition. Even Hyde Park was still being suggested as late as November 1945, until its greatest supporter Winston Churchill was at last persuaded that aircraft stood as much chance of landing on surrounding houses as the runways. But money still had to be made available, a commodity which often did not exist in the first place.

Civil airfields here thus had no option in initial peacetime but to survive on shoe-string budgets. Private flying was extremely limited, both for light aircraft and gliders, while new opportunist airlines frequently proved short-lived. The end was nigh for independent operators when nationalisation created British European Airways on August 1 1946 to take over the domestic and European services of BOAC and end the activities of RAF transports which had flown many routes until the establishing of national airlines. Most of the previously privately operated internal air concerns subsequently passed over to BEA on February 1 1947 out of the hands of the Associated Airways Joint Committee which the new Labour-inspired organisation took over. Eric Gandar Dower's Allied Airways became the last airline to surrender on April 12.

Nationalisation of airlines in Britain created some dire side-effects. The financial results of BOAC and BEA up to March 1947 produced heavy operating losses. But its biggest drawback was to hinder those civil airfields whose purpose had been more to serve the community than make substantial profits. Airfields in northern and western Scotland allowing passenger services were terribly affected, with many of the smaller ones closing down. As people like the redoubtable E.E. Fresson had worked independently, they were understandably far from pleased to see government snatch away their aircraft, services, glory and, of course, airfields. Pathetically rewarded after years of self-sacrifice, Fresson left for Africa, totally embittered with Britain as a whole. And who could honestly blame him?

Civil airfields and aviation in Britain generally badly needed a boost, and again events in troubled Berlin would play a major part in shaping their future. Whereas the USAF only operated military transports, Britain used both RAF and civil aircraft types. Our airfields became heavily involved in the Berlin Airlift, in spite of RAF aircraft having to be detached to German forward bases and only coming home for maintenance. Most notable individual site turned out to be Tarrant Rushton in Wiltshire, from where civil Avro Lancastrians of Sir Alan Cobham's Flight Refuelling Limited ferried in liquid fuel.

Here lay one of the flaws in early post-war civil airfield operations. Most British-built transports of this era comprised of ex-military machines like the Lancastrian and Handley Page Halton, a civilianised Halifax. Although cheap, they were not wholly suitable. The situation almost exactly resembled the first few years following World War One when converted bombers ruled; the introduction of captured German Ju 52/3ms in BEA service proved a dismal failure. Indigenous replacements were not forthcoming for a long period, so this in turn badly affected activities at civil airfields.

A lesser factor became a prolonged reluctance by the RAF to let go of many military sites. The Labour Government had drawn out in 1947 a list of over 40 places outwith Greater London for possible scheduled air service use by large towns and cities controlled by the Ministry of Civil Aviation. But military needs, red tape and the usual lack of money contrived between them to foul up this plan. MCA-managed airports also started running up big financial losses and local authorities soon had to be induced to take them over. This is why such large settlements as Hull, Lincoln and Sheffield have not been able to receive airports of their own since the end of World War Two; Sheffield is actually the largest city in Europe which does not possess an airport – at least for the moment.

All in all, the British civil airfield brigade were having a quite uncomfortable time, most curious when peace should have heralded happier days. Success stories did appear – transports of Silver City Airways became famous for carrying not only tourists but also their cars between Lympne and France – but generally their time would not be for some while yet.

Meanwhile, the 1950s managed to conversely invigorate

military airfields. Three reasons were responsible for this apparent revival. The total of British airfields closing had decreased considerably since the end of 1945, going under 300 only by the beginning of 1947, this downward spiral bottoming out during 1948-50 at 280. Ironically, the actions of our struggling civil airfields were primarily responsible for most of the time as they gallantly tried to stop the haemorrhage, and had all but closed the wound in 1947. Totally forgotten airfield pioneer Noel Pemberton Billing later died in obscurity during November 1948, but he had at least lived long enough to see his brain-child once more surge ahead. Now National Service had been introduced, while the outbreak of war in Korea on June 25 1950 resulted in another fillip for home bases. Official recognition came on August 30 of that year when the Government said it would increase domestic defence forces. Airfield numbers duly increased from 1951 to over 300 towards the end of 1952 and an average of 305-310 sites in 1953/54, a welcome move, though not anywhere near as much as might have been expected in the long run.

Training and second-line sites still enjoyed a noticeable change of fortunes as flying schools thrived. Already EFTSs had become Reserve Flying Schools to provide refresher practice flying for RAFVR personnel. OTUs were now known as Operational Conversion Units too, both types of training element being later joined by other instructional units, especially FTSs of various kinds. Life proved not all sweet as Basic FTSs were thought wasteful because training took up most of the two years of National Service. The complexities of aircraft then forced the reserve training programme to close in 1954 but happy days were generally here again for instructional bases after their major immediate post-war rundown.

The scene at these airfields surprisingly resembled World War Two all over again. Ansons, Wellingtons and Tiger Moths remained in RAF service, though the little de Havilland biplane was later phased out in favour of the de Havilland Canada Chipmunk. The Hunting Provost, a single piston-engined monoplane like the Chipmunk, became another familiar basic training type of the 1950s.

Reserve and support airfields also came out of their enforced slumber in droves at this time by providing good service in less glamorous roles. Ground training, technical, gliding and storage duties were required, usually handed to airfields with poorer landing surfaces. Winch-launched Air Training Cadet gliders abounded after the organisation formed in February 1941. Hawkinge returned to the land of the living by becoming tremendously involved with both the ATC and the Women's Royal Air Force. Other reserve bases were retained for possible future use, seeing little or no flying from their refurbished and enlarged runways. The Americans sent in some Air Base Groups and Squadrons to keep their airfields ticking over should policies change.

Training and other second-line airfields for once seemed to be in a better overall state than their operational equivalents. The reason could be seen in the equipment used. Quite simply, several of the British wartime aircraft superstar types still remained in service by the end of the 1940s and showed their age. Spitfires had held their place in the front line until 1948, Lancasters for a year longer, while Mosquito night fighters lasted until 1952. Newer piston-engined types such as the de Havilland Hornet fighter, Avro Lincoln heavy bomber and another Lancaster spin-off in the Shackleton maritime patrol bomber were only interim visitors – at least that was the intention with this last design. Britain had placed its faith in jet military aircraft. While the country duly prepared to make this giant technological step, its airfields had to wait for these new machines to appear. And wait. And wait . . .

As World War Two era aircraft types could not go on for much longer, Britain turned to America and asked for the loan of stopgap equipment until jets arrived. The official embarrassment was obvious. Striking 'new' aircraft called Boeing Washingtons came to RAF Bomber Command airfields in 1950, but these four-engined heavy bombers were ex-USAF B-29s. What made matters even worse was that they had formerly resided in storage. August 1951 reflected desperation when USAF North American F-86 Sabres moved into Shepherd's Grove in Suffolk as the first foreign fighters ever to defend Britain. Best hidden was the fact that their pilots comprised of mobilised National Guard or territorial members. RAF-manned Sabres then had to be ordered from the Canadian aircraft company of Canadair – and paid for by US and Canadian taxpayers.

The jet gamble would only partly pay off. Home bomber stations became equipped with the magnificent English Electric Canberra, a simply pleasing craft which later showed how it could turn its hand to other roles. Futuristic new aircraft known as V-bombers would soon make their mark too. The Hawker Hunter jet fighter proved another superb machine. But fighter airfields enjoyed considerably less luck when the truly shocking Supermarine Swift entered service and, though the de Havilland Venom was competent enough, it consisted of being little more than a superior Vampire. Both its predecessor and the even older Meteor thus had to soldier on, reliable equipment yet becoming increasingly outdated in an ever more technologically baffling world. Rearmament had to continue nevertheless on account of the friction in Korea.

Why did British military airfields have to gear up during the early 1950s because of a war which raged on the other side of the world? This question may seem difficult to answer today. But it must be remembered that atomic bombs came within an inch of being used in action for the first time since August 1945; relations between America and Russia also stayed at extremely poor levels. Both of these reasons were evidence enough for an albeit limited British military airfield buildup to stop any possible Communist spread. This expansion placed further economic strain here but was highly necessary. Even Labour Prime Minister Clement Attlee admitted as much in a speech of the day.

An armistice reached in Korea on July 27 1953 meant our airfields could settle down after this threat virtually evaporated. Little had changed, though, as stations remained busy by continuing to mostly act as homes for either fighters or bombers. Training sites kept strong, and AA co-operation units surprisingly still used airfields to a fair extent, despite being lumbered with the new jargonised role title of target facilities. At an individual level, Burtonwood still served the USAF by maintaining aircraft and keeping American airfields in Britain well stocked up. Airfields even continued to give Britain the occasional world record, just as they had done before World War Two for many years. Everything generally looked stable as the healthy average of 300 active sites during 1955/56 showed. Suggested transfer of the FAA to RAF control in October 1953 rightly came to nothing: the enormous influence of naval airfields – as was the case with all British ones in so many areas of daily life – had seen to that.

So ended the first dozen years for Britain's airfields after the end of World War Two. The future had not looked at all good for them if what had happened following World War One was to be taken as a yardstick. Peacetime had indeed dished out some heavy blows, resulting in many casualties, but our huge array of stars had weathered this series of punches and hit back, rather than falling to the canvas and nearly not getting up again. Yet the airfields of Britain would suddenly be plunged into their most fearful crisis, in some ways even worse than the events after World War One. One man and a few pieces of paper would see to that.

Absurdity, Perversity And Stupidity

Once upon a time, there existed a man who gained a position of some power. No sooner had he achieved this than he determined to do something spectacular. His was not a benevolent action. Only this man would benefit, not the many friends who helped him get on in life.

This was no fairy story, and certainly one which did not seem to have a happy ending – at first. The man in question was Duncan Sandys, Conservative Minister of Defence and then Aviation from 1957 to 1962. It was his White Paper which created a massive sensation during the first week of April 1957. Sandys' incredibly far-fetched plan was to basically replace military aircraft with missiles. Fighters would be succeeded by Surface-to-Air Missiles or SAMs, and the V-bomber force be at least supplemented by Intermediate Range Ballistic Missiles or IRBMs. Sandys actually had the audacity to forecast the end of manned aircraft. How kind was he to state that they could be used in '. . . some roles, for example in minor wars and anti-submarine work.' No wonder most servicemen despised him. Perhaps the most remarkable feature of this man was his father-in-law: Winston Churchill, as much in favour of British aviation as Sandys was against it. Rarely has the old saying about chalk and cheese been more appropriate.

Where did our airfields figure in all this? Those pieces of paper had many consequences, two of which would be immediately disastrous for certain airfield types. An ultra-heavy reliance had been placed upon fighter stations, seen as the V-bombers' protectors, so these places became prime candidates for the chop. Airfields had already created miracle after miracle but the hoped for 100 per cent interception rate against enemy nuclear bombers was a hopelessly impossible task, so RAF fighter bases had to defend V-bomber airfields instead. Maybe the new all-weather jet fighters like the big Gloster Javelin had been designed to withstand the fiercest

(above) Women's Auxiliary Air Force personnel push a Miles Master II advanced trainer of No 9 (P) AFU into a T1 hangar at Errol near Dundee during the night of January 21 1944. The names of training units changed rapidly: not so much their airfields. *(IWM)*
(below) The Fleet Air Arm brought individuality to many British airfields with their different types of runways, hangars or control towers, such as this three storey example at Crail in Fife.

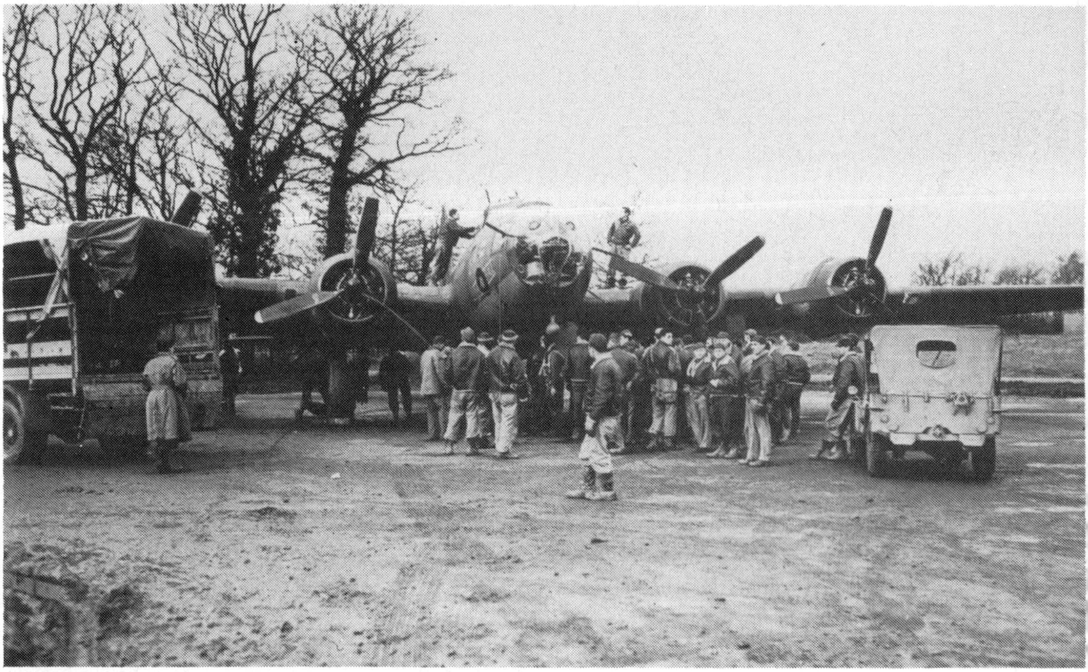

BUSBY STOOP
INN
BUSBY STOOP INN

(above) Transports became much more prominent in peacetime at civil and military airfields. One familiar type stayed around for many a year: a Dakota 6 at Eastleigh (Southampton Airport) on March 28 1964. *(C. Walker)*
(below) The aircraft that revolutionised Britain's airfields. A preserved Gloster Meteor beside a Bellman at Crosby-on-Eden.

(above) An Avro Vulcan B2 and its frightening hitting power at Waddington. The control tower shows how our airfields had to change with the times too. *(RAF Museum)*
(below) Hemswell's No 77 Squadron says goodbye and good riddance on June 14 1963 to one of its Douglas Thors, the missile that tried to wipe out Britain's military airfields. *(RAF Museum)*

THE BUSTARD
FLYING CLUB

G-ARNG

(top left) By the 1960s our airports had finally got into their stride. Heathrow on December 30 1963. *(C. Walker)*
(centre left) Recreational aviation still suffered for long enough post-war because of ageing flying equipment, as typified by this Tiger Moth at Old Sarum on September 15 1963. *(C. Walker)*
(bottom left) But newer American types helped save the day, like this Piper PA-22 Colt 108 taxying towards Thruxton's perimeter track in the early 1960s. *(C. Walker)*
(above) Our airfields steal the glory yet again as an FAA British Aerospace Sea Harrier FRS.1 of No 800 Squadron is surrounded by a television crew on return to Yeovilton from the Falklands in 1982. Airfield relations with the mass media have always varied considerably. And what does the future hold for the military? *(RAF Museum)*

(above) Solid airports like Wick are essential to the economic and social prosperity of a region. The scene here has changed fairly little from World War Two.
(below) Timelessness is a most notable quality of Britain's airfields: they still provide lots of enjoyment for people as well. This scene of Royal Aircraft Factory SE5As belonging to the Bustard Flying Club at Boscombe Down flying down Old Sarum's runway 06 towards its firing butts could easily date from World War One, never mind today. *(L.J.E. Goldfinch)*

conditions natural elements could create, but their airfields had no answer to the totally unnatural artificial storm brewed up by Sandys.

The other instantaneous axing would be the tragic ditching of hordes of disused airfields by the Air Ministry. Their last chance of glory had gone for ever. Batches of 50 at a time were listed in national newspapers like men up for execution. Some sites were not even granted their last request of having their names spelt correctly.

These doomed heroes would still have the last laugh. To slightly modify the words of a genius in another field: 'Politicians shouldn't meddle with airfields. They don't know anything about them. Of course, you could say they don't know anything about politics, but that's another matter . . .'

The ultimate nightmare had in effect already started. On March 10 1957, the RAuxAF had ceased to exist, with 25 squadrons all officially disbanding on the same day. Another eleven squadrons of the Royal Naval Volunteer Reserve simultaneously shut down during this horrifying day. Airfields based around heavily populated areas were sudddenly either deprived of military activity or greatly reduced in importance. In a few cases, the enforced removal of 'weekend' fliers killed airfields immediately: Bramcote, Hooton Park in Merseyside and Honiley in Warwickshire became examples which died instantly amid the carnage. RAuxAF/RNVR jet fighters, AOP Austers and anti-submarine types gave MU bases more scrapping work to do, the only British airfields to benefit as a result of this tragic tale.

Numbers of British airfields fell from just under 300 once the White Paper was revealed. Among other military sites to suffer were the massed ranks of reserve bases. Despite much modernisation and reconstruction work, their hopes of seeing American bombers would never be realised. The monstrous Boeing B-52, which many reserve airfields had hoped would come, was rarely seen after first appearing at Brize Norton in January 1957 and never permanently based in Britain. Sited over large tracts of this country, the USAF finally let go of its stand-bys after not even bothering to keep aircraft on most of them. Airfields under American control could be rated as lucky if they held a single C-47 transport in permanent residence. Smaller numbers of places classed as stand-by RAF V-bomber bases were similarly unused. A further blow proved the closure of Burtonwood in 1959, though Mildenhall was able to take over its USAF support role.

Such drastic cutbacks as these emphasised how vast sums of money spent post-war on military airfields were often wasted by politicians. Everywhere officialdom went, its bloody axe was sure to follow. Experimental airfields now showed signs of strain too as the amount of test work gradually reduced. Defford in Worcestershire, where *Window* and other brilliant radar-associated devices had been developed and tested, closed by a quirk of fate in 1957 during September. The great Martlesham Heath would not be all that long in following it: for the highly popular Suffolk base, life had never been the same when A&AEE failed to return from Boscombe Down after World War Two.

Another experimental casualty would be the demise of MAEE at Felixstowe in 1958, but 1957 became remembered as the year when flying boat activity in Britain effectively ceased. One could say in hindsight how the decline had started by the middle of World War Two. New landplane sites had then been created to fight U-boats, not marine ones. Nonetheless, it was a sad day when Nos 201 and 230 Squadrons disbanded on February 28 at Pembroke Dock. The authorities had not sought a successor for the Sunderland 5 variant, so marine airfield closures were inevitable. After 1945, Calshot and other members of the old guard had slowly faded away, Sunderlands occasionally visiting them to give a poignant reminder of the good old days. One or two bases were fortunate to stay with the RAF in ground roles as they could accommodate marine craft for rescue duties.

This became the only part of British aviation post-war where military and civil airfields were jointly involved to their cost. BOAC had found flying boats increasingly disadvantageous to its needs. Quite apart from company aircraft being too expensive, its marine bases and support services just could not be maintained. While local authorities paid for airports on dry land, BOAC had to fork out its own money. When the new terminal at Southampton Water opened in April 1948, a gloomy speech predicted the worst and BOAC was forced to give up in due course in November 1950. A defiant effort by Aquila Airways only lasted until 1958.

Despite many misgivings among those in the know, the politicians blindly pressed on with their absurd new plans. Duncan Sandys was renowned for his stubbornness. He personally badly wanted to see in place the Blue Streak missile, which not surprisingly never materialised in the form he would have wished. A number of airfields along eastern England from East Anglia to Yorkshire were selected instead as sites for American-built Douglas Thor IRBMs: so confused had our politicians become that Scotland had been originally scheduled to hold these weapons. Thanks to the thoughtless closures of most English sites after World War Two, the Air Ministry had to ashamedly step in and retrieve parts of them for missile use. Building estimates quoted in January 1959 of £2½ million did not seem correct but forbidding concrete missile pads were still constructed to hold the 60 Thors due in Britain, RAF squadrons reforming to control three each. Wings were created at four firmly established airfields – Driffield, two other famous former RAF bomber stations at Feltwell in Norfolk and Hemswell in Lincolnshire, plus major Leicestershire training airfield North Luffenham. Each of these four places controlled four satellites, all austerity era airfields. What a change for Carnaby, the sole casualty of the three massive ELGs. Thors were brought in by USAF Douglas C-133 Cargomaster transports, with Feltwell first to receive its quota during the summer of 1958; the remainder were installed during the following year. Soon V-bombers had extra support in ranks of white missiles looming skywards, though no Thors were ever launched for test purposes from Britain because of local geographical factors.

As bomber airfields needed every kind of protection possible, more missiles arose in the shape of Bristol Bloodhound SAMs. It was totally different from the strike Beaufighters of yore when No 264 Squadron became the first such unit at North Coates in December 1958. Although these defensive missiles proved successful, the infinitely more offensive Thors quickly attracted many critics. They were far too inflexible for a start, unlike V-bombers which could freely shift from airfield to airfield; Thor complexes could not be strictly described as airfields. Another failing lay in the missiles' interminably long launch run-up procedure by nuclear speed standards. The word 'nuclear' itself also became worrying, and Ludford Magna in Lincolnshire endured a potentially lethal accident during December 1960. The Thors were finally phased out from the start of 1963 after a statement to this effect made only in December 1962, the last being ferried away in September from North Luffenham to the relief of many, not least more conventional airfields.

Dire uncertainty among politicians marked the Thor saga as national government chopped and changed its defence policy. Preference originally switched on February 16 1960 from ground-based nuclear missiles to ballistic ones launched from aircraft or submarines. But ballistic missile development was then abandoned on April 13 to fully rely upon a V-bomber deterrent armed with the American Skybolt missile, another hare-brained and astronomically expensive scheme never to reach fruition. Politicians had to swallow their pride and accept that both airfields and aircraft were here to stay.

Even allowing for this apparent victory, terrible losses occurred among British military airfields at this time. The years since 1957 had produced a long line of casualties, with Duncan Sandys helping to abolish conscription in 1960 not assisting matters. Heading the list of famous fatalities in 1957 was none other than Hendon: what must have gone through Claude Grahame-White's mind as he lay on his deathbed in France two years later? Castle Bromwich had fallen a year earlier in 1958, Croydon and Kenley following in 1959. 1961 brought more crisis as the total of active airfields fell below 260, and from then until 1964 closures of such immortals as Felixstowe and Hornchurch (1962) plus Martlesham Heath and Netheravon (1963) steadily continued to leave just 250 by the second half of 1964. Another bad winter of 1962/63 and all it entailed had only increased the gloom.

A Parliamentary statement in July 1964 revealed how money was yet again the reason for another downward swing in fortunes for our airfields. A total of 53 RAF stations had closed during 1961-63 in order to save £10 million per year, while another 14 bases intended for closure would save £4 million more. Much of the blame must go to Prime Minister Harold Macmillan who, as recently revealed Cabinet papers have shown, was a disaster when it came to economics in general. What he really meant was: 'You've never had it so *bad*.'

Hard-earned airfield reputations built up over many years now bore out this theory as they counted for nothing. The Duxfords and Hawkinges of this world found this out to their cost. Fighter airfields, exceptionally strong since the late 1940s, were not immune to the axe. Those previously secret official papers just mentioned belatedly but sensationally stated that the Government was actively considering abolishing Fighter Command in 1957 purely to save money. Training and support airfields were also ruthlessly dropped as might have been expected.

The FAA was similarly affected, after having unusually acquired a few inland bases such as Bramcote and Benson after World War Two, but retained its individuality until the bitter end. Naval airfields did not open, they were 'commissioned': now, instead of closing, they were 'paid off'. In any case, the constantly transient squadrons at FAA airfields had by now largely become a thing of the past. Their aircraft equipment possibly hastened the end by continuing to consist of World War Two types such as Fairey Fireflies and Grumman Avenger piston-engined torpedo bombers. The few modern machines in Navy service included the Supermarine Attacker jet fighter – and even this machine was becoming long in the tooth.

As the military was forced to cut back overall, so aircraft companies and factory airfields directly suffered. Duncan Sandys played a big part in speeding up their fates as his lunatic 1957 Paper had severely hampered aircraft company development, so creating a lack of independence and allowing in more aircraft from abroad. Great names of the past steadily disappeared or linked up to slowly come under the uninspiring name of British Aircraft Corporation in 1960, today known as British Aerospace. Sandys, to our airfields the devil incarnate (or should that be inconsistent?) personified, then failed to save the potentially brilliant English Electric TSR-2 when Labour won the 1964 General Election and dropped this wonderplane. More airfields which had extensively prepared to hold this jet type were left in the lurch. Factory airfields, whose 1,800,000 workers had performed magnificently to turn out 124,109 aircraft and over 250,000 spare engines during World War Two, wondered just where on earth they had gone wrong.

To produce ever better aircraft, companies still found it necessary to make a steady progression to increasingly bigger airfields. Back in the 1930s, de Havilland had to move from Stag Lane to Hatfield, Armstrong Whitworth likewise from Whitley to Baginton and Handley Page from Cricklewood to Radlett. Factory airfields had subsequently worked almost tirelessly throughout World War Two, being tremendously busy places in their time. But now Brockworth, Chilbolton, Moreton Valence and various others were destined to shut down. This mixture of old or converted production and test centres had never been much in the public imagination, strange considering how active and interesting they normally were. It is sad to say this attitude has always prevailed right from the moment airfields first appeared in Britain. By the 1960s many factory airfields had reached a cul-de-sac, a dead end, with the emphasis on dead.

These ailing sites would also have a fateful influence on storage airfields, where the huge lines of aircraft could no longer be seen. MU casualties grew heavier as one progressed further north in Britain. Cumbrian neighbours Kirkbride and Silloth typified another downward airfield trend by both closing in 1960. Well known Scottish east coast MU base and victim of surely the most inane of the few airfield obituaries in British history Edzell II had already been dropped three years earlier.

Somehow, military airfields could still point to a few good areas of activity. Britain's trio of V-bombers had become established on various greatly extended sites, though even this great success story was tarnished by the Vickers Valiant's grounding at the end of 1964 and abrupt withdrawal from service because of fatigue problems. Handley Page Victors and Avro Vulcans nevertheless retained a nuclear role until July 1969 before changing to conventional bombing duties. The 90 B-29s which had arrived in Britain during mid-1948 had been intended to scare the Russians into thinking that these machines held atomic weapons – whereas in reality they did not. But now V-bombers carried not only examples of the bomb but British ones too; the 140 or so aircraft on their few airfields could achieve far, far more devastating results than the 2,000-3,000 heavy bombers on their scores of airfields during World War Two. In little more than 40 years, the bombs lifted away from airfields had progressed from the 20 and 100 pound Hale devices of 1915 to the 4,000 pounders or 'cookies', 14,000 pound *Tallboys* and 22,000 pound *Grand Slams* of World War Two to fearsome nuclear bombs capable of delivering an explosive force of thousands of megatons.

Such was their success that V-bombers gave RAF airfields a further role to add to their myriad in air-to-air refuelling. This was a much deserved victory for Sir Alan Cobham of Flight Refuelling Limited after years of being shunted around airfields, enduring a general lack of official interest – and only then from abroad – in his scheme, not forgetting how the Luftwaffe nearly bombed his company to oblivion at Ford in 1940. He could now thank the V-bombers for realising his dream.

This new breed of jet 'heavies' inhabited only a relatively small number of British military airfields, unlike very different machines which catered for a revived role. Helicopters, toyed with by the RAF in the mid-1940s, helped make more military bases fight back by appearing from 1953 over most of Britain for Search and Rescue or SAR duties, ASR under another name. However, the airfield side of operations remained the same as in World War Two, with squadrons still sending small detachments to places far from the HQ base. This practice has never changed: SAR helicopters are only more efficient these days. Initial types with limited range and payload capabilities such as Bristol Sycamores have given way to increasingly better Westland

Whirlwinds, Wessexes and Sea Kings.

In more general terms, helicopters had actually turned the corner in being regarded as worthwhile machines rather than freaks. These rotary-winged craft had started to show their combined airfield and social value during 1948-50 when civil BEA helicopters flew a mail service between Peterborough and Norwich. No 705 (FAA) Squadron at Gosport almost immediately fully introduced 'choppers' to the Navy, and the Korean War soon turned into a personal triumph for helicopters. Airfields did not have to worry any more about helicopters depriving them of activity by operating from places not recognised as such. No 705 Squadron's previous guise as a detachment of No 771 Squadron had resulted in its Hoverflies using a non-airfield at Haslemere in Surrey, a place whose only previous airfield experience had been holding an extremely obscure civil landing ground during the 1920s, from September 1945 for over two years. Tremendous pressure later arose in 1950 to create special landing areas for civil helicopters, particularly around London, but heliports and helipads such as Britain's first commercial one which officially opened on April 23 1959 at Battersea could not hope to match the adaptability, versatility and sheer self-sufficiency of airfields. So at odds did the pro-helicopter lobby become that they could not even fix a proper name for landing sites: some liked using the term 'helidrome', others absolutely hated it!

A radical new departure for military airfields which would place heavy reliance upon helicopters came with formation of the Army Air Corps on September 1 1957. In the past, Army aviation had been left to RAF Army Co-operation Command and RAF/Army Auster squadrons. Both elements were prominent at many an airfield up and down Britain until the Command disbanded in June 1943. Remaining Auster units in peacetime showed how largely neglected Army-related flying had become, therefore the Nos 650 and 660 class squadrons were transferred to the AAC. Battle of Britain superstar Middle Wallop became the headquarters for this new organisation, and RAF old boy Netheravon was taken on during the 1960s after its former employer had closed the veteran airfield.

Carnage on far less fortunate military airfields than Netheravon finally brought their civil counterparts more into play. A number of luckier ex-RAF bases were earmarked for more peaceful uses and switched to Ministry of Aviation control. The long-awaited airports at last started to appear and soon remorselessly expanded. Heathrow eventually showed its paces as London's airport after a painfully slow climb to the top since taking over from Croydon in 1946, so slow that Northolt effectively reigned as gateway to the British capital until October 1954. London would also be served by Gatwick from 1958, Glasgow later switching its allegiance from Renfrew to Abbotsinch in 1966. Similar takeovers happened elsewhere in Britain during both decades as the airports for Belfast, Bristol, Cardiff and Derby at Nutt's Corner, Whitchurch, Cardiff/Pengam Moors and Burnaston were respectively replaced by Aldergrove, Lulsgate Bottom, Rhoose and Castle Donington.

Better management and decreasing Government control also meant that our airports were not losing money hand over fist as in earlier post-war days. But still most struggled to just break even, let alone make an operating profit. Politicians were entirely to blame; they then totally disgraced themselves by running like rats from a sinking ship in 1961 when the Government produced a White Paper stating it would divest itself of those airports still under national ownership. No state subsidies would be given to airports except sites thought essential for transportation in Britain. A further proposal in this official document quoted how Britain's main airports at Heathrow, Prestwick and Gatwick plus the controversial rising new star of Stansted in Essex should be taken over by a public corporation. This led to the British Airports Authority owning this quartet from April 1 1966; other sites have since joined the list as this company has evolved into being known by its present title of BAA.

Large British airports had by now quickly learned to adjust to big American jet airliners coming and going from their runways. The appearance of these aircraft brought mixed reactions from airport personnel: Air Traffic Control staff liked them for not cluttering up surrounding airspace but most other workers feared coping with hundreds of passengers and their baggage departing from just one aircraft. What about the expected mountains of accompanying paperwork as well, wondered office employees. Whatever one thought, everyone would have to adjust.

First of this new breed of airliners had been the Boeing 707. Although first seen at Heathrow in October 1958, this four-engined type had been originally spotted on a British airfield seven months earlier in its military KC-135 air-to-air refuelling tanker form at Brize Norton. Severe structural problems with the de Havilland Comet earlier on in the 1950s had lost Britain its trail-blazing lead in jet airliner development, after having started the world's first jet passenger service between Heathrow and Johannesburg in South Africa on May 2 1952, but this flaw was compensated by the world's first turboprop-engined airliner in the popular Vickers Viscount entering BEA service in 1953. Britain had, it should not be forgotten, invented this cross between a piston and a jet engine, originally testing this powerplant in an experimental Gloster Trent-Meteor at the unrecognised Derbyshire airfield of Church Broughton on September 20 1945.

As airline operations suddenly became more frequent at airports, so too did air freighting as aircraft carried increasingly bulky or awkward items. The transportation of mail and newspapers had been popular in the past, but aircraft needed both airfields and to make drastic changes in their fuselages to make freighting a total success. By using opening rear doors and noses or even swinging fuselages, heavy cargoes could be taken straight off an aircraft on to an airfield and then immediately away to their final destinations. No wonder shipping companies looked on with envy.

The superb social advantages of airfields in work practices could hardly be missed. So it also applied to leisure as recreational light aircraft similarly became much more prominent at civil airfields during the 1960s. For them, the path back to recognition had proved a long and tortuous one. Several reasons were responsible but the most notable factor lay in the aircraft themselves. Pre-war British types such as the Moth family and British Aircraft Swallow monoplane had previously reigned supreme. Just over 1,000 flying club and privately owned aircraft were then impressed for World War Two use as communications types and station hacks. Many examples survived to enjoy post-war use by being resold to civilians, Kemble holding famous disposal sales during 1946, but equally many others were rejected and left to rot, put in storage for wartime duration, impressed only as instructional airframes for ATC cadets or simply smashed up. British recreational aviation hence became difficult for many years into peacetime with the glut of tired ex-military machines. Government statements that flying clubs would have little, if any subsidies post-war hardly helped either: it was perhaps just as well that Sefton Brancker did not live to witness this new policy. But now importation problems regarding Cessnas, Pipers and other American-built types had at last been solved. Supported by greater numbers of gliders, they gave a new lease of life to many airfields.

Everyone and everything connected with light civil aviation still had to accept two hard facts of life. First, the days of uncontrolled airspace had disappeared for good with the standardisation of Air Traffic Control procedures, centred around airfields. There was only one further problem: where could recreational light aircraft settle at?

While military airfields had shut down in droves after World War Two and continued to close, the Air Ministry still owned them in a loose sense. Although civil organisations were allowed to use a number of redundant airfields, changing RAF requirements made their lives uncertain. Variable attitudes of farmers and landowners only added to the confusion. Flying and gliding clubs were forced to adopt nomadic existences by shifting from site to site; sometimes civil aviation existed on a purely unofficial basis. Fairwood Common in south Wales typified this trend in the 1950s until becoming Swansea Airport in 1957. Other concerns went a stage further and risked all in every way by flying from utterly disused airfields as in the form recognised today.

It became inevitable that some brash fliers would create a certain amount of annoyance around airfields which they had no permission to use. The impromptu flying of 50 years or so earlier which farmers alleged led to crowds damaging crops had only been possible in those days because of a lack of designated airfields. Things were becoming extremely serious when places like former bomber OTU base Westcott in Buckinghamshire, already heavily involved in rocket research such as the ill-fated Blue Streak, had to virtually beg glider pilots not to make emergency landings there.

This perilous situation had improved by the mid-1960s. As hundreds of former military airfields were being sold off at this time, clubs gradually settled down in one place. Old hangars and support buildings could be used to good effect. Gliders began using formerly redundant military airfields with concrete as well as grass runways such as Lasham. Other clubs created their own recognised airfields, brand new grass sites with small but compact facilities. Angular cropspraying aircraft appeared to totally destroy the myth that airfields have irreparably damaged farming techniques: they have actually enhanced agricultural methods. Business or executive aviation has since gained popularity too at smaller civil airfields, thereby saving professional travellers long journeys to airports. Loganair has led the way in passenger services at these airfields by using the excellent Britten-Norman Islander transport; the company was responsible for opening several new Scottish island airstrips from 1967, creating a slight rise in active airfield totals. Air shows returned to prominence in the 1960s as well as millions wallowed in a mixture of the past, present and future at Farnborough and numerous Battle of Britain commemorative displays.

For all the tremendously benevolent social effects British airfields were giving, the 1960s brought ominously perverse new trends into everyday life as a whole. Warped thinking dogged our airfields as objectors constantly protested about noise and environmental factors. Prime example became the third London Airport saga as plans for sites at ex-USAAF heavy bomber station Nuthampstead and Cublington (better known as World War Two bomber OTU airfield Wing) were systematically rendered useless. The most curious suggested place of all was Maplin Sands in Essex, for it was here that pioneer American aviator Robert Macfie had come in November 1909 after being the last person to use Fambridge. The War Office reacted quickly by forbidding him or any other pilot to use Maplin, so forcing Macfie to make another hasty departure, but now all of a sudden government officials wanted aircraft to come. Just as crazy were the three public enquiries, two decades and an immense amount of money it took to say no to airport development at Stansted as prototype NIMBYs, to briefly and mercifully lapse into yuppie-speak, stopped yet another airfield creating yet more jobs. And once again out wheeled those old anti-airfield groups, the Sunday flying lobbies, this time campaigning against BEA services at airports which did exist, particularly in northern Scotland.

Yet it turned out to be subversive pacifist forces who managed to make more lasting marks in their fiercely anti-airfield tirades. The Campaign for Nuclear Disarmament and other protest groups tried constantly to hamper military airfields in ways which made the Suffragettes look even bigger nonentities than ever before. Such narrow-minded opposition was nothing new to service sites – but what did transpire was a dreadful catalogue of damage and security scares. Pacifists displayed incredible levels of crass stupidity by blatantly invading sealed-off areas, symbolically cutting barbed wire fences and even driving around perimeter tracks. 'Why don't we know what's happening?' chanted these morons who, if the places they were trying to scupper had not won two World Wars, would never have been able to enjoy the freedom of speech.

When the Thor nuclear missile sites appeared in eastern England from 1958, events took a further turn for the worse as pacifists widened their choice of targets. By 1961 this already serious situation reached critical proportions as the left-wing Committee of 100 had the nerve to draw up plans for huge sit-downs at airfields in general. Thor bases such as the great Polebrook and its more unsung fellow Northamptonshire airfield Harrington were now subjected to unwelcome visits by covertly evil elements. As one local inhabitant later bluntly but effectively put it: 'They marched here, they marched there, they marched every bloody where – and for what purpose? They only managed to nearly ruin our lives and despoil the local airfields too. God, I still shudder when I think about those bastards.'

Such, ah, illegitimate children did not require to be anywhere near as active to lambast airfields. Yet another twist occurred during the 1960s in the curious love-hate relationship between our heroes and the mass media, a tale which needs considerable explaining. There had been tremendous airfield reporting before World War One as great enthusiasm was given daily to civil and military activities and developments – and equally great reports given on aircraft accidents. But, after World War One, reporting rapidly tailed off. News of airfields in the 1920s and 1930s proved considerable compared with today, but somehow the conflict had altered things. Was it because of the attitude towards the Great War? Or more simply that aviation in general no longer remained a novelty and so became a nine day wonder like everything else in media eyes? In any case, World War One airfield reporting had been effectively non-existent, and in World War Two sloppy to say the least. One could mention the fact of censorship, but this in reality had little to do with it. Journalists never really bothered in the second conflict about going to more faraway places, preferring to visit cushy Expansion Period airfields. The Bassingbourns *et al* represented glamour – nothing wrong with that – but much more coverage should have been allotted to austerity period sites: they exuded gritty glamour, what airfield life in both World Wars was really all about.

Startling changes followed once peacetime returned. Implied left wingism silently screamed out at newspaper readers; CND and other pacifist groups undoubtedly realised this fact and started pandering towards the mass media. Military airfield reporting fell away rapidly and, unless a civil airfield was an airport, flying clubs and other organisations could not expect much joy either as before World War Two. A good test is to examine yearly reference books issued by newspapers for libraries both before and after the conflict: one cannot fail to notice the absolute dearth of articles published after 1945. Most regrettable of all turned out to be the treatment given to our American friends during the 1950s and 1960s and a steady stream of extremely unfavourable publicity. From frightening aircraft accidents to murders and shootings and more minor errings: the British Press reported it all without fail. Pacifists, and many disgruntled neighbouring civilians too, sadly tended to regard USAF airfields and their personnel almost as if they were aliens from another planet – and certainly the enemy – by the 1960s.

Another baffling factor of this quite dreadful decade proved an inexplicable turn-about on airfield policy by local councils. Officialdom had desperately sought sites in the 1930s; now, 30 years later, nobody in high office could care less. Portsmouth Airport became a classic case of how aeronautically deficient minor officials would chop off their own arms to prove a political point. The immovable faced the impossible as Labour did not want to betray its pacifist policies, while the Conservatives stuck doggedly to their monetarist dogma. If neither side could win, they could not lose either: only Britain and its airfields would be worse off.

Political immobility certainly did nothing to alter the fact that the 1970s resulted in being the least eventful decade in British airfield history to date. War had occurred three decades earlier and then another three before that, so perhaps the law of averages' failure had a lot to do with it as well. At least civil airfields went from strength to strength, though a number of seemingly minor problems contrived at first to take the gloss off their glory.

The decade had started badly when the Beagle aircraft company at Rearsby in Leicestershire went into liquidation in February 1970 as a result of lack of Government support. Any dwindling hopes Britain had for a resurgent light aircraft industry all but disappeared. But even this tragedy was nothing compared to the incredible procession of avoidable agonies airports had to endure. Sites on the south coast of England surprisingly struggled – and, as in the case of Portsmouth, failed in 1973 – mainly because of their grass landing areas; rising fuel prices caused by the 1973 oil crisis pushed up airport running costs; the Court Line airline collapse a year later showed how airports could not become complacent with operations; frequent strikes inevitably created trouble; and passengers complained about canned music in terminals! The last thing needed was a major accident, but then a Hawker Siddeley Trident jet airliner stalled and crashed shortly after take-off from Heathrow on June 18 1972, killing 118 people in what became at that time Britain's worst aircraft accident. Times had really changed when troops and armoured vehicles invaded Heathrow on January 6 1974 to counter terrorist threats of destroying airliners taking off or landing. Technology had somehow managed to defeat the days of supreme safety at airports after having only recently made it possible.

It was not a completely bad time for home airports in the 1970s. Regional ones at last firmly established themselves in areas away from the main cities. BEA and BOAC became British Airways (no relation to the 1930s airline) as well, but a most important development turned out to be the first shuttle service in Europe Tridents started flying on January 12 1975 between Abbotsinch and Heathrow. A passenger seat could now be guaranteed without having to book one and then wait for an increasingly interminable time at an airport. It is still regrettable how Scotland continues to have few direct international air services: farcical is the only word to describe how a businessman in Glasgow wishing to go to America has to fly down to London and then travel back over central Scotland in order to cross the Atlantic.

On the military airfield front, main event of note became a mini-cull of RAF stations during the mid-1970s. Another twelve airfields bit the dust. It resembled the bad old days of the early 1960s, only on a smaller scale. The cause was different too for, instead of pure economic cutbacks, the RAF was contracting administratively. Commands had steadily merged since 1968, and has since left the service with now only two – Strike and Support Commands. As the latter organisation consisted of the old Maintenance and Training Commands until September 1 1973, their airfields bore the brunt of further cuts. Colerne, Little Rissington, Tern Hill, the popular Lincolnshire double act of Manby and Strubby: these and other stations which had served gloriously but quietly in more unsung RAF duties such as training and aircraft storage/preparation became 1970s victims. Standard training types seen at these places also disappeared, notably the Vickers Varsity advanced trainer, to leave only the BAC Jet Provost basic trainer and a sprinkling of other types such as the Scottish Aviation Bulldog to soldier on.

RAF transport airfields suffered perhaps even more at this time as their tremendous luck since the end of World War Two finally ran out. Such was the severity of reduction in their aircraft strength that certain types had to be completely phased out of service. Fairly few examples of the Bristol Britannia, de Havilland Comet and Short Belfast existed at Lyneham and other central England transport stations, yet all were badly missed. Even the venerable Hastings made its final swan-song. About the only factor in their favour was that the excellent American Lockheed Hercules remained.

The FAA endured similarly crippling losses as its aircraft carrier fleet disappeared. Carriers had always received the glory in their time but, despite vessels with angled decks appearing in the 1950s to facilitate operations, this was not enough to postpone their downfall. Airfields had smoothed the path for carriers by doing the donkey work; airfields made naval military aviation feasible; and, unlike tactically-orientated aircraft carriers, airfields possessed both tactical and strategic value. Withdrawal from Royal Navy service of the *Ark Royal* in late 1978 became the final terrible blow. But this ironically, yet inevitably helped military airfields as the FAA needed land-based sites, even though the organisation had lost nearly all of its fixed-wing aircraft by the close of the 1970s once the de Havilland Sea Venom fighter and Fairey Gannet AEW or airborne early warning type retired from active service.

It was left to happier operational RAF airfields to witness a new generation of aircraft move in. Gone were the days of types such as light, medium or heavy bombers, and less faith placed in 'straight' machines like the English Electric Lightning defensive jet fighter. Multi-purpose aircraft were now all the rage, fighters in particular being given an additional role of ground attack.

This idea of aircraft serving in variable roles was nothing new for their airfields, as they had already been displaying their supreme adaptability and versatility for more than 30 years. The grand old duo of post-war British military aviation, the Canberra and Hunter, slipped with ease into other duties. A steady arrival of new front line types in the BAC Jaguar ground attack fighter, Hawker Siddeley Buccaneer strike bomber and McDonnell Douglas Phantom fighter posed airfields no problems, nor did the revolutionary Hawker Siddeley Harrier fighter with its vertical/short take-off and landing flying characteristics. Developed from the Rolls-Royce Flying Bedstead experimental vehicle which lifted off from Hucknall in Nottinghamshire on August 3 1954, the P.1127 or Harrier predecessor's first flight from Dunsfold in Surrey on October 21 1960 suggested here was an aircraft which did not require airfields. This, of course, was not to be.

The appearance of new military aircraft failed to prevent a further decline in the fortunes of factory airfields. More casualties resulted during the 1970s, notably Brooklands and Radlett in 1970, followed by Brooklands' aide Wisley in 1973. A rump of sites was left, though at least most of these have since survived. The British Aerospace flag straddles most of the factory airfield old guard such as Brough and Hatfield.

Stubbornly independent manufacturers also hold firm at their long-established bases, especially Shorts at Sydenham in Northern Ireland and Westland's veteran Somerset airfield of Yeovil. One fact is certain: great production runs of indigenous aircraft will never happen again, instead co-operation with foreign countries to jointly build aircraft. The Jaguar, Panavia Tornado fighter-bomber and civil Airbus airliner are prime examples of shared or component production.

One totally unique aircraft closed an otherwise relatively quiet 1970s chapter in remarkable fashion. King Bladud and others must have looked on in wonder as the American-designed and piloted Gossamer Albatross became the first man-powered aircraft to cross the English Channel on June 12 1979. This frail machine seemed briefly as if it would leave from Manston but took off instead from The Warren, half-way between Folkestone and the old World War One airship station of Capel. Departing from a place not recognised as an airfield was fitting in hindsight, as Louis Bleriot had landed at another non-airfield just 43 days short of 70 years earlier.

Factory airfields, not forgetting their military equivalents, managed to play an extremely important part in the Falklands conflict of 1982 – even though they lay over 8,000 miles away from the action. It proved a new experience for British airfields as they had a supporting role in an important struggle instead of starring in it as before. Their response to this emergency which perhaps more than any other factor epitomised the elements of absurdity, perversity and stupidity so evident since 1957 still remained as rapid as ever, with the first Hercules transports leaving Lyneham for Wideawake on the Atlantic island of Ascension a day after Argentina captured the Falklands on April 2. Many home-based airfield residents subsequently flew there or embarked upon newly-built aircraft carriers up to the Argentinian surrender on June 14.

So much for the victory. But the 1970s antics of politicians had taken their toll upon Britain's airfields, and their part in the conflict was not so easily achieved as is since thought. More aircraft had to be pressed into service for air-to-air refuelling duties. This conversion job was carried out by factory airfields at such phenomenal speed it seemed impossible how they could have done so after the fearsome reduction in their numbers since the late 1950s. The FAA could rejoice at having fixed-wing aircraft again in navalised Sea Harriers, based at the famous West Country station of Yeovilton, but the lack of AEW aircraft proved a major tactical flaw as the heavy loss of Royal Navy shipping showed. RAF transports could not come in enough numbers either, forcing the authorities to embarrassingly take over again from their new civil owner the Belfasts tossed away only a few years earlier. Of all the home airfields involved, Brize Norton became arguably the most important by serving as a reception centre for wounded servicemen: slight shades of 38 years earlier, except that a flight back to central England now involved somewhat more than a quick flip across the English Channel.

One aspect of the Falklands fighting which passed unnoticed proved to be how airfields were actually named: no more the highly censored received pronunciation voices of World War Two telling a largely ignorant audience how certain anonymous stations were going to give Johnny Kraut what for. While combats and casualties resulted in being tiny compared with both World Wars, one wonders why certain restrictions were still not placed on airfield names and activities in case of clandestine enemy espionage operations. Extensive televising emphasised this peculiar openness, leading to the popular joke about how Argentinian military planners would gather round a television set and say, 'Now, according to the retired British generals, this is what we should do next.'

As the Falklands conflict demonstrated, the airfields of Britain showed yet again how vital they have always been to their country. What a devastating reply to Duncan Sandys and his political cronies, people who had previously tried their damnedest to write them off. Ultimate if unrecognised humiliation for Government had come during 1979/80 when three RAuxAF Regiment squadrons were revived to give AA protection to airfields.

However, political bungling has tragically ensured that no British military airfield will ever be so crammed with units again. One big unit can be found nowadays and not much else. World War Two brought totally different memories of all the smaller elements which used to be present: training schools of varying sizes; one-off experimental concerns; BAT Flights; Bomber Defence Training Flights; AA co-operation detachments; communications Flights; or those unsung heroes, the ground units. Is there any conceivable limit of thanks climbers can give to Llandwrog in north-west Wales, the airfield which created Mountain Rescue Units?

Maybe the good old days have gone, but Britain's service airfields remain. That is more important than anything else. Imagine trying to train airmen without airfields! If we had not been blessed with so much common sense, we might have seen politicians destroy our entire airfield network. The thought of total reliance upon missiles, as might have happened, just does not bear thinking about. What would Britain have done with your beloved missiles instead of airfields during the Falklands conflict, Duncan Sandys? Nuke Argentina?

And what, incidentally, became of the chief villain of this piece? Sandys had fallen away from the political front line after 1962 once far more sane people had seen through his lunatic proposals and other dubious methods in his political life. He still later received the inevitable life peerage, changing his name by deed poll to Duncan Duncan-Sandys to keep his name in the public eye – an obvious case of egomania if ever there was one. The ignoble Lord died in November 1987, only a couple of days after America and Russia reached a major nuclear missile reduction agreement. An announcement a day after his passing stated how British and Russian leaders would meet not in London or a stately home – but at Brize Norton, one of the stoutest airfield defenders during Sandys' heyday. This was surely the final nail in the coffin of a man who had admitted years earlier that his policies had not been a dream. Too true: as our Northamptonshire friend might have said, they were a bloody nightmare!

Today – and Tomorrow?

What a history, what a life, what action and excitement, invention and innovation – and still the story goes on. So much is different, yet still the same.

Today, the airfields of Britain continue to brilliantly serve their country. Sites involved with the civil scene keep in reasonable shape. Airports are today intended to give visitors an initial good impression, smaller business and recreational airfields thrive with activity, while gliding sites still abound. The former owe their present expansion to wartime improvements and concrete runways but have strangely had steady careers in the main. Airports have even seen little action, Exeter being one of the fairly rare exceptions. Airlines and other operators now turn out in tremendous numbers at airports every day, as do the passengers who help to create terrible delays, especially at holiday periods. Regional airports also suffer by still having slightly precarious finances heavily dependant on holiday rather than business traffic, but generally our foremost aerial gates of entry are improved out of all recognition to the municipal ones before World War Two which often defied the sheer meaning of the word airport.

Time has barely changed at civil airfields overall as the great British civilian companies are still present. Jack of all trades Airwork continues to appear at many a place, while Sir Alan Cobham's Flight Refuelling Limited and aircraft maintenance firm Marshall's still remain in good health at Hurn and Cambridge respectively. All three firms have made immense contributions to airfield operations both at home and abroad.

Military airfields have meanwhile been virtually pared to the bone, but the major difference with them is how the sphere of operations has changed. South and south-eastern England used to be the primary areas for operational flying: as any threat now exists from the east, front line bases have moved further north along a wide flank. How odd to think that

Coltishall remains the only Battle of Britain era fighter station to stay operational in the RAF. The 'Magnificent Seven' have disappeared for good in their best known collective form and have met vastly different fates: only Northolt still remains in RAF hands, and only three can still boast of being active. Whereas Hornchurch lies obliterated and forgotten, Biggin Hill has successfully switched to holding civil aircraft. Britain's favourite airfield and unofficial leader of this supergroup is now a huge star the world over.

Even more notable is how eastern and northern Scotland have come to the fore militarily. Kinloss, Leuchars and Lossiemouth II – never has the abbreviation KiLL ever been more apt – are vital to the defence of Britain. Considerable importance is placed upon maritime patrol, a duty performed by the superb Hawker Siddeley Nimrod jet anti-submarine type, but Lossiemouth shows how Britain has terribly neglected AEW radar. A handful of ancient Avro Shackletons have utterly shattered all records for the longest time any RAF type has remained in operational service, and will hold their place because of the dismal failure of the AEW Nimrod version.

More isolated supportive military assistance comes from airfields in the Midlands, south-west England and Wales. Places such as these are usually where to see both RAF Gliding and Soaring Association and ATC operated gliders, or sailplanes as everyone now tends to call these craft. Apart from the RAF, FAA and AAC bases give smaller but equally invaluable assistance to Britain. A few USAF stations in central and eastern England also provide everything from bombers to air-to-air refuelling tankers and tankbusters. Although American airfields in Britain are officially under RAF ownership – they are always referred to as RAF so-and-so – the British presence is in reality at best limited.

Since the diabolical cutbacks of the Sandys era, active airfield totals have not changed greatly and hovered around the 260-270 mark since the late 1960s. The 'roller-coaster' effect active figures created during the 1920s and early 1930s no longer exists as the temporary licensing of airfields from spring to autumn has ceased. Of the four home countries, England naturally has the great majority of active sites. Scotland is not too badly off, though a heavy proportion of its airfields exist on the Western Isles plus Orkney and Shetland. Inhabitants in these areas cannot thank enough the likes of Tiree for making their everyday lives so much easier. Another rugged part of Britain is Wales, notable for the high proportion of RAF support airfields to civil ones. Northern

Ireland has not fared so well, reduced to a handful of sites basically around Belfast, but the indestructible Aldergrove just keeps on going, aided by those two other Irish airfield veterans Newtownards and Sydenham. Four more pre-World War Two era airports ensure the Isle of Man and Channel Islands are well connected with the mainland. Most major islands in Britain come complete with at least one airfield, though a few exceptions like Arran and Bute in the Firth of Clyde persist in doing without airfields, despite constant murmurings said without much conviction of what might arise one day.

Different kinds of airfield in different parts of this country have had to cope with changing times and policies. Rampantly ongoing technology has resulted in landing grounds disappearing for good, while RLGs are nowhere near as great in number. The roles of RLGs have also undergone subtle changes, for they now serve as supplementary landing areas with exceptionally little in the way of support facilities for a few extremely busy RAF stations. Personnel no longer permanently serve at these places either and only use RLGs on a non-committal day to day basis. Although these few survivors are also sometimes called satellites, this description is quite wrong: it all relates back to the previous points of current operating conditions and availability of support facilities, and satellites as of the recognised World War Two variety are anyhow as now as extinct as landing grounds.

Private civil airstrips have conversely enjoyed a second revival after their heady days of the 1920s and 1930s, yet still cannot be described as true airfields unless constantly used by aircraft. Often an airstrip belongs to a wealthy businessman or landowner and has only one aircraft permanently based on it. Scottish airstrips can be usually counted as recognised sites, on the other hand, because the regularity of air services keeps them occupied daily or weekly. Licensed and unlicensed airfields, of which airstrips form a large number of the second category, have always had subtle differences: for example, flying instruction and passenger carrying are forbidden at unlicensed sites. This is why the Air Ministry List D2 airfields after World War One had to receive permits for use, however temporary. But then the rules on licensing have hardly changed since the Air Licensed Regulations were published in 1919. Neither has the general aversion of civil aircraft using military airfields altered in the years since the Air Ministry List B category arose: relatively few machines call a service station home today, probably out of sheer awkwardness.

Not so bashful are examples of one type of military airfield noted for their daring in times of war. Forward airfields have made a certain comeback, only the term 'forward' is now taken to its extreme. Scotland is again prominent, with such unlikely places as Stornoway and that tenacious airfield survivor which has beaten all the odds Machrihanish adopting this role, in addition to their other duties, and see fighters land from time to time on exercises. Reserve airfields neither exist in such colossal numbers as they did after World War Two nor are used as much but the handful in Britain are always ready to receive aircraft at short notice.

Lastly should be mentioned Military Emergency Diversion (formerly Master Diversion) bases, which have superseded ELGs. This situation resembles the middle part of World War Two when straying aircraft tried to land at the first place available. The big difference now is that diversion airfields are recognised as such and consist of major RAF stations around Britain.

Helicopters have not proved the huge threat to Britain's airfields as many earlier expected. These machines have taken on some unusual roles since the end of World War Two such as coastal anti-submarine duties, though one could always argue that helicopters have taken over from where the *Scarecrow* DH6s of World War One left off. Heliports and helipads are now so ten-a-penny there is some truth in the joke that all you need to do to create your own is paint a circle with an 'H' inside. Helicopters can operate from mountain tops and open seas where even airfields refuse to tread, though planners had a good try at the latter during World War Two. Although military 'choppers' have also shown their ability to fly from almost anywhere, they cannot do so for long. RAF, FAA and AAC helicopters still need solid airfields to provide them with such essential facilities as fuel and spares, not forgetting weaponry or air and groundcrews. Nothing can provide support facilities like an airfield can.

Civil helicopters have had a similarly limited effect. The British Airways Isles of Scilly service between Penzance heliport and St Mary's and other passenger operations only exist because they are viewed as a public service. These helicopters and their highly limited bases are costly to run, rarely making a profit, but then they are not expected to.

It is only in oil support aviation where helicopters have greatly affected airfields, with varying results. In northern Scotland, Dyce has never looked back, though Sumburgh has suffered badly at the hands of long-range helicopters. These machines prefer instead to pass through Unst, the northerly Shetland site which must rate as top airstrip in Britain. The black gold has furthermore managed to revive one or two formerly disused airfields, or at least allow the possibility of this happening. Perhaps George Davidson's visions were not that eccentric: drawings of his elevated landing platforms are not unlike the oil rigs of today.

One needs hardly say how the oil boom will not last for ever. On that sombre note, who can therefore possibly predict what will happen to Britain's airfields in the future? Airfields are expensive to run, what with daily maintenance and aircraft landing fees, and the financial aspect is always of concern. No doubt money will have a big say at some point in many an airfield's life. The Conservative Government's policy evident since the early 1980s of putting money and greed before morality and principle has resulted in the occasionally horrific end to an airfield of late. The desperate fates which met Usworth in 1984 and Burnaston in 1989 are prime examples. Other airfields will continue to suffer the odd closure scare, no matter whether they are important military bases or small civil sites. This point about money particularly applies to civil gliding airfields. Clubs are already buying up large slices of land for flying use, but how badly will they be affected if land values soar in price? Of course, money is not everything, and so much have many active British airfields passed into folklore that no authority would dare close them, such would be the public outcry. Farnborough, Shoreham and other members of the glorious airfield old guard thus soldier on.

Incoming levels of money could also vary depending on which of the current political parties – or maybe even a progressive new one – ascends to power. We can undoubtedly be certain that the present ones will continue to considerably hinder airfield operations as they always have done. Idiotic proposals will still happen, one of the most recent being an astonishing plan to privatise RAF basic training. As if this idea was bad enough, airfield supporters were staggered to discover that it involved closing not just any training station but Cranwell, the most famous of its kind anywhere in the world. The planners will still unwittingly restrict the success of airfields on occasion, the Press still either maul or misunderstand them and pacifists try to deride them – all offshoots from political posing. But none of these opposing forces will ever be victorious, for Britain's airfields have made such visually indelible military, social, economic, technical, historical, geographical and architectural marks that will never be erased.

Politics will play a crucial part should British military airfields have to participate in the unthinkable. World War

Three would be fought on a conventional scale because of obvious fears about nuclear escalation. Our airfields would thrive at this first level; quite how they would stand up to atomic attack is naturally impossible to answer, though having not only survived but resoundingly beaten some of the most difficult opponents imaginable, who would bet against Britain's airfields even in these possible future circumstances!

Even so, certain aspects of World War Three can be predicted with reasonable accuracy. An airfield equipped with AEW aircraft will be first to detect invading aerial forces; RAF fighters will then hurriedly take off from their bases to intercept the attackers as always. Some enemy aircraft will unavoidably penetrate this defensive screen, and this is where the lessons learned from more recent conflicts such as the Six Day and Yom Kippur Arab-Israeli wars of 1967 and 1973 must be put to good effect. Strong SAM and more passive ground defences must exist at our military airfields to counter elements of surprise, enemy standing patrols over airfields and their employment of ECMs. Paratroops may try to capture British bases, as the Germans should have tried to do in 1940, and the clandestine activities of enemy Spetsnaz forces would also have to be rated as an extreme threat. That loyal airfield ally of so many years called radar will have to work better than ever before.

There are still worrying points concerning this initial scenario. Might chemical weapons be used? Will radar be able to cope with the futuristic new Stealth aircraft which effectively defy detection? Intruders, the type of aircraft airfields previously always feared most, do not exist today as they would be too vulnerable to SAMs, but Stealth could conceivably play havoc with the specialised targets such as airfields and radar stations these aircraft are detailed to knock out.

Another totally different fear remains the reluctance of home-based military aircraft to operate from airfields which do not have paved runway surfaces. Many of our present types could, and those dealing with tactical duties should. Warsaw Pact forces have long realised this aspect of tactical air warfare, while so too did the Luftwaffe in World War Two as its aircraft moved from field to field. If ever there was a case for restoring satellite airfields to Britain, it concerns this point. Operating Harriers from tiny unprepared fields is all very well but 'non-airfields' cannot possibly last long. Superiority in electronic systems is another huge Warsaw Pact tactical advantage, and in no way do our military airfields want to become involved in the one role they have yet to tackle.

Counter insurgency or COIN is impossible to win, as many wars since World War Two throughout the world have shown, or at best can only temporarily knock out enemy forces on the ground without permanently beating them.

Should the worst happen, training airfields in Britain might have to despatch their residents for light attack purposes. But even this idea is a distinct throw-back to the days of World War Two, with the successful work carried out by 'inoffensive' German and Russian machines, and since then in the Korean, Vietnam and Arab-Israeli wars. Let us still not forget how the RAF came close to using this tactic too in mid-1940.

Whatever happens, four facts are beyond doubt. Despite initial appearances, Britain's military airfields now possess quite frightening levels of hitting power. Aircraft range and offensive armament limitations tended to restrict them up to the 1930s, but such is their strength today that the huge ranks of bomber airfields once seen along eastern England or the many anti-submarine stations based around our various coastlines are now not thought necessary – or so the authorities think. (Hope might be a better word to use). Home airfields will secondly always require to be of large acreage and retain hardstandings to lessen the effects of enemy attacks; the difficulties caused by few dispersals experienced at Wideawake on Ascension during the Falklands conflict have already shown themselves to be a case in point. Someone, somewhere in a Russian nuclear missile silo also knows about Coltishall, Scampton and many other airfields in Britain. Civil ones are open to attack too as airports in particular could act as useful ELGs. The most vital of these would not be Heathrow but Prestwick, so it would thus be a disaster strategically – as well as for industry, jobs and tourism – if Scotland's greatest ever airfield is forced to close.

Talk of World War Three and nuclear weapons cannot pass without mentioning how more military airfields could once again be inhabited by these lethal but soulless devices. The spectre of Duncan Sandys could reappear to haunt us all. Although US-produced General Dynamics BGM-109 Tomahawk cruise missiles have gone from Greenham Common and Molesworth, following their introduction from 1983, only time will tell if such pernicious weapons like these have made their final bow. Fewer airfields but with more settled lives or more airfields but with a certain uncertainty as to their futures: the issue of whether military sites should or should not possess atomic munitions has long proved something of a Catch-22 situation since 1945.

Two really underestimated threats are the fuel stocks for

future years and the proposed Channel Tunnel. Fossil fuels will run out sometime next century, so liquid hydrogen might have to become the norm at airfields, whether their aircraft are the extremely advanced Horizontal Take Off and Landing craft or more mundane machines. We have only to look back in history to see the shattering effects fuel starvation had upon German airfields in the final months of World War Two. More recent events, notably the oil crisis of 1973 after the world had too hastily supported Israel in the Yom Kippur war, might prove a foretaste of things to come. As for the Channel Tunnel, the less said the better. Should this nightmarish plan rated by some as even more unthinkable than World War Three reach fruition, it will utterly destroy Britain's independence and levels of safety, the whole social fabric of this country and millions of jobs. The effect on Britain's airfields alone will prove catastrophic: people laughed at the thought of ships taking over the car ferrying routes from aircraft during the 1960s – but take over they did. What might happen on a more general scale poses potentially horrifying consequences unless the Channel Tunnel is stopped at all costs once and for all.

Moving to more pleasant future possibilities, civil airfields could step back in time to large-scale airship operations. The general public surely knows by now that helium is an infinitely safer lifting agent than hydrogen. Cardington and other suitably modified or even new sites could again see airships galore instead of the few which constantly threaten to make a big impact. Totally futuristic would be airfields equipped to support passenger craft able to travel from one side of the world to the other in a couple of hours. Regardless of whether the British HOTOL or other projected types take off and land vertically or horizontally, airfields would almost certainly have to be radically altered. Would landing areas have to be extended to unheard of acreages similar to the Bedford runway plan of 1945? What about all the various support facilities?

There is no doubt that vertical take-off and landing aircraft will never appear in quantity until their excrutiating noise problems are solved. Short take-off and landing airliners have recently come to Britain with the opening of London City Airport during 1987 but, although these small airports abound in America, it is doubtful whether this country will be greatly influenced. And let us not forget that ultimate threat to the welfare of airfields – the flying car! While one-off examples have successfully flown, nobody seems keen to pursue this idea.

What the future also holds for the legions of disused airfields in Britain is impossible to predict. These places have undoubtedly had an extremely turbulent time. That is a story in itself . . .

This unending unpredictability has long served as one of the trademarks of Britain's airfields. You simply never know what will happen to them next. An airfield has started life in one role, then delighted all concerned by effortlessly switching to one different job after another. Take Middle Wallop as a typical example. Opened in 1940, it was used in turn during World War Two by trainers, fighters, USAAF reconnaissance aircraft, a Servicing Pool to check fighters, then Royal Navy types. Peacetime brought more RAF fighters, plus AOP and target facilities aircraft, before the airfield's present resident in the AAC arrived during 1957. How ironical it is that Middle Wallop was planned as a bomber station, yet never saw any in the process.

Few things in life, if at all, have matched our airfields when it comes to sheer capriciousness. Just look back at the twists and turns in their lives to see the bizarre contrasts they have experienced. Airfields were born without anyone knowing their exact date of arrival; they were frequently kicked in the teeth by politicians, the one set of people who should have helped them; won two World Wars almost single-handed and yet personally lost out; thrived thanks to a war which never happened and then were twice unwittingly saved in quick succession by two of their greatest enemies; became highly profitable and were still deprived of their earnings; plus gained supreme stardom and no recognition simultaneously. But still they fought and continue to fight out of impossible situations. Take the example of Earl's Colne in Essex: disused for over 38 years, this former RAF/USAAF airfield still managed to regain active status right out of the blue in 1984. It is not alone either, for Port Meadow all but started this phoenix-like effect airfields have always possessed when the Oxfordshire site reappeared in World War One as a training base after its quite volatile early life.

Whether you served at airfields in the past or are simply interested in them, one phrase must keep entering your mind. Who would have thought . . . that Rhoose, a highly undistinguished training airfield in World War Two, would become Wales' airport; that Lakenheath, once not even an airfield meant for friendly aircraft to land at but a decoy site for enemy ones to bomb, would become one of the most powerful and controversial British bases of all time; that Heston, magnificent airfield trend-setter and inanimate diplomatic saviour of the free world, would be rewarded with virtual eradication from the face of this earth; or that Prestwick, a huge and enormously popular airfield superstar, would now be fighting year after year for its sheer existence?

Who could have predicted back in 1909 how our airfields would have to go through two World Wars, suffer many personal crises through no fault of their own but develop so successfully? Of all the various areas of aviation in this country, Britain's supersites have easily been the most efficient. All their diverse facets from landing areas to hangars to safety and so on have not suffered in consequence, despite having to constantly alter in appearance and technique as we shall see. Perhaps that is the biggest secret of our airfields, namely the ability to always keep changing and yet somehow remain consistent. A few laughs have occurred along the way, also considerable sadness, but their success and glory have always shone brightly through.

We may not be able to see clearly into the future as ever, but one fact will never be in any danger of dispute. Airfields might need aircraft, but aircraft will never survive without airfields.

PART TWO:
The Transition

Towards The Hard Stuff

There are many components needed to form this strange creature called the British airfield. An airfield could not be one at all if it does not have a landing area for a start. This might seem a silly statement – but how could aircraft otherwise land? As with airfields in general, their landing areas have steadily developed through the years. While runways must naturally take prime importance, one cannot forget their supporting cast: perimeter tracks, dispersals and adjoining roads. Although all have seen many changes over decades, it was a general change to concrete – the 'hard stuff', as someone once describe it – which helped British airfields no end.

The earliest aviation pioneers barely so much as bothered to select an open area of land where to test their flying contraptions. All they wanted to do was take off and achieve a few priceless moments of sustained heavier-than-air flight; if World War One landing grounds had existed in bygone times, they would have been rendered totally useless. But, as aircraft attempted to succeed balloons, pioneers gradually realised how their surrounding test areas could help fulfil the then impossible dream. Methods of launching took on some peculiar forms, from being towed by men, horses, cables or cars to taking off from carts, railway tracks or down ramps and using catapults or wires to assist machines in becoming airborne. None of these ideas worked, though two of them would have certain uses in days ahead.

What served as the best type of landing area in earlier airfield days was a much simpler device. It possessed three advantages in being natural, abundant and almost totally free of complication. Between the advent of airfields in Britain during 1909 and the outbreak of World War Two 30 years later, short grass able to knit together well generally catered for aircraft needs. Even so, early sites in this country had appalling landing surfaces on the whole as they were far too uneven and dogged by interminable drainage ditches. This became the main reason why Fambridge, Leysdown and their contemporaries closed prematurely.

A possible solution to these problems seemed to be the weight and derrick system of assisted take-off invented by the Wright brothers. Their reasons for using such a device were aimed at becoming less dependant on the weather and compensating for the limitations of their private airfield at Huffman's Prairie. Cables linked the aircraft on its launch rail with a tower, at the top of which was installed an extremely heavy weight: its release thrust forward the machine and meant that it could take off in a short distance. British pioneer José Weiss subsequently used the weight and derrick system at Fambridge but this unwieldy device could not possibly provide a permanent answer.

Having tried to use duckboards, early aviators sometimes switched in desperation to stretches of sand. At least the land was now flat and helped ease the impact of an aircraft landing heavily but beaches were too exposed, sand and wind not doing much good for a frail aircraft. Incoming tides also deprived sandy airfields of that essential airfield capability of being active 24 hours a day. Both of these reasons explain why extremely few British airfields have possessed such landing areas – or, with the exception of Barra, have survived tremendously long either.

Forced to persevere with grass, aviation pioneers gradually learned how to make better landing areas. Aircraft needed good stretches of firm grassland instead of marshland. Racecourses were reasonable sites, thanks to their largely level ground, while completely new places such as Hendon proved airfields could have good landing areas if sufficient planning had taken place beforehand. One lesson learned before World War One showed how a bed of concrete in front of hangars acting as a miniature apron where to park aircraft was needed, rather than soggy grass or sand at marine bases. Initial military airfields still continued to possess poor landing areas, though, and for that reason it is remarkable how Netheravon and Upavon have remained in service spheres for so long. The famous Salisbury Plain bases were formerly used by the cavalry, which may partly explain – along with inherent snobbery – why officers asked many early RFC recuits at their interviews: 'Can you ride?'

World War One ought to have brought further improvements, yet various problems still existed. Despite all the warning signs, a few airfields still had to rely upon duckboards to traverse cavernous ditches. Uneven landing areas became much more common and resulted in some alarming bumps and humps, dips and slopes. This in turn could lead to serious flooding, especially during the winter months. Aircraft movements had become far greater than before, so a combination of wheels and tail-skids brought havoc to many an airfield. If a site was lucky, it could get away with rutting, but frequently this situation developed into a quagmire. Many a tale could be told by former servicemen of wading through a sea of mud. Better drainage was required.

There were still some developments during World War One which helped in the short-term development of airfield landing areas. Sites usually became rectangular in shape, although many HD landing grounds tended to be laid out in the form of a letter L. Airship and marine bases frequently adopted adjacent grass sites to hold incumbent or visiting aircraft as well. Much more rare were twin airfields lying side by side as typified by Cranwell North and South or Upavon North and South.

Inevitably, as standardisation began to make its mark on Britain's landing areas, a certain quirkiness became noticeable too. Strangely shaped open grassy voids defied the rectangular and L shape theories. No airfield could beat for curiosity value Westward Ho with its incredible 'frying pan' layout, or the diagonally tangential landing area of its fellow DH6 anti-submarine patrol base Bangor in north Wales. One odd system used to an extent at this time was the habit of dropping practice bombs on targets sited at airfields. This method continued into the 1930s and was not unknown even in World War Two but damage could hardly be avoided. Separate bombing and firing ranges at coastlines or isolated areas were fortunately eventually developed to meet realistic training needs.

An even crazier suggestion was made in Parliament about whether grass could be grown longer to double up as hay at HD landing grounds. The MP concerned failed to realise how aircraft simply could not land in long grass.

Once the Great War had ended, planners were able to improve airfield landing areas. Increased acreage was provided, and greater thought given to countering surrounding obstacles such as buildings, rivers and trees; HD landing grounds had previously been placed in one of three classes to signify how much obstructions hindered them. A wide chalk circle measuring 100 feet in diameter and with a band five feet wide on the centre of the landing area, introduced during World War One, became a more standard feature both on military and civil airfields between the wars.

This device was meant to make the airfield stand out; its name in letters fifteen feet long by three feet wide was usually thrown in for good measure too, normally placed outside the circle. Credit for this idea is given to none other than Winston Churchill. Each chalk circle was soon found to serve a further purpose by acting as a bombing target for aircraft as earlier described.

But even with these changes, airfield landing areas basically stayed the same. Grass remained in fashion, each airfield possessing on average three or four runways defined by crisply mown stretches. All proved easier to maintain after a good cut and rolling from timc to timc. Thc bcst runway was that which offered the longest run into the prevailing wind. Grass also kept much in evidence off the landing area as aircraft dispersal remained unheard of. In spite of ever larger aircraft, Croydon and the other 1930s airfield stars continued with grass runways, happy as they were. This policy was a move many British airfields would live to regret in later years.

It is little appreciated how airfield landing areas have dictated to aircraft development in their time. Easily the greatest advances have been seen in landing-gears or undercarriages. Sir George Cayley had recognised the extreme importance of helping aircraft in this way by adding wheels to his gliders during the 1800s, and so can be credited with effectively inventing the undercarriage. However, one could always argue that the first 'landing-gear' comprised of nothing more than a pair of human legs. But progress soon sped up as Percy Pilcher created the world's first sprung undercarriage towards the end of the 19th Century for use on his hang-gliders. Pilcher realised that, regardless of where he landed in those days before airfields appeared, any landing would place a certain amount of strain upon his machine.

Once airfields did arise in Britain, undercarriages strangely tended to take a retrograde step. The Wright brothers preferred equipping their biplanes with skids instead of wheels, a practice which led to their undoing as aircraft then lost mobility on landing areas, surely the greatest advantage of wheeled undercarriages.

Standard policy was soon to place two wheels underneath the wings and a tail-skid at the rear. The latter served mainly to brake an aircraft, an important point as it is still not widely acknowledged how brakes generally failed to appear on aircraft for many years. Although France's Voisin biplane bombers of World War One became the first aircraft to be equipped with them, not until the 1930s and the advent of tailwheels as opposed to skids did front wheels start possessing brakes in strength. Before this time, aircraft had to both take off and land into wind at airfields, but brakes now enabled aircraft to keep straight while landing and greatly helped machines to turn on the ground as each wheel could be braked independently. Ground manoeuvrability was something the tail-skid could not provide, airfield groundcrews having to turn aircraft in the direction they wanted to go, though from the late 1920s skids helped combat their taxying problems by being transferred to form an extension from the lower half of the rudder.

For these reasons, grass runways were never thought recommendable right up to World War Two for large or fast aircraft; the fastest racers and biggest transports then tended to be seaplanes or flying boats. Any large aircraft which did land on a grass airfield required huge wheels with bulky low pressure tyres. Harsh braking while taxying at low speeds could also badly wear or cut up grass. Undercarriages had always endured an amount of notoriety prior to the mid-1930s for their comparative frailty, made worse when frost or hard ground prevailed, and there were even occasions when pilots suffered delayed action minor electric shocks after landing. Air/oil shock absorbers fitted on landing-gears solved this particular problem.

So grass had its limitations. As a number of airfields already had concrete parking aprons, the advantages of hard runways looked clear. Aircraft were becoming heavier, their tyre pressures greatly increasing; many types had already learned to cope with poor airfield landing areas by widening their front undercarriages. Concrete could take the strain to avoid many past difficulties, one of the least appreciated being the considerable wheel friction caused by grass surfaces. Perimeter tracks showed the way by appearing in 1938, this being a natural progression from perimeter roads for the use of vehicles. Perhaps the shapes of racecourses had influenced them. Concrete runways were anyhow only a matter of time.

The long held notion that concrete runways remained impractical until World War Two is quite false. Among people who supported the case for tougher types of landing area was Battle of Britain mastermind Air Chief Marshal Hugh Dowding. Civil owners and even some municipal authorities also recognised their value in times of war. But what prevented hardened stretches from being built in the 1930s was that the Air Ministry – not exactly a Dowding favourite – considered the cost of enlarging airfields and providing new runways far too high. Great concern also arose from this quarter about aircraft landing speeds, for planners thought

100 miles per hour too fast in the early 1930s. This second point, incidentally, served as the official reason why the excellent Bristol MIC fighter of World War One never saw extensive operational use. It possessed a high landing speed for its day of 49 miles per hour, but the real reason for top-level disapproval was that this machine was a monoplane, not at all favoured by Great War military planners because of largely misguided prejudice.

As with the perimeter track, nobody strangely seems to know which airfield became the first in Britain to acquire concrete runways. There are several contenders for the title, of which Cranwell, Gosport and veteran Army-orientated Hampshire base Odiham seem good bets as favourites. Hard runways were certainly around by the summer of 1939. Not before time too, for flooding had badly hampered airfield landing areas in December 1938. The same situation had occurred exactly eleven years earlier, so showing the usual British traits of not thinking far ahead and failing to spend money on a proven new idea. Some planners had feared in 1937 that airfields with runways might be too prone to enemy attack if more aircraft than usual had to cram into them from other sites under water. Their solution was to disperse aircraft to small fields where they would have some form of mechanical assistance to take off. This last suggestion was impractical but the basic idea led to the development of satellite airfields.

Immediately showing their superiority over grass, concrete runways began appearing in quantity by 1940. Construction was still limited in the summer of that year with every available operational airfield being badly needed. A wet autumn proceeded to further complicate building work.

The year 1941 made concrete a virtual necessity as the Short Stirling four-engined heavy bomber became the first of Britain's three 'heavies' to enter major RAF service, followed by the Handley Page Halifax and Avro Lancaster. Perhaps only the de Havilland Moth has had a greater effect on our airfields before or since. Every heavy bomber station would eventually be equipped with hard runways. Yet many grass airfields were not converted until the middle or late war period. An excellent example turned out to be none other than the legendary Scampton, which did not have paved runways until well into 1944. Gosport meanwhile went against convention entirely and returned to relying upon its grass landing area, an action no other British airfield followed in wartime.

The standard runway layout created in World War Two

consisted of three stretches placed in a triangular pattern. A tangential pattern, where the runways did not intersect, did receive consideration by planners but this idea was soon dropped because of Flying Control difficulties. It goes without saying that not all airfields had runways laid out in an A shape: some had only two stretches, others only one. Airfields such as Benson and durable Shropshire MU/training base Shawbury were simply incapable of taking on a third runway in the way their hangars and support buildings were positioned. The 'crossbow' and 'cruciform' layouts became less familiar schemes devised mid-war, while occasional curiosities also cropped up. Chief among these was a layout where all three runways shared a common intersection. A few airfields were given this style up and down Britain. It had one major flaw in that all three runways could be put out of action simultaneously if an enemy bomb scored a direct hit on the intersection or aircraft collided at that point.

Wartime runways measured up to 2,000 yards in length, depending upon the type of airfield, and 50 yards in breadth. Public roads frequently had to close to accommodate them, a fact of life which did not greatly please the local civilian population. Wherever possible, the main runway would be aligned to suit the existing prevailing wind, although land restrictions and other problems often prevented this from happening. The two shorter subsidiary runways could suffer similar difficulties. Particularly if heavier types of aircraft used these lesser stretches, their crews would find it nearly impossible to take off unless the wind was howling at them.

Runways were later frequently topped by a protective layer of bitumen but this substance proved to be a problem in future years when jets came into use as their engines or spilt fuel easily burnt bitumen-covered runways. A novel development of sorts was prefabricated bituminous surfacing or PBS, basically cloth soaked in bitumen to provide speed of construction. The wet British climate ensured that PBS was mainly only tested in this country but it did help flying units abroad after D-Day.

Safety played its part too in runway design. Provisions were made for spaces beyond runways to give larger aircraft greater clearance; no obstructions such as buildings had to be within 50 yards of a landing area. Hardly any camber existed either on runways to cut down on undercarriage collapses and other accidents.

Unlike runways, perimeter tracks did not have to go along as many set procedures. Only one rule essentially applied to them: each had to be preferably 50 feet wide for aircraft to travel along. Fighter airfields nevertheless tended instead to have 35 feet wide perimeter tracks, and training sites could have examples as narrow as ten feet across. The vast majority of airfields in World War Two, even those with grass runways, possessed a perimeter track. Like runways, perimeter tracks also varied in size, ranging from small 'circles' at training airfields to mazy ones at bomber stations. These larger perimeter tracks normally averaged about three miles in length. Again curiosities existed, notably those which did not enclose the landing area. Certain airfields could have done with more perimeter track as runway extensions resulted in a long stretch with no supporting roads. This could be quite a problem if an aircraft suffered an emergency on take-off. Where could the pilot have turned to if no perimeter track existed? A partial solution turned out to be the installation of turning circles at the ends of exposed runways, though this idea did not serve as a total cure.

More of the 'hard stuff' came into play early on in World War Two with the arrival of dispersals. Official thinking decreed that aircraft should be placed around airfield boundaries to stand less chance of being successfully attacked. Aircraft could now resist the elements far better than their World War One counterparts and, in any case, too many aircraft in a hangar now spelt trouble.

The first dispersals or hardstandings were fairly simple, consisting of lay-bys, but far more abundant became the frying pan and spectacle types; shaped as such, they looked quite distinctive. The frying pan, or panhandle as it was also sometimes known, had a circular apron of 125 feet, complete with a taxiway joined to the perimeter track. In practice, however, the spectacle type showed how it was better for positioning aircraft. This system of loops could either merge with the perimeter track or be linked by a taxiway. Spectacle hardstandings came in a variety of shapes, though many formed B or 8 patterns. Frying pans and spectacles frequently joined forces at airfields, a rarer dispersal type being one shaped not unlike a star.

Rules finally applied to dispersals too as RAF airfields had to have 36 hardstandings, while bases used by the USAAF required 50. Needless to say, this policy was not always followed: although airfields could have more than their fair share of hardstandings, sites would more likely not have enough. It was also not unknown for dispersals to be placed on the landing area side of the perimeter track, a ploy which surely negated their purpose.

The best types of dispersals were those which involved as

little taxying track as possible and easy parking allowances for aircraft once they had landed. As that modern day theory now suggests drivers are most prone to accidents close to home, so it applied to pilots – and, of course, a war was going on. But dispersals so lived up to their name that bicycles became a must for airfield personnel.

Runways and their supporting tracks underwent continuous refinements as World War Two progressed. Tarmac runways supplemented concrete ones; Dalcross is reputedly the first British airfield to have received this material. Other flexible base runway types as opposed to rigid base concrete included asphalt/bitumen, hardcore or building rubble, stone pitching or quarried material or various combinations/permutations of these materials. Of airfields built in World War Two with paved runways, the ratio of concrete to stone pitching was about 3:1, the reason being stone pitching proved slow to lay. While these two surfaces could be mixed with tarmac, asphalt or bitumen, five-eighths of airfields had concrete alone. Wartime economies brought narrower runway ends at some sites; these could also act as possible extra stretches should the runways have to be lengthened. Extension work became accepted as aircraft kept increasing both in size and weight, though flying was rarely badly affected.

Vast aircraft movements at busier airfields in Britain still created tremendous wear and tear. An incredible rise in the weight of aircraft was mainly to blame. A Sopwith Snipe fighter of World War One had a take-off weight of less than one ton, but now even the dainty Spitfire balanced the scales at about three tons, and a fully laden Lancaster at over 30. Yet what really mattered was not so much the weight of an aircraft but its wing loading, the gross weight of an aircraft divided by its wing area. Early machines had enjoyed such low wing loading that they could take off from almost any airfield. Their vital lifting agents were not encumbered with retractable undercarriage systems, engines, fuel tanks, guns, bombs and bomb racks because of the frail wood and fabric composition of wings. Biplanes naturally held a vast superiority over monoplanes too and so enjoyed considerably greater lift.

Metal aircraft construction totally changed matters once it became more common from the mid-1920s. Wing loading ratios started to soar – but the same could not be said of aircraft as they made increasingly lumbering take-offs from airfields. So about this time came the invention of trailing edge flaps and leading edge slots fitted on wings to greatly help aircraft with taking off and landing at airfields. Both flaps and slots also vastly reduced the chance of stalling near airfields, from which there was no possibility of recovery at low level. These two devices had soon become established by the 1930s, deceptively simple items which have since revolutionised aviation in so many ways.

Such heavy aircraft as seen on airfields during World War Two similarly forced landing-gears to make great technological strides. Undercarriages adopted twin-wheel gears on each leg and higher tyre pressures, so tarmac runways had to give ground to concrete ones. Rougher landing areas meant introducing bigger landing-gears with long shock struts to allow smoother touchdowns or taxying at airfields. This in turn created high wing aircraft which could operate better from poorer sites and so avoid damaging their engines and propellers. Tailwheel aircraft suffered in their thousands as well during World War Two from both the pressure of swinging on take-off or landing because of wrong power settings and the great stress involved in turning an aircraft on its spot. Steerable instead of fixed tailwheels had not appeared tremendously long on the scene since replacing tail-skids.

Airfield landing areas were spared from their daily battering when World War Two finally ushered in the widespread use of tricycle undercarriages. These devices immediately showed a marked superiority over tailwheels with their better steering qualities and helped aircraft to have better all-round visibility now the fuselage stood level with the landing area. Tricycle undercarriages were not new by any means: Sir George Cayley had invented them, and World War One era aircraft possessed tricycle layouts of sorts, though then the front wheel served more as an auxiliary force as emphasis was still placed on the tail-skid. It was 1940 when the Douglas Boston/Havoc light bomber/night fighter became the first aircraft in RAF service to have a tricycle undercarriage, our first similarly-equipped indigenous type being the Armstrong Whitworth Albemarle transport which reached squadrons mid-war.

Despite such magnificent efforts by aircraft to ease the pummelling of their many airfields, constant attention had to be given towards every part of a landing area. Runways and perimeter tracks therefore often had to be patched up rather than fully repaired. Breakup became fairly common and forced units to occasionally detach to other airfields. Resurfacing has since become accepted as necessary at some point in the life of an airfield.

Camouflage was another excellent aid in protecting airfield

tracks from more unnatural causes in the form of enemy aircraft. Paint was cleverly used both on and off runways; painted 'hedges' proved quite effective – provided no aircraft stood over them! This form of deception could be equally useful off the landing area, especially with access roads. Expansion Period airfields were superbly built but wartime showed up an unexpected flaw: roads at these sites were too straight. Their more austere successors produced winding tracks less distinctive from the air. Storage airfields surpassed them all, as MU taxiways stretched incredibly long distances to dispersal sites far away from the landing area. Look at any storage site on an Ordnance Survey map and you can usually still see these roads marked, seemingly going nowhere. These airfields really do have enormous acreages.

Two types of airfield runway are worthy of special mention at this point. As ever, the Royal Navy went its own way with a completely different runway layout, provided the airfield concerned was not one transferred from the RAF. FAA stations normally came equipped with four runways instead of three, all short both to counter crosswinds and imitate aircraft carrier landings. To aid pilots, these runways had grid-like white lines painted on them to simulate carrier decks, and a few strips can still be seen today. Aerodrome Dummy Deck Landing or ADDL training became quite common in World War Two. Whereas naval airfield runways proved short, they were also narrow, only being 90 feet wide in the main.

At the other end of the scale, World War Two created the three enormous ELGs at Carnaby, Manston and Woodbridge. All were benevolent monsters with their single extra-long, extra-wide runways. Each stretch measured 3,000 yards by 250 yards, not including another 500 yards of grass at each end for overruns. The runway was split into lanes: the south lane was for emergencies, having white day lights and green night lights, the middle lane had white lights for night use, while the northern one had yellow lights. Three aircraft could theoretically land at the same time. Far less obvious was a revolutionary development in runway construction, for the three ELGs had stretches made of condensed sand topped with a layer of bitumen. Surprisingly devised at Benbecula in the Outer Hebrides because of soft ground conditions there, this type of runway proved to be flexible, yet easy to mend. This special surface – sometimes known as 'sandmix' – was a great help as ELGs often witnessed bad landings by aircraft.

At least Carnaby, Manston and Woodbridge possessed runways made of fairly straightforward materials. World War

Two still had one more surprise left up its sleeve for airfield landing areas. First there had been grass runways, then concrete and other harder ones: now came metal runways. Although prefabricated and essentially temporary, metal runways did offer quick and easy installation as only locking pins needed to hold them in place.

A wide variety of metal types existed, but four stood out from the rest in terms of use. First of its kind became Sommerfeld Track, named after its inventor, consisting of rolls of wire mesh measuring 25 yards by ten feet held together by steel bars and rods. Coir or coconut matting (itself tested as a runway material) was occasionally used to support the wire mesh if the ground underneath became swampy. Soon certain ground units could lay a 1,000 by 52 yard runway in 11¾ hours. Sommerfeld Flexboards, later introduced as a portable temporary road over any suspect ground, should not be confused with Sommerfeld Track as they were quite different.

Bottisham in Cambridgeshire became the first airfield to receive Sommerfeld Track during 1941, and its viability led to increased use of metal runways. A handful of British airfields later arose solely for experimental metal runway testing purposes, such as Huggate Wold in Yorkshire, where fighters would arrive to land and take off from metal stretches over the course of a few days. A good number of grass airfields all over Britain latterly saw engineers swiftly lay down many millions of yards of metal on their landing areas as a result. Heavy traffic had made grassy fighter and training airfields begin to crack up under constant pressure as in World War One. Metal did not only have to go on runways, for it could be also used as perimeter tracks and hardstandings. Lengths placed just off the sides of runways helped to marshall gliders at airborne forces airfields for a quick take-off.

Unfortunately, remorseless pounding by aircraft tended to wear down Sommerfeld Track. Wire mesh, British Army Track and the different American Army Track suffered as well, so more durable metal runway types were needed.By 1943 ALGs had come into existence, airfields which right from inception relied heavily upon metal. Each site required two runways at right angles to one another, taxiways and dispersals. The most famous metal runway type in Pierced Steel Planking or PSP hence appeared to cover many a temporary and more permanent airfield. Although the best of its kind, PSP was not a cheap material and often bent up at the edges if the ground beneath had not been properly prepared.

This defect in turn frequently caused burst tyres. The tendency of PSP to bring mud to the surface became another hindrance.

While PSP and other metal runway types proved successful, each had its own peculiar shortcomings. The two other main variants in World War Two were typically good but not perfect. Square Mesh Track or SMT came either in rolls or panels, unlike PSP, and turned into another runway backbone. Heavy picketing and much general maintenance still remained most important in order to hold SMT to the ground. Bar and Rod Track was another American type like PSP, a form of grids mainly used off runways at taxiways and other points to strengthen these areas. Its main shortcoming was that Bar and Rod Track could not be easily produced. A much rarer third type in Channel Track bore a similarity to SMT in requiring a lot of checking.

Until the end of World War Two, these and other metal runway designs performed sterling service on Britain's airfields. British firms produced over 75 million square yards of metal alone. ALGs in particular employed vast amounts during the better months of 1944, having seen improvements carried out upon them during the previous winter. American ALGs now possessed much stronger landing areas to cope with their heavier fighters, so Sommerfeld Track became less popular. When Allied forces secured a foothold in Europe, a great deal of metal – especially PSP – was transferred from closing ALGs to foreign airstrips. Metal had served its purpose.

When peacetime returned, airfields in Britain finally fully accepted concrete for their landing areas. Metal quickly disappeared, while grass now bowed in submission to jet aircraft. The world has encountered some major abbreviated ailments in its time, from TB to that preventable disease of modern times. Our airfields could be said to have endured another,GRS or Grass Runway Syndrome, and the remedy was simple: change or close. Planners had generally recognised by 1944 that grass airfields had had their day, though how sad it became to see so many famous airfields close down because they lacked hard runways.

Despite these changing times, jet aircraft performances dictated that bases equipped with concrete runways did not go scot-free either. Acreage had to increase still further. Runways had to grow in length to 3,000 yards to handle jet fighters and bombers; if runway extension work involved heavy demolishing of houses and other items, the airfield concerned was more than likely to be dropped. More extensions meant more road closures, more crash exits for safety use and more perimeter track. The main runway grew out of all proportion to its two subsidiaries, and standard practice is now to withdraw the latter from use. One of the least noticed developments lay in how runways had to be smoother than ever, especially as radar systems could be damaged by a bad bump on landing. The infamous rise on St Eval's main runway could be said to have hastened its demise in 1959 because of this reason.

Returning more to basics, the sheer speed of jet aircraft and their wing designs remained the major factors in runways having to be greatly extended. The new swept wing aircraft as pioneered by Germany during World War Two did not create much lift at low speeds in relation to straight wings and so needed far greater take-off and landing speeds. Variable geometry or swing-wing aircraft such as the American General Dynamics F-111 bomber became a great advantage in this respect when they appeared by being able to fly quickly but slow down around airfields. Otherwise, jets have had to slam on their brakes while quickly landing, often also deploying parachutes from their tails to help slow them down before releasing these devices on the runway. USAAF Liberators devised this idea during World War Two in somewhat enforced circumstances when their brakes failed after being damaged by enemy action.

Due to continued improvements, the story of airfield landing areas does not have an ending – and probably never will. There were two early post-war developments which have since gained acceptance as speed is so vital these days. The self-explanatory Aircraft Servicing Platform is sited close to an airfield's technical site, while Operational Readiness Platforms exist at either end of the main runway. ORPs give runways a widened look and are designed to allow quick reaction by fighters. Less familiar, but still of note, has been the practice of supplying airfields with huge parking aprons. The Americans made this feature fashionable in the 1950s for their bomber fleets, usually acquiring concrete by tearing up the subsidiary runways at an airfield.

Today, the 'hard stuff' undoubtedly rules at active British airfields. It is almost unthinkable for an airport or operational military airfield not to possess hordes of concrete. Even the humble airstrip now frequently has a hard surface. Totally new runways have risen at Edinburgh (Turnhouse) and Liverpool (Speke) Airports to improve operations. Runway reconstruction during the 1950s and 1960s saw airliners land at such unusual places as East Fortune and Ouston in

Northumberland while airports temporarily lay closed. There is still plenty of grass, though, predominating at more minor military and civil airfields; gliders prefer grass too. Sometimes grass runways have enjoyed the last laugh over their concrete opponents when the latter surface becomes disused and grass takes over for light aircraft use, as has happened at Thruxton. Of metal, hardly anything is to be seen nowadays at disused airfields, and to spot a stretch still in position is a justifiable cause for rejoicing. A greater amount does remain for fencing purposes if you look closely around the countryside.

There is one final type of landing surface we have not mentioned so far in water but, as flying boat and floatplane numbers dramatically fell away in the 1950s, hardly any aircraft spectacularly takes off in spray these days. Watery landing areas have perhaps been the easiest of all to maintain: all one needed were deep water free of shipping, sheltered moorings and at least one slipway. This said, there was always a certain trickiness operating marine aircraft in rough water that possibly contributed to their downfall. World War One had shown how flying boats fared better than seaplanes in such conditions. The introduction of stepped hulls helped to reduce drag but a flying boat on its step still produced greater drag than a land undercarriage, so limiting wing loading and forcing engines to go longer flat out at full power. As freezing ice could also squash an aircraft hull as much as any ship, landplanes and 'dry' airfields would inevitably come out on top. But marine bases only went down fighting when amphibious aircraft such as the Catalina and Walrus later arose in World War Two to use either land or water.

Landing areas which have survived now experience a mixture of the old and new. Runway obstructions continue to give problems, whether they are birds or people, vehicles or accidentally discarded objects. Worries arose about animals grazing at civil sites with limited licences during the 1920s and 1930s, and it is remarkable to think that Manchester's airport at Ringway still had to contend with livestock straying on to its main runway as late as December 1963.

One acceptable obstruction these days is agriculture, as economic measures have forced the peripheries of RAF airfields, especially those on a lesser or reduced footing, to serve in this auxiliary role. Yet this idea is far from new, for surplus land intended for use as unit gardens first came into practice during World War One, was revived in the early 1930s and gave excellent service in World War Two by keeping the mess larders fully filled.

More aggressive military requirements for rough fields and

forward airstrips call for aircraft with strong undercarriages and large tyres. Standard Russian training is for Red Air Force tactical aircraft to exercise for a fortnight or so every year at crude places where machines have to use huge low pressure tyres and operate at gross weight. A Jaguar has taken off from a British motorway but this potentially highly advantageous technique, introduced by Luftwaffe fighters towards the end of World War Two, has not seen any development elsewhere except in Sweden. The obvious drawback from using such primitive landing areas is that support facilities can never hope to match those at an airfield. Supporters of the scheme state how munitions dispensers or cluster bombs can cripple a hard runway, though the best way remains dropping a stick of bombs at 30 degrees to the runway so at least one weapon hits its target. But if the runway lies on solid ground, little damage is caused.

Landing areas are not as vulnerable at first glance: they can fight back on their own. Land mines became a viable deterrent to enemy forces when introduced to some airfields in southern England during 1940, joined during World War Two by even more effective pipe mines. The idea was to prevent Luftwaffe aircraft from using any British airfield equipped as such should the worst come to the worst. Soon concrete runways were being built with voids specially set aside in case pipe mines had to be installed. These weapons in particular perhaps proved too good as bomb disposal teams found them extremely difficult to deal with post-war; a handful of fatalities resulted, and there is no absolute certainty that airfields which received mines have been totally cleared.

Other equally odd ideas from home or abroad have never seen the light of day on landing areas in Britain. We shall never see airfields here employ wooden runways as the Japanese did during World War Two, for once inventing instead of copying something. As flying boats have disappeared from this country, neither shall we see aircraft of this kind dropping water upon blazing forests as happens in Canada: what one might call bombing a target with your own runway. Frozen lake landing areas in Britain are just as unlikely as, quite apart from the impossibility of climate, enemy bombing could easily break up the surface. RAF Gladiators found this out to their cost in Norway during 1940. Wintry conditions such as these would require aircraft to adopt ski or tracked undercarriages. Elevated runways in the centres of big cities resembling gigantic tables were one 1930s suggestion thankfully never to reach further development, nor did a 1938 proposal for heavily loaded aircraft to start on journeys across the Atlantic by sliding down a long incline in the Pennines. Heaven help the passengers!

Yet a few ideas which seemed odd in days of yore have curiously caught on. Vertical take-off and landing aircraft have managed to do without runways, though these machines have to make considerable aeronautical sacrifices in other ways. Winch launching is useful for gliders if tugs are unavailable or the landing area is too small. This system of winding a cable around a drum was invented by American hang-gliding pioneer Octave Chanute. Hendon showed in 1917 how aircraft could be successfully launched from an airfield by a catapult, but this device has since proved far more useful on aircraft carriers to help aircraft become airborne quickly. And, at a more mundane level, civil light aircraft of today have been spared from the 'bounce' effect on landing which bedevilled their 1930s counterparts with the creation of smoother landing areas and stronger undercarriages. Now all someone needs to do is devise an item to spin undercarriage wheels and save aircraft tremendous tyre wear.

Runways, perimeter tracks, dispersals and supporting roads have suffered varying fates at our disused airfields. When an airfield closed to flying, white crosses were painted at each runway end to warn pilots. This has given way to gradual deterioration and even removal. Many disused airfield runways have become most distressing sights but hope springs eternal, for others now enjoy new leases of life in the most surprising of tasks. While perimeter tracks and adjacent roads have followed much the same pattern, with some aircraft now using disused airfield perimeter tracks as runways, the many thousands of dispersals built have largely disappeared either entirely or under thick mossy growth. It has reached the point where frying pans and spectacles have become comparative rarities.

As aircraft depend so much upon airfield landing areas, round-the-clock maintenance is a must. Daily runway checks at airports alone are vital: each stretch should remain in good condition for at least ten years. But, in this allegedly perfect world, runways and the rest continue to have their oddities. We need look no further than Heathrow with its runways – tangential ones at that – not in line with the prevailing winds. No British airfield has a layout like our top airport; nor was any intended to possess nine runways, easily beating the record of five at a handful of World War Two era FAA stations, even though Heathrow has finished up with just three. Nowhere either is there a runway longer than the two

12,800 feet examples at Heathrow, yet these stretches could have been utterly dwarfed by others almost twice as long if plans of 1945 had gone through.

What has become most noticeable of all is how the 'hard stuff' remains after its long battle to gain supremacy. Concrete runways have beaten off such unusual opposition in their time as piggy-back or pick-up mother aircraft or airships and ship catapult launchers. Grass runways have been vanquished too – but this is not to say they are far from needed. All these unique areas need to be saved from their main enemies: the weather, wind – and greedy landowners.

The Airfields' Eyes

Confusion frequently occurs when someone tries to describe the control building at an airfield. Should it be called a watch office, watch tower or control tower? The difference is easy to remember: the latter exists where radio is in general use. This is now standard but was not always the case. Standard is also certainly the last word in describing control towers, these distinctive all-seeing buildings.

Airfield building has always followed a logical process over many years. First of all the landing area must be prepared. A building must then arise to control aircraft before work starts on the hangars and support facilities after that. After a suitable name has been chosen and safety checks made, the site is ready to open to flying. So simple is this formula. However, construction techniques followed a different pattern before the mid-1930s by going straight from the landing area to hangars. Part of the reason control/watch towers did not exist in those days lay in the inability of most aircraft to carry r/t sets to communicate with the ground. Radios which did exist – as on flying boats – usually had short ranges, proved most unreliable and formed a cumbersome array of knobs and wires. While all these reasons were perfect excuses, one still has to wonder why nobody thought of installing watch towers at Great War airfields to provide visual contact with aircraft.

To the Americans can be credited the idea of control towers, in the same way as their popularisation of the word airfield. Until the mid-1930s, buildings dealing with such matters merely consisted of small wooden offices where pilots checked in and out; occasionally, they could be adjoined to a hangar. A tiny brick building which could be easily mistaken for a garden shed was erected at Brooklands in March 1911 as a booking office for flights, is recognised as having been the first of its kind in the world – and still stands today.

The first true control tower in Britain also became our most famous individual example. Croydon's building was completed in 1928 and set the basic style for future years. It was tall, distinctive, possessed good visibility and had radio telephony capability at hand.

Nevertheless, r/t did not become standard in aircraft until the late 1930s. As the Expansion Period had already got under way, advances in aerial control and buildings for this purpose were carried out. The first standard type of building was a design built to pattern 1959/34, '34' relating to 1934, significantly when the Expansion Period began. This small building was better known to all concerned as the 'Fort' type. Many Expansion Period RAF airfields had these neat little towers by the outbreak of war in September 1939. Examples can still be seen, usually intact if not always used for flying purposes.

A second type of watch tower which similarly belonged to the pre-war period looked much more like the squarish buildings of World War Two and beyond. Known as the 'villa' type, this sumptious building was undoubtedly the most attractive ever designed on account of its curved features. It also introduced the standard elements of a control tower: a control room, general, meteorological and movements offices plus a rest room and night flying equipment room – not forgetting toilets! Most 'villas' have enjoyed the same fates as 'Fort' types.

Almost unavoidably, World War Two brought an end to extravagant designs. New types of control tower (a name which gained acceptance during the late war period) were devised. All became much more box-like in appearance, increased in size and were better positioned. Most buildings were now sited inside the perimeter track and near the technical site, not close to the parking apron as before. Exceptions inevitably arose: RAF heavy bomber station Pocklington in Yorkshire, for example, had a control tower opposite the technical site, while bomber OTU training satellite Finmere in Oxfordshire had its building right in the centre of the airfield.

Perhaps more than anything else, World War Two showed how control towers had suddenly become more isolated from other airfield buildings, a fact of life which both helped and hindered them. Enemy action proved the perfect point as there might now have been little chance of a tower suffering blast damage from bombs directed against the technical site, but its detached position conversely provided Luftwaffe crews with an attractive target which to strafe with cannon and machine-gun fire. Control towers were also more at risk from erratically taxying aircraft, and the conflict did see several occasions where errant machines badly damaged and even destroyed buildings which just happened to be in their way. The Bodney incident during the morning of D-Day undoubtedly became the most notorious of these incidents but special mention must go to Shropshire OTU base Sleap, whose control tower was twice rammed by Whitleys in 1943. It says much for construction techniques that this particular building still stands today.

Britain possessed a great variety of control tower types during World War Two, ranging from fairly common designs to some real curiosities. No set pattern basically existed but two structural features introduced at this time soon became very noticeable. Whereas the pre-war 'villa' type bore a walk-round balcony supported by the ground floor, now the balcony simply projected from the wall. The other innovation was also easily visible, for wartime control towers were frequently provided with external stairways in addition to internal ones.

Typical of the new breed of austerity period control towers were two prominent types to designs 12096/41 and 12779/41. This second building helped develop the 13726/41, a scaled-down version with four windows instead of six. Several other types of varying sizes existed, though the basic layout remained. Of note were the large 518/40 and 13079/41 control towers which had internal and external stairways respectively.The 343/43 type was a later style of control tower but still retained the standard squarish appearance, six windows and external staircase of the 12779/41.

Various refinements were carried out to control tower design as World War Two progressed. Windows differed in size by either remaining all the same or the three upper ones becoming larger. Apart from acquiring better views of the airfield, each control tower had to take black-out procedures into account. Teleprinters for transmitting typed messages arrived during the conflict, showing themselves to be most valuable machines, while added visibility could be provided by the installation of small square observation tops. Policy changes and/or land limitations naturally meant an airfield did not have to possess only one control tower. A new one could be built if the original building was too small or too far back from the landing area.

Two further developments arose in widely different types of airfield. When SLGs first appeared on the scene at the end of 1940, a special type of control building was needed to preserve their secrecy. As a standard austerity type would be far too prominent, bungalows were devised to mingle perfectly with the surrounding countryside. The Royal Navy also had its own distinctive control type in a building with three storeys instead of two as with RAF control towers. This indirectly influenced RAF airfields, a number of which later had three storey buildings as well.

Since the end of World War Two, little general change has resulted in control tower design. Buildings perched high on stilts briefly became popular but the sole major alteration has been the positioning of bigger observation tops, known as Visual Control Rooms or VCRs, especially on military airfields and airports. Unlike the 'boxes' of World War Two, VCRs are broad at their flat tops, tapering down in width to the control tower's original roof. Devised in the 1950s, these seemingly heavy structures also have angled windows designed to cut down on reflections which cause visual distortions. All-round visibility is now considered essential, an ability which World War Two era control towers did not completely have. Every type of this period had certain blind spots, though to be fair the importance of black-out dictated affairs.

Mention of control towers cannot be made without also referring to their largely ignored ally the signals square. This simple but most necessary device situated in front of each tower has remained prominent for many years. One could say how it is descended indirectly from the chalk circles and lettering placed on landing areas between both World Wars. Built of whitewashed concrete, the signals square is particularly valuable for communicating with aircraft which do not have r/t. In it are primarily a horizontal white sign shaped like a dumb-bell which can be modified to explain take-off and landing procedures, a white landing T to show the required direction to do so and the airfield's *Pundit* letters, two of them, which form part of its name and give the pilot further assistance in helping to identify the airfield. The practice of writing out the full name of an airfield in chalk as in pre-war days was a non-starter in World War Two for obvious reasons, so clever *Pundit* abbreviations appeared, SA for Scampton being just one of hundreds of examples. Inspiration surely came from the 1920s system of a single letter as in C for Croydon as part of a navigational aid for pilots. Wartime meant not every airfield could have appropriate letters – that was just impossible – and there were a few duplications, but it is easier these days with fewer sites. Signals squares at disused airfields are now almost untraceable because they are so overgrown or have disappeared altogether.

The story of control towers has produced its oddities as in all walks of British airfield life. While you might well see one of the types already mentioned, there is just as great a chance of encountering a strange design. Various British airfields had or still do have some of the most peculiar buildings; one-offs not resembling any standard design remain fairly frequent. Single story control towers which could have passed for a 'Fort' type minus its upper storey became fashionable for a short while early on in World War Two at satellite airfields used by fighters but their marked lack of height meant these buildings were soon replaced. Another anomaly is the sight of a Royal Navy airfield with an RAF style two storey control tower: this immediately tells you that the site was originally owned by the RAF before the Navy took over.

As for the disused towers which were once so active, they have met differing fates. Some have been demolished, others left as eyeless empty shells, sometimes even still displaying the faded words 'Flying Control' above their upper windows. More have enjoyed successful conversion into offices or private dwellings. And no prizes for guessing what house owners usually tend to call their pride and joy – 'The Tower'. Service personnel and civilians alike have always called any control tower as just a 'tower', but this is as much a misnomer as calling any type of runway 'tarmac'.

Control towers at active airfields still continue to have considerable presence. These examples will always be manned, unlike the proposal that lighthouses will eventually become totally automatic. When Air Traffic Control facilities have closed at an airfield, its 'eyes' are blinded and, although emergency landings can still safely happen, they give a whole new meaning to a blind landing. Distinctive in their original roles, equally unmistakable in retirement, control towers have certainly played a major part in the development of Britain's airfields.

'It's Only A Hangar . . .'

If an airfield research expert or supporter was paid one pound every time on hearing the above expression, he or she would probably become a millionaire. Of all the various unkind things which still far too many people continue to say about the airfields of Britain, 'it's only a hangar' is still best guaranteed to bring an anguished look to the face of either party. We can at least happily report how fewer people now make this thoughtless statement. They now recognise the massive historical and architectural value of these often huge structures which continue to serve the community in various ways outwith aviation circles.

Perhaps more than any other building, even the control tower, the hangar is most associated with an airfield. Larger examples did and still do signify the presence of a site by standing out on the landscape. On a broad basis, hangarage development can be split into four distinct periods:

(1) The advent of airfields in Britain to 1934
(2) 1934 (beginning of the Expansion Period) to 1939
(3) World War Two
(4) Post-1945

So many origins involving our airfields are shrouded in mystery, but it is safe to say that the airship hangar or shed – the term garage never caught on – was the first specifically designed building of its kind. Its appearance basically never altered by having a length of several hundred feet and being extremely tall but narrow. An airship shed had to be huge, mainly for the reason that airships have always suffered from limited payload capability, regardless of whether they have seen military or civil use. Trying to overcome this shortcoming, these craft grew to massive proportions and airship sheds followed suit.

The first airship sheds arose at Farnborough from 1905.

These structures soon showed how much they were needed whenever bad weather occurred. The Admiralty was obviously thinking ahead when it considered building sheds along the east coast of Britain in 1910, though procedural difficulties delayed any start to proposed plans until 1913. World War One helped speed up matters but airship sheds proved difficult to build; a big capital investment also arose as construction costs for a single building soon frequently reached six figures.

Not many airship sheds have survived since those days but Cardington's two monsters have become famous landmarks, forever evoking memories of the doomed R-101. It is worth pointing out that the southern hangar is shorter and was actually transferred to Cardington from one of our other noted airship stations at Pulham in the late 1920s.

The infinitely more common aircraft hangar began life usually as a converted shed or similarly unrelated building. Fambridge's main example was typical as it had seen previous service as a hydraulic crane factory. World War One forced a change in policy and resulted in hangars being built to standard designs. The type best known to airmen of that period became the Bessoneau. This temporary hangar built of wood and canvas was installed at many Great War period airfields. As the word hangar itself is French, the Bessoneau was a doubly apt choice. The RFC adopted it in 1915 after having tried out various other mobile hangar types, the best of which had proved to be the RE7. Stations which possessed this newer successful design normally had about a dozen kept close together in lines.Bessoneaux looked frail structures but, provided they were firmly secured to the ground, could withstand poor weather conditions.

Such was their durability that a number of these hangars survived to see service in World War Two by usually acting as stopgaps pending more suitable buildings. Even today, the faithful Bessoneau has not totally disappeared. It is often said how the RAF keeps several dismantled examples in stock if a dire emergency should arise. You need only to look at Halton today to spot a few glaringly evident examples. An odd Bessoneau pops up elsewhere from time to time as well.

For all its success, the Bessoneau could not provide a fully effective answer to combating aircraft frailty. Permanent hangars (or aeroplane sheds, as the authorities liked to describe them at this time) were needed. Leysdown had set the ball rolling before World War One by going against the converted shed philosophy and introducing the RE hangar for the use of Shorts. This particular type caught on and could be seen at early World War One era airfields. A handful of REs up and down Britain still hold fast today as in the case of Montrose.

Corrugated iron hangars with metal frames also predominated during the initial stages of fighting but one most significant type turned out to be the wooden RFC 1915 Pattern design. Marvellous examples still proudly stand at Yatesbury of radio training fame and Tadcaster in Yorkshire. From this design developed the RFC 1916 Pattern and then its bigger 1917 equivalent. This latter type was also called the GS or General Service hangar but to most individuals became best known as the Belfast. Unlike the RFC 1915 Pattern, the Belfast had brick walls, and about its only wooden components were Belfast trusses (so giving the hangar its name) which supported its distinctive curved roof. Some Belfasts were built separately, while others could be joined together in groups of two or even three. A fair number still survive all over Britain, and a few extremely sensible local authorities have seen fit to place some of them under preservation orders.

Belfasts and Bessoneaux served as the main types of hangarage during the Great War period. An incredible array of types nevertheless existed, as may be seen by official listings of the time which curiously quote buildings not by their names but by their dimensions, such as 170x100 feet or 90x60 feet to give but two of innumerable examples. Among other types were notably storage sheds at AAP airfields. These structures were well named, for there is not much else one can say about them except that they consisted of sheds of varying sizes, though a popular measurement proved 200x60 feet. A World War One era airfield for AAP use usually came equipped with a large number of storage sheds. About the nearest equivalent to them since has been the Dutch Barn of World War Two, a tiny hangar with shed-like qualities seen at one or two FAA airfields.

One quickly acknowledged fact in World War One was that the operation of opening and closing hangars could be improved. Not only was considerable energy required, doors occupied a lot of space when open and in the process of opening and closing. Doors were thus made into sections, instead of an ordinary sliding door, and better doors castors provided. Eventually they became recognised in a totally different way as the RAF expression 'close the hangar doors', meaning stop talking about work, grew in popularity.

Greater worries than heavy or suspect doors soon arose, for not all that many hangars managed to survive after World War One, regardless of design. Bessoneaux were naturally only for use during hostilities, yet even Belfasts and other more permanent hangars succumbed in considerable numbers – if not as quickly. Airship sheds conversely disappeared with astonishing speed, while the handful left continued to grow in length: only their width remained the same as aircraft hangars. Joy-riders and other early post-war civil operators strangely preferred not to use hangars to any great extent, choosing to service their aircraft in barns during the winter months of the 1920s. The de Havilland Moth, despite helping to resuscitate general airfield activity in Britain after its appearance in 1925, had little cause to employ hangars either on account of its folding wings and could be feasibly held in a big garage.

So it was that the 1920s saw hardly any change in this area of Britain's airfields. Hangars still kept grouped together; aircraft, still structurally frail for their age, were stored in them at night. E.E. Fresson realised the advantages of hangarage at civil level as a wet aircraft would be slower, heavier, carry less passengers and earn less money. Aircraft Repair Sheds meanwhile further enhanced their cause after considerable use latterly in World War One. These buildings were really Belfasts in the main under another name: if a TDS airfield was equipped with seven hangars, one would be an ARS.

Only one major change occurred in hangar design during this period which proved a foretaste of things to come. The late 1920s saw the 250 feet long A hangar appear, like the Belfast in possessing brick walls but also having a steel frame and a ridged roof complete with strong asbestos sheeting. Several examples of the 30 or so built remain in place today.

Although the 1920s also produced the rare Hinaidi of 1927, it was the A which had a far more telling effect on British hangar design. From it developed the most elegant hangar type of all time – the C. Not surprisingly, this design first appeared in 1934, the year which saw the Expansion Period come into being. The C was basically a larger version of the A as it also had brick walls and steel frames. Two versions existed, the Gabled and the later Hipped, and it is extremely easy to distinguish between both types as the much more common Hipped had a flatter roof, whereas the Gabled C had a greatly ridged roof. The Hipped version further differed in having squared-off ends and being only 30 feet in height, compared with 35 feet for the Gabled type of C hangar.

Cs were built in various lengths as this depended on what type of airfield was being planned. If the airfield was intended for use by fighters, a small version with six or seven bays was available. Bomber stations would receive a larger version in one with ten or twelve bays. Regardless of size, C hangars were and still are most impressive buildings. Most of Britain's current military airfields have Cs; this explains why they have lasted so long. Cs have distinctive positioning too as they stand in the shape of an arc. Normally there is just a single row, but there are still cases of hangars standing side by side. Another planning idea was to leave space for more hangarage, though future developments meant these vacant areas were rarely occupied. Certain material shortages resulted in the C1, which lacked the C's squared-off ends and employed much more external toughened asbestos.

The C1 was significant because it helped to signal the beginning of far more austere hangars. Future designs would lack the C's elegant qualities, although this did not mean they would be any less effective in their intended purpose. Other changes slowly became evident as well, especially the dispersal of hangars around an airfield instead of concentrating them in one area. This would lessen the chance of a hangar being hit by bombs during an enemy attack. Hawkinge and Lympne learned the hard way during the Battle of Britain as the Luftwaffe blew their closely ranked hangars to smithereens. In fairness, one must say that the Kentish veterans would never have seen 1940 had it not been for their Belfasts, whose permanent construction saved both sites from closure after World War One.

Two other changes in general hangar design also became noticeable, for metal was now being extensively used for hangar construction. Metal sheeting saved time, money and weight. But perhaps the greatest change of all arose in how aircraft hangars were used. Before World War Two, aircraft had been stored in them at night: now aircraft would only enter these buildings for major servicing. Quite apart from the fact that aircraft were now made of much stronger materials, the threat of enemy bombs wiping out a crowd of aircraft huddled together in a hangar settled matters. We must briefly return to poor old Lympne to demonstrate this point, where ten aircraft of the Cinque Ports Flying Club were destroyed in August 1940 while in enforced storage.

Apart from the C1, an early austerity type was the D hangar of 1936. The later J and K hangars of 1939 looked quite like it in being the same size as a twelve bay C of 300 feet but with curved roofs. Bearing a door clearance of 150 feet, J and K steel framed types were identical from the outside and only differed internally. Even these types were later overwhelmed in vast numbers by the three most common hangars of the

World War Two period: the Bellman, T series and Blister.

The Bellman hangar was actually a pre-war design dating from 1937 and named after N.S. Bellman, formerly of the Air Ministry. The 400 or so which appeared were built by Head and Wrightson Co Ltd at Thornaby-on-Tees, an example standing at the nearby noted two World Wars veteran of Thornaby. Bearing a usual length of 175 feet and a clear opening of 87 feet 9 inches, the Bellman could differ in height. Still extant at many a British airfield, Bellmans can be distinguished by a lack of any panelling above their doors before the roof commences. Another fairly obvious feature is how short single-spar door runners project from the top of each door.

While Bellmans existed in considerable numbers, the T series outnumbered them by more than two to one. T stood for transportable, the members of this series being mass-produced by the Tees-side Bridge & Engineering Company and its subsidiaries. The first numerical variant in the T1 was made of sheet steel with measurements of 175 feet by 97 feet 2 inches, but most common T type became the T2 with its greater usual length of 239 feet 7 inches, though smaller sizes could be provided. The T2 was built in two versions, the Old Type T2 of 1940 (a year earlier than the T1) and the much more common T2 (Home) of 1942. It is pointless describing their various dimensions in full as not only would it be downright boring but defeat the pledged purpose of this book to cut down as far as possible on unnecessary facts and figures. Great simplification can be achieved by saying that the T2 (Home) was constructed with cheaper sheeting and positioned more randomly around an airfield instead of congregating in the general technical site like the Old Type T2.

The T2 and other T variants were a revelation in hangar design. Of prefabricated construction, they were easy to build and could be erected relatively quickly. Unlike Bellmans, T series hangars did possess panelling between the doors and roof. Not so apparent was the vast difference in weight between the austerity period Ts and their Expansion Period predecessors. A T2, for example, weighed less than 30 per cent the weight of a C. Other T variants also existed, the T3 being a vastly reduced T2 with measurements of 75 by 66 feet. Extremely rare was the ½T2, a special version for airfields in the Western Isles such as Benbecula. It was designed to offer less resistance to the fierce winds in these remote areas.

Although the T series of hangars became common sights on our airfields, even they were swamped by Blisters. Over 3,000 of these remarkable buildings were constructed to make the Blister Britain's most numerous aircraft hangar of all time. This aptly-named type was developed from the pre-war Lamella of German origins and first seen in Britain at Heston during 1930. A natural covering of earth and grass to provide additional camouflage proved even more useful than expected later on in World War Two as enemy incendiary bombs harmlessly burned themselves out on the roofs of Lamellas.

The Lamella developed with success to become known in RAF service as the E or L, the former type built of reinforced concrete and the latter of steel. Blisters as most people came to recognise them in fact only appeared in strength from 1941 and were built in many versions. They could be split into the Dorman and far more common Miskin designs, which could be divided again into an amazing array of sub-variants: Over Blisters, Enlarged Over Blisters, Double Blisters, Super Blisters and Double Over or Enlarged Over Blisters. Hangar widths could be either 45, 65, 69 or 90 feet. Most Blisters were built of steel but a few earlier ones did have some wooden components. (It is worth mentioning at this point that the Blister's German counterpart was built wholly of wood, an example of which still stands at Jersey). Despite all their differences, Blisters could still point to two similarities among them. Each was intended to house one aircraft, while there were no end doors as such; canvas curtains or even bricks could be provided if necessary.

Unlike the larger Lamella/L/E types, buildings which tended to stand at storage airfields, the Blister could be seen almost anywhere. Whether the airfield was a fighter station, training base or whatever, some Blisters could usually be spotted dotted around its perimeter. Only bomber airfields remained devoid of them as Blisters lacked enough height for bigger types of aircraft.

Bellman, T series and Blister hangars have to be set apart from the rest not only because of their vast numerical superiority during World War Two but as they tended to stand at certain types of airfield. Research will show you how Bellmans existed at early austerity period sites, T1s generally installed at fighter stations or training sites originally intended to hold fighters, and T2s at bomber airfields. Apart from major fighter or training airfields, Blisters stood in numbers at RLGs and satellites where they proved a great advance on before. In the early part of World War Two, aircraft never stayed at these sites at night, being flown back to the parent station. Machines were later held down with pickets before Blisters appeared on the scene.

As for the airfields themselves, little similarity occurred among them when it came to hangarage. It is no exaggeration to say that a thousand and one variations existed. For a start, there were the Expansion and austerity period types as already described. Hangars – not forgetting all airfield buildings – were naturally not always built at the same time. Fighter and bomber sites could have almost anything, MU stations a wide variety of Ds, Js, Ks and Lamella/L/E types, while the south of England ALGs were normally equipped with a few Blisters. ELGs, on the other hand, were not meant to have hangars.

One needs hardly say that there were many exceptions to the rule. If veteran airfields remained fit and well, they still had some equally old hangars. Other cases existed where hangars built for certain types of aircraft then received totally different machines. One particular complaint was that many lesser sites did not possess enough hangarage, this being true to an extent.

However, a pattern of sorts did become evident at bomber airfields in World War Two. Provided the original hangarage remains in its entirety, this ready reckoner will give you a good idea of the role these airfields once performed when you visit:

Hangarage	*Type of Bomber Airfield*
One J and two or four T2s	Early austerity period RAF heavy bomber station
Four or six T2s and one B1	RAF heavy bomber Base or controlling maintenance station. (Extra T2s could also on occasion signify an airborne forces airfield, with the T2s being used to store gliders). Look out in either case for three T2s in a row.
Three or four T2s	Early USAAF heavy bomber station. Also RAF heavy bomber station, but this fairly rare
Two T2s and one B1	Standard RAF heavy bomber station
Two T2s	Standard USAAF heavy bomber station. Very common.
One T2 and one B1	RAF bomber OTU satellite station

We must not forget how World War Two brought with it many other hangar types to British airfields. All were not so common as Bellman, T series and Blister hangars, but some are worthy of note. One example was the B1 of 1942, fairly common on bomber airfields and used for major overhaul work. It had two distinctive features in a steep roof and supports to the door runners. A development was the B2, similar to the B1 but more than six feet shorter in height. Two more types which have to be mentioned are the A1 with its steep roof finishing fairly close to the ground and the Callender-Hamilton of 1940, notable for its greatly projecting door runners. This second hangar had been built by the Callenders Cable and Construction Company since 1937, the same year as the Bellman appeared, seven Callenders (a bigger version) being erected in Britain by July of that year.

The Royal Navy had its own hangar types during World War Two, proving quite different from those in RAF service. If the Navy took over control of a former RAF station, it had to use the existing hangarage, yet three types were designed specially for naval use. The Tees-side Bridge & Engineering Company of T2 fame had also found time during 1940 to create the S Shed, a diminutive building either 50 or 70 feet long and 60 feet wide. In 1942 came along the Mainhill or Mains, two or fourteen feet longer than the second S Shed version but with a sloping rear and sidewalls for better wind resistance and a curved instead of angled roof. A standard FAA airfield would be equipped with a large number of S Sheds or Mainhills. Such hangars could afford to be on the small side as naval aircraft had folding wings in the main, a design feature intended for aircraft carrier use when machines had to be kept close together on deck or lowered underneath. Much bigger but less frequent was the Pentad, a hangar the same length as a Callender-Hamilton at 185 feet for servicing aircraft. Sloping sidewalls were its distinctive feature as was the case with the Mainhill, for FAA airfields were notoriously windy. Royal Navy hangars have themselves enjoyed notoriety in a quite different way, for World War Two maps only list their dimensions in a style reminiscent of World War One, making things difficult for the general airfield researcher.

For all Britain's incredible variety of hangars, whether RAF, FAA or USAAF, camouflage was never considered too much of a problem. Hangars were simply painted in black bitumen after 1942 instead of draping them in cumbersome nets prior to World War Two. In between these periods, policy was to make hangars look like houses with painted dummy doors and windows, a ploy the Germans also used at their captured French airfields. In 1941 came the Robin, a design which resembled a house more than any other type of hangar. MU airfields and SLGs made tremendous use of Robins, which measured 62 feet 6 inches long by 44 feet wide and only had doors at one end. The Super Robin was a larger version; the same size as a small Mainhill, it had six hangar bays instead of the Robin's five. Some people have said how Mainhills and Robins bear certain similarities: anyone with a trained eye must surely be astounded at such statements, and the easy way to distinguish between them is that a Robin or Super Robin has a fairly steeply pitched roof as opposed to the Mainhill's curved upper covering.

The Robin and Super Robin were among the last of World War Two's aircraft hangar designs. After 1945, both they and many other different types gradually faded from the scene in their intended role. The military returned to placing heavy reliance upon its magnificent Cs, so any airfield which possessed some examples was virtually guaranteed a long life.

Extremely few new types of hangar have arrived since then. The Gaydon (named after the first of Britain's V-bomber airfields) exists at a few military bases, though it is nothing more than a J with minor modifications here and there. Rarer still are cantilever hangars, huge buildings designed for equally big aircraft. Construction costs have undoubtedly severely limited their numbers. Fitting aircraft into hangars has never been a great problem. It was only the ungainly but unfortunate Short Stirling which suffered greatly from being unable to squeeze inside most hangar types during World War Two. The heavy bomber was not to blame as the Air Ministry had stupidly ordered its wing-span to be no more than 100 feet. As a result, the Mark I version had a span of 99 feet 1 inch, meaning that it could not go inside hangars such as the Bellman or T1. Government orders for it to conform to hangar widths of the time were more than just senseless. The Stirling was a big aircraft, and its forcibly reduced wing-span resulted in a poorer ceiling and altitude performance than either the Handley Page Halifax or Avro Lancaster.

Apart from the veritable myriad of civil hangars, still not following any set pattern after all these years, it has been left to the 1980s to produce a new kind of aircraft hangar in quantity. Hardened Aircraft Shelters have become common sights at military airfields today. Honington was the first airfield to use them at the turn of 1981/82. These are self-supporting buildings, able to withstand a direct hit from a 1,000 pound bomb. Each major military airfield in this country now has several HASs or hard shelters as they have become popularly known.

Hard shelters will surely last for a long time, but nobody in the past envisaged how Britain's older types of hangarage would survive just as well. Many have enjoyed remarkable careers for supposedly temporary buildings. Bombing destroyed few hangars during World War Two, though some were wrecked so badly they had to be pulled down. Hangar collapses have proved to be rarer still. The beauty of T series and certain other types is that their metal sheeting can be easily reclad, therefore further prolonging their lives. Blisters were often moved between airfields in World War Two, and it has become not unknown since then for larger hangar types to have enjoyed or suffered – opinions vary on this point – the same process, showing the advantages of wartime prefabricated construction. Some of the distances involved have defied belief: the record so far as can be ascertained seems to have been several Bellmans at former training airfield Shellingford in Oxfordshire which moved to the African state of Chad.

If not in use for holding aircraft, hangars are superb places to accommodate both industrial and storage concerns. The 'grain mountains' occasionally mentioned from time to time are largely held in various hangars all over Britain. The idea of this kind of storage has strange links back to World War Two, when many RAF hangars were heavily stocked with the *Window* radar jamming device. The authorities dithered for long enough over when was the right time to use these metallic strips. Only in the summer of 1943 was *Window* first used operationally for a big night raid on Hamburg. RAF losses were extremely light, thanks to *Window,* and soon hangars were able to find room for other items than these devastatingly effective devices.

An even more unusual wartime auxiliary use for hangars which has no links with today was accommodation for service personnel. This applied to airborne forces airfields in the months preceding D-Day as vast numbers of paratroops waited at these places before dropping into France. Normal sleeping quarters were already stretched for space, so there was nowhere else but the airfield's hangars which could be pressed into service. Hangars have also served as temporary mortuaries for the permanently instead of temporarily sleeping both in peace and war, though happily such has been the safety record of Britain's airfields this task has only arisen on a handful of occasions.

Such general hustle and bustle no longer reigns at our disused airfields today. Personnel, let alone those sleeping paratroops, have gone; so too have the aircraft – and colossal numbers of hangars. Far too many British airfields have been either totally or partially deprived of their prominent trademarks. There are more hangar types we have not yet mentioned because of their infrequency: the side-opening F of 1930s vintage and the Butler steel-framed canvas type used by the Americans, notably at ALGs, are just two of them. Most of these designs have also disappeared to leave great voids where they and others of their kind once stood. Sometimes the concrete floors of hangars remain today, maybe even their metal door runners.

A particularly sad fact about hangars now is how the Blister has left British airfields in droves. Incredibly few remain in their original positions. Farmers have seen to that by either needlessly destroying them or carting Blisters off to totally incongruous places for use as farm storage buildings. Those few which have held their ground and staggered through the fire are employed for more suitable forms of storage, while a handful of others have become skeletal ruins. The more one considers the Blister, it was surely World War Two's answer to the Bessoneau.

Although other hangar types have become more fortunate than the Blister, many of them have also been ruthlessly cleared, when conservation should have happened instead. In both World Wars, the average airfield was equipped with a large complement of hangars, but today the story is quite different. Our smaller civil sites look fairly empty nowadays as they try to get by with just one or two buildings. Although the hard shelter at military airfields has helped to increase the current total of hangarage in this country, the ratio of hangars to active British airfields is still far down in comparison with times past.

We shall never see a few types of highly unusual hangars. 'Underground' or semi-submerged buildings were considered in World War One but proved both expensive and extremely difficult to build. No building of this type was actually built, though a start was made at Manston and faint traces of foundations can still be seen. Even thatched hangars were tried out in the 1930s.

The most successful British aircraft hangar of all time? It has to be the C, surely the most durable and elegant design ever built. Comparing it with other major British types, the C has proportionately suffered far fewer losses among its numbers. It is worth noting how most former military airfields now in Army hands are equipped with some Cs. They are certainly prized facilities. Why else would one or two Expansion Period airfields like Middle Wallop wait years, even decades before their bomb-damaged C hangars were rebuilt?

Extremely few individual hangars have managed to achieve great fame. Only a British airfield could have a hangar

An aerial view of Bradwell Bay, a fairly typical World War Two airfield, taken on May 1 1946 after it had closed to flying. Easily visible are runway extensions plus 'frying pan' and 'spectacle' hardstandings. Twelve Blister hangars lie off from the northern and eastern perimeter; curved objects near some of them are dispersal pens for aircraft bomb blast protection. The lines parallel to the main runway mark Bradwell's FIDO fog-clearing aid: three round fuel storage tanks can just be spotted on the far left. Off the southern perimeter track, directly south of the third 'spectacle' going east, is the control tower (now a house). Further south and east are numerous support buildings. Today a nuclear power station and farmers use this famous intruder base. *(RAF Museum Crown Copyright)*

(above) Pierced Steel Planking or PSP, the best type of metal runway, can still be found here and there.
(below) How it used to be – now. An imitative old style control building, perched alongside a hangar, at Sibson. The C system of indicating where a pilot should report when requested dates back to 1935.

(above) The first major control/watch tower design was the 'Fort'. Two C hangars stand to the rear of this one at Bircham Newton. *(below)* By World War Two control towers had become more angular. A typical 343/43 type with runway board at Odiham in 1948. *(RAF Museum)*

(above) Three Bessoneau hangars at Throwley during World War One. A temporary building but a great success. *(IWM)*
(below) The other hangar mainstay of that era: a superbly preserved Belfast at former Aircraft Acceptance Park Bracebridge Heath near Lincoln. Bessoneaux used to be here too.

World War Two's equivalents to the Belfast and Bessoneau: a T2 *(above)* at Pocklington and a Blister at Panshanger *(below)*.

Two more familiar hangar types of the 1939-45 era were the Mainhill or Mains and Robin.
(above) Side and rear views of two Mainhills standing on the edge of ex-FAA Lancashire station Burscough.
(below) A Robin concealed among trees at the remote Cumbrian SLG of Hornby Hall, now used for farming purposes.

(above) The Expansion Period gave our airfields magnificent support facilities during the 1930s. Brick buildings such as this one at Martlesham Heath have proved easily durable, if not always for flying use.
(below) World War Two inevitably created more austere buildings: two Nissen huts at Ingham/Cammeringham in Lincolnshire.

(above) Fairly intact dispersed airfield sites can still be found. This old D/F station for Prestwick stands over three miles away, perfectly sited as the rising ground behind would have given excellent protection against aircraft noise and bomb blast damage.
(below) Yes, it's that concrete igloo again: Langham's Dome Trainer.
(bottom) A Pickett-Hamilton retractable pillbox on show at Tangmere.

(above) Other airfield support buildings are just as distinctive – even more so when further modified for current use. Delete the windows, insert a door, make the roof's right side match its opposite number and you have a parachute store as it used to be at Matching in Essex.
(below) Airfield names often say it all. This Suffolk USAAF heavy bomber station has already lain disused for several decades but its phenomenal socio-economic relevance is plain for all to see.

(far top left) A Drem Mark II runway light fitting at a disused airfield. For obvious reasons, its location must remain secret.
(near top left) A Chance Light, an important safety aid of World War Two, helps illuminate a runway. *(IWM)*
(centre left) Approach lights off the southern end of Waddington's main runway.
(bottom left) Heat and flames distort the shape of a Lancaster taking off from Graveley with the help of fog-clearing device FIDO. *(IWM)*
(above) One of World War Two's most remarkable airfield photographs. All hell breaks out at a USAAF 8th Air Force heavy bomber station (unknown and virtually impossible to identify) as pyrotechnics help RAF Lancasters in the darkness attempt to land after being unable to land at their own base while returning from Germany. *(IWM)*

(above) A British 'airfield' – for enemy use! Trelow Downs, St Eval's decoy Q site, intended to lure Luftwaffe aircraft away from its real neighbour. This empty countryside served its purpose.
(below) More unsung heroes. British workmen at Boxted on December 28 1942, just a few of the vast army of airfield builders. *(IWM)*

famous for being non-existent, a C at Tern Hill destroyed by the Luftwaffe in 1940. But then every hangar, regardless of its type of ownership, is special. Both in military and civil minds at least, there is no such thing as 'just a hangar . . .'

Hundreds And Thousands

One of the most fascinating features one can see while wandering around a disused airfield is the extreme variation among its support buildings. They truly are as the title suggests – and were much sweeter than often portrayed. It is not difficult to imagine what workshops, domestic huts, training buildings and the rest must have been like in their heyday as they thronged with activity. As airfields in Britain developed, so did their support facilities in quantity and quality, at least on the military side of aviation.

Early British military airfields not surprisingly heavily relied upon the good old tent. Wooden huts gradually appeared during World War One to help rescue the ordinary airman from soggy canvas but neither huts not tents gained any major superiority over each other. Bigger types of airfield like TDSs employed wooden support buildings such as Armstrong huts for the accommodation of large numbers of trainees, while the many landing grounds in Britain had hardly any buildings, if at all. The general lack of concrete meant daily airfield life was none too comfortable for the average airman. Mud remained a big problem throughout the winter months. Only officers were well served in their requisitioned large country houses or hotels. But ask anyone who served at a British airfield during World War One which was more preferable – a safe, fair-to-middling green(ish) field at home or the highly dangerous, wretched, disease-prone hell-hole that was the average Western Front airfield – and there was no contest as to which site would win.

The sheer rudimentary aspect of military aviation at this time showed itself in the relative simplicity both in design and layout of airfield support buildings. Few facilities were needed for defensive purposes because of the ineffectual range and offensive capabilities offered by enemy aircraft. This allowed buildings to be either placed together in one corner or along one side of a site. Despite great technological advances during the conflict, World War One also resulted in few buildings arising for instructional or other unusual purposes as aircraft still had considerable limitations. Specialised buildings were limited to items such as gas plants at airship stations.

The nationwide British airfield closure programme after World War One brought widespread clearance of support buildings. As tents and wooden huts could be removed with relative ease, Great War era airfields soon disappeared from trace. Hardly any buildings which belonged to this period survive today. The small and most fortunate number of airfields to remain active were improved as previous experience had shown how far more permanent buildings were needed. Not only more domestic buildings either, for aircraft and airmen badly required facilities for technical and instructional duties. Building work was still exceptionally limited during the 1920s and early 1930s in line with official policy.

If the airfield support building could not win at this time in the race for numerical supremacy, another kind of support facility could – vehicles. Cars and especially lorries could help with daily airfield operations such as local communications, rapid transit of airmen and arming. After a period of using anything to hand, World War One saw military airfields start using the Crossley general purpose tender. Just as familiar from 1917 became the Hucks Starter, named after famous aerobatic pilot of pre-war days B.C. Hucks, for starting aircraft engines. A shaft was linked to an engine on a Crossley (or, in early days, a Model T Ford) and interlocked with a propeller boss, saving airmen the strenuous – not to mention risky – job of swinging the propeller.

Mechanical Transport – as airfield vehicles were quickly collectively titled – helped quietly but efficiently at home airfields for the remainder of World War One. But then the 'Geddes Axe' declared in February 1922 that Crossleys, Hucks Starters and others of their kind were actually unnecessary. Hardly believable, but true to form the politicians took note of this suggestion. It would take another war before MT vehicles would once again show their paces. The only real development between both world conflicts strangely occurred at civil level just two months after the 'Geddes Axe' as Croydon adopted the bowser system of petrol handling. Tankers could pump fuel into aircraft far faster than airmen armed with cans. Yet not until the mid-1930s did the famous Zwicky bowser enter RAF service.

As with vehicles, not much happened to airfield support facilities in general for well over a decade. Immense changes to buildings came with the Expansion Period of 1934. Military airfields built between then and the outbreak of World War Two were equipped with most attractive support buildings. All were intended to tone in well with the surrounding countryside, less appealing structures such as boiler houses being heavily camouflaged. No matter where an airman stood in rank, his place of work was bathed in near-luxury. Built of brick, Expansion Period buildings bore a Georgian appearance, distinguished in many cases by their flat roofs. Lesser ranks had as accommodation H-shaped barracks. Some airfields were even given fountains! As the technical, domestic and communal sites were officially rated as permanent, it is no wonder that most 1930s era military airfields were retained for future use after 1945.

Despite these colossal advances, airfield buildings still grouped close together like hangars. World War Two made dispersal an absolute must to counter the effects of enemy air attacks. The number of support buildings also vastly increased: most standard airfields now possessed around 500 each, many a considerable distance from the landing area. An airfield could now have ten or more dispersed sites to its name.

One particular structure would soon become familiar to military personnel and the civilian population alike. Austerity had replaced expansion, a fact plainly evident in this building. The Nissen hut was surely one of the symbols of World War Two, despite having already appeared in strength during the Great War. A cruel twist of fate was how its namesake had died before his invention's greatest hour in 1930. Romney and Iris huts looked similar but mainly used for storage purposes. Whereas the Nissen varied in width from 16 to 30 feet, Romney and Iris huts were wider at 35 feet.

These prefabricated buildings swamped many a British airfield during World War Two. But plenty of other types existed as well: Handcrafts, Maycretes and Secos to name just three of the better known makes. Temporary though they may have been, all these products were an enormous improvement on tents and far more functional. The main complaints by servicemen were that Nissens and other kinds of hut became too cold in winter, too hot in summer. Dampness could be a problem if the building had not been properly constructed, but the health of service personnel at airfields always remained excellent on the whole. No serious bouts of illness – and certainly no epidemics – ever occurred, while the surprisingly varied types of leisure facilities from football pitches to squash courts ensured that everyone kept both happy and in trim. Although metal and concrete buildings existed everywhere, the wooden hut did not disappear entirely, still being noticeable at many airfields.

Nissens and other types of huts now greatly figured in how accommodation levels always had to be taken into consideration. In contrast to World War One when airfields had personnel attendances ranging from one or a handful at landing grounds to several hundred at bigger sites, World War Two stations could have less than 100 personnel present or 2,000 to 3,000. Many civilians could also be seen at military airfields in another change from earlier days, usually for aircraft maintenance and repair duties by factories, and numbers of the Women's Auxiliary Air Force further bolstered station personnel strength. So too did the youngsters who formed the Air Training Corps, spending their holidays by helping out at RAF airfields and receiving a quick flip in an aircraft as a reward if they were lucky enough. The irregularly placed ranks of huts continued to expand into all parts of the British countryside no matter who was in residence.

To further explain the types and functions of World War Two airfield support buildings in a simple manner, we must divide them into areas. This is only natural, for the military themselves put certain kinds of facilities into numbered categories. One of the most crucial airfield areas was the technical site. Kept well away from domestic sites, it was the scene of much activity. Workshops and other associated buildings carried out maintenance and repair work on aircraft and their components; at Expansion Period airfields, workshops were usually placed along the sides of C hangars. Other common features at standard airfields included engine test bays, photographic facilities, briefing rooms and squadron or Flight offices. Various stores existed at technical sites, these ranging from aircraft equipment huts to armouries, parachutes to pyrotechnics. The last-named were always kept close to the control tower along with the fire tender shed for rapid responses to any forms of distress.

Moving away from the technical site, the airman would encounter the domestic and communal sites. Here could be seen various messes according to rank, sleeping and NAAFI quarters plus vast dining rooms. One wartime quirk was that not everyone could have their meal at the same time; shifts were needed, hardly surprising when you consider that for every 200 aircrew at a heavy bomber station, 1,000 groundcrew were available. There were also usually sick quarters buildings, and maybe such items as pigeon lofts or a gymnasium. Spaces were eliminated and areas calculated, again according to rank. It was always the sign of a bad day or night at RAF or USAAF heavy bomber bases in particular with the lines of vacant beds when crews failed to return from operations. Members of the WAAF originally had their own communal buildings, but this policy did not continue after 1942. Sewage disposal was most necessary, being conducted on sleeping sites, and many supporting services stayed close at hand: these could include barbers, shoemakers and tailors. Some painted lettering denoting these and other activities can still be occasionally seen above the entrances of old airfield buildings.

Airfield personnel might have been well catered for in World War Two, far better than anyone really appreciated at the time, but inconvenience became unavoidable. It was something which just had to be accepted. The first few months of an airfield's life proved particularly chaotic as its builders were too busy trying to get the place into flying condition without bothering greatly about its support buildings. Construction work therefore could go on for some more months. Once finished, many moans arose regarding the distance between the sleeping quarters and ablutions. The latter were never near enough for some people!

An important part of many airfields was the instructional site. Buildings differed with the nature of the training conducted but, to take a few examples, there could be included Bombing Teachers, Link Trainers for pilots which first appeared in Britain during 1937, or gunnery, navigation and radio trainers. A whole range of buildings arose to cope with synthetic training, supported by lecture buildings for mass training of each course. One special structure which must be noted was the weird and almost spooky Dome Teacher or Trainer, a hemispherical building used for either gunnery or navigation training, for which simulated star groups could be cast upon the roof. Examples of these still futuristic-looking objects remain up and down Britain today; most have survived, and the example at Langham must count as one of the most individually photographed airfield buildings of all time. These striking oddities are so fascinatingly different that this is probably why Dome Trainers have remained, while more conventional buildings have not.

To keep instructional and other duties at a reasonably safe level, airfield defences were required. Little thought had been given to protection in World War One, though as it turned out extremely few British airfields had to endure attacks in that conflict. World War Two was a completely different matter but many sites still remained woefully defended at the beginning of fighting. Army units detailed to major bases were poorly armed and co-ordinated to deal with possible invasion attempts. Lesser airfields often only had stretches of barbed wire early on to keep out the enemy, while their bigger brethren would have some more of the 'devil's rope' and the odd machine-gun. A proposal to use tanks, the weapons which along with airfields had helped Britain win World War One, was not practical in a defensive sense, nor was a scheme in September 1940 to enlist sportsmen volunteers, and artillery was more often than not unwieldy and not over-useful. At least this last area of airfield defence enjoyed better fortunes when the superb Swedish-designed Bofors AA gun appeared. But the main fear among airfield personnel was the thought of German parachutists capturing bases, a ploy which had already achieved success in other parts of Europe.

Pillboxes were the answer, small concrete defence points built around airfield perimeters with wide angles of fire. The six-sided pillbox began to appear in strength by 1941 to establish itself as Britain's standard type. Two less familiar examples became the Oakington, devised at the noted East Anglian bomber airfield and bearing a mushroom-shaped head, plus the Seagull Trench, a flat installation shaped like a W. Other crude 'home-built' pillboxes of no recognised design were built all over Britain as well.

Developments came thick and fast in airfield defence during World War Two. The Battle HQ controlled the defensive positions of an airfield. It was built in two types for operational and training sites, the former being bigger. As these buildings mainly lie underground, a torch is needed if you want to look at one today.

Replacement of Army units by formation of the RAF Regiment in early 1942 brought more co-ordination to airfield defence. This new force's arrival virtually coincided with the abandonment of another pillbox type. The Pickett-Hamilton had seemed an ingenious device on its introduction. It was a retractable pillbox, situated not on an airfield's perimeter but its landing area, which could be operated either hydraulically, by compressed air or balanced weights. But Pickett-Hamiltons proved disastrous in use: apart from suffering frequent flooding and faults with their retraction systems, they were too isolated and unmanageable for defence purposes. Dropped after over 300 had been built, at a normal rate of three per airfield, most Pickett-Hamiltons have been left in place. They are far from easy to spot, only marked by a concrete circle on the ground. Utter failures they might have turned out to be, but these pillboxes have in recent years acquired a cult following among airfield research groups, who prefer to lift them out of the ground if possible for display elsewhere. As has been said about hangars in the previous chapter, though, many British airfield supporters regard these acts more as vandalism than conservation.

Our military airfields fortunately had more successful structures to deal with various jobs. This did not mean they failed to match the Pickett-Hamilton's distinctive qualities. An airman entering an airfield first had to go past the guard house by the station gate. Once through, he would see air raid shelters and MT sheds, both essential airfield facilities. Bedford lorries, Zwickys and bomb trolleys became familiar in World War Two, as did the Queen Mary transporter, the one vehicle airfields did not want to see as this long lorry was meant for taking away wrecked aircraft. The Jeep inevitably made its presence felt too as the Americans brought in their own vehicles, equipment and stores from 1942. And then there were bicycles: thousands upon thousands of them arrived at airfields during World War Two to help save petrol. Six British companies had delivered 170,000 bicycles by 1942 – and still it was not enough.

MT vehicles carried considerable influence at airfields as special roads had to be constructed to enable them to safely carry about bombs and fuel. Both of these dangerous materials were naturally stored well away from other airfield sites. Bomb dumps consisted of underground buildings covered with grass mounds, and woodland often helped to give further concealment. Underground tanks provided high octane aviation fuel for aircraft, plus much smaller quantities of petrol for MT vehicles. Somewhat more prominent were huts sited at dispersals to shelter groundcrews involved with tasks such as rearming and refuelling, though their detached positions have made them easier to remove than packs of other airfield buildings.

One of the terrific advantages airfields had over other wartime installations was their ability to support themselves. While villages did not have their own power and water supplies, airfields had both. The water tower was one of the most important items in particular. Fambridge had one, and flat areas such as East Anglia and Lincolnshire also needed a high structure to acquire enough water pressure before any could be released. The type familiar to most people was known as the Braithwaite, a box-shaped tank built in sections. Examples of this type can still be seen from afar, for some continue to be used for their original purpose. Another notable type of water tower was one built of brick, erected at Expansion Period airfields, and like other support buildings of this era meant to look good amid its surroundings.

Not all British airfields were so lavishly equipped. RLGs only received the bare minimum of buildings as far fewer personnel were needed to man them. SLGs and the three huge ELGs had even fewer buildings – for quite different reasons. The supplementary storage sites did not want to draw attention to themselves, so SLG buildings were both few and as 'civilianised' as possible. ELGs could hardly be described as insignificant, but these big sites were only designed to receive distressed aircraft. Buildings were therefore limited to hold the various emergency services. Worst off of types were ALGs as the tent still ruled supreme. This was a deliberate measure because ALGs were not used all year round, only during the summer months. Hardly any traces of these simple airfields have survived as a result.

Airfield structures which have survived far better than ALGs came in the most amazing shapes and sizes during World War Two. Firing butts positioned near the perimeter track for gunnery practice were fairly common. These curious structures resembled brick walls, yet were quite important. Despite their apparent simplicity, the firing butts of World War Two were much more advanced than those of World War One: they only consisted of mounds of earth. Deceptively important too were D/F stations for aircraft navigation purposes throughout Britain. They could be identified by their tall radio masts and fencing which protected each site.

Not so near an airfield were two other buildings, quite like one another but used for different purposes. Fighter sector airfields, reorganised during 1940 and 1941, were equipped with grim operations blocks, most of which remain today. Such buildings later proved particularly invaluable for controlling RAF night fighter operations against Luftwaffe bombers. Possessing no windows, these installations differed considerably from their earlier brethren as the original type of operations block had stood on the surface in the main airfield site. Too open to attack, the Battle of Britain dramatically showed up its faults. Luftwaffe aircraft scored direct hits on the operations blocks at Biggin Hill and Detling to cause great death and destruction.

The new breed of operations block learned from these past mistakes and became far more detached from other airfield buildings. Reinforced concrete offered much better resistance against bomb hits, while the building now lay partly underground. Further equipped with air supply and gas filtration systems, even an emergency reserve building stood nearby.

Much like the newer breed of operations block was the decontamination centre. This building had also arisen before World War Two as gas was viewed as a deadly threat. Again like the operations block, the decontamination centre had tall chimneys which could weed out fresh air. Showers and fresh clothing were available too, though the importance of these buildings gradually decreased as the Luftwaffe bombing threat did likewise. Later austerity period airfields were built without them.

Ironically, had the Germans used their chemical weapons against Britain, decontamination centres would have proved useless. Not even the gas mask every Briton dutifully carried during World War Two would have been of the slightest value against Tabun and other highly advanced lethal substances. It is a complicated story why they were never used, but basically Hitler feared massive Allied retaliation. Germany was however so far ahead of any other country (with the exception of Japan) when it came to this kind of warfare. The quality and quantity were there but, when Hitler actively considered using his special bombs, Germany's massive fighter programme had largely edged out bombers in the Luftwaffe. Had more bombers existed at the right time, perhaps not even our airfields could have saved Britain, save destroying every Luftwaffe machine in sight.

Once Germany's threat had been totally overcome, all British airfield support buildings could afford to slightly drop their guard. Expansion Period buildings soon returned to the fore, quickly showing a marked numerical superiority to their austerity successors. Airfields became brighter again when now largely freed of drab camouflage. Disguising of buildings had begun in World War One, although painters were sometimes too enthusiastic with their paint. Some buildings bore so much dazzle paint they looked like the Q-ships used in that conflict to lure unsuspecting U-boats, presenting even more of a target.

If camouflage had been the order of the day in World War Two, so too was improvisation. Requisitioning of houses and hotels still proved relatively common. Marquees – 'posh tents' – were occasionally seen. Almost anything would do. Scotland displayed its usual ingenuity in two extreme cases. One was at the famous Fife FAA base of Donibristle in 1941, where the forward cabin of *Helena* (one of those magnificent Handley Page HP42 biplane airliners) was transformed into a squadron office. An ATA unit at Prestwick used even more bizarre materials for offices – an old bus and an aircraft packing case.

Expansion era buildings firmly put an end to such makeshift contemporaries after World War Two. British airfields were in effect witnessing a regression in support facilities rather than an advance. Not that anyone was complaining, considering the tremendous luxury Expansion Period facilities offered. Look at active military airfields today and 1930s style buildings are usually still in abundance.

Nevertheless, times keep changing. Modernisation has slowly crept in since the end of World War Two, bringing with it a neat trimming of airfield buildings. Modern support buildings have appeared in the 1980s. Jet aircraft are so advanced these days that they have certain needs which the old type of airfield support building simply cannot cope with. Even such mundane items as fuel systems have had to be changed. Jets only needed low grade fuel right from their early days and, with the necessity of speed today, fast-feeder systems have had to be introduced in order to tank up a machine as quickly as possible and let it take off.

Despite these advances, the ideas of more recent years still owe much to wartime developments. Concrete blast pens were fashionable at a small number of airfields for a while post-war, replacing the W-shaped dispersal pens of World War Two. Designed to save fighters from bomb blast damage, the first pens consisted of little more than sandbags or wood, good but slow to construct, until the standard design of grass-covered earth appeared. Two fighters could be held in each pen with relative safety; a limited number of pens were also built for bombers up to the size of a Blenheim. Some dispersal pens remain around the perimeters of disused airfields, although most have become worn through general decay.

More offensive forms of airfield defence similarly owe something to World War Two. Barbed wire still encloses many a military airfield, the only real difference being that much of it is now in the 'razor' form which is considered more effective these days. Far more exotic are fearsome devices like the Falklands combat-proven Rapier AA missile system, deadly against low-flying aircraft. This mode of thinking can again be traced back to World War Two and the limited use made of the Parachute and Cable installation. The device fired projectiles from the ground into the air, releasing parachutes which were attached to cables. With luck, a low-flying enemy aircraft would plough straight into them. As with the Pickett-Hamilton pillbox, theory was one thing, practice another, and hardly any success greeted the 40 plus cumbersome devices installed (mostly at fighter airfields) in the early war years, apart from one spectacular day at Kenley during the Battle of Britain. Germany used a broadly similar airfield defence weapon to PAC known as RSK 1000 later on in World War Two.

While on the subject of missiles and airfield support facilities, one cannot forget that more recent saga involving the controversial Thor nuclear missile. The story of Britain's land-based 'bomb' has already been told, but its special buildings are worthy of mention. When the Air Ministry had to quickly requisition parts of formerly disused airfields in the late 1950s, decaying austerity period huts were given a new lease of life. However, they were easily eclipsed by vast concrete missile launch pads placed in the centre of the 20 airfields involved. Built in groups of three, Thor bunkers have long outlasted the missiles themselves and still provide inhabitants of eastern England with an eerie reminder of activities not so long ago.

Another highly durable airfield installation has turned out to be the pillbox, thousands of which are still dotted all over Britain. All defence points only had at most a rare exchange of gunfire with the odd low-flying Luftwaffe aircraft but these fortifications never actually saw use in action. Contrary to the usual warped thinking of farmers and landowners, this does not mean pillboxes were expensive, colossal flops – quite the opposite. Pillboxes have been among some of the best and most cost-effective deterrents Britain has ever had. The moaning today is almost certainly because farmers, landowners and their ilk find pillboxes virtually impossible to remove thanks to their great strength.

Whereas pillboxes displayed a fair amount of structural regularity, the same just cannot be said of support buildings at civil airfields in this country. As already said in this introduction of this book, it is pointless trying to describe or find major common structural links among civil buildings – there simply are none. Only their roles are similar, such as clubhouses, workshops and stores at flying club and gliding airfields.

It has been left to the military to help regularise civil airfield support buildings. Walk around Britain's smaller airports, such as Inverness (Dalcross) or Exeter, and you will see many World War Two era structures still in use. These places are a curious mix of old and new. Only at Britain's big airports have wartime buildings been largely dispensed with. Here modernisation rules, with vast terminals catering for everything from refreshment to religion. Croydon's famous terminal building undoubtedly set the trend in the 1920s: a grand structure swathed in glass and intended to impress visitors. Terminals now have to process millions of passengers each year.

Sadly, thousands of airfield buildings in Britain today do not look so impressive. Nissens and many other types have been disgracefully left to rot in the countryside. Of course, they are not to blame for their dereliction: the authorities and farmers/landowners are. But these airfield buildings are now happily fighting back, as are our disused airfields generally; many are being returned to excellent service as offices, workshops, light industrial or storage areas and, in a few cases, even housing. All these activities are quite astounding when you remember these buildings were only supposed to be 'temporary'. Airfield support buildings once helped to save their country; today they help to serve the community.

An inevitable progression has been the transformation of some airfield buildings into museum pieces. A start has occurred but much more work could be achieved in this field. It is not too difficult to look around disused airfield buildings and find some remarkable relics from the past. Paint above doors has lasted to show the visitor which building he is at. Interiors of some buildings still reveal more extravagant artwork, ranging from squadron badges to cartoon paintings, where drawings of somewhat nubile young women not surprisingly predominate. Tell-tale graffiti is another giveaway, though most inscriptions have now disappeared underneath the filth inflicted on buildings by disused airfield destroyers.

Specialised buildings such as operations blocks are always worth having a close look at. Blackboards detailing operations still remain on walls, even with the original chalk marks on them. Always remember to bring a fairly powerful torch with you in this case, not only for your own safety but also that you can see these inscriptions.

The operations block demonstrates perfectly how British airfield support buildings both gradually developed and spread so widely. On the first count, every airfield had to start from scratch. Even Heathrow had to use tents for a while in the late 1940s before its terminals came along. The expansion of buildings was just as gradual, undoubtedly reaching a peak in World War Two. We could spread the net further still in one or two cases by including special housing estates for airfield factory workers. Cardington's Shortstown and Farnborough's Rafborough have obvious links in their names alone.

Above all, always remember two things when looking at

support facilities. Never just inspect the landing area itself, for most buildings are far from this area. The other point is to appreciate support facilities as more than just a domestic hut, firing butt or whatever can be seen. Each item might not look much on its own: collectively every building has worked wonders. At these ostensibly insignificant places wars were won, lives saved, local communities revolutionised in social terms and considerable happiness created for all. It is absolutely disgraceful how many of them have been rewarded. Surely the wide variety of airfield support buildings achieved infinitely more for Britain than those damnable castles and stately homes?

The Simplest Task Of All?

Airfield construction has always proved a long and difficult business. Once its facilities neared completion and the airfield opened – what site ever opened absolutely complete – the planners still had one job to do. They had to give their latest creation a suitable name. It seemed so simple: in reality, choosing the best name for an airfield required a phenomenal amount of care. World War One began to show the problems involved to an extent, although the next world conflict really highlighted the difficulties for planners. How Britain's airfields received their respective names is a little documented and surprisingly interesting tale.

In hundreds of cases, home airfields have been named after the nearest village or parish. No problem existed if a settlement of some note lay close by. Our first two airfields at Fambridge and Leysdown led the way by both taking their titles from adjacent villages. But Leysdown displayed that unmistakable airfield trademark of unpredictability by introducing two new aspects to the name game: one, it had an alternative title in Shellbeach; and two, Shellbeach did not exist! This name was derived from a compound mixture of partly using the title of the Isle of Sheppey's most easterly point at Shell Ness, 'beach' referring to Leysdown's position alongside the sea. As events transpired, though, everyone preferred to call this place Leysdown.

Early British airfields also began to adopt the names of towns as well as villages. Again the origins of this policy could be traced back to the early days of flying as aviation pioneers selected places relatively close to large conurbations. Airfields needed room, hence their siting out in the country among villages, but the canny men of aviation such as Claude Grahame-White quickly realised how their designated flying areas should not be stuck out in the wilds if thousands of visitors were to attend special events. Doncaster, Lanark and many other places set the trend to ensure that dozens of towns all over Britain gave their names to airfields in the future, only being outgunned numerically by villages. It was not long before a profusion of Greats and Littles, Highs and Lows, Olds and News, Norths and Souths, Easts and Wests, Churches and Saints started appearing. The great majority of airfields conformed to this pattern of being named after either a village or a town – but not all. Exceptions to the rule quickly made their mark, to the delight of some, the despair of others.

Virtually anything could lend its name to an airfield. Hamlets, as opposed to villages, became occasional choices if an area of countryside was sparsely populated. Carnaby, Lulsgate Bottom and Tarrant Rushton seemingly arose from nowhere to capture the imagination. One could anyhow always argue how airfields were villages or small towns in themselves.

Farms and isolated houses could also be selected by planners. This trend started in World War One as landing grounds frequently tended to be in remote areas, so they were often named after the local residence. The passage of time has meant that some landing grounds have since disappeared from trace; as places either change names or are demolished as well, any researcher is soon put off the scent. A perfect example is Kincairn in Scotland's Central Region: as far as one can gather, this landing ground lies somewhere north-west of Stirling near the village of Gargunnock. But where? Does anyone happen to know a former RFC pilot who just by sheer chance served with No 77 (HD) Squadron during 1916/17?

The much better known Bentwaters, Britain's last all-new airfield to open in World War Two, was named after another residence to bite the dust, though at least we know in this case how the house met its end. It stood on the path of the proposed main runway!

Buildings such as Barton Abbey, Coleby Grange, Down Farm, Dunholme Lodge, Lindholme, Marwell Hall, Snipe House and many others became not the only inspiration for airfield names, for various distinctive features could be used too. How many people know that Britain's (and the world's) two main airports at Heathrow and Gatwick are named after a hall and a racecourse respectively? Here are a few other examples, taken at random from throughout Britain:

Islands – Papa Westray, Tiree, Tresco. Thorney Island is not one, despite initial appearances.

Water – Hell's Mouth (bay), Hornsea Mere (lake), Strathbeg (loch), Sullom Voe (sea loch).

Large Areas of Land – Aston Down, Davidstow Moor,

Elsham Wolds, Hockley Heath, Weston Park, Wratting Common.

Geographical Areas – Bolt Head, Donna Nook (promontory), Edgehill (escarpment), Middleton Sands, Prawle Point (headland).

Oddities – Akeman Street (Roman Road), Balado Bridge, Hooton Park (racecourse), Larks Barrow (tumulus), Lopcombe Corner (road junction), Shepherd's Grove and Spanhoe (both woodland), Stonehenge (earthwork).

Before we go on, let us not forget that other oddly-named British airfield, Andrews Field in Essex. This place remains the only active airfield in this country to be named after a person; another site existed during the 1930s on the Isle of Man, known as Hall Caine (also as Ramsey) after the Manx author. Originally called Great Saling, the former place was renamed when US theatre commander Lieutenant-General Frank M. Andrews died after a flying accident in Iceland during World War Two. One must point out how personalised airfields are extremely common in America, unlike Britain.

As Andrews Field demonstrates, many British airfields did and still do have alternative names. World War One again acted as trail-blazer, for airfields of that period could also be known by the name of a larger settlement. The noted RNAS/RAF airship station of Capel was typical by being additionally known as Folkestone; landing grounds among other types often employed the same technique. Possibly the reason behind this thinking was that airfields had taken Britain by storm and invaded so many previously unheard of areas it helped airmen, planners and just about everyone else if a site possessed a second more familiar name. Hardly anyone would have heard of the DH6 *Scarecrow* coastal patrol base at Chickerell, but back it up with its secondary title of Weymouth and the picture became much clearer to all.

At the same time began the practice of adorning airfield names with brackets. Nowhere was this better illustrated than with Dover's three airfields: Dover (St Margaret's), Dover (Guston Road) and Dover (Marine Parade). As with many other Great War airfields, this meant that each site was primarily known as Dover and secondly by the name within brackets. The introduction in future years of oblique strokes – such as in Kirkwall/Wideford of E.E. Fresson air mail fame – showed a difference as either name was now regarded as acceptable, yet brackets still largely rule to this day. These points may seem extremely pedantic but are highly important all the same, especially when dealing with reference work.

Between both World Wars, a reverse process occurred when the larger place's name held greater importance instead of vice versa as in World War One. Municipal airports of the 1930s particularly liked to bear the name of the town or city they supported. World War Two then proceeded to bring the situation back to square one and have airfield names relating to nearby smaller places. There was a difference from before as not many airfields had alternative names to keep things simple.

Since the 1939-45 period, guess what has happened? Yes, the authorities have changed their minds again. Airfields and especially airports now tend to adopt the names of places further away from the immediate area. Most people simply refer to their local airport as Glasgow, Manchester or whatever, usually not bothering to call them Abbotsinch or Ringway. Look at any airport terminal entrance and you will be greeted by large signs such as Glasgow (Abbotsinch). Even minor civil airfields are beginning to resort to more general titles as in Peterborough (Sibson).

Some people are starting to ask as a result of all this continual changing: is generalisation a good idea? The answer must be no. This situation could reach a point where everyone refers to an airfield named after a large town or city – but nobody knows where it is exactly. Ridiculous? Far from it. Problems could easily arise if a foreigner is visiting this country. Suppose he wants to go to 'London Airport' – which one? The unlucky person could finish up at Heathrow, Gatwick, Stansted or even Luton, the odds being he would probably arrive at the wrong place.

Worse still has been the introduction of regional airports, which to an outsider could be anywhere. You might well have heard of East Midlands, Humberside and Tees-side Airports, but do you know their real names? Or where they are? One suspects, with total understanding, most of you will say no. (The answers are, in turn: Castle Donington, south-east of Derby; Kirmington, south of Hull; and Middleton St George, south-west of Middlesbrough). As if this is bad enough, who knows what might happen in days ahead? If you do not know the real name of a British airfield, what chance does an overseas visitor have? Think about it . . .

Military airfields have also suffered from an element of confusion, although they have been spared from the effects of current generalisation planning. Most of their problems arose in World War Two as airfields reached huge active totals. You could hardly go anywhere and not encounter one, so a similarity in names almost became inevitable. Strangely, the most famous example of a mix-up in airfield names happened not during World War Two but in 1924. A place known until 1920 as Scopwick in Lincolnshire had requested an item, still being unable to receive it as the months progressed. The equipment had gone to Shotwick in north-east Wales! The RAF recognised its mistake and changed the second airfield's name as well; another odd factor which may have influenced matters was how Shotwick village existed in England. So Scopwick became Digby and Shotwick Sealand, gaining a fair amount of fame afterwards in their own separate ways, Digby as a famous rearward fighter airfield and Sealand as a major MU base.

In World War Two itself, planners had to be extremely careful in choosing a name as a direct result of the Scopwick-Shotwick escapade. Although there is no actual proof of general naming policies, matters became so intricate that they must have had to start dividing names into syllables to avoid accidental nominal clashes. Places which contained parts such as -field or -ham, -ton or -town, -well, -wick or -worth undoubtedly required constant checking and rechecking.

To show how incredibly complex selection procedures could be, six airfields beginning with the letter W chosen at random from all over Britain are listed below. The ways in which their names were exactly determined will never be known for sure, but these explanations show the probable methods used. Problems had already existed long before World War Two: when the site now known as Newcastle Airport opened in 1935, the authorities had to name it Woolsington as the only other settlement of note was called Prestwick! But, once fighting started, for every easy choice came more often than not a host of nightmares:

WHEATON ASTON, Staffordshire. Training station. Opened 1941. Airfield two miles from village of same name. A nearer tiny settlement called Marston would have created too much confusion with Warwickshire bomber OTU satellite Long Marston and Yorkshire HCU station Marston Moor, both of which opened at around the same time towards the end of 1941 as Wheaton Aston. The only other feasible alternative would have been the village of Church Eaton to the north but four other airfields incorporated the word Church in their names: Church Broughton, Church Fenton, Church Lawford and Churchstanton (itself later renamed Culmhead).

WHITEFIELD, Tayside. Training RLG. Opened 1939. In Cargill district, already the name of another of Perth's RLGs, and not anywhere close to a village. Named instead after various surrounding farms bearing the name.

WINKLEIGH, Devon. Odd job (night fighting, FAA, USAAF etc.) station. Opened 1943. Airfield near village in an isolated area, so no problems about selection.

WOMBLETON, North Yorkshire. HCU training station. Opened 1943. Active as a civil airfield before World War Two, known as Welburn Hall or Kirkbymoorside, later named after a nearer village. Harome village to the west too obscure, and Riccal Moor to the south-west far too like fellow Yorkshire HCU station Riccall.

WOODBRIDGE, Suffolk. ELG. Opened 1943. Airfield sited considerably east of town, but Sutton Common (a) too reminiscent of Sutton Bridge and (b) several Commons already existed such as Fairwood Common and Greenham Common among others. Nearby Rendlesham Forest far too similar to East Anglian USAAF heavy bomber station Mendlesham. And not tremendously far north-east lay another stretch of woodland incorporating the name of Staverton – far more associated with today's Gloucester/Cheltenham Airport.

WOOLFOX LODGE, Leicestershire. Heavy bomber/HCU station. Opened 1940. Village of Stretton lay to the north, a non-starter with the well known FAA station in northern England. Pickworth to the east not only sounded too bland but would be adopted by a decoy airfield. A farm immediately south-east with the name of Hardwick would soon prove impractical as well, and no other place of note appreciably near, so Woolfox Lodge named in recognition of a settlement which had to be felled to make way for this airfield. An adjacent wood helped by also having the name Woolfox.

However, despite such unprecedented levels of care, occasional likenesses in names still cropped up. Hatfield Woodhouse in Yorkshire soon required to alter its name to Lindholme, therefore cutting any unintentional links between it and de Havilland's famous factory airfield at Hatfield. Another Hertfordshire site innocently involved in a clash of names was Bovingdon, when a Staffordshire impostor called Bobbington appeared on the scene; the latter was duly renamed Halfpenny Green. Shropshire similarly experienced two examples of wartime confusion, one being Whitchurch Heath, later retitled Tilstock to avoid any difficulties with Bristol's first airport of Whitchurch. The other necessary alteration resulted in Ollerton becoming Hinstock because it sounded too much like Tollerton alongside Nottingham. And then there was a long-running saga involving two airfields near Bury St Edmunds in Suffolk, when one site bore its name before changing to Westley but a second arose on the other side of town, being known initially as Rougham and later as Bury St Edmunds. The reason for this change in 1944 was that Westley closed to major flying that year: Rougham had stood fairly far away but the village of Blackthorpe posed too many problems, while another small settlement called Cattishall sounded tremendously like the great Coltishall.

Of all these special cases, though, perhaps the most interesting coincidence occurred in July 1941. The satellite to famous RAF bomber airfield Upper Heyford at Brackley in Northamptonshire had already been active for several years when opposition appeared in the shape of a new training airfield in northern Scotland, south-west of Nairn. While the fresh site was called Brackla, Brackley became Croughton. No apparent reason has been given for this strange action, especially as Brackla lies extremely close to the village of Cawdor. If approaching Cawdor from the east, to visit Brackla you only have to turn right and the now disused airfield is a few hundred yards ahead. The mystery deepens when you discover how no other British airfield sounded like Cawdor. Curiously, though this point may not have any great relevance, a residence named Brackley stands east of Dalcross: today's Inverness Airport had strong links with Brackla during World War Two.

Another great cause of wartime confusion became the heavy censorship which had to prevail. Airfields in Britain had not been named in World War One, and the same happened again in World War Two. Even crashes remained vague in detail – '. . . near a farmhouse in north Lincolnshire . . .' – but just every now and then came reports of accidents at unfamiliar places. 'Where's Deenethorpe?' 'Chedburgh – never heard of it!' the general public must have cried out. But by adding two and two or, if the person involved was a real aviation buff, trying to master the highly complex art of unit markings on aircraft, everything suddenly became a lot clearer. The Germans naturally helped slip this mysterious air of secrecy off Britain's airfields by occasionally revealing their names in official communiques and radio broadcasts. Some airfields were anyhow so famous because of their pre-war activities that little point existed in not naming them. This had already occurred during World War One with Hendon, arguably the world's best known airfield of its day.

The incredible exploits of our airfields furthermore meant that they would become familiar to the civilian population via word of mouth. 'Careless talk costs lives' the home propaganda machine continually told everyone, but it is fair to say that this official message failed when it came to Britain's airfields – not in the sense of impending death, rather the trivial side of daily airfield affairs which some undesirable might just have overheard and put to the enemy's good use.

Local inhabitants often unwittingly created more turmoil during World War Two as, when an airfield appeared in their area, they could bewilder anyone by giving the place a completely different name. Woe betide an airman in transit who asked for directions! Each airfield could hardly proclaim its arrival to all and sundry, hence the secrecy. But alternative names frequently stuck, and some are still used today. Another hindrance of sorts became the USAAF's wartime policy of also giving their airfields station numbers, as in Station No 485 for Andrews Field, though now military bases in Britain display large name boards at their entrances. Mistakes are highly unlikely, unlike in the past. Holmsley South in Hampshire is often said to have a good claim as Britain's most misspelt airfield – it is not Holmesley. East Kirkby in Lincolnshire is likewise often erroneously called East Kirby.

One other clanger amazingly became accepted by the RAF. The airfield involved was none other than Spittlegate, where Britain's mighty strategic bombing force of four Vickers Vimy biplanes had once stayed and the Tiger Moth and Harvard trainers first entered RAF service. Named after a hill, Spittlegate was renamed Grantham in 1928, then Spitalgate sixteen years later. Although the RAF eventually realised this error years later in 1952, it strangely did not bother to drop the name of Spitalgate in favour of Spittlegate, despite intending to do so. This famous spelling mistake is generally thought to have been the result of a momentary mental aberration on the part of a typist, yet no firm evidence has come along as proof. But – and this is an unprecedented suggestion – the author has discovered that an old part of Cirencester is known as Spital Gate; alongside is Spitalgate Lane. So did the typist come from the old Cotswolds town or around this area?

More airfield names which have popped up over the years and seem correct are actually figments of the imagination: they do not technically exist. Although places such as famous intruder airfield Bradwell Bay and Crosby-on-Eden (now Carlisle Airport) looked genuine enough, they were really fictitious. Several reasons were responsible, all evident in these two particular examples. Neither site lay in even moderately populated areas; neither was surrounded by notable settlements; numerous other non-airfield places named Bradwell and Crosby existed all over Britain; and, in Crosby's case, two nearby places were called High and Low Crosby, too many Highs and Lows already existing in airfield names. As Bradwell was situated near the open sea and Crosby not far from the River Eden, planners realised how they could take the liberty of making slight alterations.

An occasional airfield has conversely proved totally false. Nowhere existed places like the Great West Aerodrome, Heathrow as it was known in the 1930s, or the Hanworth Air Park close by at Feltham. This second idea still lives on today with Wycombe Air Park in Buckinghamshire, the former Booker. Essex became notable for pioneering all encompassing names like the long-forgotten Essex Airport at Abridge; even old Fambridge was alternatively referred to as the Essex Flying Ground. A comparable small scale example of present times is the recreational light aircraft site at Fenland in Lincolnshire, but pride of place must go to two of our major airports. Rhoose suffers from the grandiose title of Cardiff/Wales, being miles away from the city, while Prestwick is sometimes inanely described as Prestwick (Scotland) Airport – well, it could hardly be in Mongolia!

Some of you may think that a few more nominal mistakes are evident in the forthcoming series of books to accompany this one. Airfields bearing the same name will be referred to as I, II, III and, as in the case of one or two sites such as Skegness, IV. Nobody ever talked about Lossiemouth I and Lossiemouth II to distinguish between J. Ramsey MacDonald's own civil airfield and the extremely famous military base still active today, but this intentional move is still made to make clear differences in time. To take the example of Skegness, some sources refer to its four airfields as Burgh Road, Skegness Beach, Winthorpe and Ingoldmells: while these names will be mentioned, their primary titles will be Skegness I, II, III and IV. Why does this scheme not apply to the three Dover sites mentioned earlier in this chapter, you may ask? The answer is that all remained an exception to the rule in World War One; they were also so well known and so different – one each belonging to the RFC and RNAS and the third being a marine base – that numbering proved unnecessary.

Numbering of a different sort still tried to appear during World War Two. Whereas foreign airfields received letters and numbers such as A-1 and B-2 after D-Day to signify American and British-operated airfields, RAF fighter airfields had previously used a broadly similar system for a while, with the letter denoting a sector and the number an airfield.

Bomber Command later introduced a scheme of more permanency on September 16 1943 whereby stations were to be known by Base numbers instead of names. The first number would denote the Group and the second the airfield, the number 1 in the second group of numbers being kept aside for airfields employed for instructional purposes, so that Scampton became known as No 52 Base or an operational bomber station within No 5 Group. No 7 Group formed as a new organisation in November 1944 and took over all the training Bases, making No 51 Base at Swinderby turn into No 75 Base, with '5' standing for the Group. Despite initial appearances, this proved a far from confusing system, but to many airmen numbers always seemed to be far less welcoming than names.

One preferable way of ensuring an airfield fame would be if it could help devise an aviation-related product. The Gosport Tube communications device and Felixstowe series of flying boats were obvious examples. But other items soon came to light as well: the Lindholme ASR aid, Drem lighting system, Hawarden and Silloth flight simulators, Oakington pillbox, Harwell Box for radio operators and Gaydon hangar. Nobody could possibly mistake where these products originated from.

Nevertheless, as you have seen, this fascinating tale which remains so bereft of hard evidence of choosing the right name for an airfield turned out to be far from easy. As they multiplied in strength, all kinds of names arose: short (Eye, Mona), long (Holme-on-Spalding Moor, Wellesbourne Mountford), strange (Findo Gask, Kingston Bagpuize) and humorous (Little Snoring, Middle Wallop). How on earth Twatt in Orkney slipped through the net is yet another airfield mystery! The Americans in World War Two loved to provide their homes from home with striking names such as Seething, quaint ones like Deopham Green or long-winded ones like Grafton Underwood. Perhaps inevitably, our friends from across the Atlantic provided a good deal of the few nicknames bestowed upon Britain's airfields, Duxford becoming known as the 'Duckpond' and, logically, its neighbour and one-time satellite Fowlmere being christened the 'Hen Puddle'. Most other nicknames usually comprised of abbreviations as in 'Lossie'. All of these unofficial names retained a common link by being made almost without exception in an affectionate manner, for our airfields were extremely popular, contrary to the claptrap suggested by politicians and farmers/landowners today.

Certainly the greatest asset of airfield names became how

they provided untold fame to hundreds of previously obscure places. More often than not, airfields have shown far greater consistency than their inspirations as villages have turned into towns or suburbs or even disappeared; a few airfields, as in the case of West Freugh, have actually outlasted the landmarks they were named after. Various parts of Britain had already become famous without needing any help from an airfield. Catterick had centuries-old Army connections, Prestwick historic links with golf, Westward Ho was the title of a famous book, and so on. But what are Acklington, Aldergrove, Biggin Hill, Coltishall, Cranwell, Hawkinge, Leuchars, St Eval, Scampton and Tangmere – plus scores of others – otherwise famous for? They have seen infinitely more history in sometimes only a handful of years than the places they are named after have in centuries.

So-called 'historians' and 'travel experts' conveniently miss out our airfields in their guides. Should they now be reading this book, here is a tip. For the general public's sake, stop waffling on about castles and stately homes. These places are all irrelevant, worthless, deadly dull, socially selfish and an affront to the sheer meaning of the word history. It was once jocularly suggested that the 'interest' in castles and stately homes is a form of brainwashing by the Establishment, aristocracy, farmers and landowners to try and snatch vast amounts of money off the gullible among us. But this has since sadly gone far beyond a joke. People want real history, not trivia, exciting history which means something to everyone and creates massive impact at every level. The airfields of Britain totally fit the bill by being tremendous places to visit, thanks in no small part to their respective names. So, all you 'historians' and 'travel experts', start mentioning our airfields and cater for the general public – or else. Millions of us cannot be wrong . . .

Safety And The Airfields

Especially in this highly sophisticated age, one factor more than any other is taken for granted at Britain's airfields. Safety acts like a huge invisible hand as it carefully guides in or leads out aircraft time and time again. Despite what many may say about it, war is remarkable in how it can either effectively invent something or drastically improve an existing item or system. Such was the case with our airfields and safety during World War Two when tens of thousands of Allied aircraft filled up the surrounding airspace daily. Due recognition must still be given to before the conflict instead of showering it with all the glory, for various ideas did see initial development in those days. The story of airfield safety remains largely unknown to the average person, and is one best split into four areas: Flying Control (now known as Air Traffic Control), airfield lighting, the weather and ground safety.

When flying began, regardless of the country concerned, control of airspace was about the last thing fliers thought about. Each of them kept too busy trying to master the complicated theories of flight; as few aircraft populated the skies in any case, there was hardly any chance of a mid-air collision. Planners had to watch out for hindrances such as ever-growing suburbia or railway lines, but these obstructions could also help with safety if an airfield lay near a distinctive landmark. Any worries pilots had related to the reliability of their aircraft, which required constant maintenance, and the possibility of bird strikes. Our feathered friends soon became used to aircraft but have never like helicopters, probably because of the unusual wind effects these machines create. The RAF and FAA have tried on occasion the novel solution of introducing birds of prey to kill or scare off wandering birds on or around airfields in addition to the more usual vehicles emitting simulated noises or firing of guns.

Even when World War One brought many more aircraft, then throughout peacetime years up to the advent of World

War Two, Flying Control remained largely non-existent. If ever general safety procedures ought to have taken effect, it was during the Great War as aircraft after aircraft met a sticky end. Thousands of machines were lost in training in Britain at this time – some say as many as 15,000 or the equivalent of almost exactly ten aircraft crashing for every day of fighting. The prohibition of airmen wearing parachutes needlessly pushed up fatality figures, though it must be said that early types of parachute such as the Calthrop proved bulky to wear.

What equally concerned airmen were flying at night and the lack of radio telephony sets in aircraft for communication with the ground. Only thorough training and constant practice would help combat fears about darkened skies, but r/t still required much development. Although flying boats could talk to some ground stations during World War One, r/t sets could not be relied upon because of their unreliability, poor range and the sheer mish-mash of wires and instrumentation they represented.

Surely in recognition of what had just been experienced, certain advances resulted in basic airfield safety. Easily the biggest and most apparent was to provide civil aircraft with G-xxxx registrations after May 1919. Circuit rules were also devised in the same year. Yet Flying Control continued to blunder along in no direction whatsoever. Although radar was not invented until 1935 and r/t in aircraft still a comparative rarity until the late 1930s, nobody seems to have considered a national system. A few people realised the need for Air Traffic Control – a term strangely not adopted for some years – in 1938 but met with little support. So the standard system continued of a pilot signing in at a watch office on departure and arrival, having to rely for himself in between times, with constant observation a must. As for emergency landings, the main solution from 1914 to 1939 was to divert to an emergency landing ground. Who could the pilot contact? This explains why landing grounds became so common, first for RFC/RNAS/RAF use and then employment by both civil airliners and the Automobile Association.

For the first two years of World War Two, Flying Control continued to operate either on an *ad hoc* or localised basis. Radar performed miracles in the Battle of Britain, while r/t was much improved, yet airspace supervision over airfields and surrounding areas left a lot to be desired. The more operational and second-line aircraft which appeared over Britain, the far greater likelihood there was of accidents. Just as many, if not more aircraft were lost through accidents instead of action; huge Queen Mary transporters became depressingly evident. Night flying hours turned into the worst time each day as all airfields had few safety procedures. Certain British airfields in World War Two were just unsuitable for night flying and not recommended for use during these hours.

The turning point proved the winter of 1941/42 as Flying Control procedures began to be standardised. Before this period, the Aldis lamp and Very pistol had reigned supreme. Both served as the usual items employed to warn aircraft of possible faults or dangers. During the later war period, these two devices were still used for training and second-line aircraft with no r/t, but by then more complicated methods had come into use. Many would still be the bomber crew accustomed to seeing the twinkle of a green Aldis light from the control tower, allowing them to take off as radio could not be used at that stage of operations.

Part of the change in Flying Control could be attributed to the majority of World War Two airfields now having three hard runways. These were split into six sections, numbered in a clockwise direction starting from the stretch facing north or as near to this position. If an aircraft suffering from no mechanical difficulties wanted to land normally, the arrangements differed depending on whether r/t was used or not. If in use, there was the simple matter of giving an aircraft the relevant runway number. However, if the aircraft did not possess r/t, two landing Ts would be shown, one in the signals square and a second at the runway's downwind end. Runway caravans with their highly distinctive black and white square colours alongside the landing ground helped too, as could boards or painted numbers on the side of the control tower. A change of direction in the wind saw a smoky device being lit to inform aircraft not to land until the Ts and runway caravan were off their original positions on the landing area and suitably adjusted.

A most important change occurred in March 1944 with runway safety, for since that time runways have been known by their magnetic headings. These range from 00/18 upwards through a 360 degree circle. If there is a heading of 145 degrees, this is increased to 150 degrees or 15.

Back in the secretive days of World War Two, other Flying Control procedures were needed for aircraft landing. Airfield names could hardly be quoted, so they were only given in code on r/t. If you have ever visited the squadron memorial at East Kirkby, no doubt you will have seen a tablet alongside. On it is a most moving poem, entitled 'Old Airfield', which ought to be imprinted on everyone's conscience. This brilliant composition ends with the line: 'I was your home, your friend, *Silksheen*.' This was East Kirkby's secret name.

Other devious naming methods were used for night identification. A beacon on the ground flashed in Morse code the airfield's *Pundit* identity. Morse could be also used in the air as a pilot requiring to land would flash his downward-facing identification light. It would then be up to the Aerodrome Control Pilot (who preceded the specialised task of Airfield Controller like our despairing friend at Sawbridgeworth) to give instructions with his Aldis lamp. A green light gave the all-clear to land, a red one advised the pilot to wait until further notice, while a white light gave the rather harsh advice to go away and try somewhere else. Once the green was shown, the pilot would change his flashing identification light from an intermittent to a constant beam, retaining it in the latter manner until he had secured a safe landing.

So far, we have dealt with what happened when an aircraft landed without difficulty. Emergency landings involved just as many requirements – if not more. All RAF airfields stuck to a standard frequency to listen out for distress calls. The Observer Corps helped out where airfields were few in number by using a mixture of radio, sight and sound; the large number of D/F stations developed in the 1930s also did their best. These aids were particularly crucial on cross-country sorties where no Flying Control existed. The usual technique among transient aircrews was to listen at set periods of time on their particular radio frequencies in case they had to return to base, divert or be warned of oncoming poor weather.

There were several ways of requesting to land at an airfield if an aircraft had got into trouble. A machine possessing r/t could summon the control tower with the call-sign *Darky*. *Darky* (just imagine trying to use that term today!) was an emergency homing system for use at night, and the great majority of airfields monitored *Darky* calls for safety purposes. Aircraft without r/t, whether by accident or design, could attempt a number of quick flashes on their navigation lights. The same could be done with an Aldis lamp, while another method was to release a while Very light. On the airfield itself, help could be given with the use of Sandra Lights, a group of three searchlights which created a cone shape in the sky. These became the main systems used: some others did exist, such as night fighters being used as guides and various light-emitting devices.

For these reasons, most British airfields had to constantly

watch their circuits or surrounding areas during World War Two. Control amounted to about 3,000 yards outside the perimeter and for a maximum height of about 2,000 feet. Both rules have provided the foundations for today's military Air Traffic Control, even taking into account the vast technological advances in aircraft. Around every station is a Military Aerodrome Traffic Zone or MATZ, which is normally five miles long beyond the runway in use, four miles wide and 3,000 feet high.

Landing rules have also largely remained the same when applying to aircraft in trouble. It was deemed necessary in World War Two that, once on the ground, an aircraft should get to the perimeter track as quickly as possible. For airfields with hard runways, the aircraft would turn to its left at either the perimeter track or a runway intersection. Landing on a grass surface would require the quickest route to the perimeter track in the same direction.

Although a safe landing at an airfield has always been vital, an aircraft first has to find its destination. Flying in darkness or poor visibility would still be hazardous were it not for the second aspect of airfield safety – lighting. Like Flying Control/ATC, it took a war to grab the system by the scruff of its neck in order to improve it out of all recognition.

By 1939 contact lights were the most advanced form of lighting available. Flood lighting had previously been the norm, though Croydon had an early form of the first system by September 1921 with rows of lights sunk into the ground and covered by sheets of thick glass to avoid aircraft breaking them. Introduced in America, Ringway became the first airfield outside that country to have contact lights when they were installed in January 1939; Heston followed a month later. Each light, sunk into the ground for aircraft to roll over them, lay apart from one another at intervals of 50 feet. These safety devices proved adequate but had one major failing in that they were not hooded: enemy aircraft could spot them shining upwards.

At least contact lights were a big improvement on oil-burning gooseneck flares as the former could be terminated at once when an enemy aircraft came close. The gooseneck (named as such because of its general shape) was very basic, although it continued to be used in strength until well into World War Two and still remains available if required at some smaller airfields today.

Goosenecks worked on much the same principles as World War One's crude 'lights', old petrol drums filled with some kind of burning material, usually cotton. While they no doubt helped the intrepid pilots of that time to a limited extent, night flying was then regarded with considerable awe. Taking off was bad enough – and landing worse. But then British airfield lighting during World War One had become notorious for its desperate crudity: whereas we used petrol flares, Germany used searchlights and France electric lights. This was despite the fact that even home authorities realised how petrol could not be switched on and off at a moment's notice; cans could only be turned over for quick extinguishing.

Airmen themselves could have told everybody where the real problem lay. A pilot might be able to see a lit landing area – but lights defining the surrounding airfield area had not been thought of. Obstructions also had to be properly and effectively marked. A giant stride in safety seemed possible if the problems of definition could be successfully tackled.

Peacetime duly brought some results. A few civil airfields dallied for some years in the 1920s with aerial lighthouses. The standard method of indicating obstructions at RAF airfields from 1921 became the placing of two red lights six feet apart on the final obstruction nearest the landing area. Boundary lights appeared in the mid-1920s, aircraft complying by subsequently always having their navigation lights on at night. Soon neon beacons and obstruction lights sited on hangars followed. All of these measures helped but so much work still had to be done.

The first really helpful lighting arrangement became the Airfield Lighting Mark I, better known to most personnel as the Drem Mark I as it was developed at the famous east of Scotland fighter airfield. RAF stations started to be equipped with outer circle lights complete with V-shaped lead-in approach lights or funnels. Those alongside the runways and perimeter track were hooded, therefore eliminating any chance of enemy aircraft noticing them from above. Newer types of friendly aircraft and the greater approach angles prior to landing they made showed how an improved version was needed, so the Drem Mark II arose. Outer circles now had a greater diameter of roughly 3¾ miles, lighting became more intense and lead-in funnels more advanced. Drem Mark II now had three more sections in Outer, Intermediate and Inner Funnels to help keep pilots on course for a safe landing. These were preceded by the Lead-in String, the point at which aircraft moved in from the outer circle, showing how smooth the turn was before approaching the intended runway. The Mark II also saw airfield lights being better spaced apart, with its 52 fixtures (more than twice those employed by Drem

Mark I) separate from each other by over 400 yards and installed on poles to be more noticeable.

Developments occurred so quickly in this area of airfield safety that soon any site worth its salt was equipped with Drem Mark II lighting by the latter part of World War Two. The same applied to QDM (meaning, in the International Q code introduced just before fighting, 'a course to steer with zero wind to base') radio for magnetic runway headings.

Runway lights became standardised with even quicker speed. By mid-war contact lights, gooseneck flares and the equally awkward Glim lights had given way to more sophisticated devices such as Angle of Approach Indicators or AAIs to help a pilot assume a safe approach angle. Other familiar items useful in the art of landing were the groups of lights placed above one another on posts and oddly known as totem poles. Maybe World War Two runway lights proved frugal in comparison with Ringway's pre-war ones by being spaced about 100 yards apart down both sides, but they made up for this shortcoming by being consistent. Just as the motorist knew the proper colours for traffic lights, so the same applied to airfields as follows:

White – active runway, outer lights and approach funnels
Orange – outside border of perimeter track
Blue – inside border of perimeter track
Green – runway threshold
Red – obstructions

Various airfield lighting measures were available during World War Two to deal with aircraft in difficulty or possible danger. If a pilot wanted still more lighting, he could request 'Floods' over r/t and the Chance Light could provide this. It was a mobile floodlight aboard a Brockhouse trailer developed not long before the war in 1937 by Chance Bros and Co Ltd, a company which did so much in its time to advance airfield safety. Should an aircraft not possess r/t while intruders were on the prowl, two airfield lighting devices existed to help it. If the friendly aircraft did not spot a hooded red light above the control tower, more red lights would be available alongside the *Pundit* identity beacon some distance from the airfield. Like the Chance Light, these secondary obstruction lights were not always in use and formed the shape of a triangle. When warning lights flashed, any friendly aircraft could either fly a short set route or hang about the circuit until given clearance to land.

Having mentioned circuits, no detailed history of airfield

lighting would be complete without describing the problems of circuit overlap, that peculiar airfield problem of one site's surrounding airspace converging upon that of another or even several. Nobody had recognised this difficulty in World War One, though it had started then with the hundreds of airfields available. This may well be the reason why twin airfields such as Cranwell North and South never caught on: for them the problem was not so much circuit overlap, more circuit immersion.

But it was in World War Two that circuit overlap difficulties reached their height, when the numbers of British airfields increased dramatically to unparalleled heights. Perhaps the best known example occurred in Lincolnshire during late 1944, when Dunholme Lodge had to close to RAF heavy bombers because it interfered with the almighty Scampton; possibilities of mid-air collisions had become too great. Among many other places, Scotland had two excellent examples of airfields being too close to one another – Abbotsinch and Renfrew, Glasgow's current and former airports, plus Prestwick and Ayr II (Heathfield). Stand on Ayr's now dreadfully mauled landing area and you can easily see its remarkable neighbour's 1950s era subsidiary runway stretching into the disused airfield. It killed any hopes of a return to flying at Ayr II, which suffered enough from circuit overlap problems with Prestwick and vice versa. Although difficulties here were contained, circuit overlap could and did cause trouble in many parts of Britain. Of equal concern became how some flight paths travelled over other ones. Airfields could be so close to each other that even outer circle lights could overlap, so six flashing lights would be laid in a 1,000 yard line 200 yards apart to show pilots the outer circle limit.

Another problem with outer circle lights concerned British coastal airfields. Their lights ought to have theoretically extended out to sea. While some were mounted on buoys, the majority became duplicated along the coastline, complete with a small searchlight to act as a guide. Flying boat bases not surprisingly stuck more rigidly to theory by employing buoys to support their lights: the days when they only had to watch out for floating debris had long gone. But the light-absorbing qualities of water always meant that marine base landing areas could not be as effectively lit as 'dry' runways and resulted in variable lighting systems.

Airfield lighting, not forgetting Flying Control/ATC, greatly assisted pilots in safely landing their aircraft. However, sometimes even these two areas of airfield safety could not provide enough protection. Britain's weather is a most odd creature: some safety aids have therefore been required to appear from time to time to specifically deal with it. Many have succeeded but our highly unpredictable climate will always win in the end. How often frustration resulted at heavy bomber airfields during World War Two as poor weather cancelled operations at the last moment or delayed take-off, the two USAAF Schweinfurt raids of 1943 suffering badly from the second problem.

The weather first made its mark on Britain's airfields in the form of strong winds. Gales tried with considerable success to blow away aircraft and buildings as happened at Barking Creek and Port Meadow before World War One. Airborne machines were similarly subjected to the perils of this invisible enemy, though conditions then proved nothing to the notorious westerly winds which so severely dogged Allied airmen on their rudimentary airfields in the Western Front during the war itself. The numbers of men unnecessarily lost as their aircraft struggled back to base in strong headwinds became all too sadly clear.

A suggestion arose in 1918 which seemed the answer to their troubles. A member of the public thought that a piece of whalebone, an old shirt and a pole '. . . which any housewife would gladly provide . . .' could create a wind cone and enable pilots to know where to land and in which direction. His letter sounded utterly daft, but from such basics was born that familiar airfield item known as the wind-sock. It has since become immediately recognisable to anyone visiting or passing by an airfield, yet strangely nobody seems to know who actually invented this device. There was terrific debate in 1938 over its origins: many possible answers were given but it appears that wind-socks were carried aboard Dutch sailing ships in the early 1800s. They certainly were around for aeronautical use at airfields in the Middle East by 1916. The smoke trail wind indicator was a later development, along with from the early 1930s an illuminated T wind indicator with lights on top produced by Chance Bros and Co Ltd.

Airship stations in World War One tried to counter the wind by having wind-breaks project from their large hangars. This idea influenced a less successful type of wind-break tested at Manby during 1937/38. This device consisted of a steel framework with a protective outer layer of metal sheeting. The idea was feasible as crosswinds, particularly at airfields near the coast, could be quite fearsome when an aircraft was trying to make a steady approach. The wind-break's main drawback was its immense size: 500 yards long and 50 feet high, it would have been most vulnerable to attack. For all its cleverness of concept, this 'corridor' was later moved to Rollestone in Wiltshire but eventually dropped.

Not much could be done as a result to counter the wind at airfields. Virtually nothing at all could help where snow was concerned, except either clear it as best as possible or roll snow into a hard-packed surface, a technique first tried at Bradport in America during 1936. But overcast weather and total darkness could be beaten. The first really forward step was taken during World War One when the RFC created several squadrons at places such as Rochford (Southend) and Throwley solely for night flying training. Their activities certainly helped to lift off some of the mysterious allure surrounding the sky in its pitch black state.

The 1920s later saw small but equally useful advances in this field of airfield safety. The D/F stations so familiar to pilots in the 1930s and World War Two started to appear, initially being sited at Croydon, Lympne and Pulham. These places could provide an aircraft with its true bearing, the negative bearing of the D/F station from the aircraft and the aircraft's position, obtained by cross bearings, at the time of observation in each case. More mundane, but necessary for aircraft not equipped with radio, was a series of white rectangular panels laid out in a line – almost like a pack of cards – showing in turn the airfield's initial letter, then symbols to denote the current weather, visibility and height of the lowest cloud. Biggin Hill, Croydon and Lympne became the first airfields to have this system.

Blind or poor weather flying had gained increasing accceptance by all come the 1930s. And it was during this particular decade that tremendous development work brought forth excellent results. CFS at Wittering started the world's first training courses in blind flying, while the D/F station network gradually built up. Yet still some primitive ideas tended to suffice. One could be seen at Croydon, consisting of nothing more than a white line on the grass which guided pilots in the correct direction to take off in limited visibility. Blind flying techniques had by then arrived on the scene, but still a Douglas DC-2 pilot of the Dutch airline KLM relied upon Croydon's white line while attempting to leave London's airport in thick fog on December 9 1936. Suddenly he became disorientated, and the DC-2 crashed seconds after take-off; fifteen people were killed, notably autogiro inventor Juan de la Cierva.

This dreadful accident for its day ironically occurred in the same year that airfield trail-blazer Heston became the first British airfield to acquire the Lorenz or Standard Beam Approach landing system. Germany had recently developed this radio beam which guided pilots along the correct approach path to an airfield by way of positive and negative 'bleeps'. Lorenz/SBA was the world's first modern landing aid, an excellent one at that, and the Air Ministry decided in November 1938 to equip 40 RAF airfields with it, eventually phasing out the earlier ZZ and QGH landing aids. Common at airfields by 1942, BAT Flights had to appear in force to teach pilots on SBA. Training was conducted at the real unsung airfield hero of Watchfield in Oxfordshire, a place which has since been rewarded for saving countless lives by being totally flattened. Unusual opposition to SBA equipment later came from television transmitters, of all things, as they caused interference post-war.

BAT Flights also employed a totally different device during World War Two for their widespread activities. Sodium lighting was a synthetic training aid which consisted of using coloured light absorption filters to isolate the wavelengths of monochromatic sodium light still visible through otherwise dark filters. Filters could be used by wearing goggles in daylight to simulate night hours and ensure that pilots could only see an airfield's sodium flarepath and their sodium-lit instruments. Instrument flying involved another method, whereby blue and amber coloured filters cut off the light in two stages. Amber filters covered the cockpit windows of aircraft, trainee pilots wearing blue goggles. The degrees of darkness could be varied by the intensity of filters in either method. So secret was sodium lighting that any public demonstration of its capabilities did not come until March 1946 at Hullavington in Wiltshire.

Lorenz/SBA and sodium lighting between them helped to beat the dual enemies of darkness and poor visibility. Fog was a totally different opponent. Surely the biggest fear of any pilot, it could arise without warning to make life almost impossible both on the ground and in the air. World War One first tried to deal with this problem, flares being used to assist aircraft while they attempted to land. Such crude devices had some value but flares could only be expected to burn for a few minutes.

Despite fog clearance by artificial means first being discussed in March 1921, the major change only came in 1943 with the arrival of FIDO (Fog Investigation Dispersal Operation). Petroleum was now used to clear fog, large pumps feeding out thousands of gallons of fuel to burners lying parallel with the main runway. Not only were both sides of the runway covered but also the threshold. As the burners started to light up, some smoke arose, though this quickly cleared. FIDO might now seem an odd way to have dealt with fog: each occasion expended tens of thousands of gallons and there were obvious risks from explosion, but FIDO was worth the cost in lives saved.

Graveley in Cambridgeshire became the first airfield to possess FIDO, and also the first to operationally use it in November 1943. Not before time, for the following month saw a terrible accident when 29 Lancasters crashed due to fog after a raid on Berlin, more than had been actually lost to enemy action that night. Fourteen other British airfields subsequently similarly received FIDO, including the three big ELGs at Carnaby, Manston and Woodbridge. According to wartime records, FIDO's pipes, nozzles and fuel tanks helped 2,486 aircraft land safely. The airfield aid was expensive but think of the thousands of lives saved, not to mention aircraft.

Ironically, it seems that hardly any aircraft landed with the assistance of FIDO post-war, despite the device being made ready frequently. On only one occasion was it used for civil aircraft when a Vickers Viking transport took off from Blackbushe on November 30 1948. By the 1950s the RAF began to think twice about FIDO's continuing existence because of its high operating costs. Manston still had its fiery installation, while Blackbushe retained its device for a number of years as well in reserve, but now electronic systems deal with fog.

Provided an aircraft had battled through all sorts of weather conditions to land at an airfield, its worries about safety had not yet ended. An accident on the ground could happen as much as one in the air. The early days of flying in Britain required aircraft to strengthen their frail structures and undercarriages. Our airfields had to improve their landing areas too. By the 1930s, markings made of chalk, white stones or temporary white fabric strips had appeared to point out bad ground to aircraft. Worries over the parking of RAF MT vehicles were voiced in the same decade, fears which perhaps ushered in perimeter roads, the forerunners of perimeter tracks.

World War Two brought more problems with ground safety. Strict controls had to be placed upon taxying aircraft and MT movements. Perimeter tracks might now have become standard, but surprisingly no provision had been made for lighting beside these stretches, except for taxying post lights fitted at the end of each runway to guide pilots.

This deficiency was soon remedied, further improvements being made by making perimeter track lights closer spaced at any bend. Yet many taxying accidents of various kinds still occurred. Aircraft could run off the perimeter track and become stuck in soft ground. Maybe the biggest concern was how meandering perimeter tracks exhausted the brake pressure on tyres as aircraft taxied along to take-off so much that they could sometimes not brake sufficiently on landing, making overshoots at ELGs most welcome. Arrester wires tested in World War Two failed because of their inconvenience but RAF fighter and training stations started using the Swedish-designed and built Safeland safety barrier on runways by 1960. This far more useful system which is still used today can be raised or lowered in ten seconds when electrically operated from the control tower. The Safeland's one drawback is that it is not designed to stop propeller-driven aircraft.

Sundry airfield aids have not needed to be so complicated. Simple verbal ones proved very useful in World War Two when German intruders were at their most evident during mid-1941 and March 1945. A friendly aircraft could be warned over r/t by the phrase 'Hun about' should it be in danger. Another spoken r/t order was 'Scram', notably used during the fearful Luftwaffe intruder mission of March 3/4 1945. This instruction would have two effects: the airfields under threat would shut down, and their aircraft make for safer inland areas.

Two other methods dealing with warning procedures must be included, although both really lie outside the context of this book. IFF (Identification, Friend or Foe) was a transmitting signal which had to be given at all times, except when over any stretch of water well away from the British coastline. If radar did not pick up the signal, an aircraft was to be regarded as hostile. Several occasions resulted when RAF aircraft fell to the guns of their own fighters because IFF was not being used. Aircraft could also be regarded as unwelcome if they failed to display their navigation lights at heights above 5,000 feet at night over Britain. Both these measures were necessary, particularly with the advent of the notorious Luftwaffe wing Kampfgeschwader 200, which flew many types of captured Allied aircraft on various controversial missions.

So much has been mentioned in this chapter about general airfield safety in World War Two and relatively little about today for one reason. From ATC to airfield lighting, from dealing with the weather to ground safety, the various techniques described fundamentally remain the same. The old

Flying Control became operational as Air Traffic Control on January 15 1948 and still operates on its original principles. The main differences lie outwith its control, namely sophistication plus much faster and more reliable aircraft heavily trusting in technology. Britain is divided into airspace sectors nowadays. The oil support aviation scene has required special techniques to deal with hordes of helicopters taking off and landing, while radar is now incredibly advanced. Grave concern however now exists about heavy aircraft movements around airports, particularly around London. Gatwick's single runway worries many people, and the by now excessively long queues for holiday flights have meant ATC personnel 'stacking' airliners above one another in circuits to allow them to land in a safe orderly fashion. Circuit overlap has otherwise disappeared, though one could always say that it was a blessing in disguise in the sense how more airfields were present.

Airfield lighting has changed even less. Only three major differences have occurred since World War Two. Runway threshold lighting has become a standard feature to replace the various funnels of yore. Of course, peacetime has had a lot to do with this change as there are no current enemy aircraft around. Even more specialised is the Calvert bar landing light system, common today in Britain, Europe and some other parts of the world. This device was developed in the mid-1940s and consists of six crosswise lines of lights at right angles to the axis of approach; the bars shorten as an aircraft approaches the threshold. Heathrow became the first airport to use the Calvert system. The third change? If nothing else, airfield lights are just more powerful than ever before in their history.

Britain's weather has meanwhile been considerably frustrated in its never-ending war with our airfields by the introduction of three separate guidance systems. One shortcoming of Lorenz/SBA was how pilots still had to use some judgement in regard to the altitudes of their machines, a flaw solved by the introduction of instrument landing systems able to guide aircraft both in altitude and direction. A Boeing 247 transport historically landed with the help of an ILS at Defford in October 1944 but this aid did not appear in numbers until after World War Two. Ground Controlled Approach or GCA talk-down radar similarly took time to become evident after experimentation at several wartime airfields. Automatic landing systems developed from ILSs in the 1960s, where an aircraft's autopilot linked itself to its ILS. No more does fog greatly worry pilots, standard Civil Aviation

Authority rules now permitting airliners to take off in not less than 150 metres on a lit runway and smaller executive aircraft in not less than 600 metres on an unlit runway.

Airfield ground safety has perhaps changed the least of the four areas. Tricycle undercarriage aircraft have helped with their improved visibility. Traffic lights such as those at Manston help stop vehicular traffic on public roads whenever an aircraft is on a runway. This system can be traced back to the famous level crossing at Plough Lane to assist Croydon's airliners. Recreational aviation has since brought its own problems as people blunder on to airfields, whether accidentally or deliberately. There was the occasion a man took along his son to do some aircraft spotting not so long ago, and an aircraft propeller decapitated the youngster that same day . . . Parachuting accidents – especially charity jumps – have also given great cause for concern in more recent years, these culminating in a dreadful accident at Thruxton in 1987 when a woman on her first jump fell into the blades of a hovering helicopter. Cases of people being sucked into jet engines have proved equally horrifying. But it has to be said that most of these accidents can be blamed upon the persons themselves, for they should not have been in the area they were killed or not on the airfield altogether. Airfields are extremely safe places – their huge acreage undoubtedly helped to cut down on fatalities whenever bombing occurred – provided you follow their basic safety rules.

Of course, such stringent safety levels can always be caught out by those two deadly elements of human error and sheer bad luck. Our airfields have seen it all, from bombs abruptly exploding to falling out of aircraft, unmanned machine-guns firing unexpectedly to aircraft sometimes finding difficulty selecting the correct runway at the correct airfield or swinging on take-off and crashing into buildings. Crashes and forced landings will always occur; it is odd why the successful Pyrene foam system used at a few airfields from the 1960s to cut down on any fire risk from wheels-up landings by pumping foam on to a runway fell into disuse about 1980. At least the old aircraft dispersed around airfield perimeters to give fire-fighting crews realistic practice are still there.

Not all that many disasters have occurred at Britain's airfields since 1909 to have collectively enforced their claims of tremendous safety records. Charles Rolls' fatal crash at Southbourne in 1910 caused quite a stir for being the first of its kind in this country, and most newspapers of the day gave no help by providing deceptively huge lists of aircraft crashes which often involved single deaths. The first really serious airfield accident on December 14 1920 when a Handley Page 0/400 civil transport crashed on take-off at Cricklewood and killed four people on board was notable in another way as it proved to be the first fatal accident involving a British aircraft on a scheduled service. Llandow in south Wales was unfortunate to be branded through no fault of its own as scene of the world's worst aircraft accident in the early 1950s when a civil Avro Tudor transport crashed near the airfield on March 12 1950 with the loss of 80 lives, but other crashes have been thankfully few. In not one case has an airfield been shown to be negligent: the two big British airfield-related disasters at Staines in 1972 and Lockerbie in 1988 are the perfect examples, the first incident caused by pilot illness and the second through poor security at a foreign airport.

Rarer still have turned out to be fires at airfields over the years. Major blazes of note have occurred at Acton in 1911, Port Meadow (1913), Cranwell (1920), Hooton Park and Maylands (both 1940), St Athan (1944), Broxbourne (1947) and Old Sarum (1987). Many aircraft, hangars and other support buildings fell victim to these often bizarre incidents, yet no amount of airfield safety procedures could have saved some of them as several fires could be attributed to blatant arson.

Like so many other things in life, airfield safety has never received the thanks it deserves. Next time you visit an airfield or take off in an aircraft, give a moment's thought to the stunning mixture of wizardry and simplicity which make airfield, aviation and everyday British life infinitely safer for all concerned.

The Clever Dummies

The 1930s dream of National Flying Services Ltd nearly became reality during World War Two. Its vision of 1,000 airfields in Britain never happened – only over 800 sites appeared – but for a while Germany thought many more did exist.

If there was an area of airfield research which could be best described as baffling, the story of Britain's decoy airfields must come high on any list. These modern equivalents of the Druids remain enigmatic as hardly anything is left of historical records, artifacts or even the sites themselves. Research therefore becomes all but impossible. Dig deep, though, and the basic facts of this odd tale can at least be found.

What was a decoy airfield? The answer to that question is simple enough to explain. During World War Two, many British airfields were equipped with supposed surrounding sites not too far away. Yet these airfields were not real ones, rather fakes to attract enemy aircraft into attacking them and leaving the genuine site well alone. Thinking along these lines had first arisen during World War One when the Captain-in-Charge of RNAS Lowestoft suggested in a letter to the Admiralty on March 10 1916 creating dummy landing grounds with flares to lure Zeppelins. His thinking had been influenced by a recent night raid on Holt, one of Great Yarmouth's aides mistaken for the town itself.

Nobody in authority seems to have taken any note of this suggestion, and the idea of decoy airfields lay unnoticed for more than two decades until a far more extensive plan was put forward to the three main RAF Commands in May 1938. Both Bomber and Coastal Commands liked the thought of giving every major airfield in Britain a decoy when consulted, although the former organisation proved somewhat cautious in its reply. But Fighter Command was conversely not happy at all: it alleged that identification between a real airfield and a decoy would prove to be extremely difficult. Its concern was understandable, what with virtually every pre-war airfield possessing grass runways, only the different operating conditions of World War Two forcing a change to harder types of landing areas.

Despite Fighter Command's lack of keenness, plans for one of the most widespread deceptions ever seen were put into action. Fast and furious work followed an official meeting held on the subject on September 27 1939. Notes made were passed on for top-level approval on October 2, plans for the first decoy sites completed that same month and a list of decoy airfields sent to Bomber and Coastal Commands for approval on December 13/14. Provisions were being made for telephone links between 35 decoys and real airfields by early January 1940, training of 36 separate detachments starting by the month's end at Hook, an RAF ground station in Surrey later known as Chessington.

The first type of decoy airfield became known as the K site. Expansion Period stations would have been far too expensive to reproduce with all their stylish C hangars and support buildings, so Ks were designed to resemble the new austerity period satellite airfields instead. Each decoy held about ten dummy aircraft cleverly placed here and there, fake buildings built of wood plus vehicles, especially lorries, which had seen much better days. Two main disadvantages proved high construction costs and the necessary employment of 24 RAF personnel at every K site, but the authorities accepted these shortcomings.

How to produce the dummy aircraft just mentioned turned out to be an equally elaborate process. In the long run, five main types were chosen: the Hawker Hurricane fighter, Fairey Battle light bomber and Armstrong Whitworth Whitley, Bristol Blenheim and Vickers Wellington medium bombers. Members of the film industry mainly manufactured them and used all their special effects skills. Constructed fairly quickly, decoy aircraft were collapsible for easy transportation by lorry. Stilts sufficed for undercarriages as they were not considered necessary: decoy airfields looked very real from the air, so a pair of stilts would not be spotted from any height except at virtual ground level, where the decoy site itself would be revealed. Few details remain of production costs, though it is known that a dummy Hurricane cost around £50.

The first K site became operational at the end of January 1940. A total of 34 were ready by July, with another two still to come, but these false airfields would be heavily outnumbered by a second type of decoy. Whereas the K site was intended as a daylight dummy airfield, the Q site would serve for night purposes. It consisted of dummy flarepath lighting or landing Ts, contained no dummy aircraft, and was generally far less costly to operate in terms of money and manpower; only two men could be called upon, though some Q sites eventually held as many as six. Thc land did not even have to look like an airfield: the less level a Q site was the better for daylight hours when it was not in use. Like the K site, one Q had also started to function as 1940 started.

By mid-1940 Britain's remarkable decoy airfield programme had got well under way. Q site coverage reached all over Britain after June once France capitulated to greatly increase the 42 decoys then available. Already showing themselves to be useful, many K and Q sites joined forces to become doubly effective. Some real airfields could have more than one decoy to give added protection, sometimes even as many as three. Not uncommon either became the procedure of transferring a decoy from one real airfield's control to that of another. Each decoy airfield was always nearer the coastline than its real counterpart, allowing the genuine site to escape unscathed, but never too far away. A few miles would suffice to enable easy contact between personnel.

Various improvements were carried out to K and Q sites as time passed. No sooner had the first Q appeared than every site of this type had to have its flarepaths lengthened by 100 yards. A subsequent aerial inspection of completed Ks on April 30 1940 showed how more work was needed to make these places more conspicuous and lifelike. Later in 1940 on September 22 Ks received machine-gun posts for further protection. Soon Q sites had helped develop other types of decoys: QFs were meant to resemble small fires, while factory airfields adopted QLs which pretended to be factory and furnace lighting. From December 1942 QFs were operated by remote control, and only a month had passed when mobile Q sites started to crop up.

But for all these significant advances, what mattered most in decoy airfield design were how to stop real aircraft landing by mistake and the best way of creating fake aircraft movements. To solve the first problem initially involved equipping an airman with a red Aldis lamp on the downwind stretch of the 'landing area'. Q sites also switched off their lights when friendly aircraft tried to land but the original type of Q decoy with its landing Ts bore certain shortcomings. Planners gradually realised that small yet still discernible differences in lighting systems which pilots could recognise had to be devised. The first Q site equipped with a Drem flarepath therefore became operational at Middle Wallop's decoy assistant Houghton on September 15 1941. Each Drem type Q later received in January 1942 a bar of red warning lights (known as Red Bar) across the lighting system's funnels, a further method to prevent aircraft landing being the creation of single line hooded flarepaths from July 1943. All these developments took time to arise, still only two-thirds of all Q sites being equipped with Drem lighting systems by June 1944, though a mixture of careful instruction and not a little luck ensured that very few aircraft accidentally landed on decoy airfields during World War Two.

As for those 'aircraft' which did use them, personnel had to go to considerable trouble at decoy sites to create fake movements. The landing area was marked to show alleged undercarriage tracks or painted over to represent hedges: real airfields had already adopted this second form of camouflage. Lights were also moved about until an ingenious system was devised to place lights upon carriages fixed to wires and driven by an explosive charge. Each carriage could travel about 1,000 yards and decelerated part of the way as the charge burned out to imitate an aircraft landing.

How decoy airfields in Britain basically operated is not too difficult to discover today. So much for the theory – what about actual operational results? This is where problems really begin for the researcher. Try as hard you might, little evidence of results can be found. Few official records specifically state how each decoy site was used or how often enemy aircraft attacked them; perhaps there is a passing mention, but this is all. Parts of the RAF such as Fighter Command certainly tended to treat decoys with disdain for various reasons, and this factor can also be attributed to the lack of information. Another reason relates to the bombing of real airfields, for only from January 1 1942 were attacks against all RAF airfields recorded to leave huge question marks about what had happened in the preceding period. But this policy itself creates a whole new mystery in the decoy airfield story as we shall soon see. Inquiries among locals provide a bit more insight into this strange tale, bringing back memories of odd Luftwaffe attacks upon seemingly open country, but recollections become understandably vague as time progresses.

Generalisation therefore has to almost entirely rule when recalling Luftwaffe attacks upon decoy airfields. The first raid upon a Q site occurred on the night of June 6/7 1940, with 36 attacks being recorded that month on Qs in general. Six K site raids were also registered by July, 30 by the end of 1940 and six more in 1941, the last in June, to make a total of 36.

Some dummy aircraft were positioned during 1940 on a number of real airfields. Driffield became the first when it accommodated 'Whitleys'. In this type of situation, dummies would be positioned around the airfield perimeter. One may argue whether such a move was wise in hindsight. Driffield had only accepted its strange visitors after a highly successful Luftwaffe raid had severely damaged the airfield. Dummies would give German airmen overhead the impression Driffield remained active, when really it lay closed for extensive repairs. Why then would dummy aircraft be present? They could always have encouraged the Luftwaffe to have another go at causing more death and destruction.

But a handful of genuine airfields conversely turned into fake ones that same year to be deliberately bombed. As the Luftwaffe had made ferocious assaults upon airfields in Kent, three of the county's worst hit sites – Eastchurch, Lympne and Manston – had their complements of aircraft removed and decoy types installed in their place. This idea of creating dummy K landing grounds, as they were officially known, seems to have worked as the Luftwaffe made eleven attacks upon this trio before the practice ceased in May 1941.

The previous month gave a rare insight into decoy airfield bombing tallies as a number of enemy raids are listed in official records. To take a few select examples, two Dornier Do 217 bombers dropped six HE devices on Houghton on April 17, while a single raider presented Warmwell's Q site at Knighton with three anti-personnel bombs on the 25th, Suffield (Q site for Coltishall) then being strafed on the 28th.

Whatever the RAF thought of them, Britain's decoy airfields were easily fulfilling all expectations. Whereas Luftwaffe aircraft had made 90 night raids on real RAF airfields by the end of 1940, they had unwittingly attacked almost double this number of Q sites. While this gap in figures considerably narrowed from mid-1941, the overall total of Q site raids still outnumbered those incurred upon genuine airfields. These figures, especially earlier ones detailing the events of 1940 and 1941, however still fail to explain who calculated the tally of real airfield raids if no official records were kept before January 1 1942. Our decoy airfields performed an excellent job, though, and that is what essentially mattered.

Other dummy aircraft types such as Spitfires started to appear on false airfields in smaller quantities. Yet the end was nigh for K decoys as a rundown in their strength began in February 1941. Twelve inland sites closed in June, and then sixteen out of the remaining twenty on October 31. One factor became the increasing scarcity of Luftwaffe bombers over Britain: most had travelled east to tackle the Russians. Carelessness in the operation of Ks could also be counted as a reason for their downfall. But it seems enemy aerial reconnaissance had discovered the vast majority of K sites, and this was confirmed when a map found aboard a Luftwaffe aircraft shot down over Britain in October 1941 showed half the Ks left in service as recognised false airfields. The last three Ks finally ceased to function on June 11 1942.

This was not quite the end for dummy aircraft in Britain. Collapsible aircraft were introduced in August 1942, differing from their predecessors as they could be packed into a couple of fairly small bags instead of lying like long flat boards when dismantled. Neither were collapsible aircraft meant for decoy airfields but operations in the field. 'Bostons' came to north-east Scotland in 1943 for a spoof invasion of Norway. From July 22 Operation *Tyndall* involved placing twenty of these dummies at Peterhead, plus ten each at Fordoun and Fraserburgh. These fake aircraft were removed on November 26 but returned for a second period of deliberate confusion in 1944 between the end of April and June 17 to deflect attention from the proposed Allied landings in Normandy. Again the same three real airfields saw use, one slight difference being that Peterhead this time held twelve 'Bostons' and eight 'Spitfires'.

By D-Day many Q sites still existed in Britain in considerable numbers. Perhaps enemy aircraft had become nowhere near as frequent over Britain but still the total of attacks upon Qs steadily increased. What scraps of information remain show how less experienced Luftwaffe bomber crews had not learned as well as their veteran brethren now fighting in the Eastern Front the differences between real and false British airfields. Among the few final attacks documented, Gravesend's two Q sites at Cliffe Marshes and Luddesdown attracted 25 bombs between them on the night of February 3/4 1944, while Knighton managed as late as the night of May 14/15 to further save Warmwell when it was attacked three times.

Three more raids upon Q sites occurred during June. Once D-Day had passed, it became clear that these places might not be required in the long run. Despite their success, the RAF still had mixed views on decoys: they undoubtedly saved many lives, but many planners and personnel continued to voice the opinion that decoys took up a lot of manpower. Could these disapproving servicemen be the real reason why K and Q sites merit hardly any mention in official records? Whatever the explanation, the Q sites left in Britain were not destined to survive much longer and became non-operational in September 1944. Other types of non-airfield decoy sites outside the context of this book, such as the Starfish and SF decoy fire devices, were still active by December 30 but never lured any more enemy aircraft into bombing them after the Allied invasion of Europe.

What happened to Britain's decoy airfields, their 'aircraft' and sundry equipment? Like so many parts of this modern mystery, the answers are largely unknown or uncertain. As regards the airfields, most of their positions are known but not all, primarily because lists of active decoy sites were only published from August 1941. It is virtually impossible to even trace the exact positions of those sites which are known among the vast empty stretches of farmland or moorland, sometimes crossed by roads.

We do at least know what happened to a small number of decoy airfields with complete certainty – they turned into real airfields! So great proved the potential of various sites that planners thought it would be a shame to waste them, while one or two other decoys lying not on but extremely close to future genuine airfields became highly influential in deciding where to place yet another new base. Major USAF station Lakenheath and Lossiemouth's faithful satellite of 30 years Milltown must rank as the most successful direct and/or indirect conversions of all. Panshanger is noteworthy too as the Hertfordshire airfield began life as a real site, became a decoy, then reverted to being a true airfield. This place served as one of the four dummy aircraft factories constructed during World War Two, which helped to attract Luftwaffe aircraft into bombing them nine times by day and another fourteen times at night. The last dummy factory site (Chatham for Rochester) closed in the spring of 1943.

If the fates of our decoy airfields are at best hazy, obscurity prevails over the subjects of what happened to the hundreds of remaining dummy aircraft and hordes of supportive devices. In May 1943 Army forces in the Middle East gained possession of the surviving aircraft but these decoys failed in this area as they looked just too artificial. Enquiries then draw a blank, though it is probable that the dummy aircraft were used for somewhat destructive purposes, for none survives today, a great pity. No sundry equipment remains either.

The story of decoys did not – and has not – come to a finish with Britain's abandonment of the scheme. Germany later used decoy aircraft on a smaller scale. Strafing Allied fighters still tended to mistakenly shoot up a few fake types standing at dispersals on real airfields towards the end of World War Two. Enemy decoy airfields continued in use as late as the autumn of 1944 as well. The sorry-looking grounded military types at RAF stations today which stand around their outer edges owe much to wartime thinking by acting as decoys, and the Americans have experimented with 3-D paintings on dispersals at real airfields to create a 'shadow' effect.

Back in their heyday, everyone had totally forgotten about decoy sites in Britain soon after World War Two. They received brief, if public, acknowledgement in November 1945 – and that was all. A claim was made at the time that all 500 decoys in this country (including Starfish and other non-airfield devices) had absorbed about five per cent of enemy bombs dropped. This might be so overall, but surely the 300 or so decoy airfields helped relieve their genuine overlords of a much higher percentage. While the 29 QF sites had proved disappointing in action by having only five of them lit and two attacked, the numerous K, Q, combined KQ and dummy factory sites had given marvellous service. Qs alone each drew on average seven HE bombs and 2½ attacks to every one made upon a real airfield.

Now we can do little more than hope that certain deceptively quiet fields might reveal their secret pasts. Remarkably, virtually no information concerning the activities of decoy sites was leaked during World War Two, despite farmers and others having to billet RAF personnel. Perhaps even more surprising is that only four cases of casualties to civilians living in the surrounding area occurred during the 730 officially noted attacks on all British decoys. Historical excavation would also be pointless today as not only are the positions of many decoy airfields obscure, nobody knows how their materials were disposed of. Was equipment taken back to the controlling real airfield? Or could personnel have just thrown items into a convenient ditch? This makes the chance of finding some discarded rations or maybe even a landing light more minute. Photograph research is another hopeless area as hardly any photographs were taken of decoy airfields and those shown in past books dealing with Britain's airfields have more than done the rounds.

A novel suggestion could be the use of aerial infra-red photography. It is a known fact bomb craters, some dating from as early as World War One, can still be discerned when fields are newly ploughed. Infra-red could well pick out the differing shades of earth where Luftwaffe bombs fell. By using this method, research could pinpoint exactly decoy airfield positions or at least narrow the area of study.

A TOWERING CONTROL

Hopefully someone sometime will uncover an item of interest relating to arguably the most curious chapter in the history of our airfields, their mainly unappreciated 'cousins' which were nowhere near as foolish as they looked.

A list of Britain's decoy airfields is being prepared for the final volume of *The Airfields of Britain* series. Included will be the opening and closing dates of each decoy, the name of its parent or parents, records of bombing attacks and Ordnance Survey map references – if possible. As you have seen, the general details of decoy sites are heavily cloaked in mystery. Do you know about the activities of any site or its precise position? Or what became of any equipment? The author would be most interested to hear from anyone with any information.

Decoy Airfield Numerical Strength

Date	K	Q	QF
31 Dec 1940	36	79	29
31 Dec 1941	3	112	17
31 Dec 1942	–	168	NA
31 Mar 1943	–	170	NA
31 Dec 1943	–	146	NA
31 May 1944	–	143	NA
31 Aug 1944	–	126	8

*Decoy Site Attack Totals**

K	36
Q	443
QF	9
QL	72
Decoy Factory	23
Dummy K LG	11
Starfish/SF	79
Cover Plan**	2
Naval Decoys	55
Total	730

Totals of Attacks Upon Real Airfields and Q Sites at Night

Date	RAF Stations	Q Sites
31 Dec 1940	90	174
30 Jun 1941	304	322
31 Dec 1941	358	359
31 Dec 1942	393	396
31 Dec 1943	414	418
30 Jun 1944	434	443

* At least 524 of these attacks directly associated with airfields. Probably more but uncertainty with certain types of decoy sites such as naval decoys.

** Apparently relating to Operation *Tyndall.*

Here, There And Everywhere

It has been one of the biggest – if not the biggest – games of musical chairs the world has ever seen. The game started in 1912, has never ended since and almost certainly never will.

When describing the history of each military airfield in Britain, one particular feature figures every time. Units, regardless of whether they are squadrons, Flights, schools, miscellaneous or foreign elements, have to move from one place to another. Sometimes, not often but sometimes, units can remain in the one place throughout their existences – but they still have to form and disband. A glance through often tremendously long unit movement lists reveals a whole collection of airfield names: some famous, some not so well known and others largely obscure. Look behind this facade and the reasons why units had to be constantly on the move become extremely involved. Airfield names are fascinating in themselves, yet only tell a small part of the story. This chapter concerns the military, but first of all we must look at early British civil flying activities, for the tale of airfield unit movements really began there.

Aircraft movements of any real note between airfields before World War One hardly existed at all. Machines just did not possess the necessary duration to do so at first, their engines could not be greatly relied upon, airfields did not lie fairly close to one another as they were then not so common, and Britain's highly unpredictable weather forced matters further. Pilots therefore had to content themselves with circling an airfield – if they could steer their aircraft, for in those days ailerons on aircraft wings had not succeeded wing warping, the art of controlling an aircraft by twisting its wing devised by the Wright brothers.

Events in France had already shown that these problems could be overcome. Henry Farman had flown the first officially observed one kilometre circle on January 13 1908; he then made the first cross-country flight on October 30 by covering 17 miles over various obstructions. Duration, however, remained the main problem in Britain. J.T.C. Moore-Brabazon's opening flight at Leysdown on April 30 1909 had managed only 450 feet. Sam Cody soon flew the first mile flight at Farnborough on May 14, but he then made rapid progress and had travelled 40 miles at one go by the autumn of 1909. No more did Cody have to wonder if he had taken off by looking to see if skid marks on the grass had stopped for a short while!

Several events during 1909-11 in the British civil aviation scene emphasised in their own ways how aircraft were capable of moving from place to place without trouble. Louis Bleriot's trip across the English Channel in 1909 and Claude Grahame-White's London-Manchester heroics the following year took prominence and really changed everything. Perhaps less well remembered these days are how Charles Rolls flew from Dover to Calais and back without landing on June 2 1910, or Pierre Prier's non-stop flight of 250 miles in under four hours in a Bleriot monoplane between Hendon and Issy-les-Moulineaux on April 12 1911. Any doubts about long-range activities ended with the inaugural *Daily Mail* Circuit of Britain race in July 1911. This 1,010 mile competition started at Brooklands, pilots having to go via northern England to central Scotland, down to south-west England, up to Salisbury Plain, down to Brighton and back to Brooklands. All these events proved tremendous preparation for days ahead.

The military possibilities of aircraft and increasing tension throughout Europe at last enabled military machines to appear in Britain and officially start the unit movements story. When the RFC came into effect on May 13 1912, three squadrons also formed: Nos 1 and 2 at Farnborough and No 3 at Larkhill. It was a reasonable start, but all three units resided in the Salisbury Plain area; while this move may have made good sense as regards the surrounding heavy Army contingent, military planners still looked to be too cautious about deploying aircraft over a wide area. Or so it seemed . . .

January and February 1913 were two momentous months which, if nothing much happened in the world as a whole, became notable for fully starting British unit movements instead of just letting units form at airfields. What happened in this period is often considered irrelevant today but was in fact subtly revolutionary. The first and most famous of all unit movements was announced in January with the proposal that No 2 Squadron travel from Farnborough to Montrose on the Scottish east coast. Personnel must have wondered what was the reasoning behind such a move, yet the transfer served three highly useful purposes. It would test the mobility of aircraft, bring military aviation away from Salisbury Plain and into Scotland, while Montrose had long-established military connections, so support facilities in the form of former Territorial barracks at Panmure were available.

Plans were quickly drawn up, and by January 20 the War Office had secured an airfield to the south of Montrose at Upper Dysart. No 2 Squadron's air and ground personnel had hoped to leave Farnborough next day but poor weather and the Panmure barracks being not quite ready for use delayed everyone. Eventually the advance ground party reached its destination on the 28th, the remaining non-flying personnel arriving by road and rail by February 18, but the flying element and its supporting road party following the machines were really held up. Yet another change of plans had arisen as now only five aircraft were to fly north instead of the twelve originally scheduled to go. The pilots had changed too: among the initial list had been the future father of flying training Robert Smith-Barry, but the eventual choices became Captains C.A.H. Longcroft, J.H.W. Becke and G.W.P. Dawes, plus Lieutenants F.F. Waldron and P.W.L. Herbert. Dawes and Becke later commanded No 2 Squadron in the early part of World War One, while Longcroft became highly influential in airfield affairs of a more unusual way as will be revealed later on in this book. These five men may nevertheless mean little to most people today, yet all of them must be recognised for their supreme courage in literally flying into the unknown.

At last the aerial movement began on the afternoon of February 13 – and then had to be aborted. Fog had arisen south of Towcester, the first proposed landing stop, even though sunny conditions existed in that part of Northamptonshire. So it was that Longcroft's BE2 and Herbert's Maurice Farman S.7 Longhorn had to stop at Reading, while Becke, Dawes and Waldron – Becke operating a second BE2 and the two others Longhorns – had to return to Farnborough. A fresh start was made on Monday, February 17, and it is from this particular day that it is best to show what happened in diary form:

Monday, February 17: Herbert and Longcroft, who started from Reading, reached Moreton-in-Marsh and three miles west of Oxford respectively. Waldron landed at Port Meadow and Dawes Banbury, but Becke made the day's best flight by going from Farnborough to Towcester, with one refuelling stop at Blakesley to the west of Towcester. The other four pilots similarly stopped once each to replenish their fuel tanks.

Tuesday, February 18: Herbert flew a few more miles to

land near Banbury.

Wednesday, February 19: Longcroft and Herbert joined Becke at Towcester, while Dawes had to stop two miles short because of engine trouble. Waldron suffered the same problem and called in at Bicester.

Thursday, February 20: Becke, Herbert and Longcroft arrived at the second arranged transit point of Kelham near Newark in Nottinghamshire, while Waldron at last reached Towcester.

Friday, February 21: Waldron made up for his poor start by flying to Newark, refuelling and then going on to York. Herbert and Longcroft followed him there. Dawes meanwhile landed at Newark, slightly damaging his aircraft, and Becke had to land near Doncaster with engine trouble while trying to reach York.

Saturday, February 22: Herbert, Longcroft and Waldron flew on to Gosforth Park at Newcastle but had problems trying to land in fog, and a minor landing accident meant that Waldron stopped at Benwell to the west of Newcastle. More problems cropped up for Dawes after leaving Newark as he had to land after travelling only eight miles and then again just three miles on, though he struggled on before stopping 20 miles south of York.

Sunday, February 23: Rest day.

Monday, February 24: Having had a new engine fitted to his aircraft, Becke travelled from York to Gosforth Park, Dawes making the same trip.

Tuesday, February 25: Becke, Dawes, Herbert, Longcroft and Waldron all set off as one for Edinburgh and touched down near the Retford Barracks except for Waldron, who had to land 28 miles south of Berwick at Stamford Bridge with engine trouble. He took off again to reach Berwick.

Wednesday, February 26: Waldron enjoyed much better luck from the previous day by going straight from Berwick to Upper Dysart. Becke, Dawes and Longcroft soon followed him, while Herbert arrived in the afternoon.

By the standards of the day, it had been an epic journey, notable for the bad weather encountered, occasional cheering crowds en route and comparative lack of mechanical failure. The gamble had paid off handsomely. No 2 Squadron did not rest on its laurels there, for Longcroft then flew a BE2 from Farnborough to Montrose in one day during May 1913 with only two stops at East Grimsby for petrol, then Ellington near Morpeth. He then made an even longer flight the following August with only one stop at Alnmouth. Perhaps the biggest test of all came a month later when the entire squadron travelled via airfieldless south-west Scotland and the Irish Sea to Ireland to participate in Army manoeuvres at Limerick. Everyone returned to Upper Dysart despite poor weather and such fearsome geographical obstacles as hill ranges and a large stretch of water.

For all its unrecognised heroics, No 2 Squadron's flights here and there did not particularly rub off on the few other military squadrons of this period. The 'concentration camp' held at Netheravon in mid-1914 roused RFC units out of their lethargy to a certain extent but World War One totally blew away the cobwebs of stagnation. Already it had become clear that any fighting would occur in the central part of northern Europe – a different country or countries, across a major stretch of water, *abroad.* How to get there was the problem.

Britain's two military flying elements adopted totally different approaches to reaching the Continent. The RNAS' Eastchurch Squadron decided to go backwards to go forward by flying from Kent to Skegness (Burgh Road) in Lincolnshire for coastal patrol duties during August 1914, back to Eastchurch later that month and then on to Belgium. What Charles Samson and his men exactly achieved remains questionable but at least the RNAS now had experience of long distance travel between airfields under its belt.

As the RFC and RNAS had no great affection for each other, it was not surprising that the former organisation decided to go abroad in alternative (and easier) fashion. No 2 Squadron, having already flown down from Montrose to Netheravon in the summer of 1914, joined Nos 3 and 4 Squadrons at Dover (St Margaret's) on August 12. This move to Kent was marred that day by the deaths of Lieutenant R.R. Skene and Air Mechanic R.K. Barlow of No 3 Squadron when their aircraft crashed shortly after take-off from Netheravon, these men having the unfortunate distinction of being Britain's first aerial fatalities of World War One. The subsequent move to France happily proved uneventful, though, and soon many more RFC and RNAS squadrons would travel across the English Channel.

One drawback from this collective move could be seen in the number of flying units having to abruptly disband in Britain during the early part of World War One. Most of the RFC's front line aircraft and many trained personnel had gone abroad to leave perilously little on airfields in this country. Still too few sites existed for aircraft, most machines were anyhow at best of doubtful airworthiness if not completely unflyable, mechanics and motor vehicles proved thin on the ground, while no real policy remained as to how make the maximum use of aircraft in wartime. The flow of squadrons to France therefore temporarily stopped for a while but by 1915 new units were not only able to form, their nuclei could help create other squadrons.

Unlike in World War Two, British unit movements to and from airfields possessed no tremendous complications during the Great War. Front line squadrons would form at one airfield and then either move straight to the Western Front after a period of training or go there via another British airfield nearer the Continent. St Omer in France became a popular transit airfield and gave several dozen British units their first taste of a foreign airfield. Once abroad, units stayed there almost without fail, the only exceptions being a handful of RFC fighter units being rushed home in 1917 as an emergency measure to counter Gotha bombers and some RNAS squadrons coming to Kent in the winter of 1917/18 to rest and re-equip with aircraft.

Training establishments, whether they were Reserve Aeroplane, Reserve or Training Schools, followed much the same course of action as their operational counterparts without leaving Britain. No worries existed about major tactical or especially strategic considerations as in the second world conflict. Enemy aircraft proved at best only a negligible threat to Britain as well, so training units could freely move from one airfield to another at will without any fear of air attacks. About the sole major difference lay in how groundcrews moved about in trains or more readily available numbers of vehicles instead of ships across the English Channel.

Front line forces which remained on British airfields during World War One strangely tended not to travel about so much – if at all. Nowhere was this more evident than with RNAS/RAF coastal and maritime patrol units: the sheer fact of aircraft coming under a station's control effectively cancelled out unit movements until 1918 but, even when the RAF appeared in April, the new 200 class patrol squadrons still preferred to largely stay put at one airfield. Airships technically made no unit movements as they did not form squadrons but remained separate entities, yet also stuck to one airfield like most fixed-wing aircraft. RFC Home Defence squadrons similarly moved little either, though there was a noticeable movement eastwards during 1917 as Germany's Zeppelin threat decreased. The effect could be seen in Flight Stations and landing grounds sited well inland prematurely closing once deprived of aircraft.

Why was there such a dearth of unit movements on our

airfields during World War One? It all had to do with the poor range of aircraft. Matters had barely improved since the days of No 2 Squadron at Upper Dysart in this respect: even the Independent Force's heavy bombers had to be based in eastern France to attack targets in western Germany. Although aircraft had also benefitted a bit in terms of structural strength and engine reliability, every machine still badly needed landing grounds. A few of these sites such as Scale Hall in Lancashire were later specially created not to aid HD or other units but aircraft travelling between airfields in areas mostly devoid of landing places.

1918 and the last year of World War One should have brought an increase in unit movements but, if anything, the opposite happened. While the general advent of airfields in Ireland naturally had its effect, the three main types of British airfield – those used for HD, training and patrol duties – witnessed units rigidly sticking to them. TDSs and more specialised schools hardly ever moved to another airfield, trainees being deprived of using various sites with all their distinctively individual conditions and quirks.

What became particularly worrying during 1918 was the chaos in RAF organisation which arose as new squadrons had appeared like wildfire during the autumn of 1917 and spring of 1918. Too many airfields had under their control units without any real hope of becoming operational, grossly undermanned, uncertain in purpose or equipped with too diverse aircraft, too few machines or none at all. The massive reorganisation required in turning the RFC and RNAS into one service had left Britain with a vastly overstretched air force. Massive administrative surgery had to be carried out, and so on July 4 thirteen front line squadrons at nucleus or non-operational level were disbanded, their crews reinforcing squadrons already in France. Another thirteen units folded in the coming weeks before the Armistice of November 1918.

It could be argued that the events of July 4 and not the Armistice changed our Great War airfields' fortunes for the worse. There was certainly no doubt about how that summer day gave a foretaste of the dreadful times to come. Squadrons had flown from Britain to the Continent in wartime: hardly any flew back in peacetime. Instead of the roar of piston engines, military airfields resounded to the noise of boots as units returned home without their aircraft in the form of cadres comprising of little more than a dozen men. Scores of airfields about to close themselves acted as bases for these sorry-looking elements which gradually faded into obscurity. Worse still became a few phantom 'paper' movements of units not even existent at cadre level.

Not all RAF squadrons which formed in this country for service overseas came back to Britain in the immediate post-war period, if only as a cadre: indeed, some of them never did. The lethal cocktail of politics, money, pacifism and misguided long-term military planning had forced Chief of the Air Staff Hugh Trenchard into another of his major battles with officialdom. Trenchard had already fiercely opposed the large RFC movement from Dover (St Margaret's) to France in 1914: now, five years later, he struggled just to hold on to any of the RAF's squadrons, whether in Britain or abroad. To keep the RAF in business required unconventional tactics to outfox the politicians, hence Trenchard decided to hold three-quarters of the pitifully few squadrons left in the Mediterranean, Middle East and India. Rather less than world famous airfields such as Baghdad West in Iraq and Dardoni in India thrived in the early 1920s while vastly more important British sites like Sutton's Farm – already a big name in the days before being known as Hornchurch – lay disused. Keeping obscure foreign airfields in business at the expense of closing our own stars proved an extremely tough medicine to swallow, but this policy had to endure while Army and Navy political interests tried to totally abolish the RAF as a separate armed service.

The years 1919 and 1920 saw one almighty annihilation of all types of RAF unit in a completely random fashion. Training establishments suffered the most as always. About the only notably evident common factors were the disbandment of most HD squadrons on June 13 1919 and a marked number of squadrons disbanding on December 31 as if to neatly round up official paperwork. Apart from the RAF evacuation of Eire in early 1922, nothing much of note in terms of unit movements happened for a few years until 1923 – and again fighter units figured prominently. The number of squadrons scheduled to serve in this role increased on April 1 as the RAF in general had been saved from extinction and official purse strings loosened slightly. New types of RAF unit could reform; at last there seemed hope for the future once more.

Gradually RAF squadrons and other units did reappear from the mid-1920s onwards to slowly increase the number of British airfield movements. But by very little, for the inter-wars period ushered in the age of units staying enormously long periods at one airfield. The RAF Area philosophy prevalent from 1925 to 1936 virtually dictated that squadrons of Fighting Area stay in southern England and those of the

Wessex Bombing Area a bit further inland in central and eastern England. Again the lack of range in aircraft played its part too. Only one country's air force had the potential to assault Britain – and that was France's Armée de l'Air.

Yet this policy of rigidity made sense for more mundane reasons as the RAF's permanency brought with it personnel intending to serve long careers in the service, people with wives and families to support. The introduction of Auxiliary Air Force and Special Reserve squadrons from 1925 followed along the same line of thinking in that these units were manned by part-timers living and working in surrounding areas who could not readily move to another airfield in Britain and therefore had to stay put. More than ever since 1909 did the social side of daily airfield life make its mark.

So it was that for almost two decades RAF units doggedly resided at one station. Squadrons visited Armament Training Camps in summer and flying boats often made yearly cruises in the same season, while fighting in Abyssinia sent a number of squadrons scurrying to the Mediterranean and Middle East during 1935/36, but on the whole British-based forces remained remarkably static. No 25 Squadron's fighters stayed non-stop at Hawkinge between October 1923 and September 1938; the army co-operation aircraft of No 16 Squadron likewise at Old Sarum from April 1924 to February 1940; while the Auxiliaries of No 502 Squadron worked through seven different aircraft types and three separate roles during their time at Aldergrove between May 1925 and January 1941.

One remarkable civil experiment conducted during 1927 showed how RAF aircraft could rapidly move about if they wanted to. Mrs Sophie Elliott-Lynn, a noted pilot of her day later known as Lady Heath, decided to carry out an aerial survey of Britain's airfields and landing grounds on July 19. She left in her Avro Avian from Avro's factory airfield at Woodford at 03:20 hours and finally stopped for the night at Cramlington in Northumberland at 21:27 hours. By then Elliott-Lynn had flown 1,200 miles and made 79 landings at over 50 airfields and another 17 or so 'open spaces'. This exercise had only been of a recreational nature and served no practical military purpose, not least because RAF machines required considerable administrative and mechanical ground back-up, but still demonstrated how mobile aircraft could be flying between airfields.

Another event of huge significance like the outbreak of World War One had to rouse RAF units out of their extreme torpor. It turned out to be the war that never was – the

Munich Crisis. Suddenly squadrons sped towards their war stations in September 1938, in No 25 Squadron's case Northolt, to await what for several days seemed like the inevitable. Thankfully for Britain, war never did break out and resulted in squadrons moving back to their normal peacetime homes in early October, No 25 Squadron staying at Hawkinge until August 1939.

Unnerving though it may have been, the Munich Crisis had one beneficial effect as it forced RAF units at home to think hard about how to quickly move to another airfield in an emergency. The new satellite airfields enabled units to test their rapidity of transferral from parent sites in the final peacetime months; despite always having an air of a barely controlled madcap cavalry charge, both air and ground echelons could shift from one place to the other in several hours.

Theory suddenly became reality with Germany's invasion of Poland on September 1 1939. As war this time looked far more likely, RAF squadrons moved into action on the 2nd as fighter units in particular once more proceeded to their war stations and ten Fairey Battle light bomber squadrons of the AASF flew from central England to France. Those bomber forces left behind in Britain soon departed from their usual bases in eastern England for safer rearward airfields as part of the *Scatter Scheme* after this country had declared war upon Germany. Many training units meanwhile either disbanded, merged with others or re-emerged under new titles at the same time. All this activity had occurred in just three or four days. British airfield unit movements had rocketed in quantity: World War Two had arrived with a bang.

The next six years resulted in a veritable blizzard of arrivals and departures at our airfields. Infinitely more units appeared, supported by enormously improved ground echelons to speed up moves between airfields. The vital pieces in this gigantic jigsaw had themselves greatly multiplied in numerical strength to provide planners with many more possible permutations. If nothing else, the eventual trebling of Britain's airfields offered units the chance to acquaint themselves with a whole variety of places and keep their personnel fresh without complacency setting in.

To explain the reasoning behind every single movement during World War Two remains a monumental task, for so many explanations can be given. One odd cause had fortunately disappeared for good after briefly manifesting itself in World War One, namely the closing of some HD airfields in 1917 to aid food production. Those three social factors so important in pre-war days – the wife, kids or job in civvy street if an Auxiliary – conversely had to be put into abeyance for the duration of fighting. But examine World War Two movement lists more closely and a pattern does start to emerge. Causes can be split into the following sixteen categories:

1. Unit formation/disbandment.
2. Strategic or tactical developments.
3. Aircraft operating range.
4. Training.
5. Aircraft re-equipment. While like the above four categories basically an old factor in forcing units to move, World War Two brought such major advances in aircraft that they appeared in a bewildering array of variants and sub-variants unlike earlier days. A Spitfire Mark IIA might have seemed to be hardly any different from a Mark IIB but both types of aircraft carried greatly contrasting armament, the IIA eight machine-guns and the IIB two cannon plus four machine-guns. No matter how subtle the alterations in aircraft, conversion always took time. And there were eighteen Spitfire variants – about forty sub-variants!
6. Change of role. More and more squadrons were by now switching tasks; the greater the alteration, the increased probability that a unit would be at the wrong type of airfield for various reasons. When No 415 Squadron was ordered in mid-1944 to change from flying Albacore and Wellington anti-shipping types to Halifax heavy bombers, Bircham Newton could hardly expect to continue holding this RCAF unit as the station came under the control of Coastal Command, had no hard runways and lay in the wrong area for strategic bombing operations. The Canadians therefore moved to East Moor in Yorkshire, where so many RCAF heavy bomber squadrons already resided.
7. Rest periods. Whereas World War One front line squadrons stayed in action without a break, many in the next world conflict could expect to be transferred to calmer pastures new after a hectic period of action. Fighter squadrons could reside in southern England one minute, then as remote an area as Orkney the next. Units could be tasked with such less strenuous tasks as convoy patrols in these less turbulent places,

while building up their strength once more.

8. Aircraft leaving for or coming from overseas.
9. Exercises. Many large or small-scale tests became accepted as normal for both operational and non-operational units.
10. Airfields opening, closing or becoming inactive. Occasions did arise when units arrived before airfields officially opened, while training establishments and minor non-operational elements were not averse every now and then to using sites theoretically on C&M. Stations forced to temporarily close for repair work or especially runway building now tended to increase the number of unit movements.
11. Airfield suitability/availability. Suitability played a crucial part in World War Two with the diversity of aircraft and roles. Lancasters could not use a grass airfield with only Blisters for hangarage; an ASR unit would hardly move to central England; an airfield equipped with bomb storage areas and firing butts would not exactly be of much use to an unarmed PR squadron. The design limitations of certain aircraft types directly affected their choice of suitable airfields, one example being the Halifax's lack of altitude which precluded its use at 'high' airfields. So many airfield-related factors such as runway lengths, hardstandings, hangarage, support buildings and night flying facilities proved heavily influential in where to place units. As for availability, even an airfield could only hold so many occupants at a time.
12. Official policy. Unit movements could be affected by a change in emphasis in top-level thinking. The several Bomber Command squadrons which formed in April 1940 and then abruptly disbanded a month later typified such sudden caprices. Operational and training elements could hastily form or disband if the war situation called for more or less types of certain aircraft or aircrew. These forces could equally stay at the same airfield but still change title to more correctly define their new roles. Such was the case with the pre-war Armament Training Stations, which in turn became Air Observer Schools in September 1939, Bombing and Gunnery Schools two months later, AOSs again in mid-1941 and (Observers) Advanced Flying Units from February 1942 onwards.
13. Change of Command or Group. Any RAF unit

transferred from either type of organisation would more often than not have to change airfields.

14. Provision of support for another unit or airfield. Whether a BDTF providing affiliation for an OTU or an ASR squadron covering an area of water frequently used by operational aircraft, many forces had to work in tandem with others.
15. The weather. Our unique climate has always played its part in the story of airfield unit movements – but a small one nevertheless. Its effect upon World War One proved negligible, and the same could be said in World War Two. If any type of airfield was vulnerable to the weather it was the marine base, but even here little impact resulted, not least because of the relative self-sufficiency of flying boats. Since the mid-1920s these machines could use almost any harbour during their travels, thanks to the clever employment of support facilities, groundcrews and dinghies carried aboard each flying boat.
16. Any enemy threat to an airfield or airfield area. As with the previous category relatively rare in occurrence but still always a possible reason for moving elsewhere.

These sixteen categories may seem confusing today but in reality detail in a nutshell why friendly aircraft moved around Britain's airfields during World War Two; take any case you care to mention and at least two of the above could be quoted as valid reasons.

Categories 2, 3, 8 and 12 were why more RAF squadrons belonging to the AASF and Air Component proceeded to France throughout the remaining months of 1939. But category 16 had replaced 3 as Blenheim and Lysander units fled to Kent once Germany started surging west. Battle and Hurricane squadrons stayed on a while longer until the situation in France became completely untenable and either returned without aircraft by troopship or flew back in totally disorganised fashion to any old airfield in Britain. Once Nos 17 and 501 Squadrons had hurried from Guernsey and Jersey in mid-June, no British or Allied flying unit would fly from the Continent for just under four years.

The Battle of Britain dominated its airfields for the second half of 1940. Much of their success could be put down to the scores of unit movements which resulted. First the flying schools situated in southern England had to be evacuated prior to the system of rotating fighter squadrons favoured by

Air Chief Marshal Hugh Dowding could come into full effect. RAF fighters had at first moved daily or in rapid rotation from Sector to advanced airfields in the early months of World War Two, No 504 Squadron alone making an incredible eighteen trips to and from Debden and Martlesham Heath between December 1939 and May 1940, but once France fell appeared for longer stays at either satellites or forward airfields under the Sector station's control. Satellites enabled unit movements as a whole to greatly increase from the spring of 1940, though some confusion exists in records about satellite airfields, their parents and where units were precisely based. Did squadrons disperse only at the satellite, were they only serviced at the parent or which site saw use for operational flying: such questions as these still remain arguable as both official records and memories become blurred.

Fighter Command had developed its prolonged rotational system into a fine art as the Battle of Britain drew to its close. Units would move down from a rearward airfield for a month or two, see some action and then leave again for a rest period. No 41 Squadron's Spitfires made six trips from Catterick to Hornchurch and back again during May 1940-February 1941 as in line with policy. Both Catterick and Hornchurch feature very prominently in Spitfire unit movement lists of 1940, as do Biggin Hill, Duxford and Middle Wallop, for only these places were able during the Battle of Britain to repair the Supermarine fighter which employed far more metal construction than the Hawker Hurricane.

Soon the problems of keeping Spitfires up to scratch were solved and they became able to move to any airfield just like other aircraft types. By the middle of World War Two movements had reached huge levels as airfields, aircraft and units alike swamped Britain. Hardly anyone now worried about the range of aircraft, even less so when those simple inventions called drop tanks were introduced underneath the wings of aircraft.

Structurally strong and large aircraft such as transports or heavy bombers especially revolutionised the art of moving personnel around during World War Two. MT vehicles naturally still played their part but increasing numbers of people found themselves flying to their next base instead. The transports of No 271 Squadron at Doncaster IV specialised in this type of ferrying from 1940 onwards. Even gliders were used on occasion, one noteworthy movement being the transferral of No 228 Squadron's groundcrew in Horsas towed by Albemarles from St Angelo in Northern Ireland to

Talbenny in west Wales on May 4 1943, the aircrew meanwhile going in their Sunderlands from Castle Archdale to Pembroke Dock. Heavy bomber squadrons were also not unknown to take off from one airfield on a raid and land at their new home. German soldiers just could not understand why bicycles lay aboard machines shot down over enemy territory, passing off such finds by denouncing these 'crazy British airmen hoping to cycle back to England'.

Those units not involved on operations tended to shift about with greater frequency in Britain. Training establishments now had no qualms about sending Flights to RLGs or satellites. RAF Army Co-operation Command squadrons were notable in often residing at one particular airfield but still regularly flying to other sites for short stays to participate in exercises. Movements of this nature reached a new peak with Exercise *Spartan* in early 1943 as Army Co-operation units went to different airfields almost daily in what was effectively a test run for D-Day. Unusual sites such as heavy bomber stations were employed to further enhance the expected realism of having to operate from strange foreign airfields. Constant home airfield changes continued once the Second TAF replaced Army Co-operation Command in June 1943, squadrons being grouped into Airfields (later Wings) to transport themselves rapidly between sites. This increased mobility worked but the fly-by-night nature of Second TAF lodger units made them unpopular with airfield personnel.

Even Army Co-operation Command/Second TAF squadrons of World War Two looked immobile compared to FAA units. Look at the wartime movement list of any naval element and you cannot fail to be amazed by its sheer length. The advent of aircraft carriers at the end of World War One had a terrific effect as it was impractical for aircraft to permanently stay aboard these vessels. Previously placed under the No 400 series of Flights in April 1923 and then becoming squadrons again exactly a decade later, FAA squadrons have always suffered from poor documentation of records – especially before World War Two – but reached frenetic heights during the 1939-45 period. Fleet Requirements Units and other second-line squadrons normally held their ground at one airfield for fairly long periods but their operational equivalents dementedly dashed around. A few days or weeks at a shore base, then on an aircraft carrier, back on dry land again, perhaps off to another airfield after a short while, once more on a carrier . . . FAA squadrons simply never stopped.

But if World War Two brought with it a blizzard of unit

movements, two particular features stood out from all the rest: the hordes of detachments and miscellaneous units. The process of detaching part of a squadron to another airfield had occurred since the beginning of World War One, one early example of that era being 'C' Flight of No 4 Squadron remaining at Dover (St Margaret's) in August/September 1914 while the rest of this unit left for France with Nos 2, 3, and 5 Squadrons. Further separations for short-term tactical reasons resulted now and again over the next 25 years until World War Two made the detachment its own. Enormously complex detachments happened from the start of fighting as day fighter, Army Co-operation/Second TAF, ASR, AA co-operation, radar calibration, maritime patrol and strike units frequently split up for special requirements at other airfields. Gradually detachments reached tremendous distances as PR and maritime patrol aircraft dared to roam overseas or night fighter squadrons based in northern Britain sent sections further south to find more available 'trade'. Probably the most remarkable of all wartime detachments were made not by an operational unit but No 11 SFTS at Shawbury, which in the second half of 1941 despatched aircraft from its beleaguered Shropshire base to such distant areas as Lincolnshire and even northern Scotland to maintain training schedules. Detachments were essentially tactical ploys not liked by everyone because of the administrative work involved to keep in touch with everyone, but the temporary movement of Nos 9 and 617 Squadrons from Lincolnshire to the Moray Firth area of Scotland in November 1944 to sink the *Tirpitz* showed how they could provide devastating firepower if need be.

Any airfield not subjected to 'lodgers' usually had a miscellaneous unit hanging around instead. The most obvious of these were flying schools present for every role imaginable. A decrease in their numbers seemed to have occurred in 1941 when SFTSs left for abroad as part of the Commonwealth Air Training Scheme until (P) AFUs and (O) AFUs cropped up in their place a year later. Experimental units meanwhile prospered to cope with the massive advances in aerial warfare, fitting in at airfields whenever front line elements allowed, but particularly prominent became the myriad of individual Flights up and down Britain. Initially numbered to be compatible with RAF Groups (No 5 Gp Target Towing Flight) or squadrons (No 35 Squadron Conversion Flight), they were eventually classed in the Nos 1300-1600 categories as more elements appeared. Of note became the low 1400 Met Flights, Nos 1451-1460 Turbinlite night fighter Flights, BAT Flights and those for TT (later AA co-operation) duties in the first half of the 1500 and 1600 categories respectively, and BDTFs in the high 1600s. Their numbers were strengthened by the Command or Group Communications Flights which used the nearest available airfield to their HQs, and no self-respecting airfield came without its own Station Flight for local communications, often employing requisitioned civil aircraft as runabout 'hacks'.

Nightmarish it may have been to the administrators at times, yet unit movements never went out of control during World War Two. By mid-war a certain clanship was evident as heavy bomber units settled down more in one place for longer periods than medium bombers. RAF 'heavies' resided along most of the east coast of England, the Canadians in Yorkshire, the PFF in Cambridgeshire and Huntingdonshire and No 100 Group's bomber support types in Norfolk. USAAF Groups stayed together almost entirely after their uncertain beginnings in 1942, the 306th BG at Thurleigh spending more time at one British airfield than any other American combat unit between September 1942 and December 1945. It made sense for three or four squadron Groups to be fairly immovable because of administrative and operational reasons. The 92nd BG had become the first Group to make a non-stop flight to Britain from America in August 1942, and afterwards 8th Air Force air echelons took either the northern or southern Atlantic routes once they had formed at home; only the 482nd BG at Alconbury formed in this country during August 1943. Such became the preponderance of operational American units here that few second-line or miscellaneous establishments appeared.

Despite the subtle standardisation of airfield design in the second half of World War Two to help relieve the difficulties for units moving about Britain, as typified by the installation of two T2s at each second generation American heavy bomber station, plenty of other factors kept units on the hop. The unsuccessful Dieppe Raid of August 19 1942 saw an abnormally large number of RAF fighter squadrons arrive at almost every available airfield in southern England, broadly the same thing happening again a year later with the similarly hopeless Operation *Starkey*. Luftwaffe fighter-bomber raids tied down defensive fighter units in the south, while more offensive RAF forces concerned themselves with *Rhubarbs* and other tactical missions. The new ALGs had to be tested, and there were increasing visits of a few days at a time to important APC airfields scattered around Britain for weaponry training.

As ever, units continued to move abroad, just as the Americans and Canadians had come to Britain. RAF aircraft had flown via Shetland to Russia in late 1941 and anti-submarine types to the West Indies in mid-1942. Many light and medium bomber detachments travelled to Malta, North Africa and the Middle East during 1941/42, Flights at home eventually evolving into new squadrons. But these movements were primarily only of a token propaganda value to help out other areas badly needing air power, and it was not until the North African invasion of November 1942 – mounted from Cornish airfields – that British airfield unit movements really made an impact abroad. The airfield capability of the Azores from October 1943 later enabled maritime patrol aircraft to secure another mid-Atlantic hole in their war against the U-boat. Not recommended, however, were the RAF and USAAF 'shuttle' raids of 1943/44 as maintaining heavy bombers in extremes of climate at faraway airfields after highly arduous flights was not a practical scheme.

A number of RAF fighter squadrons returned home from Italy in the spring of 1944 as D-Day drew ever closer. This year saw unit movements reach their all-time peak as tens of thousands of aircraft played musical chairs around Britain's 700-plus airfields. Some sites remained greatly associated with certain roles: Benson for PR, Tempsford for Special Duty spy-dropping or Aldergrove, Bircham Newton and Tiree for meteorological reporting aircraft. But these places proved comparative exceptions as most units arrived at virtually any airfield, so long as it was suitable and available for their aircraft. The cramming of operational forces into southern England brought about a massive imbalance as Second TAF squadrons filled sites such as Tangmere almost to over-capacity as these three squadron Wings moved about in virtual unison. ALGs were most welcome in relieving the strain when they reappeared in April 1944.

AOP Auster squadrons, of which nine of the eventual total of sixteen had formed at Old Sarum, went a stage further by moving everywhere regardless while training. Frequently these little monoplanes appeared at large fields not recognised as proper airfields for very brief stays. Such places are now so meaningless that they are normally omitted from squadron movement lists. By April 1944 Auster squadrons had settled down at ALGs like Allied single-engined fighters, though to use this airfield term when applied to Austers proved somewhat tenuous.

It was an Auster squadron that became the first Allied flying unit to operate from the Continent following D-Day when No 652 dared to leave its ALG at Cobham in Surrey on June 7. No 144 Wing led the way for high-performance aircraft to fly from France three days later on June 10 when its Spitfires crossed the English Channel from Ford, a place through which many units would pass, more Spitfires of No 222 Squadron at Selsey in west Sussex being the first purely British element to also nervously venture abroad on the 10th after the Canadian Wing. Yet it was advisable at that time for Allied fighters to still officially remain at their British bases and only use numbered Normandy airstrips for brief refuelling and rearming stops during daylight hours as these crude French places still came under fire from enemy ground forces.

Units had permanently moved to France by the time P-47s of the 368th FG at Chilbolton heralded the US 9th Air Force's arrival on June 19. Over 30 Allied squadrons were on the mainland of Europe less than three weeks after D-Day and never returned to Britain, except for aircraft re-equipment or firing courses at APCs. Just as RAF fighter detachments in France had been few during May/June 1940 due to various complications, the reverse process of sending sections back to Britain four years later rarely happened as well.

This major departure of British and American tactical units had far-reaching consequences for our airfields. Retreating German forces compelled Allied light bomber elements to make increasingly longer raids until their operating radii could barely take the strain. From the late summer of 1944 Bostons and other types had to go either straight to France or via more southerly English airfields. Lines of communication almost stretched to breaking point too and forced abroad many RAF and USAAF transport units.

But the most affected of all units during the latter part of 1944 were those involved in airborne forces duties. Mainly situated since mid-1943 at airfields in central England, British squadrons and American TCGs had sailed through the D-Day period with ease. Arnhem, though, was a completely different matter. RAF airborne forces squadrons in particular suddenly found how their Midlands bases lay too far away from the action. Many aircraft badly damaged by enemy fighters or flak over the Low Countries crashed unnecessarily while limping the long journey back to Oxfordshire and elsewhere in appallingly bad weather. Nearer airfields had to be found urgently: the answer lay in various East Anglian sites recently vacated by US 9th Air Force Groups, these places being occupied by RAF transports instead from October.

Front line RAF fighter and bomber squadrons helped to

make up for the general decrease of Allied aircraft in Britain as more units formed after D-Day into the early part of 1945. Lancaster and Mosquito squadrons still arose, especially Lancaster ones, forming at one airfield from an already existent unit and then quickly moving to another base for a much longer stay.

While RAF heavy bombers put down their roots as usual, maritime patrol squadrons tended to move more towards northern Britain after France was recaptured and Germany's U-boats lost the use of their concrete pens alongside the Bay of Biscay. Strike Wings wrought carnage among ships and submarines once installed in their eastern and northern haunts. Unit movements had played a major part in defeating the enemy naval threat, for patrol squadrons began achieving greater success when they started changing airfields more often instead of staying at their pre-war bases as No 502 Squadron had done at Aldergrove until January 1941. More good fortune resulted once the clumsy practice of passing Bomber Command detachments to temporary Coastal Command control during 1939-42 ceased. Movements between airfields in Britain or to Iceland, Gibraltar and eventually the Azores became more pronounced when four-engined types such as the Liberator entered RAF service. Still the old favourites received visits – Ballykelly, Bircham Newton, Chivenor, St Eval and Wick among others – but Scottish bases such as Milltown and Stornoway came more to the fore from mid-1944 as U-boats were forced to hunt elsewhere.

Apart from the tentative return of training schools to southern airfields fairly secure from enemy intruders in the final months of World War Two, the last major unit movement of the conflict occurred in March 1945 with Operation *Varsity*. This airborne invasion of the River Rhine and its surroundings became the only time transports tried to imitate their fighter counterparts by making considerable use of forward airfields. A number of redundant or little used airfields in the southern half of East Anglia lay available for use: being nearer the Continent, and perhaps also aware of the Arnhem experience, RAF and USAAF aircraft decided to make good use of these sites. No sooner had the transports arrived then they were gone.

The end of World War Two in Europe did not signal the end of massive unit movements at Britain's airfields. But many dramatic changes could be easily seen in terms of both domestic and foreign military planning. At home, many squadrons and other units gradually disbanded from the second half of 1945 as financial cutbacks took their toll. Training and support organisations were devastated. Other elements such as RAF airborne forces, ASR and radar calibration squadrons disappeared for the often highly debatable reason that all were no longer considered necessary. Many squadrons began to shift from closing airfields too and, with the massive reductions in both aircraft and personnel, sites which stayed active began holding a larger than average number of major units. RAF heavy bomber stations which previously held a couple of Lancaster squadrons in World War Two could now expect to see four resident. Soon a tremendous renumbering of first-line units occurred to recreate famous RAF squadrons of years past.

Yet the changing political situation throughout the world as a whole had a far greater impact upon British airfield unit movements. Most Second TAF squadrons disbanded in Germany, not even bothering to send cadres back to Britain as RAF units did after World War One, but the most immediate effect could be felt in the USAAF's departure from East Anglia and elsewhere. America's first British-based Group to return home (the 489th BG at Halesworth) had actually left in November 1944: following VE Day, 8th Air Force Groups subsequently left in droves until Honington became the last airfield to be given back to RAF hands in February 1946. A total of 2,118 American four-engined heavy bombers had crossed the Atlantic Ocean in just 51 days by July 11 1945. While air echelons frequently left Britain's airfields with almost alarming suddenness, their supportive ground echelons usually stayed on another month or two to clear up administrative matters before leaving in ships, notably the *Queen Mary* and *Queen Elizabeth,* from either the Clyde or Southampton. Yorkshire-based RCAF heavy bomber squadrons also quickly flew home to form *Tiger Force,* though like the 8th Air Force never managed to bomb Japan with the advent of VJ Day in mid-August.

Yorkshire proved a hotbed of activity at this period in more ways than one. Just before the Canadians had departed, so RAF Bomber Command Halifax squadrons in the area changed allegiance to Transport Command as Germany capitulated. Britain still had its Empire to maintain: in aviation terms, that meant many more transports were needed to maintain air links. A noticeable shift south resulted, the ex-heavy bomber units intensifying the strength of a number of airfields in southern England which had already seen new transport units form since the autumn of 1944.

Only now did communications and trooping flights to the

Middle and Far East begin – but soon the glare of publicity would move considerably closer to Britain. Many RAF fighter squadrons had left Britain's finest for Germany's bomb-shattered and patched up flugplatzen as part of the occupying forces. The rapidly increasing threat posed by Russia towards the West reached its pinnacle in the blockade of Berlin, forcing our transport airfields to participate in the famous Airlift – or perhaps not, depending on how one views history. For the first time in British military aviation history, RAF transport forces worked en masse abroad as they tried to keep German civilians alive. Ostensibly transport bases in southern and central England, East Anglia and Yorkshire – where some squadrons had ironically returned – did not seem to be involved. True, most transport elements were only nominally based in Britain while spending months at a time detached in Germany, but aircraft maintenance still had to be carried out at home.

Once this political crisis of potentially disastrous consequences had been averted in 1949, British military flying units began to settle down more to resemble to a large extent the situation before World War Two, the only major difference being the deployment of fighter squadrons right along the eastern half of Britain instead of just south-east England to deal with the new Communist threat. The Empire slowly receded but events abroad still took RAF fighters and bombers to some far-flung places. Lancasters so accustomed to eastern England had a habit of visiting Shallufa in Egypt during the late 1940s to give their crews long-range flying experience, while Lincolns temporarily sent abroad performed good work against the Communists in Malaya during 1948-56 and Mau Mau terrorists in Kenya during 1953-55. Not so successful proved the impetuous rush of RAF and FAA units to Cyprus and Malta for the ill-fated invasion of Suez in the autumn of 1956. However, the long periods of time spent at one airfield as typified by the thirteen year stay of No 54 Squadron's jet fighters at Odiham emphasised how unit movements had generally decreased again.

By the 1950s the Americans had already been back in Britain for some years and not followed the example of their British opposite numbers. USAF heavy bombers had operated from various airfields here since July 1948 to threaten Russia during the Berlin Airlift. First site to welcome back our American friends after a gap of 2½ years had not turned out to be one in East Anglia but RAF Bomber Command's all-time favourite Scampton, which led to a laughably absurd British film news commentary of the time proclaiming that the B-29s were '. . . the first American bombers to be seen in Lincolnshire since World War Two.' The USAF jet 'heavies' never failed to amaze in terms of their size and complexity, but what also became noticeable was Strategic Air Command's Temporary Duty (TDY) policy of sending Groups on 90 day rotations to British airfields to enable a quick response to any enemy attack. Many ABGs and ABSs remained on hand throughout to provide vital material support. The TDY method of deployment lasted well into the 1960s.

The cessation of TDY helped bring about an air of crisis to Britain's airfields during this decade. No replacements seemed apparent to keep every base busy. Duncan Sandys had done his dastardly work too to help wipe out as many RAF squadrons as possible. Missiles did not technically move: the 60 Thor IRBMs could not in any case while imprisoned in their launch pads. RAuxAF squadrons had long passed into history on March 10 1957 after restarting somewhat hesitantly on May 10 1946. Life in these units carried on much the same as in pre-war days once recruiting problems had been overcome, only their aircraft being more advanced. But Duncan Sandys' challenge to the entire basic concept of military aviation in Britain still managed to wipe out all RAuxAF and equivalent RNVR squadrons.

Fighter squadrons manned by RAF regulars were also hammered numerically to end their halcyon days since the end of World War Two. Notable in making many brief movements from their permanent stations for firing practice to Acklington and Germany during the first few post-war years, fighter units had even increased in strength in the mid-1950s until you-know-who came along.

Time had similarly run out for training establishments since their rebirth in the early 1950s. Closure of the reserve training programme was the first major blow but later policies reduced instructional units to virtually nothing. Even the small Reserve Command ATC Gliding Schools had had their day: 84 had existed by May 1945, the same number by October 1947, but this figure was slashed in 1948 to 53 as officialdom considered that the numbers of ATC cadets trained and passed were too small for so many GSs and their cost. By the end of 1962 GSs existed at only 28 airfields.

This constant reduction of units finally hit RAF transports by the 1970s to markedly reduce squadrons involved with this duty. Although some transport units had disbanded once the Berlin Airlift ended, their aircraft still enjoyed many years of quiet glory by flying about the British Empire. But when this country started to pawn off its various outposts, transports found less and less jobs to do to leave them with a gradually increasing hangover.

Nobody needed to tell the FAA about hard times either. Its monumental list of unit movements had carried on for a few years after World War Two until 1950s defence cuts took their toll. Navy units were forced to become less transient as their aircraft carriers were progressively scrapped or sold abroad, but when these vessels disappeared altogether from Royal Navy service during the 1970s FAA squadrons ironically started making more airfield movements again.

RAF airfields continued to see FAA elements drop in for brief stays at this time as had always been the case. Still more stations kept closing, though, indirectly forcing certain aircraft types to be centralised at one airfield. Canberras congregated at Wyton, Lightnings at Binbrook and Hercules at Lyneham. Fewer airfields were becoming available but the RAF was also considering aircraft servicing and maintenance factors, particularly with regard to older types such as the Canberra and Lightning.

If detachments and 'lodgers' served as the trademarks of unit movements in World War Two, air-to-air refuelling and helicopters have been their post-war equivalents. The RAF has employed airborne tanker aircraft since the late 1950s to enable military types to make ultra-long detachments. Such is the commonality of these movements plus the speed of aircraft that nobody bothers now to quote such quick trips in official listings. A squadron might fly to Cyprus for armament training lasting a week or two – surely noteworthy enough, one might say, but in this day and age not really. RAF, FAA and AAC helicopter squadrons suffer the same fate in this respect because of their use of 'non-airfields' which even AOP Austers would have baulked at flying from in the past.

The Empire has steadily disintegrated since 1945 – but homebased units were able to put a new place on their agenda in 1982. Argentina's invasion of the Falklands resulted in many RAF and FAA squadrons having to hastily form during the fighting. The Atlantic island of Ascension served as a most useful staging post, and continues to do so, though air-to-air refuelling has helped to break several operational range records. But the increase in squadrons was something of an illusion, as it showed up the RAF practice of sharing aircraft between operational and training units. Turning an OCU into a first-line unit bears more than a passing resemblance to the *Saracen Scheme* of World War Two when OTUs became squadrons if required in an emergency. This method of aircraft sharing first started on a small scale during the 1930s, is frighteningly reminiscent of those days and does not bode well for the future.

The future has already arrived as unit movements continue to take place on our military airfields. Certain aspects have changed, quite apart from the now accepted use of air-to-air refuelling and helicopters, particularly how the vast mixture of units as seen in earlier times have disappeared. Many things however still stay the same: most of the sixteen categories relating to World War Two apply today, RAF formations and disbandments still almost entirely occur at Expansion Period stations, and very few unit movements take place in one day. This last fact can frequently confuse researchers when they see exact dates quoted but the easy way to sort out a date is that if it is in wartime, the date reveals when the unit's aircraft moved base; in peacetime, it is when the unit officially moves. For once it pays to be vague when writing about unit movements between airfields as being too exact can bring problems, especially if comparing station and unit official records.

Scan unit movement lists and you can also spot not only elements continually reforming but certain airfield names recurring again and again. How many units have made such cyclical moves back to a place each used perhaps months, years or even decades earlier? It is remarkable to see the alterations in aircraft roles and equipment which have resulted. If any one airfield emphasises the cyclical effect, it has to be Thorney Island, for No 22 Squadron was the first unit there in 1938 and also the last when this famous airfield closed in 1976. By then the squadron's equipment had changed from biplane torpedo bombers to SAR helicopters.

The amount of time units have spent at airfields has varied wildly. FAA squadrons could pass through one and even two airfields in a single day to leave everyone gasping! At the other extreme, no British-based unit has stayed longer at an airfield than No 781 Squadron, a communications element which spent almost 35 years at Lee-on-Solent between June 1946 and March 1981 – not forgetting over five years more during World War Two when it similarly formed and disbanded at the same airfield.

Perhaps the best tribute one can pay to Britain's airfields in the unit movements story is that not one unit has ever had to disband because of enemy action, though No 793 Squadron's Blackburn Roc target towing monoplanes came perilously close to doing so when the Luftwaffe raided Ford on August 18 1940, only being saved by luckily having a detachment at Warmwell during the attack. No airfields of any country in the world which have seen prolonged front line service and action can boast such a record.

This book scores yet another first among others of its kind by describing the here, there and everywhere style of units, aircraft and their crews. Whenever people ask about an airfield, they want to know the site's name, when it opened, closed, its architecture, present use and who has used it in the past. Unit movements are crucial to every military airfield's history. Regardless of what the future holds, it is impossible to imagine British airfield unit movements ever ending. Musical chairs goes on.

To Those Who Made It All Possible

The story of British aviation is a classic chicken and egg situation. People needed aircraft; aircraft needed airfields. The first two have previously received all the praise through the years, and now airfields are belatedly gaining the credit too. But even airfields needed the people who devised and built them: they never receive any praise. Let us now try to redress the balance and give due recognition to these largely anonymous heroes for their foresight and effort over decades.

Anyone who says that all one requires to do to create an airfield is to select a large area of flat land has no idea of the work involved. Certain cardinal rules have always existed in the selection and construction of any site. Unfortunately, the more experience gained has brought with it a baffling array of problems. To achieve one necessary stage of an airfield's path to fruition, designers and builders have often had to negotiate some astonishingly difficult obstacles.

Early British airfields showed how little pioneer aviators had thought about selection of suitable sites. Finding an open space was easy enough but they had reckoned without marshes divided by ditches. Noel Pemberton Billing, after having gone right over the top as usual and purchased 3,000 acres of land for his proposed Fambridge site, learned the hard way. Landing areas of the time were also too rough for aircraft, the wind and natural obstructions created problems, and leasing difficulties were made worse by suspicious officialdom. Farnborough proved different by lying on a common which was both open for airships or aircraft and suitably free of drainage plus contractural problems. No wonder it is still active after all these years.

By the time World War One arose, military airfield selection was left to the War Office and Admiralty for RFC and RNAS sites respectively. The latter department chose some landing grounds too before the War Office took over in early 1916. Wartime saw necessary airfield selection requirements expand slightly as grass sites were chosen if possible rather than arable land. Not every lesson had been learned from the Fambridge and Leysdown days, though, as ditches and obstructions still brought many aircraft to grief. Landing areas themselves often remained rough as well, a fact attributable to two causes. Senior military officers largely chose HD landing grounds instead of official surveyors, so it was perhaps inevitable how some sites would prove unsatisfactory. Strategic requirements, particularly when it came to countering the U-boat threat, meant some coastal airfields had frighteningly uneven landing areas.

As they lay in exposed positions, coastal bases tended more than most to feel the effects of that uniquely British obsession – the weather. An airfield had to be serviceable in all climates. Construction workers hated rain and snow. Rain usually brought heavy flooding; snow was even worse as, after a freezing winter, the resultant thaw saw flooding become more intolerable than ever. There followed mud, which seemed to stick to aircraft wheels and just about everything else. Planners, builders and airfield personnel alike hated mud more than any other problem. Storm damage could badly affect frail aircraft and less strong airfield buildings too, and planners quickly had to recognise the unexpected additional effects of crosswinds and circuit turbulence around each site.

World War One resulted in various nationalities appearing to build military airfields. Such diverse groups as Americans, Canadians and even Chinese struggled to construct the 500 sites in Britain at this time. Government authorities have always found suitable airfield construction labour hard to find, and World War One was no different. Minister of National Service Sir Auckland Geddes, brother of the infamous future Axeman, implied as such in a speech on November 12 1917 when, amid a lot of typical political blustering, he stated: 'What I do want at present is a steady supply of labour to build aerodromes . . . I definitely appeal tonight for 10,000 men for aerodrome work . . .' Many of the unfit or unemployed – '. . . anyone who can lay a brick . . .', as Geddes put it – dutifully crawled out of the woodwork, but this plan backfired on the Government as many farm workers badly hampered agricultural operations when they switched to airfield construction.

An unusual remedy was the use of German PoWs as forced labour during 1917/18. Various airfields were built by this method, especially in southern England, one being Old Sarum. It is a sad reflection on the society of today that prisoners built eight Belfast hangars in 1917, their free offspring bombed one 24 years later, but British arsonists made a much better job of destroying two in 1987.

The employment of rather less than friendly helpers did not mean they would produce poor airfields: after all, Old Sarum is still active. But conversely British assistance produced some real 'disaster' airfields. One was Westgate's landplane airfield, as opposed to the far superior seaplane base in Kent, which had to prematurely close in mid-1916 after its landing area literally crumbled away! Responsible for this strange phenomenon were eroding cliffs which made take-offs highly dangerous.

Even Westgate proved nothing compared to the Loch Doon saga, a fiasco of quite mind-numbing proportions which still creates many red faces in Government circles. For those of you who have not visited the area, Loch Doon is a beautiful part of southern Scotland, south-east of Ayr, but an airfield is the last thing to be expected in this area. Intended as a training station, its builders (including German PoWs) finally gave up in the first half of 1918. To cut a long and best forgotten story short, Loch Doon was sited on a bog! Media reports still unusually named it in Parliamentary reports despite naming restrictions of the time. The Government had spent a colossal sum – figures vary wildly from £400,000 to around £3 million – and all for nothing. An equivalent sum in current monetary terms would be running well into eight figures.

Human instead of sheer geographical factors also made British airfield planning and construction an extremely tricky business to co-ordinate. Parliament tried to cover its Loch Doon tracks by constantly complaining about land requisition, workmanship, wages, levels of workrate and strikes. While many of these complaints were totally unwarranted, Government accusations seemed to have a certain amount of validity when it came to fraud. Extensive allegations of this nature arose over the construction of Renfrew's AAP and adjacent Aircraft Repair Depot: it was claimed how books or time sheets had been falsified by entering the names of men in reality not employed on construction duties. So great did this row develop that an action was brought to the Scottish courts in February 1920 by the Air Council against Renfrew's contractors Messrs F.C. Cowieson and Company for the alleged overpayment of £49,908. The case was only settled on March 31 1921 with Cowieson being cleared, a decree granted against him for only £1,000 as assessment for the amount appropriated by dishonest employees and even being entitled to expenses.

Not so apparently convincing was part of the Select Committee on National Expenditure's third report of August 1919 in its analysis of workrate. After mentioning how work at Halton had started and then stopped, Administrator of Works and Buildings Sir John Hunter was asked why such enormous wages were paid by contractors. He stated that it was all settled by the Government, nobody had written more strongly on the subject than he had, and that no man employed on airfield construction had earned the money he had received in his opinion. This formal account was highly dubious in its presentation, and Hunter did nothing to endear himself to the gallant 70,000 airfield builders – an even greater total than in World War Two – by saying that his comments covered '. . . the whole lot of them.'

Airfield planning and construction otherwise continued with great success for the rest of World War One. Official policy at the Armistice of November 1918 was to stop work on stations under construction whenever possible but building kept going at some airfields until policy deemed it had to stop. Destruction now replaced construction, followed by general stagnation for the next 15 years or so, again in line with Government thinking.

Two items of note still occurred during this prolonged fallow period, one as the doldrums started and the other as this phase ended, which had far-reaching consequences. The Civil Aerial Transport Committee suggested at the beginning of 1919 in its ultra-thorough report various ideas for airfield construction, many of which were later put into operation. Sites ought to be fairly clear of houses, free from obstructions and poor weather, provided with good support facilities and be capable of expansion. Now civil airports and airfields had a good yardstick as to their successful and continued existences.

The second noteworthy event received nothing like the same media publicity as the Civil Aerial Transport Committee but, at least militarily if not overall, became of even greater importance. The War Office had previously endured great criticism for requisitioning a number of proposed HD landing grounds in World War One and then abruptly discarding them. Allegations of reckless commandeering resulted with similar claims of hundreds of acres containing corn and wheat being wasted at considerable cost. It was left to Noel Pemberton Billing to ask in Parliament during December 1917 whether a proper committee would be formed for airfield selection. For once the Government took notice of this unrecognised genius, though not until 1934 did the Air Ministry Aerodromes Board become established to choose suitable future airfields, regardless of whether they were intended for RAF or FAA use. One of its heads turned out to be none other than Air Vice-Marshal C.A.H. Longcroft, the same Captain Longcroft who had taken part in that epic journey from Farnborough to Upper Dysart during February 1913.

The work-load of the Air Ministry Aerodromes Board immediately piled up as the Expansion Period started that same year. Yearly Air Estimates of huge six figure sums for each new airfield became regularly published. Selection techniques had now been refined and split into three procedures. Surveyors came first to inspect the proposed site, farmers or landowners being notified by letter in the 1930s of official visits. However, these officials unwittingly created yet another problem by sometimes coming before the letters arrived! Fierce arguments often resulted.

How did surveyors know where to look? Although there is no firm evidence as such to prove it, many new airfields lay on or near World War One era sites, so it is quite feasible that engineers may have waded into old official files for some kind of inspiration. Detling, Feltwell, Montrose and Scampton were a few typical examples of airfields resuscitated after two decades of disuse. Other chosen airfields with no past history were probably discovered as Air Ministry men branched out from these sites. A handful more arose out of sheer chance when aircraft made forced landings on empty fields; two of the 'Magnificent Seven' in Debden and Tangmere came to prominence in this way.

Once surveyed from both the ground and air, the proposed airfield had to undergo consideration of its suitability. This period of contemplation took quite a while as geographical, geological and topographical issues had to be pondered over. Civilian areas were avoided both for their closeness and possible industrial haze from towns and cities. An aircraft would not want to crash into an important factory either. Yet a future airfield still needed good communications to allow vital supplies to arrive quickly. Planners had recognised this fact in World War One when airfields were linked up to the rail network. Roads now mattered too as vehicular traffic improved.

Provided a site met these and other requirements, the Air Ministry Aerodromes Board would make a compulsory purchase. Problems could occur even here if more than one owner of the required land was involved. A contract with a construction company would be let in due course. Airfield builders have always remained the same, a vast number of firms from big names such as Laing, McAlpine and Wimpey to local ones. Construction companies came under the control of the Air Ministry Works Department, which became colloquially known in the RAF as 'Works and Bricks'. Their men and equipment would move in to grade the landing area, reseed the grass or returf it wherever necessary. Already the massive importance of preparing the landing area at the expense of everything else had become evident. Official statements of the 1930s often said how an airfield would be available from such a date, before the Station HQ opened, though no facilities of any kind could be provided, hence proving how the landing area was all important when it came to construction techniques. Villages, houses, farms, trees and whole woods often had to be felled, regrettable actions which led to much bitterness but were simply unavoidable. The forthcoming war knocked out all other considerations.

No more of those fine Georgian style buildings which characterised the Expansion Period were built from scratch after September 1939. Surveying periods became shorter and queues of construction workers longer as Britain's airfields rapidly increased in number and their boundaries became ever more jagged. Despite many former unemployed men joining building squads, a scarcity of labour still existed, so large numbers of imported Irish labourers moved in. The Army, Royal Marines and Canadian engineers helped out initially too. Heavy requisitioning began again of farms, houses or hotels and often met considerable local opposition.

One particular thorn in the Air Ministry Aerodromes Board's side proved the War Agricultural Executive Committee, which fiercely opposed the whole concept of British airfield construction. Airfield planners were nowhere near as narrow-minded but, in reluctant deference to the farming fraternity, had to take two new factors into account. What was the land used for? Was it available or suitable? Food production had to be considered – however unenthusiastically.

The question of suitability became especially crucial by the time World War Two started. While all the old area advantages like good communications remained, proposed airfields did not want to be sited on too high or too low ground. The former would be terribly exposed, subject to low cloud, make aircraft approaches tricky and also require longer runways as thin air provides less lift for aircraft. But low sites, particularly those in valleys, could suffer from fog, mist and flooding.

Ground as opposed to area suitability now gained a far greater place in planning thinking as well. Yes, airfields had to be flat, but not supremely flat as to gently undulate and allow drainage; draining a landing area has always proved more costly than levelling. Ground slopes and gradient limits therefore became more flexible. Tremendous advances occurred during World War Two in soil and sub-soil stabilisation, the process of mixing soils and/or special stabilising agents with the normal soil. Soil types became far more widespread than in World War One because of concrete runways and better aircraft undercarriages. Heavy, solid soils were excellent; clay soils could get by, though they created problems in wet weather. Marshy or boggy land like the Fens in eastern England was naturally unsuitable, while peat was definitely not good for airfields with its high water content.

Now that the area and ground suitability of an airfield had been accepted, building work could begin. Construction techniques were honed still further into a fine art during World War Two. Basic moves would be to order civilians off the designated land, then have tractors fitted with steel hawsers uproot trees, wrench out hedgerows, fill in ditches and avoid dykes. Road closures also came into force: hundreds were sealed off in wartime, including famous ones like the Fosse Way which crossed Kemble and Long Newnton. Both stretches of this ancient highway remain closed to this day, even though Long Newnton has long fallen into disuse.

Next stop in airfield construction was the removal of major obstructions. Telegraph wires often had to be buried to make way for power supply lines, though the latter were also placed underground on approaches to airfields for safety reasons. Obstructing buildings were naturally next for removal, being frequently cleared with explosives, before runway laying and construction of buildings started. But some obstructions became useful landmarks and so escaped demolition. Church spires and similar structures could be fitted with red warning lights. Woods did not have to be removed either as they could help conceal vulnerable airfield support facilities, notably bomb dumps.

It soon became apparent how airfield construction was posing problems as soon as workers moved in. Again a lack of manpower resulted. This led to building material shortages and a shortfall in sophisticated machinery: the spade still ruled. General confusion as to who should be doing what arose and occasionally created unruliness among builders. The subsequent delays were highlighted by a Government Select Committee on National Expenditure in April 1941, stating how some airfield building contracts had fallen months behind schedule. One unnamed site was claimed to have only

500 workmen when 1,000 of them were needed instead. Although allegations about corruption remained unsubstantiated as in World War One, contractors were encouraged to make greater use of sub-contractors. The report surprisingly ended by saying that the Air Ministry should be more considerate when dealing with landowners. Had the War Agricultural Executive Committee been flexing its political lobbying muscles?

Despite these difficulties, the tens of thousands of construction workers ploughed on through all weathers to finish scores of new airfields. They had to learn the new techniques of prefabricated construction and how to scatter support buildings amid the countryside; Ayr II is generally thought to have revolutionised the general idea of support facility dispersal. A lot of time had to be spent on laying hard runways. One airfield had seen 180,000 square yards of concrete laid in a month, another 18,000 square yards in just one day, but these feats were rare as runway laying tended to be a laborious process. Another Government report in May 1941 claimed that the costs of landing areas were being greatly exceeded; one case revealed how the excess amounted to a staggering 1,600 per cent. The money spent still turned out to be totally worthwhile.

These forgotten heroes called construction workers never received any publicity worth talking about from the mass media as they slogged it out day after day trying to build airfield after airfield. Yet the people whom every site was eventually intended for did not display such ignorance as RAF personnel often made public relations visits to urge the workmen along and show how they appreciated what these civilians were doing for the war effort. Airfield builders liked these calls as they felt wanted, just as in the same way did those other ignored stars of the air war during World War Two, Britain's aircraft factory workers. Soon service personnel began appearing in greater numbers at new airfields not quite ready. First came the equipment officer to get in petrol and stores, then ground staff of various kinds. Once a senior medical officer had passed the airfield fit for use, its permanent staff moved in.

Construction work to complete a new airfield took on average about a year during World War Two – but hardly any fresh site was totally ready for aircraft and personnel. The conflict had brought with it various new dimensions to airfield building. Light, fuel, power and water systems often became delayed for weeks or even months as the vital landing area was prepared. It is a common misconception that the runways alone bore the greatest priority, for actually the perimeter track of an airfield did to allow builders' vehicles a mud-free approach road. Domestic sites suffered as a direct consequence from such a lack of basics as stoves for cooking: even when completed, the speed at which they were created meant standards often did not reach perfection. Complaints from personnel not surprisingly resulted, people who perhaps only weeks earlier had been praising airfield construction workers to the skies. Contractors' lorries also frequently still remained present in abundance and their equipment tended to litter newly-opened airfields. This led to collisions between lorries and aircraft either taxying, taking off or landing and a few unfortunate fatalities.

If World War Two had brought with it certain advanced problems in airfield construction, these proved nothing compared to the various unexpected difficulties which cropped up. One that became familiar in time was how planning strategies for airfields changed dramatically, so a site could be caught short in support facilities for its new role. Limited refuelling facilities or insufficient accommodation levels for major operational units served as two examples. Once active, aircraft use became so tremendously heavy that runways and perimeter tracks suffered terrific wear and tear. Repairs frequently had to take place, often while flying continued as had happened with the laying of runways. Then came the problem of circuit overlap, caused by the awesome numerical strength of airfields. Planners now had to take into account the distances between each site to avoid mid-air collisions between aircraft.

One World War Two problem was not unexpected but potentially posed the greatest difficulty of all: the Luftwaffe. Just because an airfield was under construction did not ensure it immunity from enemy attack: far more the opposite as lorries and machinery churned up fields into distinctive shapes. The dangers of the airfield construction business became all too sadly clear when Stanton Harcourt suffered a disastrous attack on August 16 1940. Luftwaffe bombers ran riot over the unfinished Oxfordshire bomber OTU satellite to leave nine workmen dead in their wake. Such ferocity was fortunately never again repeated, especially as AA guns were specially set aside afterwards for the protection of unfinished airfields and their builders, though several other British airfields in this state would be attacked during the remainder of World War Two. Fears of enemy aircraft or gliders landing earlier in the conflict saw anti-invasion obstructions such as old cars, trip wires and poles being laid on airfields and surrounding fields but the use of cars ceased after November 1940 as towing them on and off repeatedly badly cut up grassy landing areas.

Not every Luftwaffe airfield raider was able to find its target. Camouflage was the reason, a passive deterrent which cost a lot of money but surpassed all its planners' expectations. Building workers had to be diverted in order to make support buildings seem less regular or distinctive and 'dissolve' airfield landing areas into the surrounding countryside. Reflection became a serious problem, especially with runways, and so various camouflage coverings were introduced. Bitumen, pre-coloured slag chippings and stones helped, though the latter type of substance tended to burst aircraft tyres and unnecessarily damage their propellers, a defect which could only be avoided by manually brushing runways and other tracks. But wood chippings became the unusual best answer for runway camouflage, for not only could they be easily produced, they stuck to runways. All this work could be a waste of time if an airfield lay on thin ground which could be heavily scored, but the relative absence of enemy aircraft over Britain late on in World War Two meant less time and money needed to be devoted to camouflage.

Enough Luftwaffe aircraft still made their mark for both planners and builders to realise how repair work had become another part of their busy daily lives. The Pioneer Corps was initially used for airfield repair but the Battle of Britain proved how neglected this duty had become as any available airmen were summoned to fill in craters. Works Services Flights (later known as Airfield Construction Squadrons) were thus devised, mobile units assigned to carrying out repairs and complete with their own equipment and transport. Routine airfield maintenance became another standard task, a Flight having 70-80 personnel stationed at each site. The RAF formed its own engineering corps in early 1941.

The frantic British airfield building programme reached even greater intensity once the Americans appeared during 1942. US Army Engineer Aviation Battalions moved in, with Andrews Field becoming the first American-built airfield in Britain. Work here finished three months ahead of schedule, not least because it went on at night with the help of screened lights. Another EAB was claimed in July 1943 to have taken only 89 days to clear an area of land, lay out runways and make it ready for bomber use. A total of 4,153,590 square feet of concrete had been put down at this unnamed airfield, plus seven miles of water main, four miles of sewer line and 26 miles of electrical wiring installed. This was a remarkable feat by any standards but American construction elements otherwise found putting new airfields together as prolonged a task as their British compatriots.

The US Army Engineer Aviation Battalions, RAF Airfield Construction Squadrons and Royal Engineers' Airfield Construction Groups later found themselves building, then being attached to the ALGs in southern England. Not only did this work help in furthering the strategic and tactical cause, it provided these military forces with invaluable operational training for when they had to cross the English Channel after D-Day and build airstrips in France. Considerable requisitioning of surrounding farms and houses became necessary to accommodate ALGs, but then the whole of southern England was already one gigantic requisitioned area.

Two types of British airfield in World War Two turned out to be poor beneficiaries of the building programme. Flying boat bases had always been ramshackle – Pembroke Dock had required to use a floating dock for maintenance duties before the conflict – and bases such as Hamworthy/Poole or Bowmore on Islay left much to be desired. Part of the problem lay in their cramped situations, while no amount of camouflage was going to help cover their distinctive outlines.

FAA airfields also suffered at this time. Although the Admiralty had its own building programme, as opposed to the Air Ministry, the latter's Aerodromes Board chose sites for both the RAF and FAA. But the RAF was always given preference, so airfields transferred to the Navy were not always perfect for its special needs. The FAA had a rough deal as not many of the overall total of sites under its control during World War Two came purpose-built for its aircraft and personnel. The situation had however been remedied to a certain degree by 1944 as true FAA airfields like Anthorn, Burscough, East Haven, Henstridge, Rattray and Ronaldsway came on stream. Yet it is a sign of how unfairly the service was treated by the fact that two of the last three airfields to open in Britain during World War Two belonged to the FAA: Rattray and Oxfordshire base Culham.

Many became the airfields which would never materialise during World War Two – at least FAA sites had been better late than never. The increasingly hopeful war situation for Britain meant they were not necessary; strategic or tactical considerations could change too. But other proposed sites only saw rejection because agricultural land would allegedly be lost. Unlike World War One, when several sites were only half-completed, only one airfield – Millisle in Northern Ireland – remained unfinished in the second conflict.

As Millisle had shown, little wastage resulted from airfield building during World War Two. It was revealed in January 1944 how Britain had become one huge airfield, covering more than 250,000 acres of land. By then the limit of suitable ground had almost been reached – but room still existed for more ALGs, new FAA stations and noted RAF bases like Bentwaters, Wiltshire's Blakehill Farm and Full Sutton in Yorkshire. The Air Ministry estimated at this time that the building programme for both the British and American air forces would be £615 million, though the final figure was surely more like £1 billion or just short of that total.

Further information quoted at the start of February 1944 managed to illustrate to an extent the incredible effort already involved. The total area of paved runways, perimeter tracks and hardstandings then reached almost 160 million square yards or the equivalent of 9,000 miles of road 30 feet wide. Ballast totalling 30 million tons, one million tons of steel and cast iron, 18 million cubic feet of wood and over one million accommodation huts were needed for airfield tracks and support facilities. These required in turn almost 7,000 electrical transformers, 9,800 switchboards and 336,000 miles of cables: not surprisingly, the RAF became the Post Office's biggest customer when it came to wiring. More official information released after World War Two said that airfield paving had increased to 175 million square yards or about 10,000 miles of road, while £645 million had to be spent on airfields to accommodate the USAAF in Britain. This last figure is significant as not only does it prove how the overall monetary total stopped much closer to the £1 billion mark, Britain bore £605 million of the cost to emphasise how this country nowhere near entirely relied upon America for financial support.

Peacetime inevitably brought another rapid rundown in airfield construction work, but rampant technology and 'the bomb' factor meant this job never effectively ceased as had happened for the first 15 years after World War One. Famous FAA station Culdrose in Cornwall still had to be completed, the only all-new British military airfield built since World War Two. The 1950s and the advent of jet aircraft saw considerable revamping of military bases, with special attention being given to extending runways or radically redeveloping their entire layouts. Measures had to be taken to counter the constant damage caused by pacifist sabotage and lack of security. Planners now became worried about possible subsidence from old mine workings as well to put some airfields under threat. Whatever task was required, it provided builders with a steady source of employment.

This low-key work continues at military airfields in Britain as construction workers still beaver away with hardly any recognition. Hardened Aircraft Shelters and ultra-modern support buildings keep appearing, as do new operations blocks, fuel storage tanks and greater than ever amounts of fencing to ward off terrorists and protestors. Load factors of runways need to be constantly checked too as they have to cope with the incredible weights of aircraft.

Civil aviation has for once seen more building work in more recent years than that carried out at military sites. Vast work has been carried out at airports in particular to provide them with new terminals, support facilities and even new runways. Yet the old airfield planning thinking of how a site ought to be near good lines of communication still applies as every major airport in Britain stands near major roads and railway lines.

For all the massive amount of airfield building in Britain down the years, World War Two will always be remembered above all. But perhaps the greatest tribute to the tens of thousand anonymous heroes who made it all possible came from the Secretary of State for the RAF Lord Rothermere in April 1918, when he said to airfield workers: 'Without your help he (the average airman) can do nothing . . .'

The tragedy was that most of their efforts counted for nothing.

PART THREE:
The Tragedy

A Horror Story To Beat Them All

If you have ever visited one of Britain's disused airfields, the scene is far too often one of wanton destruction and desolation. A few World War Two era sites, like Kimbolton in Cambridgeshire and Tuddenham in Suffolk, have reached the stage where resemblance to an airfield is all but nil; a few World War One airfields can be rated exceptionally fortunate to even look like one. How on earth was this decay allowed? After countless years of complete dismission, the story of how our premier historical sites were betrayed in their moment of need is now told in detail for the first time. It is a horrifying and quite sickening tale: one of deceit, personal greed, government incompetence and a sheer lack of appreciation.

An indication of the heinous crimes to come occurred after the end of World War One in November 1918 as hundreds of airfields, of all types, fell unwillingly to the axe. Any site was in dire trouble once the Air Ministry reduced its state of condition from List C (Station temporarily retained for service purposes) to List E (Station no longer in RAF use, passed to the Ministry of Munitions' Surplus Property Disposal Board). Then, just as after World War Two, the ignorant voiced the usual glib remarks as to why airfields ought to disappear in droves. Each site was too costly, not required for future needs, strategically and tactically obsolescent, times were different and that peace could be achieved in other ways without using force to counter force. Are these attitudes not reminiscent of today?

Airfields in Britain closed with almost indecent haste following the Armistice, 1919 being the worst period. A total of 116 airfields and landing grounds had already been released for cultivation by May 1 of that year; 52 airfields, 147 landing grounds and 11 marine bases were later stated as either available for relinquishment or to be disposed of by August 6. A further check during 1919 on November 6 revealed how 122 permanent stations plus 124 landing grounds and what were described as 'camping grounds' had passed to the Disposal Board, with six more airfields having been released but their buildings still retained for RAF purposes.

In duly stepped the aforementioned Government organisation to auction off derequisitioned land and buildings. Standard procedure was to offer airfield buildings to the landowner and local authorities for housing purposes; if neither party showed interest, they were advertised for sale *in situ;* demolishing would follow if no sale was effected. As the majority of World War One airfields consisted of wooden and canvas structures, all were easy to clear at low prices. Unlike after World War Two, farmers proved to be not very active among purchasers, seemingly happy in acquiring land. Most buyers turned out to be scrap merchants, ready to dismantle airfield facilities for various materials.

Records still exist from these early days of disused airfield auctions. A good example involved Turnberry in Ayrshire, now of course scene of the famous golf course. (Is it possible to pick up a golfing book without seeing someone attack the airfield?). This former Great War training base was sold on February 26 1920 for almost £8,000, and details remain of individual items purchased. A salvage shed measuring 172 x 165 x 25 feet reached £1,150, and four hangars £420, £410, £400 and £310 each. Among other buildings, a workshop was bought for £510, a goods shed for £250, stores hut for £205, guard hut for £150, technical stores for £110 and metal workshops for £105. Huts formerly used by the Women's Royal Air Force ranged in price from £80 to £140, while other huts and stores were cleared at costs between £64 and £155. Another auction further down the Clyde coast that month at Luce Bay, the West Freugh of today, saw a big attendance from all over Britain. Heavy bidding resulted in a large airship shed being sold for £2,750, with four large wind-breaks going for £196 each. Yet no Great War traces remain at either airfield today, an appalling feature of those terrible times.

By the early 1920s disused airfields of the World War One period had all but disappeared from the British landscape. A total of 146 permanent stations had been relinquished by July 1925. Support facilities in particular went through agonies, which is why literally only a handful of buildings still survive today. Neither was our first major permanent hangar design in the Belfast excluded from the carnage. Airfields which did possess examples of this type, such as Hawkinge and Lympne, stood a far greater chance of survival, yet many Belfasts on disused airfields were demolished. No adequate reason was given by the authorities: they apparently simply wanted every possible airfield out of the way. Thousands upon thousands of memorials were erected all over Britain – but only two on airfields. Even these commemorative stones at Turnberry and Walmer in Kent each served more as a unit memorial, not an airfield one. If ever the old saying 'out of sight, out of mind' applied to anything, it was surely to our World War One heroes.

But even at this desperate period, some far-sighted individuals were already having grave doubts about such a destructive policy. Why could permanent airfield buildings not be saved for future use – and not just for aeronautical needs? Controller-General of Civil Aviation and Sefton Brancker's predecessor Major-General Sir F.H. Sykes had suggested as much in a speech during April 1919. He stated that, from an international viewpoint, airfields could either be taken over by engineering and motor industries or acquired by aircraft companies. Others proposed how disused airfields, by means of their excellent positions, could be turned into hospitals, sick homes and training centres: their awesome social benefits were already starting to shine through the gloom.

Opinions such as these at last received concrete support from the late 1920s as airfields in Britain once more began to increase in strength. Civil aviation thrived, so more airfields were needed. Unfortunately, proposed sites had been flattened only a few years earlier, therefore rebuilding work had to start from scratch. Builders quite rightly complained about what seemed to be unnecessary work. Hangars and major support buildings could have quickly and easily adapted for civil needs had they enjoyed retention. Savings in valuable time, effort and money could have resulted. Examples became numerous but one of the best was Cramlington in Northumberland. In September 1925, the Newcastle-on-Tyne Aero Club secured its position at this former World War One HD Flight Station, a place which had in fact pioneered defensive fighter operations in Britain by having the first HD RFC squadron form here. The newer civil organisation subsequently survived but Cramlington found life difficult as every wartime building had already disappeared from trace and closed in 1936. This was unusual as most civil airfields of this period usually managed to keep going until 1939 and the outbreak of World War Two.

How club members must have wished Cramlington could have found itself in the position of somewhere like East

Retford in Nottinghamshire. This erstwhile night flying training airfield, despite being closed for good years before, was an increasingly extreme rarity. Although its hangars had also suffered removal, a number of huts still remained. And this was 1929 . . .

Sixteen years and a torrent of water under the proverbial bridge had passed when the meaningless madness began to rear its ugly head again. World War Two had effectively ended for Britain's airfields when Germany surrendered in May 1945. Of course, many sites were already disused, namely the small civil private and flying club airfields which outlasted Cramlington but had to close in September 1939. The Hall Caines and Horton Kirbys, Wenvoes and Wilmingtons never saw aircraft again – tremendous technological advances in aircraft and limited landing areas became the main reasons – but some of these silenced places still possessed good support facilities and could have served a useful purpose post-war. Why they had really fallen by the wayside was the cruel fact that people had forgotten about them and not looked ahead.

Soon this mental disease spread with alarming alacrity to military airfields. All had achieved stupendous success in wartime, yet no thought was again given as to their future needs – well, almost. On November 29 1943, as our supersites continued to rain blow upon blow on Germany, the Air Ministry News Service issued this sobering statement:

> 'In a country of the size of Great Britain the construction of so large a number of airfields has involved serious encroachments on land formerly available for agricultural and other purposes. It is not possible to express in terms of money what this diversion has involved, but it is very considerable. Further, a large proportion of the airfields constructed for war purposes cannot be used either for post-war military purposes or for civil aviation. Therefore, so far from representing an asset of abiding value, the British Government will, upon the termination of hostilities, be faced with a very considerable liability for the reinstatement of sites and the restoration of land to its former uses.'

Doom-laden and, as the passing of time would show, extremely ill-judged words indeed. But worse was to come. A letter of February 1944 from a man described as the manager of a large agricultural estate who was replying to an effusive pro-airfield article quoted three days earlier, gave due warning of the 'respect' our heroes could expect in peacetime:

> 'The airfield which has been carved out of my land is one of those which are far from urban amenities . . . We are 40 miles from the nearest large city, which already possesses an excellent civil airport. What, then, is to become of areas such as this when the time arrives for reducing the number of landing grounds for military aircraft? To get an aerodrome under cultivation again would be a prodigious task, and could not in itself solve the problem of multitudes of buildings unsuitable for agricultural purposes, with wide concrete roads out of reach of the main streams of traffic.
>
> Britain may be an 'unsinkable aircraft carrier', but if such vessels are to be required at all in the post-war era I imagine that the movable type will suffice. Neither type is suitable for food production. Has any authoritative persons or body of persons given due thought to this tremendous problem, which demands a very large part of the attention of post-war planners?'

Reading this letter more closely, it becomes obvious how three fallacies appear along with a selfish attitude and general arrogance. The reintroduction of farming would not be difficult; support buildings would display considerable versatility; and runways plus perimeter tracks would actually aid motorists. But these were points to be aired in future years: what mattered in mid-1945 was that anti-airfield battle lines had already been drawn.

If you go to the Public Record Office in London and look up any airfield Operations Record Book, it is fairly easy with practice to see when an RAF station is due to close. Entries in month-by-month record sheets made by the Station Commanding Officer or senior officer present become gradually fewer; the daily comment 'Nothing to report' arises with depressing frequency. Unit movements and activities slowly wind down until aircraft stationed at the site go elsewhere or are flown off to an MU if a unit is disbanding. Closure to flying then happens before a state of C&M frequently arises, when only essential tasks are performed. Many airfields are transferred to Maintenance or Technical Training Commands, in whose hands flying becomes barely minimal or ceases altogether. ORB comments now quickly

Farmers harvest on the edge of an RAF Bomber Command airfield during World War Two as a Halifax undergoes servicing and another takes off. Were they thinking of days ahead? *(IWM)*

(above) First the runways were painted with crosses to signify closure to flying. Just any old airfield? Only the legendary Debden.
(below) Then came the closing down of airfield sites. Fading paint above its door still marks out Matlaske's sad guardroom.

(above) Eventually came the disused airfield auctions. This small support building at Shellingford continues to remember its final humiliation.
(below) Finally all too often came demolition – and still does. An execution notice at Burtonwood, once one of the world's most important airfields. But when property developers want some more houses . . .

(above) A parade ground? No, Carew Cheriton's technical site. Some call scenes like this 'tidying up': others would say desecration.
(below) Hard to believe, but this road amid a housing estate once used to be part of the western landing area of Staffordshire training airfield Perton. Those oh-so-considerate property developers have provided this area with 'suitable' road names. Up ahead on the right is Manston Road: what on earth has it got to do with Perton?

A few glimpses of the depressing British disused airfield runway and supporting tracks story.
(above) An access track at Marston Moor in North Yorkshire. A total of 175 million square yards of concrete, tarmac and other hard surfaces were laid in World War Two to provide paved runways and associated tracks. This enterprise cost £200 million – so why tear it up again?
(below) One of Hemswell's runways, virtually (and freshly) removed.

If 'lucky', a disused airfield can see its runways only being affected by chippings, cracks, pot-holes and obstructions, like this runway intersection at Banff *(above)*. But more likely will be the terrible fate of being severely narrowed to become a farm track. Multiply Lissett's main runway *(below)* by about fifteen times across and you have its true width.

Amid a sea of nothing and crying out for help: Fulbeck's last remaining T2 before its greatest crisis. Local villagers protested when the Nuclear Industry Radioactive Waste Executive (NIREX) moved in during the autumn of 1986 to assess the suitability of this disused Lincolnshire site for nuclear waste storage. While an airfield destroying organisation was bad enough, the villagers were not innocent either. Of course, when Fulbeck lay disused, they did nothing, and a military training area proposal was met with much dismay. But when NIREX moved in during September, people such as vicars talked of the irony of its arrival coinciding in the same month as Arnhem, in which Fulbeck took part. If the villagers had transformed Fulbeck into a historical conservation area, no nuclear testing would probably have ever happened. It just goes to show how our disused airfields are classic places of convenience for the changeable attitudes of people.

(above) This Lancaster propeller, acting as a unit memorial to No 9 Squadron, stands in Bardney village. But surely it should have been placed at the airfield?

(below) An airfield memorial at an airfield – but, more importantly, 121 reasons why we must always remember. Plaques on either side of this symbolic Mosquito at the south-western side of Bradwell Bay list the personnel lost on operations while based here.

(above) On a happier note, our disused airfields never fail to pleasantly surprise. 'Temporary' buildings as houses? Impossible. Yet that square dwelling behind the brick wall is a converted 12779/41 control tower at Sandtoft in Humberside.
(below) And what about this flower-bedecked Maycrete support building in Norfolk? The road signs tell you where it is: Ludham.

(above) Another Maycrete, this time at Cark, providing more people with more jobs. Disused airfields are superb for industry, whether large or small.
(below) Just look at that list! A wonderful performance from former World War Two monster ELG Carnaby as we look down its old tremendously long runway, now known as Lancaster Road (Perton property developers take note). Jobs, facilities, services and appreciation of what made all this possible – perfect.

(above) More brilliant community service: part of the perimeter track at Great Orton in Cumbria has become a public road. Our disused airfields can easily tackle more specialised tasks too. Whether potato research at Sutton Bridge *(below)* or pipe storage on Longtown's main runway *(bottom),* nothing is too difficult.

(above) Another potential candidate to bite the dust? Houses and roads with pathetically absurd names creep ever closer to Panshanger. Its owner is none too keen on keeping the airfield open either . . .
(below) And how it could be if we act now: a control tower, T2 and Braithwaite water tower in the distance at Framlingham – a disused airfield despite initial appearances. In superb condition, with the added bonus of the control tower now serving as a museum.

amount to little more than standard statements at the end of each month such as 'The men are fit and well' or 'Morale is good'. There will be a final entry eventually to obliquely signify closure of the airfield. Yet even these extensive details do not quite fully describe the intricate business of how Britain's airfields were made tragic sacrificial lambs.

RAF airfields intended for closure would be stripped bare of their contents while still in military hands. Inventories would be checked, stores removed and all the various sites on an airfield methodically shut down. Lorries would arrive largely unnoticed to ferry out those items which could be easily taken away. This winding down process varied in duration by taking either a few days or a few months, though the latter usually prevailed because a lack of personnel made this grim job more difficult. Small maintenance crews from an assigned parent airfield visited now and again to check if everything was in order. Airfields on C&M were often nominally transferred between Commands and Groups, administrative changes which really meant nothing, before being eventually downgraded to inactive (guarded) status prior to total closure.

An even quicker departure was accomplished by the Americans, considering the long journey they had to undergo. Of the 54 USAAF airfields in East Anglia alone, only 14 still remained in American hands by October 10 1945; a total of 24 others had reverted to RAF control, while 16 more were in the process of transfer. US personnel had stayed on very good terms with the local population, and everyone was sorry to see them go. Apart from the normal removal of contents, the neighbouring civilian population was treated to large amounts of surplus food, including some items then considered as delicacies. But not every American unit left with good wishes, mainly because of its wasteful attitude to food and certain equipment. Minor riots occurred at one East Anglian airfield (its name is withheld here, to avoid embarrassment on both sides) when vast quantities of food were destroyed, although much of it had been hardly used. A large tin of jam was considered unfit to eat, to take one example, only because someone had taken a single spoonful out of the container. Why the food was discarded in this particular case remains unclear.

Also squandered for no purpose on USAAF airfields were various kinds of equipment. It seems that personnel threw items of all shapes and sizes into large holes in the ground and covered them over. Whether this practice occurred on a large scale has still to be fully confirmed. Rumour has it that even

Jeeps were buried underground! One cannot discount this claim, especially if the Lend-Lease agreement is recalled. Perfectly good military aircraft were dumped into the Atlantic Ocean off aircraft carriers to comply with inflexible officialdom after World War Two. So, if people could be capable of performing such madness, who would miss the odd Jeep, last seen several feet under East Anglia?

Once an airfield had closed, its immediate life over the next few months could only be described as most unreal. Undoubtedly the most striking feature became the total silence. Buildings empty of personnel, runways and supporting tracks devoid of aircraft and vehicles; it was as if every last drop of blood had been taken out of a human body. Derequisitioning had already started before the end of World War Two, mainly limited to ALGs, but by early 1946 destiny had many more sites in line for a quick return to farmland. The last of the SLGs for dispersed aircraft storage were in the process of going, soon followed by RLGs. Neither type of airfield had a great number of support buildings, and grass frequently sufficed as a landing area.

The numerous anti-airfield elements in Britain gleefully sharpened their knives in readiness for what they thought would be another easy kill like the events after World War One. But World War Two had established the airfield with hard runways, so opponents of our disused sites met much stiffer opposition. That fact worried their collective foes called the Establishment; soon the new Labour Government plus Conservative and other extant Opposition parties began hatching a huge diabolical plot to bring down the 800 plus sites which had existed at one time or another during the second world conflict.

Considerable time was given to a debate in the House of Lords on November 22 1945 concerning redundant airfields in Britain. Just fifteen days earlier, the Lower House had revealed in passing how since May 8 derequisitioning had reached completion or was in progress at 29 airfields with a total acreage of 7,500 acres; over 40,000 acres in all had been let for agricultural use. Lord Cranworth now called attention to the great acreage of agricultural land lying derelict, Lord Meston claimed how airfields in particular posed potentially serious compensation difficulties, and cheers resulted when the Duke of Norfolk stated that operational land ought to grow food for Britain and Europe. By doing some detective work, you inevitably find a story within a story, and in this case it was all to do with vested interest. The trick in research is to check the address of anyone who has ever criticised an airfield or airfields in general; do this and you will always find that vested interest is the common denominator. This House of Lords debate served as the perfect example as Lords Cranworth and Meston both lived in important airfield areas. One resided at Cookham Dean in Buckinghamshire, between EFTS base Booker and ATA headquarters White Waltham, while the other's home at Grundisburgh in Suffolk lay between Martlesham Heath and USAAF heavy bomber station Debach.

The Government replied to the claims of these peers by saying that co-operation between the Air Ministry and the War Agricultural Executive Committee had been so close (eh?) this was why over 40,000 acres of land on airfields were presently let for grazing or hay cutting. This formed a sixth of the total land requisitioned or owned by the Air Ministry and not covered by paving or buildings. A total of 100 airfields were now surplus to flying requirements and arrangements were being made for the 'dual user' military/civil system to cope with the urgent needs for food, storage and accommodation. Land at these airfields would be placed at the disposal of the Ministry of Agriculture. Farming would come under control of the War Agricultural Executive Committee, but in suitable cases land would be temporarily let out to neighbouring farmers until the land was derequisitioned. The 'dual user' system would be extended, and the Government hoped to quickly add another 100 airfields in this fashion.

These and other views met with laughter and general derision from the Opposition. Labour was out to get Britain's airfields – but so too were the Conservatives and other parties. Lord Cranworth moaned about the 'monstrous injustice' that a farmer (or more likely himself) who had his land and livelihood taken from him in the national interest should not have the first opportunity of utilising that same land. He was and remains completely wrong, for all farmers and landowners work in areas technically owned by nobody under centuries old laws: the word 'landowner' is really a complete misnomer and should be cast out of the English language. It was *our* land, for what *we* had to do, and the greatest emergency Britain has ever encountered meant that *we* needed airfields. But now *they* were trying to win.

First moves in the ultimate Armageddon started with a hunt to derequisition larger airfields at the beginning of 1946. The Government had stated in November 1945 how it intended to review the best ways of service, civilian and industrial uses for airfields. This would take account of agricultural interests: in political double speak, that meant votes, votes, votes. Yet so little media attention was given to these covert official actions that it almost confirms how authoritative forces had other ideas in mind. The only information of any sort then released revealed how the Government did not intend to derequisition runwayed airfields except in a few cases where a site had or nearly had one owner. It was one of the most disgraceful lies ever perpetrated.

Another official announcement followed just two months later in March to say that ploughing was allowable up to runway edges. But even this statement was a lie as the Operations Record Book for Gamston in Nottinghamshire quotes how ploughing was already noticeable by February.

March 1946 also revealed how nearly half of the 650 airfields in England and Wales had been given over for farming to increase food production. A total of 195 passed that month alone to the Ministry of Agriculture: 100 for total use, 60 for ploughing up to their runways and 35 for grazing. About 100 grass airfields were already in the process of derequisitioning. Unrestricted farming covered airfields definitely not required for flying again, their derequisitioning coming when the temporary military occupation of airfield buildings ended. At some sites, though, arable farming as well as grazing and hay cutting would be allowed even if these airfields might be again required for flying. Whatever way one looked at the situation, times had certainly rapidly changed since 78 airfields considered unsuitable for future flying and potentially available for unrestricted agricultural use had been released by both the RAF and Ministry of Aircraft Production in November 1945 to other government departments.

Still more Government activity occurred in April 1946 when it was claimed that airfields had greatly damaged public roads, a view since regarded as highly unusual to say the least. A total of 39 first class and 65 second class ones had been closed, of which twelve and few respectively had reopened by this time. Tilstock in Shropshire only closed because the Government wanted the A41 reopened. But surely all of our airfields had primary territorial as well as strategic considerations? How many traffic jams were to be seen moreover in Britain during World War Two?

Between then and 1947, the farmers and landowners (for the sake of simplicity only, that second dubious word will continue to be used) were allowed back in as in line with official policy instead of on loan. The speed of this action surprised many people: back in November 1945, the Earl of Rosebery summed up his thoughts of an extremely prolonged official transfer with the comment ‘By which time the farmer may be dead'. Now the Agricultural Land Commission became responsible for the agricultural use of redundant airfields, though both this organisation and farmers/landowners had to leave alone disused airfields. Yet what exactly constituted a disused airfield?

Since the late 1940s, tremendous confusion has resulted over this term. Successive governments must take responsibility, for they have never been able to make clear the meaning of 'disused airfield'. This has led to much misunderstanding among the general public and even some researchers. Although the term remains highly obscure with added complications, we can distinguish between airfields which completely closed and those which only closed to flying. In theory, an airfield became disused when powered aircraft ceased to fly from it on a constant basis, but . . . This is where problems arise. In reality, a disused airfield only came into effect when the military had completely pulled out and the site was relinquished by the authorities. If neither of the two above events arose, the best one can say is that closure to flying had resulted. Despite this, the situation remained vague, especially when gliders could still be seen. This was not a phenomenon confined to the late 1940s and early 1950s, for a number of ostensibly disused military airfields continue to bewilder experts by retaining these unpowered craft.

Here is as good a point as any to make a general introduction of probably the most dreaded of all airfield-related terms – Care and Maintenance. To those of you entering the world of British airfield research, C&M can be frighteningly complex; it does not have the normally accepted meaning of the term when applied to airfields. However, for C&M read inactive and a somewhat clearer picture of the situation can be discerned. From the service point of view, disused airfields have always been split into two categories: secondary bases for useful but less important non-flying duties and those not needed or 'surplus'. As long as there is the possibility of aircraft using an airfield at some point in the future, an airfield is under C&M. The word 'inactive' is in itself a strange term but applies particularly to an airfield on C&M which is reduced further to guarded status. After World War Two, such famous places as Debden, Digby, North Coates and even Hendon were classed as inactive but still busy, yet all were or still are inactive to *flying*.

Three main uses have occurred at airfields classed as in a C&M state – technical duties, training and accommodation-cum-storage – to make something of a mockery of the term. This latter combined purpose was much in evidence on airfields which had closed to flying after World War Two. Runways and supporting tracks groaned under the weight of a wide variety of munitions. Both ends of each runway first had to be marked with a white cross to signify it was closed, not that a pilot could fail to see the hordes of equipment before him. Even so, supposedly closed airfields remained open in a sense as some sites kept their main runways open for a long time in order to act as ELGs.

On the ground, 'disused' airfields resounded to several unusual activities. Bomb storage became fairly common, every available area being stacked up with weapons of all shapes and sizes. Britain had built up an enormous stockpile of weaponry during World War Two and subsequently found its airfields excellent places where to store them. Surplus bombs lay in menacing silence for several years until the mid to late 1950s, when they were removed to isolated areas and exploded.

A far safer form of storage was retention of vehicles by the War Department, who gradually sold off to individuals or scrapped millions of items. Almost anything from cars, spares and other surplus equipment to lorries and even tanks could be seen. Perhaps Britain was short of money but many people eagerly attended WD sales in the hope of finding a possible bargain. Where have all those military vehicles gone to since then, one might ask? Apart from holding many thousands of German PoWs until the last left in 1948, redundant airfields on a sadder note could also offer temporary relief to displaced persons unable to return to their homelands. Home Communist elements unfortunately took advantage of this situation and created organised squatting during 1946, a number of airfields being among places becoming unwillingly caught up in trouble.

While it seemed as if someone cared in Britain by helping foreign evacuees, the same could hardly have been said of the Air Ministry in its attitude to this country's disused airfields. It was supposed to maintain them in good condition – and did the exact opposite. Showing why Britain has long lost its greatness as a leading world power, the Air Ministry displayed a 'couldn't be bothered' air towards our wartime superstars. As nothing was done, whether deliberately or not, airfield installations soon lapsed into decay. Buildings began disappearing in mysterious fashion – incredible when government was supposed to have control over them. Officialdom was not interested in airfields. The warning signs were there: if highly decorated aircraft such as Lancaster *Mike Squared* and Halifax *Friday the 13th* (brilliant survivors of 268 operational bombing sorties between them) could be unceremoniously scrapped after World War Two, the same could happen to their airfields. And it did for the two sites primarily associated with these two individual aircraft, Elsham Wolds in Lincolnshire and Lissett in Yorkshire, mangled being the best way to describe them today.

Highly abusive remarks now started to appear in force in public circles, emitted by people trying to verbally annihilate Britain's airfields. Similar fusillades had rarely reached the light of day after World War One: possibly the reason why so little criticism of airfields resulted was how our sites had not quite acquired such towering control over their country. There was nevertheless one statement quoted during the autumn of 1921 from the Reverend E. Rhys Jones of Amesbury Vicarage in Wiltshire which proved an exception to the rule and acted as prototype for anti-airfield volleys in future decades:

> 'To some of us in this part of the country it seems amazing that the authorities appear to be taking no steps to hurry up the dismantling of the many derelict camps of all sorts and sizes round about us. I understand that the Stonehenge Aerodrome, for example, is to be demolished. But there it still stands, like so many of its fellows, decaying, deteriorating, and falling to pieces. The cost of dismantling it is to be met some time or other. Why not now? So the lay mind naturally queries, in the presence of so much good material gradually drifting into more or less valueless rubbish, and so many idle hands that might be employed in clearing up the debris, which disfigures the landscape, and will soon be of no use to anyone. Quis custodiet ipsos custodes?'

Classic passive antagonistic waffle from someone quite clearly a trendy before his time. A quarter of a century then passed, another war was fought and won, the world had changed considerably, but still the greater numbers of anti-airfield tirades remarkably followed the same style as that set by the wayward clergyman. Another example came during the summer months of 1946 from a man resident in London which typified the general level of tone:

> 'What settled policy exists to eliminate from the countryside the many unwanted Bomber and Fighter Command aerodromes and their

> accompanying defacements? To leave some of our best land – perhaps for years to come – flecked with runways and concrete aprons can only lead to the permanent impoverishment of the nation's heritage.'

In answer to such a shameful question, hardly any policy existed. About the only item of note was how the Agricultural Land Commission continued to oversee relatively few disused airfields. Although it had taken on another 17 sites to the year ended March 31 1951, the total of airfields or parts of airfields under ALC control still only reached 53. The Cold and Korean Wars had undoubtedly forced home authorities to hold on to many silent sites, just in case foreign events worsened. A more mundane reason was the Government statement in 1954 that although land would be offered back to former owners whenever possible, exceptions to this general policy would have to be made. Airfields naturally formed the top rank of these special cases.

It is pleasing to note that by the early 1950s airfield conservationists were already hard at work, gathering vital evidence for the future prosecution. Although these admirable individuals proved all but powerless, for incredibly little news appeared about disused airfields in Britain between 1945 and 1960, they did at least help to start the ball rolling. Photographs of the time present a disturbing picture, mainly showing buildings in various poor states. Already windows are smashed and doors off their hinges; in a not inconsiderable number of photographs, huts have been reduced to flattened hulks. This was bad enough, but the real tragedy is that we are talking about major operational airfields. Only eight years had passed at most since they had helped to save Britain. What a reward . . .

Proof of how our disused airfields were badly mouldering away as early as the mid-1950s can be best shown by this sermon quoted in September 1956 from a woman living in Broadway in Worcestershire. The main point of her short statement was to condemn the construction of new runways at an airfield in her area, unnamed but almost certainly Pershore, yet this woman still found plenty of time like many of her contemporaries to blast away at some disused airfields:

> 'Apart from the question of the injudicious spending of public money, would it not be more practical to demolish what remains of the existing half-dozen or so disused airfields which are within a radius of about 12 miles and make use of the rubble for the

> base of the new runways? These airfields lie festering across the face of agricultural land like half-healed wounds, the windows of the buildings broken, roofs sagging, and a hearty crop of weeds sprouting on the tarmac. In 20 years' time it may be that the new airfield will be as obsolete as these 15 year olds and there will be an ugly scar permanently upon the hillside from which it was constructed.'

The dreadful run of misfortune continued for Britain's disused airfields less than a year later in 1957, after Duncan Sandys had got his way, when the Air Ministry's laughable control at most of them started swiftly running down. Hit lists of often long disused sites surplus to RAF needs were notified in official circles, though many were still regarded as stand-by sites or held for possible future development into the 1960s. Batches of 50 or so at a time were dropped over a period, all destined for humiliating ends.

Yet, amid these opening moves in one of the worst mass exterminations of all time, suddenly some people dared to speak up in defence of the airfields. One example stated during May 1957 came from an inhabitant of Ampthill near Bedford. His opening sentence did not give much hope, but here was at least someone who had a glimmer of conscience:

> 'It is good news that the Air Ministry are to release another 50 former airfields, and all who have deplored the waste of land and desecration of the countryside they represent will rejoice. But, Sir, lest we forget, and future generations never know, that these were the places from which brave men flew to risk death and often to find it, let something be done to mark them.
>
> If it should be found impracticable to erect inscriptions on the sites, could not they be placed in the local parish church? And if the State will not find the money required, will not the local communities?'

Further support came a few days later from a gentleman in London who suggested that most wartime personnel who served at airfields '. . . would gladly make a small contribution to some form of commemoration.' He wanted to, more recent probing research shows many others wanted to at the time – but what happened? Is there any truth in the horrific rumour which persists that officialdom quietly discouraged conservationist acts? And was there any collusion between

Government and the farming fraternity?

Farmers and landowners had waited eagerly to get their own back on the airfields of Britain. Their insatiable greed for more land was only matched by utterly disgraceful deceit. Thanks to the Air Ministry's pathetic lack of supervision, both parties became almost entirely responsible for the clearance of many buildings: you will recall they were meant to leave airfields alone. It has been said how no site was largely removed before sale, but many have since doubted this statement. Disused airfield sales quickly started, though red tape resulted in most only being auctioned during the early 1960s. Self-centred farmers and landowners contrived to make sales extremely protracted, especially if more than one individual was involved. The late Colin Chapman, founder of the Lotus motor company, found out the hard way to his chagrin when trying to purchase Hethel in Norfolk in this period. If you visit a disused airfield and see a derelict building bearing a crudely painted figure, this is its lot number.

Much hunting is required, but pour through the catalogue list at a major library and details can still be occasionally found of post-1945 airfield auctions. Dumfries is a good example; less precise details can be spotted in newspapers of the era such as the *Daily Mail.* These documents are quite revealing in several senses. As each airfield covered a large acreage, a number of different buyers would buy back the land and not just one. While they could be auctioned off in a day, airfields were more often sold over a period of months, if not years. Ex-USAAF station Chipping Ongar in Essex typified this trend by having the greater but not total part of its area sold in February 1963. But disused airfields were not difficult to sell, primarily because the Air Ministry gave farmers and landowners the chance to buy them at what they thought were reasonable prices. An absolute giveaway was more like it.

To explain this point further, we need only look at the airfields and their associated monetary costs. The price of building an airfield in Britain had risen sharply during World War Two. A major base for heavy bomber use cost over £1,000,000 to construct towards the end of fighting, roughly twice what it would have cost in 1939. Taking everything into consideration, it is thought that British airfield construction and development throughout World War Two totalled on or near £1,000 million. Let us now travel in time to 1958, when en masse airfield sales had not long started. On the market that year was Thruxton: as civil flying existed both before and after auction, and happily still does, it is not a totally perfect example but proves a point. On July 7, the south of England airfield was sold for only £27,600. As Thruxton was a comparatively modest mid-war type, we can therefore say with confidence that the Air Ministry threw away at least £500,000. Figures such as these may now seem unbelievable but many other auctions turned out broadly similar prices. Some places struggled to simply reach four figures, never mind five.

By any standards, these auctions showed up the staggeringly suicidal economic mismanagement within government circles. Think of the hundreds of disused sites sold at bargain prices and Joe Taxpayer must have needlessly parted with several hundred million pounds. Parliament admitted in July 1964 that the sale of airfield land and buildings had so far raised what amounted to the paltry sum of £4,250,000. Neither politicians nor farmers/landowners had given any thought what to do with our airfields, even though disused World War One sites had long shown how they could serve the community in other ways outwith aviation.

Now the handover had been effected, the disused airfields of Britain suffered some of the most appalling acts of gratuitous destruction this country has ever seen in what became a kind of inanimate Final Solution. Farmers and landowners had not liked how 'their' land was seized off them two decades earlier. What did it matter if these morally benevolent actions had only been for the defence of Britain? This is why the War Agricultural Executive Committee made sure it protested about every airfield plan possible during World War Two. In their perverted ways, farmers and landowners now tried their best at revenge by turning Britain's ranks of disused airfields into a nationwide killing ground. The earth trembled as sites were mercilessly hammered from all directions; some, like Turnberry, fell a second time. No thought was given towards those who had laboured long and hard to build these irreplaceable pieces of history, or towards those who had diligently served at them, or especially towards those who had given the ultimate sacrifice while serving at the airfields. No appreciation existed in these historically and architecturally ignorant minds, only blatant selfishness.

Some real horror stories have slowly emerged relating to those diabolical days. Just one of many tales concerns the famous major FAA training base at St Merryn in Cornwall. After being sold for reportedly £32,000 in 1959, plans were afoot for a large job scheme. But the selfish local inhabitants complained bitterly and deprived many people of employment; the same applied to a proposed holiday camp, and yet a facility of this nature stands alongside the old airfield today. St Merryn had the facilities but the local opposition forced them to rot, and items from specialised buildings to piping that could have enjoyed excellent alternative use lie wasting away to this day. Even so, the despicable opposition was not averse to taking advantage of poor security and stealing anything and everything down to light bulbs. It is a tragic but far from typical tale, made all the more sad as even a farmer here has agreed that St Merryn performed wonders for not only himself but also the country and local community.

Two less involved tales involve Britain's top airfield region, namely East Anglia. One farmer is recorded as saying how he strived for some hours to remove an airfield item out of deep concrete, then felt great when he had done so. Was he talking about a building of some kind, or perhaps a stretch of runway? Would you believe a single runway light? Then there was the occasion when another disused site of considerable distinction in the area was being sold and its control tower had come under offer. 'Look,' said the auctioneer, 'give me a couple of quid and you can do what the hell you like with it.' So a farmer gave him £3 and then blew the building up with high explosive . . .

Information on general disused airfield demolition activities nevertheless not surprisingly remains almost impossible to find to this day. But there was one astonishing personal assessment made during the summer of 1960 which now gives us a good idea of what must have happened throughout Britain during this period. Its unusual source appears to have been RAF Church of England chaplain at Elsham Wolds (the airfield featured) circa 1944. He later became rector of that parish, centred in the village church, a year or two after being demobbed, though extensive probing research has surprisingly failed to identify who exactly this person was. His comments are both highly revealing and quite frightening:

> 'Many a time during my year or more on the RAF station perched on top of the Lincolnshire Wolds I would wonder, What will they do with all these places when the war is over? The answer proved to be nothing at all – for 15 years or so. But now I hear that young students from several different countries have been helping the Lindsey County Council, under the aegis of the Civic Trust, to clear away the derelict Air Ministry buildings which for far too long

> have been allowed to scar the Lincolnshire countryside.'

(After talking about wandering into the airfield):

> 'The walls were still there, but most of the windows had gone. Evidently when anybody had wanted a window frame, a door or other portable pieces of furnishing, here they had been for the taking . . . Standing in the centre of the desolate room which had once been my office . . . were scraps of old notices and the more unofficial writings on the wall.
>
> Shaking myself back to the present, I returned to where I had left my car. . . I was startled by a human voice greeting me. Human, but not, I thought, English. And I was right. Six refugees from the eastern boundaries of western Europe were billeted among the old officers' mess huts, while doing potato picking in the district . . . Now, it seems, schoolboys from Germany and students from other countries in western Europe have been at work on some of the Lincolnshire airfields, demolishing the buildings that have continued to stand for far too long. Youngsters from France, Holland and Italy are among those living temporarily in the remaining huts.
>
> It will be much more tidy and much more useful when the young demolishers have completed their task.'

Considering how a man of the cloth wrote this piece, a supposedly peaceful person, his aggressive attitude is frighteningly apparent. Again ingratitude arises, as does a generally increasing obsession with aesthetic matters. His story also confirms actions of vandalism and theft, along with inefficient military evacuation procedures, but above all damningly indicts at least one local government organisation for gross anti-airfield atrocities. Not only did this particular council direct demolition work, it actually dared to bring in outsiders – young, impressionable and ex-enemy ones at that – to do the job. It made a mockery of the suggestion someone had made years earlier that airfields be turned into youth camps after World War Two. Was this organisation afraid of what might have happened if it had tried to acquire British workers?

People did not even have to read this piece to discover what it was saying. They only had to look at the title: 'Clearing Away the Airfields', subtitled 'Derelict Huts and Runways that are full of ghosts'. So were these actions at Elsham Wolds and elsewhere seen as some kind of exorcism?

Mass destruction seemed endless for a while. This is why British disused airfields now frequently look in a poor state with their roofless buildings and huts trying to hide in the undergrowth. At least their runways, perimeter tracks, dispersals and supporting roads kept holding on at the start of the 1960s, the factor which made a huge difference between now and the sheer hell World War One airfields had to endure. This caused considerable anguish among farmers and landowners, who claimed without any real foundation that acres of concrete had taken over good soil.

Tragically, the airfields' apparent upswing in fortunes was destroyed by the 1960s building boom. More bulldozers homed in to join those machines already attacking buildings, but these new arrivals were after concrete. Massive amounts were smashed where they lay before being lifted in crushed form for use elsewhere. Dispersals disappeared in their thousands, resulting in not many surviving today, while runways and perimeter tracks followed the path to oblivion to a lesser extent. No-one could possibly say exactly how much concrete has gone from disused airfields, though surely half of the total acreage has vanished, if not going on two-thirds.

It was possibly this widescale eradication of the 'hard stuff' which prompted farmers and landowners to re-examine their disused airfield policy. Twenty years had passed before both parties were able to realise that airfields could be useful without having to be obliterated. Formerly hostile attitudes gradually gave way, though their new ideas still remained controversial. Worst of this category became the installation of broiler houses on runways, so providing the operator with ready-made foundations. Quite apart from the morally questionable way of rearing chickens and turkeys in this manner, the runways themselves were badly defaced. A small number of disused airfields up and down Britain are now desecrated by these unsightly buildings. Halesworth in Suffolk is probably the best known broiler site in Britain today; its noted owner once dared to say in a newspaper: 'Airfields? Who's interested in them?' He would not have become a multi-millionaire without them for a start . . .

More mundane farm use at disused airfields was to convert runways and perimeter tracks into access roads. Where was all that moaning from farmers and landowners now? No more did they have to plough through muddy fields when tracks already lay there for them. But both parties were still keen to have their pound of flesh and greatly narrowed these tracks. While perimeter tracks became badly affected, disused airfield runways suffered vast reductions in breadth. Standard former RAF runways of 150 feet in width are not common sights nowadays, far more a tenth or so of that size. Hay or manure is often stored on them.

Other farm use has seen buildings converted into crude storage areas, once the structure's shell is left. Again the greed of others saw them stripping off vital building materials for sale. One airfield of that era had the last laugh when a huge quantity of its building material was sold for firewood: the buyer later discovered it had been fireproofed!

Our disused airfields' power, ailing though it seemed to be, had still turned out to prove more than strong enough to convince farmers and landowners that destruction was useless. The deadly duo rather should have left them alone as their removal policy-cum-vendetta had cost a vast sum of money for virtually nothing in return. But farmers and landowners incredibly still consider disused airfields with sceptism. Ruinous buildings give great concern, yet they have only themselves to blame. By first removing parts of an airfield, then wishing they had done the opposite, both parties belatedly discovered how they could not have their cake and eat it.

Of course, there have existed many other types of disused airfield criminal and not just farmers or landowners. The 1960s can also be held responsible for new breeds of these destroyers. Land started to be sold for use as quarries, so that gravel, sand and other minerals could be extracted. Financial greed was the reason for this move which not only severely blemished airfields but also the surrounding countryside. Diggers could make quick work of tearing apart an old airfield.

Property developers, not exactly renowned for their appreciative qualities either, similarly moved in like vultures. Their first thought was to ruthlessly clear all airfield buildings, even though many of these structures could have been easily converted into public service buildings such as halls. Almost as an afterthought, house builders named estate roads after airfields or famous pilots of the past – frequently bearing no relevance whatsoever to the airfield involved. If this was supposed to be some kind of thanks, we should be always wary when confronted with the intentions of property developers.

One cannot help but think at this stage of Hornchurch,

which must surely rank as Britain's most tragic disused airfield. Not only does it clearly display all the traits of an airfield savaged by property developers, extracted land lies alongside. This was only the airfield which brilliantly defended Britain in both World Wars, destroyed the first enemy raider over this country and became one of the seven vitally important fighter sector stations in south-east England during the Battle of Britain. In short, Hornchurch was one of our greatest ever airfields, to be obliterated as a reward by predatory maniacs.

How could our airfields attract so much opposition? It now seems painfully obvious that the 1960s, where lapsed morals generally abounded, had much to do with it. The low-key activities of property developers and excavators proved frightening enough but high-profile subversives were also at work. Perhaps the most alarming factor in all this was that no matter their class or political leaning, complete unison existed between all these anti-airfield parties. Those further up the social scale sneered at our airfields, preferring instead to promote unimportant and crashingly dull castles or stately homes. How many of these places saved Britain or did anything worthwhile for their country? For some reason, the mass media have always tended to ignore airfields, but then any person or organisation who calls an airfield an 'air base' deserves all the contempt he or it can get. It also hardly needs saying that pacifists and vandals continued to go about their normal scurrilous business.

Local authorities must take much of the blame in particular by showing no appreciation towards disused airfields in Britain. If not letting foresters tear them apart and obscure such historic sites with trees, authorities clear sites for faceless parkland. Their utterly contemptible cheek knows no bounds. Take the case of one or two who have mercilessly wiped out disused airfields, then had the nerve to declare the land they stood on as conservation areas! Many authorities are known to despise airfield buildings but this has not prevented a few taking over some as council headquarters or installations. Places as diverse as Kintore in north-east Scotland, Manby and West Malling immediately come to mind – what double standards. Make no mistake about it, some local authorities are hell-bent in intending to remove our disused airfields. Their members conveniently forget how those same sites fought to allow them to speak freely, something they could not do today if there had not been any British airfields.

Still spasmodic attacks continued in communications as the 1960s drew to a close. One typical letter published during

March 1969 criticised airfields in the Oxfordshire area. Defensive opposition declared how airfields had '. . . set the picture for general farm building improvement to overcome the difficulties of farmers leaving machinery outdoors at the end of harvests . . .' and finished by describing remarks made in the original letter as 'inopportune'. But then the inevitable local government gnome stuck his nose in during April and openly challenged the defender's statement. He somehow managed to quote Martin-Baker's test site at Chalgrove as a disused airfield, and called Edgehill Shennington without even spelling its alternative local name correctly.

Come the 1970s, Britain's disused airfields were in desperate trouble. Their problems had multiplied during the previous decade, for the heavy RAF casualty list had brought many more airfields into disuse. Any mention as happened in January 1963 that RAF stations were closing down was done so only mechanically. The authorities naturally still wanted their married quarters and certain other buildings for overspill use by other airfields.

Everyone now seemed against our airfields. Neglect relentlessly gnawed away at them to make some sites take on the appearance of a Roman fort in that they could only be spotted from the air. Runways and supporting tracks became cracked, being covered with chippings, fencing, moss, oil drums and pot-holes. Many buildings were shattered hulks. Vast piles of rubble lay everywhere. Salvation seemed impossible – or did it? Read on . . .

Fightback

What happened was nothing short of remarkable. Britain's disused World War Two era airfields all of a sudden found themselves with many more allies during the early 1970s. Not even their most ardent supporters could have imagined deep in their hearts such an event taking place.

The reason for this change in attitude was fairly simple. Official documents relating to all aspects of military airfield life had not been previously available because of the standard 30 year delay on their release. When writers, researchers and the general public finally managed to acquire this veritable mountain of records, they realised virtually overnight just how great were our World War Two airfields. Nobody could fail to be staggered by their enormous historical, technical, architectural and social importance.

You might be asking at this point: what about the disused airfields of World War One? Sadly, organised assistance had come far too late for them. While a lack of permanent looks and concrete had not helped their cause, pacifism had been primarily responsible for the decline of Great War sites. Another detrimental factor was that Britain still continued to suffer from post-World War Two blues when official records relating to the first world conflict became available. People, rightly or wrongly, had more pressing things on their minds. Perhaps proof of this attitude could be seen in the excellent attendances at many airfields during the first Battle of Britain Day in September 1945, but the following year's celebrations showed an alarming slump in visitors. Had post-war apathy set in? Or was the drop more down to the severe restrictions placed on people attending? At the first event, no visitors had been allowed into airfields with cameras, and a short opening period from 14:30 hours to 18:00 hours could not have helped much either.

Although World War One airfield relics had now become virtually non-existent, more than enough of their World War

Two equivalents still abounded. This stirred the minds of many people who saw the tremendous potential our disused airfields offered. Already active airfields had delved with considerable success into ostensibly unrelated areas of everyday life but it has since become astounding to see how many new roles disused sites have taken on. Most of these duties are far removed from aeronautical links.

To give you an idea of how disused airfields are employed today, here is a list of their new activities. All of these tasks are at least relatively common throughout Britain; a few specialised roles are excluded. Random airfields are given as examples, particularly less obvious ones:

Activity	*Airfield*
Caravan Site	Castle Archdale
Civil Aviation (limited flying)	
Cropspraying	Hutton Cranswick
Gliding	Dallachy
Light aircraft	St Merryn
Microlight	Metheringham
Parachuting	Kinnell
Housing	
Control Towers	Zeals
Support Buildings	Melbourne (guard room)
Industry	
Estate	Eye
Factory	Brockworth
Light	Talbenny
Market	Finmere
Military Aviation (non-flying)	
RAF	North Luffenham
Royal Navy	Gosport
Army	Colerne
USAF	Welford
Motor Racing	Kirkistown
Museum	Framlingham (control tower)
Nuclear Related Industries	
Power Station	Bradwell Bay
Research	Culham
Offices	Llandow (control tower)
Parking Areas	Turnberry
Prison	Millom
Proving Ground	Nuneaton II
Racecourse	Redcar
Roads	
Motorway	Stretton

Minor	Birch
Storage	
Indoor	Hemswell
Outdoor	Longtown (pipes)
Water Towers	Faldingworth (Braithwaite)
Wireless Transmission Site	Rattray

Various forms of industry have found disused airfields excellent places for their needs. Industrial estates and factories have been built on or around many wartime sites. Their support facilities have provided unexpectedly good service. Former aircraft factories continue as they were, only now producing non-aeronautical goods, while hangars and support buildings have similarly seen suitable conversion. Many supposedly temporary buildings such as domestic or technical huts have defied their critics by now serving as small workshops or offices. Small businesses find that airfield support buildings offer low overheads. Undoubtedly the most surprising type of office today is the converted control tower. This facility has become fairly common all over Britain and often appears in the most unusual of places. Control towers are now not always easily recognisable, a fact of life which can also be applied to hangars, but at least many examples of both types are still present. Despite this minor quibble, British industry has shown itself to be of great benefit to airfields – and the benefit is mutual. The beauty is that sites can easily adapt to whatever form of industry is required.

Disused airfields are also most effective at turning their hands to other practical uses. Storage is a familiar occupation nowadays, including some hangars in Government use which hold equipment and other items. Just as runways take on external storage duties such as the retention of factory fresh cars, hangars naturally bear the brunt of internal work, and how many famine-stricken victims owe their lives to grain storage sites like Hemswell? Housing is quite popular too, with control towers again unpredictably leading the way. Property developers have for once acted in a benevolent manner by managing to combine history and architecture with enterprise. As at some industrial sites, though, a number of privately owned control towers have been unfortunately over-modified to retain little of their original appearance. Much rarer is the odd wartime hut here and there in use as a house. This is quite incredible, as are a few Braithwaite water towers in remoter parts still being used for their intended purpose.

Much of today's new activities revolve around cars and other vehicles, for which runways and perimeter tracks are ideally suited. Roads are the most obvious, regardless of where the disused airfield is. Country inhabitants especially have praised airfields for opening up their areas. One great plus point is how versatile runways and perimeter tracks can either weave round an obstacle with ease or go straight towards the next point. The open features of runways furthermore help driver trainees at different stages. Few cannot have seen a learner driver take his or her first tentative steps on a disused airfield. Other popular – if not always official – airfield track activities can include Sunday markets and car parking, the latter of which can be more than adequately performed on runways or even parade grounds.

Disused airfields have occasionally been subjected to totally illegal activities, though happily not often. Light aircraft pilots find sites in East Anglia particularly useful for smuggling tobacco into Britain from the Continent. Illegal immigration has been another ploy tried, and there was the celebrated occasion on November 28 1971 when farmer Ray Convine rammed his truck into the wing of a Piper Cherokee light aircraft carrying five Pakistanis into Kimbolton. This incident became about the only time a British disused airfield made headline news as soon police had to be detailed to watch other airfields in East Anglia. Thankfully, hardly any criminal activities – and certainly no serious ones – have occurred since at any site in Britain.

When it comes to leisure instead of work, disused airfields are superb in serving the surrounding community. Everyone has heard of Silverstone, but Britain has other motor racing circuits which used to be airfields. This practice first started during the late 1940s and had to run the inevitable gauntlet of officialdom in early days before gaining total acceptance. Events in those days such as the Borders racing circuit helped produce a future Formula One world champion in the late Jim Clark; now the Northern Ireland racing circuits among others have become acknowledged favourites. Former perimeter tracks even have their own chicanes! Formula racing is not the only activity, for go-karts, motorcycles and dragsters frequently use disused airfields too.

Racing of a four-legged kind occurs at many racecourses which, particularly in earlier days, helped give Britain's airfields in general a reasonable start in life. Few racecourses do not have some kind of link with airfields, and several such as Newmarket still welcome in aircraft during racedays. Polo is another airfield-related equestrian sport because of its strong historical or current links with Hounslow, Cowdray Park and Smith's Lawn in southern England.

At a more peaceful level of leisure, disused airfields have been successfully transformed into recreation areas without damaging the site itself too badly, while caravanning is popular in places such as Northern Ireland. Dispersals, about the only airfield items little suited to present activities, are often employed as caravan bases.

The worlds of cinema and television have inevitably made their mark as well. Both active and disused airfields create tremendous atmosphere, although the frequently incorrect choice of aircraft often tends to ruin things for the viewer. One memorably poor film once had a Dakota in Luftwaffe markings on a supposed German-operated airfield – even though the viewer could hardly miss a couple of T2s, a B1 and even a Jeep. Of course, not an aircraft is in sight as a disused airfield stars in the introduction to the most technically and artistically brilliant television series of all time. The runway scene for *The Prisoner* was shot at Hethel, site of the Lotus works, quite fitting as the car seen speeding down towards the camera at the start of nearly every episode of this series as timeless as Britain's airfields is a Lotus 7.

Such has been the widespread alternative use at disused airfields in Britain that their popularity has increased enormously since the mid-1970s. Their renowned adaptability and versatility has extended well beyond flying days. Whatever their new use or uses, all continue to create hundreds of thousands of new jobs for a grateful population in this difficult employment age. Whereas the authorities are quite hopeless or resort to deception in trying to stop the dole tide, our airfields step in time and time again to save the day. One aspect maybe too obvious is their sheer space, thus allowing airfields to cater superbly for innumerable activities.

Not surprisingly, some people are never happy, a factor which has brought controversy to a number of former airfields. Oxfordshire nuclear research complex Harwell and Long Kesh (alias The Maze prison) are familiar enough names today, but surprisingly few know what these places originally saw use as. Britain's first controversial disused airfield was undoubtedly Aldermaston during the late 1950s because of its atomic weapons links. Others have since become linked with debatable nuclear operations, such as the power station at Chapelcross (Annan to the purists) in Dumfries and Galloway. Hardly popular either are prisons, which also began to be converted in the same decade as Aldermaston. Authorities have in addition the most distressing habit of frequently not naming prisons after the airfields they are built on or around. For example, why cannot Highpoint Prison just be called

Stradishall? One could however argue that giving an airfield now a prison an alternative title is a good idea as lesser men might detract from its glorious past.

Two other less prominent but equally controversial new uses on disused airfields are where huge aerials act as foreign listening posts to gather intelligence information, and proving grounds. Proving grounds? What is wrong with running factory vehicles around the tracks of an airfield, you might ask? Nothing – except in the secretive way this activity is conducted. Casual sightseers are not exactly popular at these places. You have been warned! Disused airfields have been given some quite dreadful tasks such as rubbish dumping over the years, often maliciously, but have taken on their opponents at their own game and made a roaring success of the job.

Despite such phenomenally successful diversification, our disused airfields have not forgotten their old traditions. If we use 'disused airfield' in its closed to flying context, the military still uses them in many ground roles from radar stations to weaponry storage. Special mention must go to the Army for its masterly performance in using airfield installations to their full potential. Why build new accommodation and training areas when many are already at hand? Disused airfields can even temporarily return to flying for exercise purposes, as was the case during November 1987 when helicopters briefly operated from Castle Kennedy near Stranraer during Operation *Purple Warrior,* Britain's largest post-war military exercise. Even though these places may be regarded as disused, they can never be totally dropped. Scores of sites would prove most useful in auxiliary flying as well as ground capacities should World War Three ever happen.

On the civil side of aviation, large numbers of disused sites continue to have links with flying, however slender. Whether it is the odd light aircraft, cropsprayer, a few gliders or parachutists, chances are there is usually something happening. Recreational flying at disused airfields helps to take some of the load off busy active airfields and disperse aircraft movements more evenly without cluttering up available airspace. Microlight flying has become more popular of late as well and disused airfields are easily able to cater for these tiny machines. Many aircraft have also come to thank disused airfields when having to make emergency landings over many years.

Official worries about hazards of aircraft landing unauthorised at such airfields were voiced by the Ministry of Aviation as early as November 1963. It stated that runways and grass landing areas were not normally maintained in flying condition once active flying ceased and would soon become unfit for use. People, animals and vehicles could be on the airfield because of farming or if roads crossed the site. The Air Ministry went on: 'At disused airfields, every effort is made to keep the runways clear, but there is no guarantee that they will be unobstructed, so pilots making use of them for emergency landings should exercise caution.' What a laugh that statement turned out to be.

No matter what suffering a disused airfield in Britain has been subjected to, every one without fail has helped the people, landscape and society in general, if only to serve as 'straight' and much improved farmland. ALGs and SLGs were largely cleared at the end of World War Two but farmers and landowners have reaped the rich benefits of some dogged airfield survivors. Quite apart from the occasional hangar or hut, metal runways have enjoyed a new lease of life as fencing. Of all the different types of airfield, marine bases have turned out to be the most difficult to convert. Few have been wasted, though there is not one new role these places have taken on which stands out prominently from the rest.

How must many former disused airfield destroyers now be deeply regretting their past attitude towards them. For sites supposed to be absolute no-hopers, Britain's disused airfields have performed near-miracles: jobs, facilities and services. The idea that 'there was no further need for airfields after World War Two' has proved to be utter baloney. Their potential for future uses as in new technology is quite endless.

It has now happily reached the stage where airfields are being transformed into places of historical and architectural interest. Control towers, hangars and support buildings now act as museum bases, run by dedicated individuals and small organisations. While such airfields at present only exist here and there, this brand of disused airfield conservation is rapidly growing in support. Memorials are also frequently arising but it has become a long-standing myth to call them airfield memorials: they are not, only unit ones. It is only natural that former service personnel should mark their own activities; even so, Britain still does not have a true airfield memorial after all this time. Such a stone should ideally have inscribed on it the airfield's name, when it opened and closed, and the units stationed at it from squadrons to Flights and so on.

Suggestions to bring all disused airfield relics to a collection centre have occasionally arisen. One must be thankful that it is the ignorant who make these statements for, if this madness ever occurred, it would effectively kill the disused airfields involved. Part of the pleasure in this activity is to travel from place to place, forever encountering the unexpected. Look around old buildings and you might come upon a wall painting. It would be impossible to move this, let alone something much larger on the scale of Tempsford's famous barn where secret agents were equipped before taking off, and the countryside atmosphere would be totally ruined by that of a plastic urban environment. You only need to look at Hendon today for evidence of this second factor.

Although disused airfield conservationists can congratulate themselves for a spirited defence of our supersites, let us not think the tide has yet turned. Our airfields have won the battle – but the war is far from over. War is no exaggeration either. On one hand, there is the growing army of individualists and specialist organisations helping to conserve disused airfields. On the other are vast ranks of surprisingly different people – government, local authorities, the upper classes, pacifists, the Press and the inevitable farmers/landowners – who just cannot see past their castles and stately homes. But there are now clear signs that this combined opposition force is slowly but surely losing support. This is most noticeable among local authorities, a few of which have at last slapped preservation orders on various buildings. Whether it is a Belfast hangar or a small hut, some airfield relics have received their belated reward. One must remember that a building of great importance does not have to be sited at a disused airfield, for many more exist on active sites, just as not every building on an active airfield is used for flying purposes.

Unfortunately, countless thousands of crucial airfield relics have succumbed before help could reach them. If a bulldozer has not flattened them, others have been moved to different locations. This point partly relates to the suggestion about collection centres. Easily the most common examples of unsuitable moves are Blisters transferred from their natural positions to finish up as sad-looking farm storage areas, often miles from where they came. Feeble excuses by their new owners only again prove, as if anyone should still be in doubt, how greed for more farmland knows no bounds.

Proof of close co-operation among the anti-disused airfield lobby is shown by the Ministry of Defence's deplorable attitude. The government organisation '. . . considers it quite impossible to justify their (the airfields) retention.' Standard MoD policy is to let the Property Services Agency, the Government's estate agent, dispose of land at the best price obtainable on the open market, not stipulating that the airfields remain as such. In other words, governments betray their saviours so that farmers/landowners and the rest can have carte blanche powers in wiping them out. Who needs friends with attitudes such as these?

Also ask yourself this question: were you truly ever interested in other alleged 'historical sites' such as castles and stately homes? Perhaps when of school age, you were attracted by all the ostentation. Do not be fooled. Always remember that castles, stately homes and their ilk have never done anything worthwhile to help Britain. This is why our disused airfields are always sniped at by the ignorant for their lack of beauty, a stupid remark as they were not meant to be so. Others go further by claiming how disused airfields are eyesores without knowing the slightest thing about their glorious histories. In any case, governmental laziness and lack of gratitude by their owners are the basic reasons for decay at many sites.

And some even dare to say people are not interested in Britain's disused airfields! If only these closed minds made the effort to see the vast numbers of interested visitors at airfield museums – and not just British tourists. People have always cared, as huge and stunned crowds showed on the evening of September 30 1959 when Croydon closed. It is nothing other than painful to watch former RAF or USAAF personnel return to their old homes as part of a unit reunion and see the sadness on their faces. Some see the often mauled remains and weep unashamedly; others look about in horror, and you can almost read their minds as they think: 'My God – was winning a war worth it when we see this?' or 'So this is what they call gratitude.' That is why the younger generations among us in Britain must work on to make up for the atrocities committed against our airfields after both World Wars.

Still remarks occasionally appear here and there about disused airfields. But no longer do they spit venom: far more the opposite. As those in society utterly obsessed with money try to sweep morality aside, as financial help for them comes from ever more unlikely sources, literally millions of people in this country have at last realised the colossal all-round worth of our airfields and are now drawing attention to their plight. About the first airfield to be mentioned in this story of Britain's disused airfields was Turnberry, and there can be no better example of a supportive message representative of today than that featured during mid-1987, written by a gentleman in Tyne and Wear:

'I was shocked and saddened to read of the sale of

Turnberry golf course and hotel to a Japanese company.

In two World Wars, the course was used as an airfield for the training of aircrews. In 1942 with many others, I trained to operate torpedo bombers at Turnberry. Presumably, the object thereafter was to fly against the Germans in the first phase, and then against the Japanese.

During the course of training, my course lost approximately one-quarter of its members in flying accidents. The popular saying was always 'They did not die in vain.'

But surely the Japanese have just proved it wrong.'

This superb statement has highlighted the latest frightening trend in the disused airfield war. Turnberry holds on – just – but already Japanese companies, disgracefully aided by the Government, have claimed the scalps of Usworth, Burnaston and former factory airfield South Marston in Wiltshire. Other sites may well be on their target list. But neither they nor any other anti-disused airfield elements will ever again find such a lack of opposition to stop the eradication of our top historical sites. The conscience of a nation has awoken.

So the disused airfields of Britain continue to fight back. The tragedy is that not all of them survived post-war attacks. Obliteration still goes on almost daily – but you can stop it. Totally. And how!

How You Can Help

The millions of disused airfield supporters in this country must look at their opponents and wonder how best to tackle them. They seem to hold all the cards. This is an understandable reaction but these combined subversives can be beaten. They are already losing.

Nevertheless, the road to victory is still far off. It must be said that disused airfield supporter victories have so far mainly occurred on a small or localised scale, a case of tactical rather than strategic successes. An individual saves a control tower from demolition, an organisation manages to create a local museum. These and similar actions are all highly commendable but suffer badly from a lack of back-up and cohesion.

This is where you can help. One people with one voice will win much more quickly, therefore massacring the sheer warped concept of 'history' castles and stately homes represent, yet retaining essential individuality as Britain's airfields themselves personify. So much can be achieved in so many ways. To show how, it is necessary to describe separately four simple steps of action. You cannot go about promoting Britain's disused airfields any other way.

(1) The Mass Media – Malevolence or Misunderstanding?

Television, radio, newspapers, the literary world and sundry components which make up the mass media are undoubtedly the most subtly pervasive elements in our daily lives. All can almost hypnotically influence us. One famous example happened in America, where Richard Nixon is said to have lost a Presidential election long before the Watergate debacle not on account of his policies or views but just because he stood sloppily behind a podium during a television debate. From our airfields' point of view, regardless of whether they are active or disused, the mass media represent their most powerful passive opponents, as opposed to active farmers/

landowners or politicians. These various forms of communication tend to either ignore, misinform about or scorn airfields. Why?

The answer lies in a lethal mixture of politics, pacifism and a total lack of knowledge in airfield affairs. Newspapers give disused airfields in particular barely any coverage because of the above three factors. Two examples demonstrate this collective point. On July 13 1984, one 'heavy' national newspaper reported how York's main runway was to be tragically removed. This snippet of news, only four lines in length, was placed in a very small area of the paper. Worst of all, the whole tone of this piece was almost jocular. Roughly two years later, another article in the same newspaper noted in greater detail the unfortunate death of a female parachutist. (Her demise was of note as it raised the question of relatively untrained persons jumping for charity). The airfield she died at was called 'Forton'. People in the know scratched their heads and wondered where this place was. The airfield concerned was in fact Montford Bridge in Shropshire, Rednal's satellite during World War Two. Through their usual sloppy research, the press had fallen victim to the old habit of local inhabitants calling their nearby airfield by another name.

The two above articles form only a microcosm of the immeasurably huge number of mistakes that have arisen over decades. If the mass media deal with an airfield story, you can be sure that they will get something wrong. The author once monitored a selection of national and regional newspapers plus television news programmes for accuracy as an exercise and discovered 308 mistakes in 120 days – chronically bad by any standards. One of these involved another parachuting fatality at a place described as an 'airport', ludicrous beyond belief as the airfield involved had lain disused for over 40 years.

At least newspapers occasionally mention Britain's airfields. When it comes to tourist guides plus geographical and historical tomes, our heroes suffer terribly at their hands. All three types of book usually tend to ignore them completely. You would never guess airfields even existed in most parts of Britain, only those dreadful castles and stately homes. Books have been written about Lincolnshire, to take but one county, totally omitting its glorious airfield history. What does it matter that Lincolnshire is Britain's number one airfield county, home of our greatest bomber station, greatest training base, many other famous airfields and backbone of the RAF today? Some books go further by openly criticising British airfields, but their authors will not have the pleasure of seeing their scurrilous remarks in this book.

Television displays some of the worst mass media traits. Quite apart from the fact that no true historical programmes about airfields have ever seen transmission, television news rarely names them. The situation is made worse still by the common habit in news bulletins of trivialising everything, easily done by using the wrong type of reporter. An airfield is usually referred to as 'a disused airfield' or 'a former fighter/bomber base' – frequently when it is not.

A most irritating recurring factor is an airfield being called an 'air base'. Is this a place where air is stored or takes off and lands by itself? Or is it a place which magically floats about in the sky? Look up any dictionary and you will not even find 'air base' in any of them. Thorough research has revealed that the Modern New English Dictionary (an American publication) of 1947 contained this term, where it was described as 'a service station for airplanes'. But a service station is surely a place where petrol is provided: an airfield does infinitely more than that for aircraft. 'Air base' is a dreadful term, probably derived from the American policy of calling military airfields Air Force Bases or AFBs for short. Why is our mass media totally unable to just call them airfields? It is sad to report that this practice was already happening as early as 1943.

Not only is television news at fault, also the odd television programme. We need look no further than the hugely popular comedy series *Dad's Army*. In one episode, a secret weapon not unlike the disastrous Panjandrum catherine wheel-like device is to be tested on 'a disused airfield'. Can you imagine it, a disused military airfield in wartime – impossible!

Returning to the mass media as a whole, the 'air base' controversy is only one of four specific complaints. The second is how pacifist and protest organisations are portrayed almost as heroes, while airfields are shown to be somewhat sinister: in reality, it should be the other way around. The Cublington saga of 1971 was typical, when Wing (why was its apt name dropped?) was proposed as London's third airport. Placard waving activists and screaming women made a lot of headlines, not to mention noise. A book written on the subject seems to praise them (and, true to form, virtually omits Wing's past) but inadvertently lets the cat out of the bag. The Cublington protestors show themselves to be sickeningly selfish. Although supposedly concerned with environmental problems, the protestors were really only worried about number one. Each conveniently forgot how places such as Wing fought to give them a good standard of living and the pleasure of free speech.

The third complaint is the constant habit of making silly mistakes like saying certain aircraft types flew from airfields when they did not. One newspaper article once remarkably mentioned how B-29s used Britain's bomber airfields during World War Two. But it is the fourth qualm which is perhaps the most worrying of all. Surprisingly, considering the mass media, they have terrible problems in just trying to correctly spell airfield names. Mistakes are shockingly frequent: literally dozens of misspelt sites can be listed. Remember the hippies of Stony – sorry, Stoney Cross? Brandy instead of Brawdy – and, talking of alcohol, Bulmer instead of Boulmer? Nobody is exempt. Even the Americans got in the act during the Libyan Crisis of 1986 by persisting in calling Lakenheath Laken Heath: at least the Russians must be credited for knowing about and correctly spelling 'Aerodromo Brize Norton'.

Airfield spelling errors are not just confined to the mass media. Look at many other aspects of everyday British life and the clangers doth flow. To go to slightly ridiculous lengths, dishtowels honouring World War Two era airfields in this country which have apparently sold very well are absolutely riddled with mistakes. One cloth dealing with the Battle of Britain mentions such strange places as Bilbury, Prembrey and Stapleford Abbots instead of Stapleford Tawney. (Heathrow, incidentally, is for once correct, even if only used by an obscure Hurricane detachment of No 1 Squadron). Another towel devoted to Bomber Command stations has been revised – for instance, there is no Snitterfield, a Warwickshire airfield never even used by bombers – but some mistakes such as Lissett with only one t and the inevitable East Kirby instead of Kirkby still appear.

If one had to pick out the two most astonishingly bad airfield spelling mistakes of recent memory, we must stay on the subject of bomber airfields. The mass media have an appalling tendency to keep misspelling Wyton of Pathfinder Force glory. Down the years we have seen Witon, Witton, Wydon and even Wyham. But even these horrors pale into relative insignificance compared to the photograph once featured in the magazine supplement of a national Sunday newspaper which ought to hang its head in shame for evermore. Two royals who shall remain nameless are depicted standing back to camera in a signals square watching the *Red Arrows* aerobatic team give a flying display. And what did the supporting caption in large letters call this airfield? Only Scrampton . . .

Would any other country in the world tolerate such

extremely alarming trends as these? Scampton and Wyton, the king of Britain's bomber airfields and its specialist consort respectively, are two of Britain's greatest ever airfields. So, if these colossal superstars can suffer such indignity through nothing more than spelling mistakes, what chance do our less familiar airfields have? No wonder people frequently complain about the poor overall standard of spelling nowadays: the computer saw to that.

How you can help reverse this dreadful general situation involving our airfields and the mass media is fairly easy. Keep pressurising their various outlets. Keep correcting them on their airfield accuracy, spelling, tone and that truly shocking 'air base' term. Bombard television and radio companies, newspapers, magazines and the rest with letters to get airfields noticed. The mass media hate this constant correction, but by utterly besieging them you can numb them into submission. It is just like dealing with enormously cruel satirists, for as one unfortunate victim once said: 'They (satirists) are always trying to destroy you, but fire back at them and they will always collapse.' How true.

This method of coercing the mass media into getting their facts correct does work. There was the occasion when one of Britain's oldest national newspapers featured an article about Brooklands. Mistake followed mistake to leave a grand total of six errors, exceptionally bad by normal standards, and then in came that word: old Brooklands is about the last place anyone should call an air base. The author followed his normal rules and sent an advisory letter to the newspaper immediately afterwards. No reply was ever received, nor was the letter ever published, but it was strange how another airfield article appeared a few weeks later by the same reporter – and not a single error was to be seen. Although it can never be proved outright, that corrective note must have come as something of a bombshell and ruffled more than a few feathers. Yet another victory had been scored.

Above all, remember that while nobody has a duty to do anything in life, you should never forget the incomparable service that our airfields and everyone who has worked at them have given for Britain, nor the scandalous treatment still being dished out to disused sites in this country. It therefore may not be your duty to do so, but you should still seriously consider spending a little time to help support their cause, just as airfields have helped and continue to help all of us 24 hours a day, seven days a week, 52 weeks a year without a break. And the easiest way of all is to correct the mass media whenever they make a mistake on the subject of Britain's airfields.

The mass media's attitude to our airfields has always been twofold. Certainly there is some malevolence, which would seem to confirm alleged left wing attitudes in some parts of the media. This can be easily overcome, though the real case for the prosecution is how their basic airfield research is haywire. Basic mistakes can be solved by basic corrections but, if you really want to know more about British airfield life, you must move to your second course of action.

(2) Airfield Research For All

Much information exists on Britain's airfields. A fair number of airfield books have appeared to deal with military histories, wartime histories, individual histories and regional histories – but never a whole one. No complete history of Britain's airfields has ever been written (though that situation will soon come to an end). The knack in researching is trying to separate the gems from the dross. Unfortunately, when it comes to research problems, this is only one of many difficulties which have to be faced. But persevere, weather any initial teething troubles and the answers to your questions will more often than not be discovered.

As regards military airfields, records greatly vary in quantity and accuracy. World War One airfield research is extremely difficult because of shortcomings in these two areas. About three-quarters of all records belonging to this era were destroyed by bombing in World War Two. Some more were simply thrown away, hard as this may seem to believe, leaving only a representative selection of records. Big gaps and question marks hence appear. When did certain airfields open and close? Where were certain units based? When did they move to other airfields? What aircraft did they use? About the most frustrating are World War One landing grounds: directions for these all too often elusive Home Defence sites were given as so many miles from a railway station. Not even compass directions were provided and so landing grounds remain vague. It has to be said that the Great War period requires you to reach new levels of inspired guesswork, rather than rely upon hard fact all the time, though this factor makes research even more exciting than usual.

While the 1920s and 1930s do not score particularly well in terms of official records either, World War Two is much better, where most facets of military airfield life can be found. The typed reports before you might look overwhelming as you plough through files the size of large telephone directories – for, as aviation developed, so too did the paperwork – but with practice the relevant information can be easily picked out.

A word of warning, though. Do not expect to find much about RLGs, satellites or SLGs. A good example is how the official records for No 18 EFTS at Fairoaks mention the acquisition of Bray in February 1941 as a supportive airfield, then never mention this RLG again. Expect even less about FAA and factory airfields, and always double check unit movement dates. A few hangarage arrangements do not add up either. Sloppiness in writing up official records sometimes appears too. This factor was recognised by the Americans' 9th Air Force Troop Carrier Command Substitution Unit in September 1944 when a memo was sent out to its Leicestershire and Lincolnshire bases at Barkston Heath, Folkingham, North Witham and Saltby, saying how insufficient attention was being paid to writing up official records, and that these files had to be as comprehensive as possible. But diligent detailing of daily airfield activities otherwise mainly occurred throughout the second world conflict.

Where can you acquire all this information? Although there are several major sources, easily the best is the Public Record Office at Kew in London. If you are based hundreds of miles from it, like the author, there are immediately obvious problems, so make sure in advance you know exactly what you want to look for. A marvellous place, the PRO contains thousands upon thousands of airfield records. All you need to do is go in, armed with your Reader's Ticket, secure a seat and a 'bleeper' for communications purposes, search through any index book for the required files, order this requirement via a computer system and then return to your seat. A few minutes pass until your 'bleeper' reacts to tell you that your files are ready for collection. The staff make you welcome and readily give any assistance, though it is best to ask for an advisory leaflet beforehand to avoid accidentally upsetting anyone. One typical rule is that only pencils are allowed as writing materials to avoid marking documents.

PRO records relating to military airfield histories are classed under the AIR category; a second AVIA category is less helpful but provides useful bits of information now and again. Document numbers can be found in index books as just mentioned or in card files, the difference being that the latter denote loose-leaf documents which can only be taken out one at a time instead of up to three with bound ones. Check right through the AIR indices, though three particularly useful sections are AIR 1 (World War One), AIR 28 (RAF station Operations Record Books) and AIR 29 (RAF units other than squadrons). Here you can see what happened at Britain's airfields day by day, from the day they opened to the day they closed. Absolutely everything is featured, both on the glamorous and more mundane areas of daily airfield life, and make fascinating reading.

It goes without saying that not all of you will want to visit the PRO. Perhaps travelling distance is too great; maybe you do not want to delve into airfield research too deeply. Provided the second case applies and you only want a good but not excellent knowledge of Britain's airfields, our bigger public libraries are the place for you. They should stock old copies of *Aeroplane* and *Flight* magazines for a start. Both come in volumes, usually complete with indices for easy reference. Since *Flight* became *Flight International,* it has vastly cut back on general airfield information, but both *Aeroplane* and *Flight* are very useful for research purposes. These two publications really score on British civil airfield activities, where information as a whole is at best patchy and at worst infuriatingly elusive; the PRO is not greatly endowed with civil aviation documents either. You can also try obtaining more specialised magazines, of which *Sailplane and Gliding* stands out from the rest. A must for civil airfield information if it can be obtained is the *Air Pilot* series of records which have been published since 1924. Detailed maps and excellent technical information are quoted, but a researcher can be counted lucky to find even the majority of books published before World War Two. The situation is infinitely worse after that conflict as available information in *Air Pilot* publications virtually dries up.

Staying with public libraries, newspapers are a more readily available source for your research. *The Times* and the *Daily Mail* come out best when dealing with overall airfield affairs, while more regional or local newspapers score when it comes to mentioning airfields in their own areas. Try all of them but, as this chapter has already shown, never read too much into their information. A handy tip with both magazines and newspapers is to largely skim through wartime editions. Severe official restrictions then resulted in no specific information or names being quoted; reports on both sides often also proved vague and wildly exaggerated. This is perhaps too obvious for some people, yet it is amazing those who forget, wasting their time looking for information they do not have an earthly of finding.

Some libraries have gone a stage further by taking newspaper clippings and any photographs which come to hand, putting them in a folder to form part of a local-cum-social history collection. These documents are usually crudely made up but often contain a small gem of information. One typical example can be found in a back room of the library in Weston-super-Mare, where amid local press cuttings lies a superb photograph of an Avro 504K joy-riding aircraft standing at the old List D2 airfield of Brean Down during the early post-Great War period.

And back to airfield books . . . You are no doubt wondering by now why they were briefly mentioned before we left for other British airfield research sources. It all comes back to the gems and dross. PRO documents are the precious gems, library records semi-precious ones and most airfield books the dross. By all means have a look at other books but, like the mass media, only do so for a rough idea of what happened at any site. Never believe them as a whole.

Why have previous airfield books turned out to be more of a hindrance than a help? How best to answer that question is far from easy. One possible theory which becomes ever more evident as you read through other books is that the greater area of Britain covered, the more flawed a book becomes. Publications dealing with just one airfield pose further problems as, though they can be rarely faulted for their technical content, these books become so ultra-specialised that they tend to create only very limited interest.

Among the increasingly varied works to have appeared has been one high-profile series of supposedly praised books. No doubt you have already come across some of them if you are a British airfield supporter. Those who really understand airfield research will tell you that this series has proved to be an utterly chaotic disaster. Unco-ordinated, ponderous, pretentious, often irrelevant – and these are only the more minor failings. Too many cooks spoil the broth, goes the old saying: these books have not only done that but dropped the broth on the floor and failed to clear up the mess.

There are three major shortcomings in this series of books. Historical and technical information is to begin with riddled with errors and omissions. Dates are far too often hopelessly wrong. Certain important airfield activities are often never mentioned. For books ostensibly dealing with military airfields in Britain, great numbers of them are not even described, let alone mentioned in passing. What happened to all our World War One airfields? The publishers at first decided not to mention them, then gradually phased in Great War sites as the series progressed to leave huge historical gaps.

To list every factual mistake in these books would be a mammoth task. Among the vast range of errors is the case of a fighter squadron reforming at one airfield after World War Two, then another volume states how the same unit reformed on the same date – at an airfield over 100 miles away. Other unit movement dates are frequently wildly inaccurate. Photographic evidence is similarly dubious, as shown by the aerial shot of one disused airfield. There is nothing wrong about the quality of this photograph: a shame it shows a completely different site. Then there is the curious policy of how the series deals with civil airfield operations; although every book is supposed to deal with military airfield history, the writers are continually at sixes and sevens as how best to describe more peaceful uses. Some civil airfield operations are quoted as a result, others are not. Take the case of one airfield which saw civil flying for a total of 17 years before and after World War Two – even becoming a municipal airport – but does not rate any mention whatsoever. The details of this particular airfield's military career are extremely vague to further worsen the situation.

The second major fault is that reports on what is left at our disused airfields are so woeful that one wonders whether many sites have even received visits. The giveaway is a glaring lack of information on remaining disused airfield relics or padding so vague you think the writers have possibly never bothered to visit a site and resorted to looking at an Ordnance Survey map to find information anyone else could discover. Of 112 airfields mentioned in one volume, 43 sites have surely not been visited, another 17 probably not visited, and 70-80 more (mainly of the World War One era) not listed at all. Akeman Street, Church Lawford, Clyffe Pypard, Fersfield, Kingston Bagpuize, Matching, Podington, Ratcliffe, Shellingford, Stanton Harcourt, Stratford II, Talbenny, Woodley . . . the list of disused airfields which are still tangible but not recognised as such is almost endless.

Sometimes architectural reporting is conversely not non-existent but slapdash or hopelessly wrong. One airfield is said to have only a B1 left of its original hangarage, whereas in reality a T2 also stands just 200 yards up a side road. If that is not careless research, then what is? Well, what about the airfield where one control tower and one hangar remain? You do not need to know a thing about airfields to see that there are two plus four respectively! The writers of these books also occasionally say how a disused airfield bears no buildings or remains when the opposite occurs to commit total literary suicide.

The third bad failing in this series is a pervasive air of defeatism throughout. Each book gloomily reports on the states of Britain's disused airfields, then seems to meekly surrender to the disused airfield destroyers amid our midst. This entire series and many other books are without doubt bad examples in every way to those of you trying to help our premier historical sites.

Away from books, maps also have varied levels of use in airfield research. The best are those in PRO or similar ownership as they are tremendously detailed in every way. A serious researcher can accurately identify any individual building, airfield track or whatever as each structure is numbered.

For the more average airfield researcher, the most prominent maps are Ordnance Survey 1:50,000 ones. Thereby hangs a tale in itself. For some time after World War Two, OS maps did not show airfields at all, only the landscape. Blank spaces then appeared, with the term 'Airfield' perched incongruously in the middle. Matters later became somewhat confused, and this is the state of affairs which remains today. Wholly active airfields are usually correctly termed but airfields of restricted activity and those disused come under some curious categories. These are: 'Airfield' (without the name being given, as with active airfields), 'Airfield (disused)' and no term at all.

Is there a pattern? Some would say yes. 'Airfield' relates to an otherwise disused airfield where gliding or some similar activity occurs, 'Airfield (disused)' where a site remains prominent on a map, and nothing mentioned where it is not. Others, with equally good reason, would immediately disagree. Why are restricted activity sites not named? Why are not all disused airfields termed 'Airfield (disused)'? Why are many disused sites, still easily recognisable as airfields, not termed at all? It truly is a strange set of affairs. World War One and other types of airfields are in addition impossible to discern on OS maps except to the expert eye. OS maps can therefore only be described as of limited value to the airfield researcher in this respect.

Relatively little needs to be said about airfield photographs. The major photographic agencies can be easily found in various guides. A short letter in a newspaper or magazine asking for photographs can suffice if you prefer. Do not forget friends or relatives either, for their old snapshots could surprise you.

The only point to be wary of is when dealing with many World War One and a few World War Two photographs. These stills have been ruined as a result of censorship: look out for the crude deletion of aircraft markings or equipment on aircraft then regarded as secret.

What has just been said is all you need as a basic guide for airfield research. How you can help is to plug the gaps in information whenever possible, make corrections or bring new areas to light. Much work can still be done in many individual branches of study: pre-World War One airfields, World War One landing grounds, civil airfields of the 1920s (exceptionally poor in terms of available records), FAA airfields, decoy airfields or civil airfields which existed in the first 20 years or so after World War Two. Some British airfields are indeed still being found.

Much of the blame for airfield information dross lies with the authorities for failing to retain hordes of documents, followed by Station COs for their slackness in writing up ORBs. With airfield books, it is not so much the writers to blame but their publishers for allowing such tame and grossly inaccurate works to be accepted, while more progressive ideas are rejected. And it is surely not too difficult to work out how you can combat them . . .

Far less blame should be heaped on the Ordnance Survey. It has at least made an effort to show Britain's airfields on its maps. You could persuade it to be more consistent by naming all disused airfields, including more early ones. Despite their shortcomings on the airfield research front, the portable qualities of OS maps are invaluable in your next course of action.

(3) In The Field

Indoor research is one thing, outdoor research another. You have made your presence felt among the mass media, then expanded your airfield knowledge by reading some documents. No matter how much you have participated in these first two stages, if you are at all interested in Britain's airfields it is imperative to get out there and visit the sites themselves.

Field-work activity brings with it one immediate advantage. Outdoor airfield research is ridiculously cheap in comparison with other pursuits. All you need to bring are the relevant OS map or maps, a camera, binoculars, pens or pencils and a notebook. Good protective clothing is also a must with our ever erratic weather! Two more optional items you can bring are a powerful torch, necessary for certain disused airfield buildings such as operations blocks, plus a long tape measure if certain dimensions need to be checked.

Needless to say, a car is also required, but the cost in fuel involved while travelling from airfield to airfield is extremely small. Costs can be cut even more beforehand by checking your OS map for shorter direct routes.

Should you be thinking of doing so, never call in at Tourist Information offices for help. Quite simply, they know absolutely nothing about our disused airfields. Take heed from the author's own experience while visiting the town of Forres in northern Scotland. Trying to ask for local sources on the disused bomber OTU satellite of the same name, Tourist Information staff originally thought that the airfield concerned was none other than Kinloss. One middle-aged woman who obviously came from the area by the way she spoke then said, 'Forres airfield? Where's that?' Here is a disused airfield just one mile west of the town, still tangible, and she has never even heard of it . . .

Another too often overlooked fact about airfield research is how many sites lie in fairly quiet parts of Britain: it is remarkable how well hidden most airfields are. Roads in these areas are often narrow, twisted and lined with hedges. Good planning is again required here. Always allow plenty of time for your research to ensure you are not rushing along country roads.

Having reached your intended destination, a good idea is to talk to local inhabitants. The so-called 'experts' turn up their noses at doing this but there is no harm in chatting to people. You can often acquire fresh information on certain aspects official documents have overlooked. Perhaps the dismay displayed by 'experts' arises from how some tales have become altered with time. A typical story tells of the occasion at a now disused World War Two USAAF airfield in East Anglia when a serviceman took a short cut in his Jeep through a nearby field to visit a lady friend. The tyre tracks are still supposed to be there! Do not let this exaggerated incident put you off talking to the locals, though, for they can frequently surprise you with what they know. If nothing else, you are always spreading the gospel plus acquiring contacts for possible future measures.

Naturally, your prime target is the airfield itself. This is probably the best point to issue the main word of warning about outdoor airfield research. No British disused airfield is listed as an historical preservation area, a national scandal. Until that glorious day comes, it is therefore always advisable to ask permission to inspect a site. Although there are many public rights of way through our airfields – notably using former runways and perimeter tracks – always check first if in doubt.

Simple but special rules apply to active and disused airfields. Surprisingly, the former present more problems in outdoor research. For all their greatness, RAF airfields are not exactly renowned for their viewing areas. Any available spectator points are usually far away from where the action is. It is all part of the peculiarly British fascination with secrecy and stems from when permits began to be issued to visitors for RAF airfields from August 1919 following trouble with sabotage and intruders in World War One. The only way to get a closer look is if the airfield holds an Open Day, which normally occurs at some time around the Battle of Britain celebrations. The Americans have been somewhat more considerate by providing better positioned viewing areas by their airfields, and Britain's civil airfields have mainly done the same. Everything is fine provided you do not get in the way of everyday activity. Any airfield researcher, no matter how innocent, seen stepping out of line is likely to be prosecuted, with a resultant heavy dent in the wallet.

This is why binoculars are most useful in outdoor research. If you have a camera with a zoom lens, all the better for doing your work without disturbing anybody. Few problems exist with photography in general, though the authorities might be touchy at one or two military, experimental and factory airfields. One case in point is Boscombe Down, home of A&AEE, where signs exist all around its perimeter to deter viewers. Prosecutions for unauthorised photography occurred as early as August 1938 but anyone with a morsel of common sense will know when and when not to take a snapshot.

Surveying of Britain's disused airfields is much easier. No more for a start those irritating trees and hedges which always seem to be there at active airfields when you do not want them. Many stretches of runway and perimeter track are now used as roads or public paths. If this is not the case, try to ask permission from the farmer or landowner. But do not waste too much time in doing this, for he will probably not be around. Should someone appear during your research, explain what your purpose is and most farmers or landowners will accept the situation, however grudgingly in some cases.

You might well encounter the odd member of either party who is rampantly anti-disused airfield. He will do all in his power to stop you entering. Easily the most memorable incident the author can remember was during a second visit to the former HD Flight Station of Helperby in Yorkshire.

A TOWERING CONTROL

Horrified to see that the last remaining hangar of its kind in Britain had disappeared, the local farmer was spotted and engaged in conversation. For reasons of sheer taste, considerable alterations have had to be made as this foul-mouthed individual used four-letter words with massive over-kill in all their noun, adjectival, adverbial and intensive forms, but this is the remarkable otherwise verbatim conversation which followed:

> KPB: Excuse me.
> F (an apt title): What do you want?
> KPB: I'm doing some historical research for a series of books currently being written. (Shows ID). There used to be a World War One hangar which stood to the left.
> F: There were no airfield here. I've written to other people, telling them there weren't any airfield here.
> KPB: I can easily show you some proof.
> F: Did you not listen? Aircraft couldn't even get into that building.
> KPB: Then when was it removed, if I may ask?
> F: I know, but I'm nowt telling you. So you can just piss off. (As our hero decides to cut his losses and depart, he notices a half brick lying on some grass).
> KPB: Look, there's a jumbo-sized bar of soap to wash your mouth out with.
> F: F- off! F-, do I hate you airfield researchers and your airfields.
> KPB: I'll be back someday . . .

So what can we deduce from this meeting? Quite apart from this moron's antagonism and extreme inferiority complex by way of his disgraceful language, he is a total liar as aircraft could enter this tragic building. But two particular comments this farmer makes totally gives his game away. No matter that Helperby is frequently mentioned in PRO records; no matter that it has often figured in past aeronautical publications; no matter that even a bomb dump existed here during World War Two; despite such overwhelming evidence, he still dares to deny it ever existed. Yet his final words not only betray his poorly concealed ignorance but confirm the thoughts of many farmers and landowners, who are desperate to get their own back on Britain's disused airfields at all costs.

Your intrepid author has had to go through a few verbal clashes over the years with garbage such as this Yorkshire farmer. And they are all the same – strutting, ungrateful, obnoxious nonentities who think they own the world. But one must quickly add that such encounters have proved very rare: for every one quarrel, there have been at least a couple of hundred occasions when people have shown considerable affability or co-operation. These wise individuals have realised the true worth of our disused airfields. Should you be unfortunate enough to endure a similar experience to the Helperby incident – and that was an extreme case, it has to be emphasised – your best defence in such a situation is to gently but firmly verbally counter your opponent by showing him the colossal all-round value of the airfield. Tell him how he has ready-made buildings for storage, hard tracks for access and so on. Past experience has shown how farmers and landowners are rendered totally defenceless to this argument – they will then meekly let you in.

What happens next is up to you. Everyone has their own special method of research. A good tip is to try and find a centrally defined position from where you can branch out. Runways and perimeter tracks are best walked along, as their often pitifully potholed states can prove too rough for most vehicles. Remember to check more outlying support buildings. Keep an eye out for any painted inscriptions. And never, ever take any item you might spot lying about which is of historical value from a disused airfield: that is as much an act of vandalism as the desecration which has been caused by farmers, landowners and all the other anti-airfield opposition.

By visiting our airfields, you are not only getting fresh air and appreciating the countryside, it is a sense of adventure. This is most certainly a family pastime and an extremely healthy pursuit. Britain's disused airfields cater for seemingly unrelated interests too. They enable nature to develop freely, allowing flora and fauna to peacefully exist. Railway buffs have come to appreciate disused airfields as World War One sites often had their own spur to assist with the transfer of munitions and other items, provided a main railway line lay nearby. These special lines linked to the network lasted long into peacetime, and Cranwell's old station is now its guardroom. Among many other interests which ostensibly seem to have no connections with Britain's airfields, we must mention those beings so much a part of British folklore: ghosts. Our airfields' two most famous examples are those in Bircham Newton's squash courts and the phantom flier of Montrose. Whatever your taste in hobbies, the airfields of Britain cater for everybody.

This chapter has so far been based solely on the assumption that our airfields are excellent places for research and recreational purposes. All of them are – but they could also provide a huge number of jobs, jobs the like of which Britain has never witnessed before. Although many people have joined up with disused airfield organisations, such groups are primarily non-profit elements only intended for research purposes. All are too diverse, too unco-ordinated and lack punch. What is surely needed is one national force, controlled by one person, a force dealing with far more than research and recreational affairs. Millions of people are screaming for jobs. Real jobs, not stopgaps. Not humdrum jobs but jobs which are worthwhile, progressive, achieve things and above all have a start and an end, instead of going in endless circles getting nowhere. There is an answer . . .

(4) The Way Ahead

To be brutally frank, successive governments – of any party – have shown themselves to be disastrous on the questions of British unemployment and disused airfield conservation. No real or feasible new ideas have arisen concerning the former, while there is not the remotest chance at present of an Act being passed to make our disused airfields official historical sites. Politicians just cannot comprehend how they would not be able to speak freely today were it not for Britain's true historical superstars. What would the dole queues now be like either had we never possessed any airfields? The answer to that question is too frightening to contemplate. It is said how eight million people directly and as many as twenty million more indirectly depend on airfields in this country for their jobs or livelihoods. Well over 50,000 people work at Heathrow alone: how on earth can the Government say that only 80,000 people are directly employed by aviation in Britain? Far more than that figure work just at Heathrow and Gatwick combined!

Apart from fairly obvious jobs associated with active airfields, both they and our far greater number of disused airfields keep all kinds of people in work from builders to shopkeepers, mechanics to office employees. The direct or indirect value of airfields in terms of employment is so huge it is impossible to fully comprehend. But far more can still be achieved . . .

We all know how tourism is one of Britain's biggest assets. A unique organisation has therefore been devised with this in mind to enormously assist both the unemployment and disused airfield conservation situations. For obvious reasons, this force's name and certain other aspects of its operation have to remain secret for the moment. Only public demand –

in other words, you – can activate it. This idea has been planned in scrupulous detail by the author for several years. More importantly, experimental semi-operational tests have already been conducted over large tracts of Britain with great success, so the system is already proven. Such was its success during early test runs, when one might have expected teething troubles to have appeared, that this scheme has massive potential. As such an organisation has never been thought of, let alone attempted before, the planning for it is so far ahead of its time that a comparable system would take many years to devise and perfect.

How do our disused airfields and the unemployed benefit? As regards the former, the first step would be to erect a memorial stone at every disused airfield. These would not be unit memorials: why, incidentally, are they erected on village greens or in churches or town halls when any stone should rightfully stand at the airfield itself? Each proposed airfield memorial stone would instead show the site's layout, name, period of use and units based there. Disused airfields with less involved histories, such as World War One HD landing grounds, would each have a stone on a slightly smaller scale. To further highlight Britain's disused airfields, the Ordnance Survey would be urged to name every site and show the position of each memorial.

Jobs could be easily created in several areas, again with tourism firmly in mind. Having publicised our disused airfields, repair work would be the next priority, running alongside the placing of memorial stones. Once the airfields are tidied up of all the mess inflicted upon them by disused airfield destroyers of the past, maintenance crews would take over while yet more jobs simultaneously arise in tourism for British disused airfield promotion. Then there would be further jobs required for monitoring duties, providing vital security to guard against more atrocities being carried out against any disused airfield by whatever opposition element.

Just think of the tourism aspect. The possibilities are quite staggering. Think of the countless tourists from the Commonwealth countries and Europe who would visit. There is also America, of course, where a market for British airfield tourism is colossal. American memorials might be unit ones – but at least their impressive stones usually stand at airfields. Imagine the hordes of ex-servicemen and women plus their relations coming to visit, regardless of where they come from. Former personnel and their descendants already visit their old haunts in droves, so this fact alone shows the plan is totally feasible. This is a practice which many Americans and

Canadians already do on a private or unco-ordinated basis. Not that you will find anyone in authority admitting this: to do so would be the equivalent of cutting their own throats.

British disused airfield tourism would lead to other things. Villages, towns and especially their shopkeepers in our remoter areas would greatly benefit from incoming tourists. Airfield personnel gave tradespeople in towns and villages phenomenal levels of business during World War Two, and the closing down of airfields in peacetime meant a tremendous financial loss which shopowners quickly came to regret. But a visit to places like Alconbury today immediately becomes noticeable for the hordes of airfield personnel boosting the local economy – and many contented shopkeepers. Tourism would result in a more equal distribution of trade generally. Many more support buildings could be returned into service for industrial or public use too, something again extremely evident today. Jobs, facilities, services: is there anything our airfields cannot achieve?

One suspects the more sceptical among you must be asking several questions by now. The first must be whether disused airfield tourism exists in other countries. Yes, it does in many other parts of the world: various European countries, America, Canada, north Africa, the Pacific – even such unlikely places as Vietnam. All of these areas receive large numbers of visitors. Yet the disused airfields in these countries are either losers, unimportant or both. Britain's sites have proved to be huge winners and enormously important in comparison but officially ignored. Such a situation is deplorable.

The authorities might hit back by putting forward another question: should every disused airfield in Britain be saved for posterity? But is it better to ask whether every castle and stately home should be preserved? Disused airfields in this country have been flattened in the past without anyone in power questioning this vandalism. Put a castle or stately home under threat, though, and the Establishment howl in protest. It is impossible while travelling about Britain to spot examples of either type of 'historical' building as derelict as any disused airfield, structures which are of absolutely no consequence but still surrounded by National Trust and other signs. Such is the case with the village of Dale in south-west Wales, where its totally irrelevant castle receives all the plaudits, whereas the highly significant RAF/FAA airfield of World War Two literally just up the road is given no attention by way of signposts or any other devices.

But would farmers and landowners react favourably to disused airfields being turned into recognised historical sites?

This is yet another question posed by the doubters. It hardly needs saying how an old pals act has long existed between both parties on the subject of disused airfields. Although they do not deserve it, considering their appalling past track record, farmers and landowners would not need to worry about this revolutionary new plan as their privacy would be strictly observed. Visitors would be kept to the convenient maze of access tracks which fill every airfield. Recognition of disused airfields as historical sites would help farmers and landowners in other ways as tourism could help them create their own cottage industries. There is also the general notion now about how the 'grow your own food' policy finally ended in the mid-1980s, so it would be simple to take land out of production and convert it into a historical site.

Perhaps your last question may well concern the facts, figures and sheer financial viability of this proposed plan. This holds no problems in explaining. Estimates show how over six million people at the bare minimum in Britain are either actively or passively interested in the welfare of our disused airfields; foreign figures are much more difficult to calculate but could be in the region of 100 million people. Proof of the domestic total is shown by the four million plus visitors who attend airshows every year: remember, however, that not everyone interested in Britain's airfields is able to attend any event or is only concerned with disused sites, hence the figure of at least six million.

Another fact is how over 60,000 men were employed on average for airfield construction during World War Two. We could therefore employ 50,000 unemployed today for starters alone to deal with tourism and related activities. As this plan gets under way, tens of thousands of more jobs would arise in indirect forms of employment. Two areas would finance this entire scheme – internal/external investment and donations. Such a programme would be far from costly, even more so once the plan became fully operational. Every Briton would only have to give a few pence each year to preserve both airfields and jobs. Have you forgotten about that gentleman from London who said in 1957 how he and many others wanted to help financially to commemorate Britain's disused airfields? So, by this combination of investment and charity, it is estimated that at least £90 million could be raised each year; with the emergence of spin-off jobs and enterprises, this total would become considerably higher.

This, then, is how the proposed new disused airfield supportive force would basically operate. To divulge any more information would play into the hands of many anti-airfield elements. But there is one inescapable fact among many others which shows how this idea can work: the massive interest in the welfare of our disused airfields. Foreigners are interested, the older generations in this country are naturally interested, and so too are the young – British airfield history is excellent for projects and other forms of study. It is only the middle-age generations who need to be converted. The 1960s must be held responsible for their generally dismissive attitude as that perverted decade changed everything for the worse while they were being born or coming of age. In came too much lawlessness, pacifism and freedom of speech: out the window went the old ideals, standards and traditions which our airfields grimly fought to preserve. And ultimately received no thanks for . . .

Today is a different story, for many moral victories have been and are being won. Airfield buildings are being placed under preservation orders; airfield museums are opening; regional non-aeronautical magazines often give basic histories of disused airfields in their areas; generally our premier historical sites are finally starting to get the attention they richly deserve. At even the smallest scale, the Ordnance Survey now prints special postcard-size tourist maps where disused airfields are shown, like Dale on one example, and on the back some historical information is given. Although there is not much, it is at least a start. Subtle ideas like this tend to get any idea noticed, whether large or small.

Now this revolutionary new idea has been revealed, whether you decide to do anything further is naturally up to you. But before making your final decision, consider these four points:

1. This plan is feasible, proven and ready to go.
2. Disused airfield conservation is already happening.
3. Countless millions of people are interested and/or involved.
4. If you are unemployed, here is a chance of finding a practical, exciting and highly satisfying job.

If you think about it for a moment, the situation of Britain's disused airfields is much like that of capital punishment. The vast majority of us want our airfields conserved and the death penalty brought back. Hardly any ordinary person in the street does not but those gutless wonders in power will not follow our wishes. If they continue to do so, we might have to take even more unorthodox action until someone is found who will. Who would not wish for a new apolitical party which could eradicate unemployment, create supreme law and order and just make Britain a better place to live in again – not forgetting the conservation of our disused airfields? Oh yes, right will eventually win over might.

The Final Countdown

The eleventh hour has passed. It is all or nothing. If action is not taken now, everything will be lost.

This simple scenario sums up the future facing Britain's disused airfields. Clusters of them in various areas of this country – central Essex, the New Forest, Orkney and south-west Wales to name but four – are in frightening danger of being totally wiped out. And what will happen to currently active sites if and when they become disused?

No type of installation has given Britain such near-flawless service in so short a period of time. The 20th Century and our airfields are inextricably linked, not just in the sense of being involved in major conflicts but also in their incessant attempts to reach greater standards, increase knowledge and help others attain their dreams. Recall those ignorant remarks made about airfields after World War One? Even today all these old opinions can be blown apart. For items supposedly too costly, look at how over 800 airfields can equal the cost of just four nuclear submarines today. This example alone makes a mockery of the theory airfields are strategically and tactically obsolescent: they will never become outdated. As a result, our airfields will always be required for future needs (look at how National Service revived many of them), while the thought peace can be won without using force to counter force is simply utter rubbish.

But times are different? Are they? Without realising it, we daily rely on our airfields for ordinary life to proceed efficiently. Exclude the normally accepted functions active airfields perform so well that are all too often taken for granted: keeping the peace, making travel easy, giving swift medical assistance and ferrying goods or mail. Take the even greater range of services supplied by disused airfields to an average family in an average week. The husband, wife and 2.4 children live in a housing estate sited on a disused airfield. Food they eat, water they drink and energy providing power are grown, stored or supplied by disused airfields. When the husband drives to work, he does so along roads which are either converted runways or perimeter tracks or made of their crushed concrete. His workplace is a disused airfield, a mixture of industry and offices. Various recreational facilities such as caravanning on former airfield dispersals or playing areas for the children are available to the family at weekends. Back at work, the husband is told to go on a training course at another disused airfield. Life goes on for the average family, safe in the knowledge they are protected by the police, also trained at disused airfields. And where do criminals go when caught – disused airfields-cum-prisons!

In short, Britain's airfields crop up everywhere in our everyday lives. We all depend upon them in one way or another. Airfield critics frequently dismiss our heroes but could not survive a day without them. By aiding everybody, whether friend or foe, airfields most certainly have an extreme sense of duty. Linked in with this social value are the millions of jobs that would never have arisen otherwise. 'Airfields are the key to creating employment,' one editorial prophetically stated as far back as the early 1960s. Look at these following random facts to show the combination of social thinking and employment:

1. Walk down any street and you will usually see building labourers at work. Where is their training given? At the Construction Industry Training Centre at Bircham Newton.
2. Where does every person in the fire service receive instruction? At former 1940s and early 1950s training airfield Moreton-in-Marsh in Gloucestershire.
3. Britain's nuclear industry would be all but dead were it not for its airfields: Harwell, Culham and Dounreay for research, Bradwell Bay and Chapelcross (Annan) for power stations, and Aldermaston for weaponry production.
4. Airfields provide the great majority of weather reports in this country. Look at the weather section in your daily newspaper and see how many you can find.
5. The maps we all need for business or recreational purposes are provided by airfields as their aircraft perform regular survey work.
6. Staying on broadly the same theme, how many serious crimes – especially murders – have British-based reconnaissance aircraft helped to solve? A lot.
7. And going from public to political crime, what would

> Britain do without all those aerials sited on places such as Anthorn, Croughton and Edzell II for intelligence eavesdropping? Most of the major listening posts here exist on former airfields.

Only a fool or an anti-airfield diehard would disagree about the devastating omnipresence of airfields in the running of Britain. The seven above examples have created several hundred thousand jobs between them – and perhaps millions more indirectly.

This unquestioning belief in the social, economic and employment advantages of airfields is already recognised in other parts of the world, nowhere more so than in America. Local inhabitants talked in a nationally broadcast radio programme in January 1988 about the 'disastrous' effects of intended closure of their nearby airfield, George AFB in California, would have on the entire community. (America has been going through a period of heavy airfield closures because of massive cutbacks in defence spending to reduce the national debt). People feared for the severe levels of unemployment among not only military personnel but non-related ones as well. The hundreds of millions of dollars pumped into local traders would be lost, as would the marvellous social effects George created as in hospital facilities. Still more jobs would disappear, house prices would plummet and, as if everyone seemed to have enough to worry about, nobody remained confident about future levels of national security. But most of all look back on this heart-breaking situation and you can see that what is happening in America is exactly what happened in Britain after World War Two.

Our airfields can already tell their distant American cousins about how politicians really feel about them. National and local government elements have always proved two-faced in the British airfield story as with any other issue. Never has any person or item been subjected to so much dog's abuse as the airfields of this country. Give a politician a chance to snipe at an airfield and he or she will readily do so. How dare a government pamphlet of recent times declare that people find smaller airfields '. . . a nuisance, especially on Sunday afternoons.' As one frustrated company said years ago, 'Private aeroplanes unfortunately meet with insufficient understanding from the authorities.'

A lot of the political criticism deliberately aimed at our airfields unquestionably results from an alliance with farmers and 'landowners' in general: the National Farmers' Union is said to be the most powerful lobby group in Britain. Still demolition work at disused airfields continues now and again as these two elements remove tracks and buildings in a scorched earth type policy. Ask a member of either party why a control tower or whatever has been flattened and his or her extreme embarrassment is plain for all to see: all know they have done wrong. But then farmers have always been against aviation. When balloons landed on their fields in the 18th Century, did farmers welcome these craft? No, they attacked balloons with pitchforks. When aircraft in trouble as a result of enemy action made forced landings on farmland in World War Two, did farmers show any concern for aircrews? No, only their farmland.

Three factors crop up time and time again in the saga of farmers/landowners and Britain's disused airfields. The first is how farmers complain that former sites have made agricultural techniques much more difficult: what utter codswallop. The complete opposite has happened; if airfields had never existed, farming practices would be infinitely harder. In line with this argument is often quoted the allegation that airfields destroyed vast amounts of hedgerows during World War Two, another statement which is completely untrue. Whereas very little disappeared during the conflict, at least 20 per cent of hedgerows were removed during 1946-70. The Ministry of Agriculture provided a grant to farmers until 1977 to rip up hedgerows to aid modern farming techniques, and 20,000 miles were removed from England and Wales just in the early 1980s as farmers preferred crops to cattle.

Factor number two after operating methods is the heavy insistence by farmers and landowners on privacy. This demand is nothing other than an absolute disgrace, for centuries old laws should ensure rights to free access for anyone wanting to visit a disused airfield: no wonder the Ramblers' Association complains. Technically, farmers, landowners, foresters and all the rest of them are criminals.

But it is the third factor, one which has far greater consequences outwith the basic idea of land ownership, which merits special examination. Exactly what is history? Had people been asked this question as little as fifteen years ago, out would come the same tired old answers: castles and stately homes. These places are not history, rather pseudo-history, places of no value whatsoever. Compare for a moment Britain's airfields with its castles and stately homes, then ask yourself these nine questions:

1. Have they saved Britain – twice?
2. Do they still keep the peace?
3. Have they provided millions of jobs?
4. Have they saved millions of lives?
5. Do they have colossal historical value?
6. Have they created worldwide impact?
7. Are they supremely adaptable and versatile?
8. Have they greatly helped the environment?
9. Have they enriched the lives of the local population?

In each case, for castles and stately homes read no, for airfields read yes. Nine-nil: what a drubbing. And we have not even asked the tenth and most damning question of all. What have castles and stately homes *done* for Britain? Nothing, absolutely nothing. For every castle which has, we can show them a thousand airfields; for every stately home, we can show them every airfield in sight.

Our historical priorities therefore should be clear. Yet still millions of people go for frippery instead of force when dealing with history. Scotland has 1,269 castles on its own – but can you honestly name one of any real historical or social note? Stately homes are a complete irrelevance, and even the politicians realised this fact for once in 1940 when Secretary of State for Air Sir Archibald Sinclair made the now famous remark, 'We are out to win this war and should not be put off by a desire to maintain intact the stately homes of England . . .'

Now you may be wondering at this point whether churches can be counted as history: the answer here is also no. These 'historical' sites have no value in this respect either but at least do possess limited local social value. The religious authorities were none too pleased by one scene in a famous but controversial comedy film of the 1970s when someone asked: 'But what have the Romans given you that God hasn't?' To which a man from the crowd replied: 'Roads, law and order, a language, education, a sewerage system . . .' and so on. Clergymen were furious – but did it never cross their minds that this person was correct? The Romans did give us roads, they did give us law and order, they did lay down the fundamentals of civilisation today. This is why Roman relics are one of only two categories which can be truly described as 'history', the other being Britain's airfields. It is worth noting how both Roman sites and our airfields have no previous historical links. 'Fame is no plant that grows on mortal soil,' said Milton, but these two types totally defy that famous saying. Neither have British Roman sites nor airfields enjoyed the poisoned fruits of nepotism while raising themselves from scratch.

Artifacts dating from Roman times have always struggled for official support, while our disused airfields have never received any help, and three reasons are responsible. Political lobbying again plays its part, as does the brain-conditioning effect of castles and stately homes. The Department of Environment displays an extremely poor attitude by only recognising buildings of 1914-39 vintage as of any historical value, which effectively rules out our airfields as few buildings dating from that era still remain, and to class airfields as industrial history is simply ridiculous. A third reason is inevitably money; one odious Government Minister unwittingly summed up the situation on May 15 1989 by grandly declaring: 'If we (the Government) were forced to save every any old monument, we would be in for a very big bill.'

Of course, money is important in life. But put money in such a position at the expense of everything else and basic values will always be sacrificed first. Such has been the tale for airfields in Britain for many years. No matter how heroically a site has performed in one or both World Wars, it might as well not have bothered judging by the attitudes of some people. We have had the sickening sight on television of an ex-Bomber Command airman going to Dresden and actually apologising for bombing the German city in February 1945 – what a gross insult to his fellow crews who failed to see freedom. This man belonged to CND, and it should not be forgotten that a leading RAF chaplain who tried his hardest to obstruct 'Bomber' Harris during many operations – including Dresden – because of alleged humaniterian reasons later became a leading figure in the organisation. We have also had a certain Jewish 'agony aunt' go on a discussion programme and tell children: 'Don't ever think you owe anyone who fought for their country a thing, for you don't.' Such famous airmen who operated from British airfields in the past as air aces Robert Stanford Tuck and 'Ginger' Lacey have died without hardly anyone recognising their enormous contributions to Britain, while massive coverage is given to total nonentities who could not even lace their boots.

The constantly increasing armies of disused airfield supporters have long realised that they are involved in not just a hobby or even an unpaid auxiliary job but a moral crusade. Too many people still have to be converted to the idea of what is really worthwhile and socially relevant history. On hearing that a disused airfield may entirely disappear for alternative purposes, people have said: 'We lose one here, we lose one there. What's wrong with losing just this one?' But then you lose another, and another, and another – until none is left. Photographs can never replace the real thing. Think of the site which served in both World Wars, starred in the Battle of Britain and gave excellent civil service for many years afterwards but the local council tried for decades to close it, and then the Japanese eradicated it for a car factory. (No prizes for guessing where that is). Developers can find loopholes in laws, and ominously more planning appeals to the Government are being granted. If Malta has won the George Cross, what does that make Hornchurch – a Victoria Cross and two Bars? Alas, for many of us money is the be-all and end-all of life.

It soon may be the case that every airfield in Britain might disappear – perhaps even life itself. Will the 'greenhouse effect' take hold and alter the entire landscape of this country? All the jokes about Doncaster-by-the-Sea would cease if this became the case. Hundreds of active and disused airfields would slip beneath the waves: Scampton among others would be struggling to survive as only a flying boat base, should these machines ever come back into vogue.

And then there is the ultimate Armageddon – World War Three. It is unnerving to say the least that famous astrologer Nostradamus predicted centuries ago how a huge world conflict resulting in terrible destruction will start some time between 1994 and 1996 in the Middle East, involving the Arabs and Russians on one side. Significantly, this war will start after an ostensible period of peace. Had this book been published when originally intended in the early 1980s, it would never have mentioned such an alarming prediction. But huge changes have occurred since then: for this apparent peace, one can interpret the collapse of Communism in eastern Europe. Now you can regard what has just been said as complete nonsense but Nostradamus predicted the fall as well as rise of Communism, plus Napoleon, Franco, Hitler and World War Two. Whether he foretold airfields is another matter entirely!

Thanks to their brilliant performances in World Wars One and Two, our airfields may well have still eradicated the chances of another war from ever happening. Talk arose of requisitioning civil airfields for military purposes by April 1913 when they were barely four years old; if the worst came in the shape of World War Three, our disused airfields could still again be requisitioned. Russia has apparently specifically targeted over 80 airfields in Britain for conventional or nuclear attack. Military bases and civil airports are naturally on its shopping list but a lot of odd places too: Barra, Mull's airstrip at Glenforsa, St Angelo, Barrow and Rochester to name but a few. The Russians undoubtedly recognise Britain's airfields for their true worth.

Our airfields have not achieved everything on their own. France invented airfields; an Italian-operated airfield in Libya made possible the world's first bombing raid; to an Austrian seaplane base can be credited the first aerial victory over a submarine; one airfield on a tiny Pacific island beat a whole country. Other countries have been notable for the numerical strength of their airfields as America or constructional skills in building them, like Canada's training sites literally hacked out of the bush. But how many countries in the world can say they have two world famous airfields or even just one? Britain can conversely rattle off with ease 30 or 40 sites. Mention any type of aircraft role – fighter and trainer to name but two – and this country has the greatest airfields of their kind in the world. Their fame is worldwide – except in Britain.

The introduction of this book says that our airfields have had no superiors in the world for history or density per square mile. Perfectly true, but they have proved unbeatable in a third respect as no other country's airfields have actively battled it out in two World Wars and won both of them. Germany, played two, lost two; France and Russia, played two, lost one and very nearly lost the other; and America cannot be counted as hardly any airfields existed there during World War One, saw only negligible action (against U-boats) in World War Two and were never bombed. Britain's airfields meanwhile have an unblemished record, a tremendous feat, yet have been rewarded for their pains by physical and verbal assassination from those in authority.

Perhaps the real reason why the Establishment in general absolutely detests airfields in Britain in general is the way in which our heroes stand for everything it is against: individualism, innovation, self-sufficiency, complete detachment from politics, self-regulated ultra-heavy fire-power, total social benevolence, no rigid red tape and putting purpose before dogma. Think of the pioneers associated with them – Noel Pemberton Billing, Claude Grahame-White, Sir Alan Cobham and E.E. Fresson among others – and all suffered either diabolical fates or met with extreme official harassment. As for their two allies in authority – Sir Sefton Brancker and, more subtly, Neville Chamberlain – perhaps even the word diabolical to describe their destinies is an understatement.

It is often said the British general public loves its failures but has no time for successes – and our airfields are roaring successes. This is why every one of those doubters and non-participants among you must be re-educated about the solely relevant modern half of British history. Things are direly wrong when contestants on a television game show say Prestwick is in Wales and, equally unbelievably, Aldergrove is the airport for Chicago. Too many people cannot even standardise on the word airfield. In one television news report from Afghanistan, one site there was described as an airport, an airfield, an airstrip, then again as an airport and airfield – in four sentences. Wot, no air base? For sites which exist close at hand and so dominate our lives, incredibly little is known about Britain's airfields by the average person, but happily many of you are learning fast.

This is why it is imperative you must act now to help give our ailing disused airfields the support they so desperately need. Time still remains for one last chance to save them – but we must act immediately, as to wait any longer could in the not-so-long run leave as few remains of Britain's disused airfields as of their ancient Roman counterparts. But these places will never totally surrender or disappear, a fact farmers and landowners with their steadily decreasing power are already finding out. If they do not learn fully, remaining opposition might well have to be crushed without mercy, as farmers and their ilk did to our airfields.

Many ordinary people now realise what really counts as British history, quite apart from the innumerable benefits which have been created for them. Those in authority must register and honour our airfields as top rank historical conservation areas at once, otherwise the future for them might be somewhat bleak. Why not for a start create a British Airfield Day? And what date could be more appropriate than September 7, that day in 1940 when the Luftwaffe realised it could not defeat our airfields unlike the rabble elsewhere in Europe and turned instead upon London and elsewhere.

It has been said of Britain generally that we are hopeless when everything is fine but brilliant in a crisis, brilliant inventors but hopeless marketeers. With our airfields, particularly those now disused, people like you must act immediately to solve another crisis. A brilliant system has been devised to save them but individuals or specialist units cannot change things on their own. No action has been taken to stop the disused airfield carnage: really radical methods are needed, hence why this proposed disused airfield organisation must be mobilised instantly.

Our airfields now exert phenomenal levels of control over every one of us. No person or type of installation throughout British history has so revolutionised daily society in such a short period of time as the 1,700 or so sites in this country. All have achieved their objectives with virtually no assistance – but many disused airfields today for once badly require some kind of help. If you saw an injured serviceman in the street, you would help him, not kick away his crutches: the same situation applies to Britain's disused airfields.

So remember the airfields of Britain. They saved you twice . . . and could do so again. Now *you* save *them.*

In Volume I of *The Airfields of Britain:*

Aldergrove, Northern Ireland's greatest ever airfield . . . the tragedy of Battle of Britain superstar Acklington . . . Bircham Newton, Britain's best preserved disused airfield . . . the 'dry' airfield that once welcomed in a flying boat . . . how alcohol helped create an airfield . . . and the one and only, Biggin Hill.

All this and more in the most extensive airfield history ever written. *The Airfields of Britain* – coming soon!